The Elusive Promise of **INDIGENOUS DEVELOPMENT**

The Elusive Promise

of **INDIGENOUS**

DEVELOPMENT

Rights, Culture, Strategy

Karen Engle

Duke University Press   Durham and London   2010

© 2010 Duke University Press

All rights reserved.

Printed in the United States of America
on acid-free paper ∞

Designed by Heather Hensley

Typeset in Monotype Dante by
Keystone Typesetting, Inc.

Library of Congress Cataloging-in-
Publication Data and republication
acknowledgments appear on the last
printed pages of this book.

Duke University Press gratefully
acknowledges the support of a University
Co-operative Society Subvention Grant
awarded by The University of Texas at
Austin, which provided funds toward
the production of this book.

To the Memory of
LEE TEITELBAUM

Contents

Table of Cases

Acknowledgments

This book is the product of years of conversations with more people than I can possibly recall. I am both grateful for and humbled by the numerous colleagues, students, friends, and family members who have made this work possible.

Though the beginning of this book—as a book—roughly coincided with my move to the University of Texas in 2002, its ideas had already begun to take shape in multiple encounters before then. I see its beginnings in interactions dating back over two decades with my law school and postdoctoral mentors, Duncan Kennedy and David Kennedy. I thank Duncan for his generosity of time and spirit, his insatiable curiosity, and his insistence on precision. I am grateful to David, not only for all the conversations and collaborations over the years, but for extensive comments on the draft of this book that were crucial to its development. I also owe much of my intellectual work to the vital space he created for critical inquiry in international law through the network of scholars he brought together in the early 1990s under New Approaches to International Law (NAIL).

The book has also been influenced by early and, in many cases, ongoing discussions with a number of colleagues from the University of Utah. I would like to thank in particular Antony Anghie, Srinivas Aravamudan, Daniel Greenwood, Ranjana Khanna, Mitchel Lasser, Ileana Porras, and Kathryn Stockton (who all participated in NAIL events as well) for growing up with me in the academy, and nourishing the seeds of what would eventually take root in this book. I have dedicated this book to the memory of my first law school dean at Utah, Lee Teitelbaum, whom many of us dubbed the "dream dean." Lee's commitment to critical, interdisciplinary scholarly engagement—and his active participation in the same—made him a unique dean and a cherished colleague and friend.

My move to the University of Texas renewed my interest in Latin America, and honed my focus on indigenous and Afro-descendant rights in the region. Charles Hale, Shannon Speed, and Gerald Torres welcomed me with open arms, introduced me to the Lozano Long Institute for Latin American Studies, engaged with me in numerous scholarly and programmatic endeavors, and supported—in part by critiquing—my scholarship in ways that I hope are evident in the book. They also worked with me to found the Bernard and Audre Rapoport Center for Human Rights and Justice, which has provided an important space for my research and inquiry. Ariel Dulitzky and Alvaro Santos have both been trusted colleagues in this endeavor as well, and have given me substantive feedback on various parts of the book. Barbara Harlow and Neville Hoad have ensured that I not forget about other parts of the world, and have offered many close reads and much indispensable advice.

The research for the book has spanned years and continents and has required the persistence of many librarians and research assistants. I am grateful to Jon Pratter at the Tarlton Law Library for his special attentiveness to the project, and to Christian Kelleher at the Berson Collection for helping me create the archive for the book. Thanks to Ashley Bryan, Mery Ciacci, Celeste Henery, Mónica Jiménez, Laura Peterson, and Connie Steele for relatively brief but intensive work on the manuscript at various points, and to Creighton Chandler, Mary Beth Hickcox-Howard, Lucas Lixinski, and Matthew Wooten for their sustained, and in many cases heroic, efforts in compiling much of the research that I relied on for the book. I owe special thanks to Creighton for his undying commitment to the project over the past two years, up through the final proofreading stage. I am also particularly grateful to Josh Clark, who began as a research assistant on this project four years ago and has remained on it since then as a researcher, trusted advisor, and editor. He and Sylvia Romo accompanied me to the Caribbean coast of Colombia in 2007, a trip that had a significant impact on this work. Many thanks to Sarah Cline, who has been key to the administrative organization of the book, and who has jealously guarded my time and graciously assumed additional responsibilities to ensure its timely completion.

I am appreciative of two deans at the University of Texas, Bill Powers and Larry Sager, for offering crucial leave time for this project and providing funding through the UT Law School Foundation. I also benefited from a number of grants from the University of Texas at Austin: two University of Texas Special Research Grants and a Mellon Faculty Research Grant supported some of the book's research, while a University Co-operative Society Subvention Grant covered some of the costs of publication. The Bernard and Audre Rapoport Foundation, through the Rapoport Center at UT, facilitated a number of advocacy projects and academic discussions that significantly influenced the book. I am thankful to Bernard ("B") Rapoport for his financial support, as well as for his passionate commitments to both social justice and the academy.

I spent seven months in Colombia in 2007, which was indispensable to the shape of this book. I am grateful to the Universidad de los Andes for its institutional support and to many colleagues in Bogotá for their academic engagement with the work. *Mil gracias* to Helena Alviar, Daniel Bonilla, Claudia Mosquera, Liliana Obregon, Francisco Ortega, Eduardo Restrepo, and Fernando Serrano. Thanks also to Manuel Tibaquirá for his research assistance and for teaching me so many nuances of the Spanish language. I am also grateful to the many Afro-Colombian rights advocates who took time out of their busy schedules to teach me and my students about their social movement. For their hospitality and openness to showing me the Isla Grande and sharing with me their struggles, I thank Hugo Camargo, Ever de la Rosa, and Javier "Cuco" Morales.

The book was also heavily influenced in its early days by a six-week stay in San Cristobal de las Casas, in Chiapas, Mexico. Thanks to Shannon Speed for encouraging me to spend time there, and to her and Miguel Angel de los Santos for providing me with a place to stay. Miguel opened not only his home, but the offices of the Red de Defensores, to me.

A number of lectures, conferences, and guest teaching engagements aided in the development and sharpening of the book's arguments. I first presented the work as a lecture for the Nordic Human Rights Research Course at the Åbo Akademi University in Turku, Finland. Thanks to Martin Scheinin for that invitation, and for many influential discussions during the days I participated in the course. Thanks also to the organizers and audiences of my presentations at the American University in Cairo, the Universidad de los Andes, the Human Rights Program at Harvard Law School, the University of Kentucky College of Law, the Georgetown University Law Center, the Wake Forest School of Law, the University of Iowa, and the University of Texas. The work benefited from presentations at meetings of the International Network on Transformative Employment & Labor Law in Cuernavaca, the Latin American Studies Association in Montreal, the American Anthropological Association in Washington, and the San Antonio Bar Association. Thanks to Judson Wood for his keen insights and love of learning and to Karen Knop for helping me articulate a number of the ideas presented here during an intensive course we co-taught at the University of Melbourne on culture, human rights, and sovereignty.

Family and friends have shown remarkable patience, encouragement, and generosity throughout this process. I especially want to thank my brother Art Wilson and my sister-in-law, Kathy Wilson, for providing inspirational work space and company at Fabra Acres in Boerne, Texas. Thanks also to my nephew Jeff Wilson for his road-trip companionship, close friendship, and intellectual camaraderie. Finally, much gratitude goes to my partner, Ana Almaguel, who, over the past three years, has supported me in this endeavor and in the long absences it has sometimes entailed. She has also spent many hours talking through the ideas with me, checking and helping with Spanish translations, and teaching me much in the process.

List of Acronyms and Abbreviations

AAA (American Anthropological Association)

American Convention (American Convention on Human Rights)

American Declaration (American Declaration of the Rights and Duties of Man)

Brundtland Commission (World Commission on Environment and Development)

CISA (*Consejo Indio de Sud America*; Indian Council of South America)

CERD (Committee on the Elimination of Racial Discrimination)

Cobo Report (UN Commission on Human Rights, report submitted by Special Rapporteur José Martínez Cobo)

CRIC (*Consejo Regional Indígena del Cauca*; Regional Indigenous Council of Cauca)

Daes Report (UNESCO publication entitled "Protection of the Heritage of Indigenous People")

Friendly Relations Declaration (UN Declaration on Principles of International Law Concerning Friendly Relations and Cooperation among States in Accordance with the Charter of the United Nations)

ICCPR (International Covenant on Civil and Political Rights)

ICERD (International Convention on the Elimination of All Forms of Racial Discrimination)

ICESCR (International Covenant on Economic, Social and Cultural Rights)

IITC (International Indian Treaty Council)

ILO (International Labor Organization)

ILO 107 (International Labor Organization Convention 107, Concerning the Protection and Integration of Indigenous and Other Tribal and Semi-Tribal Populations in Independent Countries)

ILO 169 (International Labor Organization Convention 169, Concerning Indigenous and Tribal Peoples in Independent Countries)

INCODER (*Instituto Colombiano de Desarrollo Rural*; Colombian Institute of Rural Development)

INCORA (*Instituto Colombiano de la Reforma Agraria*; Colombian Institute of Agrarian Reform)

Inter-American Commission (Inter-American Commission on Human Rights)

Inter-American Court (Inter-American Court of Human Rights)

OAS (Organization of American States)

OD 4.20 (World Bank Operational Directive 4.20)

OP 4.10 (World Bank Operational Policy 4.10)

PCN (*Proceso de Comunidades Negras*; Process of Black Communities)

Special Commission (Special Commission for Black Communities, established by TA 55 of Colombia's Constitution of 1991)

TA 55 (Transitory Article 55, or *Artículo Transitorio 55* of the 1991 Colombian Constitution)

UBCIC (Union of British Columbia Indian Chiefs)

UDHR (Universal Declaration of Human Rights)

UNAT (*Unidad Nacional de Tierras Rurales*, or National Unity of Rural Lands)

UN Declaration (UN Declaration on the Rights of Indigenous Peoples)

UNESCO (United Nations Educational, Scientific and Cultural Organization)

UN Report on Relationship to Land (UN Commission on Human Rights, report entitled "Indigenous Peoples and Their Relationship to Land")

WCIP (World Council of Indigenous Peoples)

WGIP (UN Working Group on Indigenous Populations; Working Group)

Working Group (UN Working Group on Indigenous Populations; WGIP)

Introduction

This book is about indigenous movements in the Americas since the 1970s, and how the movements have interacted with, reacted to, and participated in the creation of law, mostly international law. The book is based on the assumption that social movements formed by indigenous peoples and their non-indigenous allies have affected the shape of international law as it applies to indigenous peoples, notwithstanding centuries of colonialism, massive acts of violence aimed directly at them, development projects meant to remove or assimilate them, structural discrimination, ongoing poverty, and unequal access to education and resources. As with all social movements, indigenous rights advocates have faced internal disagreements and organizational challenges. But in their promotion of particular laws or interpretations of existing laws, indigenous peoples have in fact had a number of successes. In many ways, this book focuses on those successes by considering, for example, the appeal of indigenous rights models for other groups, specifically Afro-descendants in certain areas of Colombia, in their own organization for the recognition of collective land ownership.

The book also spends significant time exploring what David Kennedy refers to as "the dark sides of virtue."[1] That is, each victory brings with it (often unintended) limitations and downsides, which I largely pin on the reification of indigenous culture. Cultural rights have provided the dominant framework for indigenous rights advocacy since at least the 1990s. The acceptance and incorporation of this cultural rights framework by international institutions rose alongside neoliberalism, and enthusiasm for it has outlasted that for neoliberalism. As the right to culture has developed over the years, I contend that it has largely displaced or deferred the very issues that initially motivated much of the advocacy: issues of economic dependency, structural discrimination, and lack of indigenous autonomy. This displacement occurs even when the right to culture is used specifically with the aim of promoting development that is thought to accord with indigenous culture. In fact, I suggest that increased cultural rights sometimes lead to decreased opportunities for autonomy and development.

Of course, a victory for some positions within a social movement often means a defeat for others. Part of the story I therefore tell is how indigenous groups arguing for a strong form of self-determination that would recognize the right of statehood for indigenous peoples were ultimately unsuccessful on the international plane. Not only were they unable to convince states to support such a right, but they did not persuade enough other indigenous groups to follow their lead in what was thought by many to be a futile attempt to affect international law too dramatically. Some of the other groups seemed content to push for cultural rights within the existing state structure. For the most part (although I complicate this account below), the latter group won. These internal conflicts are the stuff of social movements. Thus, when I say that indigenous social movements have achieved successes, I do not mean to suggest that they have received everything they have demanded, even in any given case, or that their members are in agreement about what they want.

I also do not mean to overstate the political power possessed by indigenous peoples. When indigenous social movements began to form in the 1970s, they were faced with a limited set of options for international legal advocacy within a legal framework that had largely facilitated their conquest and subjugation. But the movements designed their discourse largely within the limits and possibilities they saw, and they often carefully chose the words they used to describe their complaints and make their demands (even if many were forced to do so in a language that was not native to them). Indigenous leaders often engaged in the production of discourse, knowledge, law, and politics, through attendance at pan-indigenous conferences. As Charles Hale explains: "The history of nearly every indigenous movement throughout the Americas is punctuated by leaders' attendance at such meetings . . . Documents produced in such events—statements of principle, analysis, denunciations, etc.—circulate among these organizations and continue to influence leaders' thinking."[2]

Nearly forty years since the start of the movements, indigenous rights advocates continue to engage in pan-indigenous networks. Although these networks and the exchange of ideas and strategies are greatly facilitated by the Internet and other forms of modern communication, it could be argued that political and legal advocacy possibilities remain largely constrained by an international legal regime that is tainted by its historical biases. Nevertheless, indigenous social movements are full of advocates who seem resolute in their attempts both to deploy and to reform the law. Part of my goal here is to attend to when and how the advocates have changed their claims to adapt to their perceptions of what the law might allow, and when they have attempted to challenge the law by arguing for new legal documents or institutions. I also consider the extent to which their articulations of rights have been adopted by, or at least coincided with, that of the international legal regime.

The book is centered around two primary paths of political and legal advocacy to which I have already alluded: those based on self-determination and those based on the human right to culture. Each of those positions manifests itself in multiple ways. The right to self-determination, for example, comes in a strong form that asserts the right of secession or independence as a nation-state, a weaker form that claims significant legal and political autonomy within existing states, and a still weaker form that is often articulated as a human right. Similarly, the right to culture sometimes implicates strong collective rights for land and territory, while at other times it is used to support individual indigenous people against indigenous groups that are attempting to limit their rights.

I first began this project with the assumption that self-determination—in all its forms—offered greater possibilities for the enfranchisement of indigenous peoples than the right to culture, in its various permutations. The process of writing the book, however, has caused me to question that assumption. Despite my general critique of the cultural rights rubric for often displacing or deferring issues of structural distributional inequalities, I acknowledge that indigenous peoples sometimes make relatively strong redistributive claims under the right to culture, or with the claim that particular human rights (like the right to property) protect their culture.

Indeed, at the risk of sounding overly teleological or deterministic, I want to suggest that an often elusive promise of indigenous development underlies nearly every strategy that indigenous peoples have chosen to pursue their claims.

At the start of this project, I also would have said that self-determination arguments were waning, at least among "internationally active indigenous peoples."[3] Although the right to culture was included in a number of international legal instruments and, when necessary, interpreted to apply to indigenous peoples, none of those instruments applied the term "self-determination" to indigenous peoples, despite many attempts on the parts of advocates to have them do so. In fact, the term's inclusion had been explicitly rejected in the drafting of the 1989 International Labor Organization Convention 169, the only international instrument at the time that specifically addressed the rights of indigenous peoples. Moreover, at least since the 1980s, indigenous advocates have couched their demands largely in terms of cultural rights. Claims centered on the protection of culture have tended to garner success before international and regional legal bodies, and the jurisprudence has largely developed along those lines (thereby encouraging more such claims).

In 2007, however, the United Nations General Assembly adopted the Declaration on the Rights of Indigenous Peoples[4] (UN Declaration). That document had been mired for years in a drafting process perennially full of political stalemates, in which debates over the inclusion and meaning of self-determination were paramount. During that process, indigenous movements generally considered the recognition of the right to self-determination, however defined, to be nonnegotiable.

Indigenous peoples' insistence on the inclusion of the right to self-determination arguably paid off with the passage of the final text. The text of Article 3 of the UN Declaration, for example, remained identical to that first agreed upon in 1993 by a UN working group and consistently supported by indigenous participants: "Indigenous peoples have the right of self-determination. By virtue of that right they freely determine their political status and freely pursue their economic, social and cultural development."[5] At first glance, it would appear to represent a victory for indigenous peoples and support a strong version of self-determination.

Yet, there was a caveat. The possibility that self-determination might imply a right to statehood or secession had concerned a number of states throughout the years. While Canada, the United States, New Zealand, and Australia had originally been among the greatest opponents of the declaration, the African Union somewhat unexpectedly led the campaign against it in 2006 and 2007. Part of its opposition was based on the ground that "the vast majority of the peoples of Africa are indigenous to the African Continent,"[6] and that "self-determination only applies to nations trying to free themselves from the yoke of colonialism."[7]

African states proposed a number of changes to the declaration. Although they ultimately relented on many of them, they held tight to the need for strong language limiting the right to self-determination. They won. Article 46 states that the declaration should not be "construed as authorizing or encouraging any action which would dismember or impair totally or in part, the territorial integrity or political unity of sovereign and independent States." Although this compromise language gave indigenous peoples significant pause, they ultimately decided to support it with the assurance that other key provisions would remain intact, including those on land and resource rights and free and informed consent, and would in some sense protect "indigenous peoples' territorial integrity."[8]

The United States, Canada, Australia, and New Zealand were the only four states that opposed the UN Declaration in the end (and Australia has since changed its position). While New Zealand claimed to be satisfied with Article 46, the others seemed categorically opposed to having any self-determination language in the declaration. The United States delegate explained that Article 3, because it "involves the foundation of international relations and stability (i.e., the political unity and territorial integrity of nation-states) [is] ill advised and likely to result in confusion and disputes."[9]

In the short time since the declaration's passage, it seems that indigenous rights advocates have begun to exploit its self-determination language, notwithstanding its limitations. As I discuss in various places in the book, the term "self-determination" is now being used by advocates who never deployed it in the past, or who seemed to have abandoned it for the right to culture. To be sure, few argue for the right to the strong form of self-determination (which, in fact, had been largely set aside by the early 1990s). But the term is being used to argue for indigenous control over heritage, land, and development.

The debates that took place over the UN Declaration offer a lens through which to view legal and theoretical differences over the promises, limits, and threats of both the self-determination and cultural rights models that have been proposed and deployed over the years for empowering indigenous individuals and groups. Contemporary disputes are simply the most recent manifestation of tensions that have been simmering in a variety of contexts. They surfaced, I believe, as a result of unsuccessful mediations of those tensions throughout the years. That indigenous rights advocates continued to push for self-determination through the UN mechanisms set up to adopt a declaration might suggest an acknowledgment of some pitfalls of the cultural rights model, in particular its failure to attend to ongoing needs for—or claims by indigenous groups to—economic and political autonomy.

Within these disputed legal and political models, this book explores the trajectory of international indigenous advocacy, primarily but not exclusively in the Americas, from the 1970s to today. Part I investigates the shift in discourse during this time and, in particular, the extent to which indigenous rights advocates have in different periods relied upon strategies of self-determination and cultural rights to make their claims. It begins with a historical account of the models of colonialism deployed in the Americas, comparing in particular England's and Spain's justifications for and forms of conquest. It then considers how the deployment of those different models influenced legal and political ideology for the next several hundred years, ultimately affecting the forms that international indigenous rights advocacy would take in the Americas.

With this background in mind, the ensuing chapters in part I interrogate the understandings of self-determination and culture that have emerged in various years of international indigenous rights advocacy and in the international institutional structures that have considered indigenous issues. Such institutions range from the International Labor Organization to the United Nations and the Organization of American States. At the end of part I, I conclude that despite—or perhaps because of—enduring debates about self-determination, the past twenty years have demonstrated an agreement, if sometimes only an implicit one, among tribal representatives, indigenous rights activists, lawyers, anthropologists, and even most states that the human right to culture provides a secure and relatively uncontroversial means by which to protect the rights of indigenous people, if not peoples, internationally.

Although calls for the use of human rights to protect culture have obviously not totally replaced calls for self-determination for indigenous peoples, they continue to provide the dominant discursive and legal vehicle for making indigenous claims. The right to culture is deployed in different ways. Although discussions of differing definitions of self-determination are abundant in the literature on international indigenous advocacy, there is little explicit discussion of the meaning of the right to culture. In part II of the book, I identify and discuss three different understandings of culture in international indigenous advocacy and law: culture as heritage, culture as land, and culture as development.

In describing these various meanings of the right to culture, I consider their embodiment in international legal instruments (which often resulted from indigenous rights advocacy) and discuss some of their strengths and weaknesses. In particular, I argue that each of these understandings of culture has its limitations and unintended consequences, with which I encourage advocates to grapple. The first, culture as heritage, threatens to alienate indigenous peoples from their heritage; the second, culture as land, makes indigenous land inalienable; and the third, culture as development, combines with the second to limit the forms of development available to indigenous peoples.

In the latter two cases, if successful in achieving land or development rights based on the protection of their traditional practices, indigenous peoples are often restricted in their ability to make autonomous decisions. In the context of land, for example, they are generally prohibited from engaging in the free market. With regard to development, they are sometimes restricted to ecologically sustainable forms of development. And while recognized indigenous peoples are expected to live up to their presumed cultural respect for the environment, land, and communal property, they are also often forced to give up those parts of their culture that are seen to conflict with universal understandings of human rights. As Elizabeth Povinelli explains in the context of the state's purported deference to indigenous customary law in Australia: "an invisible asterisk, a proviso, hovers above every enunciation of indigenous customary law: '(provided [they] . . . are not so repugnant).' "[10] That same asterisk, I argue, is built into the international legal protection of cultural rights, although not so invisibly.

Although these consequences lead me to be skeptical of many aspects of contemporary models for the protection of indigenous rights, I recognize that they are, in many ways, what indigenous peoples have called for. Moreover, these models have been seen as aspirational and powerful, particularly to the extent that they attempt to redistribute land and economic resources. In perhaps its most radical form, the right to culture makes heritage, land, and economic development inseparable; the three constitute a rights package that promises to challenge the dominant distribution of wealth and resources. The stakes to claiming indigenous identity are thus increased. Some claim indigeneity to get the rights package, while others attach the package to some other form of minority cultural alterity. For those who have not experienced the protection of even some of the most basic rights included in the package, the model is often perceived as particularly promising. Especially for those minority groups that do not desire to pursue strong claims to self-determination, the model of the right to culture is attractive for its potential to support collective title and economic resources for development. Afro-descendants in Latin America often fall into this category.

In part III of the book, I explore one such use of the model outside of the context of indigenous rights, by turning to a discussion of Law 70, a 1993 Colombian law that offers Afro-descendants the opportunity to apply for collective title for lands they have traditionally occupied. The law also provides for the protection and perpetuation of Afro-Colombian identity, primarily through education, and for sustainable development in accord with traditional cultural patterns of land and water use. As such, it includes all three understandings of culture I describe in part II of the book. Its implementation (or lack thereof) has also reproduced many of the dark sides that inhere in the various understandings of indigenous culture.

Even though Law 70 continues to be the most progressive legislation for protecting Afro-descendant rights in the region, it has led to disappointment both for those who have fallen under its ambit and for those who have not. On one hand, many communities in the Pacific region of Colombia that have been granted collective land title have found it difficult to enforce or take advantage of the rights protected under Law 70, in large part due to displacement by the war, the encroachment of megabusiness projects, and conflicting state priorities. On the other hand, some Afro-Colombian communities in the Atlantic region of the country, who do not as clearly fall under the law's ambit, nevertheless make claims to collective title under the law because they see few alternatives for development and cultural recognition. The book's final chapter considers a case study of a community living on a set of islands off the Caribbean coast of Colombia that has attempted to use Law 70 to claim collective title over part of the main island. I use the case to consider the continuing attraction to right to culture claims, and the extent to which that attraction affects the everyday discourse of community members engaged in the struggle.

ON METHOD

Because the book's aim is to study the interaction between social movements and law, it principally relies upon two types of primary documents and an eclectic and multidisciplinary range of secondary sources. In terms of primary documents, I study written texts produced by indigenous social movements in the Americas (and Afro-Colombians in the final two chapters) in the articulation of their legal and political claims. I also consider written texts produced by international and regional legal and political institutions and decision-making bodies. My secondary sources mainly stem from the fields of anthropology and law because these are the two disciplines that have been most involved in advocating for indigenous rights and in analyzing the advocacy. Though I use the terms "primary" and "secondary" here, in fact much of my method is meant to betray that distinction. That is, throughout my analysis and use of these various sources, I attempt to bring a common critical lens to works of legal and political advocacy, scholarship, international institutional reports, and legal decisions. As I explain more fully below, I am to deploy a self-conscious strategy of multidisciplinarity that refuses to distinguish between cultural critique and advocacy. In foregrounding much of the discourse produced by indigenous and Afro-Colombian social movements, I take seriously what is often referred to as "local knowledge." I read closely and carefully the statements and declarations that those in the movements have made to each other, the public, national governments, and international organizations. I quote extensively from their work. When I translate from Spanish, I do so as literally as possible, at the risk of sacrificing the nuance of the language, but in an attempt to be as true as possible to the words the movements use. The Spanish quotations are all in the endnotes, for those who prefer to read the original text.

I do not, however, claim that the knowledge is necessarily subaltern, because I essentially agree with Gayatri Spivak that the subaltern cannot speak.[11] The very act of issuing declarations and statements—generally written in one's second (nonindigenous) language—that are aimed at political actors on a local and global scale requires an articulation that, by definition, is not subaltern. That the discourse is not subaltern does not, however, mean that it cannot be subversive or challenge the frame in a variety of ways. That it is local does not mean that it cannot be co-opted.

More importantly, perhaps, I do not treat local knowledge as beyond critique. In fact, the aim of the book is to use my analysis of the right to culture to urge advocates away from the acceptance and deployment of static and essentialized notions of culture, and to raise questions about whether the right to culture—and perhaps human rights, more generally—is up to the task of the major economic and political restructuring that many advocates (if covertly) seem to seek. When advocates use essentialized understandings of culture, they do not generally do so naively. Essentialism itself has become a tool, which even indigenous peoples use. Many scholars and activists embrace and sometimes valorize this usage, referring to it as "strategic essentialism."

Much of my thinking about this book has been influenced by encounters I have had with those who argue either directly or implicitly for strategic essentialism. Gayatri Spivak is generally cited as the source for strategic essentialism, based on an interview she gave in 1984.[12] There, in the context of postcolonial feminist studies, she discussed the inevitability of both essentialist and universalist thinking, and argued that deconstructive practice requires that each be adopted strategically at different times to oppose the other. Although Spivak considered strategic deployments of both essentialism and universalism, it is the former that has had significant traction. Indeed, the term "strategic essentialism" has been used by scholars in a number of different disciplines in ways that have prompted Spivak to distance herself from it.[13]

I have encountered the term in a number of cross-disciplinary discussions in the context of indigenous rights advocacy. In particular, it often arises in conversations with academic colleagues outside law who, while critical in their own disciplines, are often reluctant to deploy critique with regard to law or legal discourse. These colleagues, I would say, tend to see law as more real and powerful than, say, ethnography or literature. They hope to channel law's power, and are often willing to suppress their own critical instincts to do so. Believing that essentialism works in or is required by law, they advocate its self-conscious and strategic usage.

Anthropologists, for example, are often asked to testify in indigenous rights cases in various domestic and international forums. They are generally called upon to describe the indigenous groups that are seeking rights, and to explain their historical and cultural ties to particular lands or practices over which the groups are making claims. A number of these anthropologists report that they have felt obliged to overly essentialize the group and avoid discussion of the inevitable gaps, conflicts, and ambiguities in the narrative. They sometimes blame the law for their strategic uses of essentialism, seeing the law as requiring anthropologists to construct what Alcida Ramos has called "the hyperreal Indian."[14]

In an article on activist research, Charles Hale thoughtfully explores his own participation in what turned out to be a seminal case before the Inter-American Court of Human Rights (*Awas Tingni v. Nicaragua*, which I discuss in chapter 4). He begins by noting that he had approached the case "in hopes of contributing useful and persuasive expert testimony; the idea of carrying out a critique of the problematic notion of culture underlying the community's claim could not have been further from my mind."[15] He continues by drawing a distinction between "cultural critique" and "activist research," which he describes as follows: "Cultural critique strives for intellectual production uncompromised by the inevitable negotiations and contradictions that these broader political struggles entail. Activist research is compromised—but also enriched—by opting to position itself squarely amid the tension between utopian ideals and practical politics."[16] He draws another line as well, when he suggests that activist researchers keep one foot "firmly planted in the rarified space of cultural critique" and the other "cautiously, but confidently, [in] law, demographics, statistics, human ecology, geographic information systems, and other technologies of objective (no quotation marks allowed) social science."[17] In short, Hale calls on the activist researcher to "deploy positivist social science methods and subject them to rigorous critique while acknowledging with acceptance the cognitive dissonance that results."[18]

I would like to resist both sets of distinctions that Hale makes, as well as his appeal to cognitive dissonance. Although I think he accurately describes many of the tensions experienced by academics engaged in activism and by activists engaged in academia, I think he also perpetuates dichotomies that we should try to break down, rather than concede. I am particularly troubled (and surprised) by his distinction between cultural critique and law because it suggests that bringing cultural critique to law would inappropriately challenge its utility, without recognizing the extent to which *not* deploying cultural critique participates in the production of legal rules that cannot accommodate the everyday messiness and contradictions of the cultural claims.

Although Hale claims not to ally himself fully with strategic essentialists,[19] he reaches some of their same conclusions in terms of rejecting constructivism in advocacy. "To state it bluntly," as he puts it, "anthropologists, geographers and lawyers who have only cultural critique to offer will disappoint the people with whom they are aligned."[20] The latter want social science, he explains, to be put to the service of their struggles, suggesting that the foot in cultural critique must give way—if through dissonance—to the other foot when it comes to advocacy. Like strategic essentialists, Hale in effect calls for a self-consciously anticonstructivist account of law that tolerates an essentialized view of culture.

Here is my concern. As long as anthropologists and others continue to provide overly stereotyped and unrealistically coherent stories of culture to fit into what they see as the requirements of the law (regardless of whether the stories comport with local knowledge), the law will almost certainly continue to require such narratives. I contend that social movements need anthropologists and lawyers in or allied with the movements to engage the social sciences and law with their critical impulses as a part of, not in contrast to, the advocacy. Moreover, there needs to be critical exchange between the would-be scientists and their clients. As social movements voice their claims in terms of law, even if through their legal representatives, they act on and interact with law and engage in its ongoing production. If they cede that job to those who claim to know what is best (and who do not want to disappoint them), they permit the discourse to control them and many others who follow in their footsteps.

These multidisciplinary discussions in which I have participated about strategic essentialism have both explicitly and implicitly framed much of my work in tracing the ways in which indigenous social movements and their allies have become increasingly enamored of human rights law and discourse. As indigenous advocates began to abandon the framing of their demands in strong self-determination terms and began to promote cultural rights instead, they turned to a legal frame—human rights—of which they had long been skeptical. As I will discuss at some length, the individualist and Western focus of the human rights regime had seemed to threaten, not protect, indigenous interests in communal land and in the maintenance of traditional economic, social, and cultural practices. Rather than seeing human rights and culture in opposition to each other, the human right to culture attempts to mediate tensions between them. Like strategic essentialism, it often assumes or promotes essentialized understandings of culture. And, as already suggested, by making the protection of culture its principal aim, it often displaces or defers a focus on the economic dependence and marginalization of most of the world's indigenous peoples, even though it was such dependence that motivated much of the activism in the first place.

Proponents of strategic essentialism in the context of indigenous human rights advocacy often suggest that exposing the incongruencies or conflicts in narratives of cultural unity is risky, perhaps providing ammunition for those who hope to deny claims to the cultural rights package. At some level, this concern is persuasive; few want their work to be used by their opponents. But I often wonder who the audience is for those who discuss these issues. They assume, almost by definition, that those who might want to use their arguments to deny such claims are not reading the works in which they discuss their strategies.[21] And, again, they reinforce the very legal paradigms they believe are problematic by adapting to, rather than confronting, them.

If an essentialized understanding of culture were to produce unequivocally positive results for indigenous peoples, I believe I would still have a difficult time with this position. But it does not. I hope to demonstrate that right to culture claims, when successful, threaten to limit the groups that might qualify for protection, force groups to overstate their cultural cohesion, and limit indigenous economic, political, and territorial autonomy. That is, I encourage indigenous peoples and their advocates to resist essentialism in a way that would not only be willing to expose the often fragile nature of the culture claims, but might facilitate the study of the background distributional inequality that both underlies and structures them.

Rodolfo Stavenhagen has noted that "indigenous opposition to domination took the form of passive resistance, of turning inward and building protective shells around community life and cultural identity."[22] Without denying the power of cultural identity and the extent to which ideas about culture organize our understandings about and presentations of ourselves and others, I suggest we consider how assertions of cultural (and other) identity claims often function as defense mechanisms to protect against real and vast material and political inequalities. As with most defense mechanisms, I would add, identity assertions work at some level to stave off or at least diminish the impact of daily threats. But they also accept as ongoing and unchangeable the threats against which they are initially created.

Studying defense mechanisms can be useful because defense mechanisms often provide gateways for understanding underlying pathologies. In exploring the multiple deployments of culture, I attempt better to understand the threats to which they are responding. Imbedded in assertions of culture are multiple understandings about indigenous peoples and their traditions, but also about their relationship and ongoing service to states, civil society, and even the future of humankind. Assertions of the right to culture are more complex, and at times even more radical, than they might originally appear. To the extent, however, that they aim to protect the group, rather than to transform the underlying power structures that work to marginalize it, I suggest that they might be short-sighted and even counterproductive. Perhaps more importantly, the assertions appear unsustainable. To the extent that the dominant societies in which indigenous peoples or their territories reside have expressed an acknowledgment of a right to indigenous culture, including special protections for that culture, few indigenous groups can live up to the cultural purity and ideal that the state and its nonindigenous citizens have come to expect in the bargain.

Far from playing into the hands of those who might aim to deny indigenous rights, my hope is that this anti-essentialist approach would not conclude that indigenous groups that do not meet the expectations of cultural performance, territory, or ancestry that have come to be expected by many settler societies are inauthentic. Rather, it would demonstrate the impossibility of that performance, and aim to create more, not less, autonomy within and among groups by rejecting the assumption that they should be empowered only to the extent that they are carriers of a culture worth preserving for the good of humankind.

PART I

International and Transnational Indigenous Movements

Setting the Stage for Transnational Indigenous Rights Movements | I

DOMESTIC AND INTERNATIONAL LAW AND POLITICS

Contemporary international indigenous movements are generally traced back to the 1970s, although their roots can be seen in the 1960s, when national indigenous organizations began to gain political momentum in a number of countries, including Canada, the United States, Australia, and many Latin American states.[1] Of course, some movements began earlier. The early twentieth century, for example, saw the formation of the Allied Tribes of British Columbia, organized by Peter Kelley and Andrew Paull;[2] the Lamista movement in Colombia, led by Páez activist Manuel Quintín Lame;[3] and attempts by Deskaheh, leader of the Six Nations Iroquois Confederacy, to petition the League of Nations to consider its case against Canada.[4] These movements tended to have a pan-indigenous element from their early stages, as indigenous groups began to identify with each other as indigenous vis-à-vis the modern state.[5]

In the 1970s, indigenous peoples began to organize more actively across nation-state borders, and to form international pan-indigenous networks. With this organization came regional and international meetings, including the 1974 planning meeting in Guyana for what eventually became the World Council of Indigenous Peoples, that council's first meeting in 1975 in Canada,[6] the 1974 meeting of the Parliament of American Indians of the Southern Cone in Paraguay,[7] the NGO Conference on Discrimination against Indigenous Populations in 1977 in Geneva, and a 1977 meeting in Barbados (known as Barbados II). Gatherings such as these were an outgrowth of, as well as a catalyst for, increasing international organization, both intergovernmental and nongovernmental. As Alyson Brysk explains: "International fora such as the International Labor Organization and transnational nongovernmental organizations such as the World Council of Churches systematically examined indigenous issues within the organizations' wider mandates and brought together Indian activists."[8] Brysk also contends that indigenous peoples were drawn to the international system out of "domestic powerlessness": "International activity required fewer resources than domestic mobilization and was more amenable to information politics. In some cases, characteristics that were domestic handicaps became international strengths."[9]

Regardless of their incentive, those groups involved with pan-indigenous movements found themselves organizing against and influenced by the background of colonialist conquest and years of domestic and international law and policy pertaining directly and indirectly to indigenous peoples. While parts I and II of this book consider in detail the demands of international and transnational indigenous movements, the purpose of the present chapter is to set the stage for that discussion by describing the political and legal landscape within and against which the movements were organizing. As indigenous rights advocates have made decisions over the past few decades about how best to pursue or articulate their claims in the international arena, they have often borrowed from, adapted, or critiqued legal and political models—such as sovereignty, self-determination, and human rights—that largely have been developed in other contexts.

I focus the first section of this chapter on the Americas—on the different models of colonial techniques that were deployed there, and on their ongoing effects. In *American Pentimento*, Patricia Seed uses the concept of a pentimento, the "trace of an earlier composition or of alterations [in painting] that has become visible with the passage of time,"[10] to revisit English, Spanish, and Portuguese forms of colonialism in the Americas and how they were driven by different economic interests. For Seed, colonists' representations of the people, culture, and forms of livelihood they encountered in the New World derived more from colonial economic desires and political arrangements than from the actual observable characteristics and circumstances of native peoples. Thus, the differences can be traced back to Europe itself—to the Christian identity maintained by the Spanish and Portuguese contrasted with the planter, or farmer, identity of the English[11]—and their ongoing effects can be seen beyond the Americas. Many distinctive aspects of English colonial models deployed in the Americas, for example, can also be found in India, Australia, and New Zealand.

I rely on much of Seed's analysis in this chapter, but I also hope to extend it by connecting ongoing debates about the meaning and necessity of indigenous self-determination to some of the same differences in colonial method. In particular, I tie indigenous demands for a right to self-determination and land to former British colonies, while connecting legal and political strategies aimed at internal autonomy and collective cultural rights to former Spanish colonies. These two lines of advocacy, I contend, respond to different histories of oppression and conquest as well as to different mechanisms designed and justified to legalize and control conquest. The first section of the chapter explores those histories.

In the second section of the chapter, I consider the development of international legal models in the mid-twentieth century that suggest the landscape for advocacy strategies that existed for indigenous peoples when they begin to organize internationally. Self-determination (in the context of decolonization), international human rights, and economic integration through international labor rights are the principal models I discuss.

CONQUEST, COLONIAL, AND POST-COLONIAL LAW: BRITISH AND SPANISH APPROACHES

Conquest and Colonial Law

A number of scholars have written on the different strategies and justifications for conquest deployed in the Americas by Spain and Portugal, on one hand, and Britain and France, on the other hand. I revisit some of this work briefly here, as a means to set up different lines of resistance that I believe we can follow through even to recent debates about the UN Declaration discussed in the introduction. My goal is not to offer anything near a comprehensive account of the treatments of native populations during conquest; rather, I hope to use some of the narratives about that treatment to foreshadow later tensions between the self-determination and cultural rights strands of advocacy.

Antony Anghie reminds us that colonial expansion and conquest of indigenous peoples involved a well-thought-through, and contestable, set of legal justifications.[12] Indeed, Spanish theologians engaged in debates about whether indigenous people were human, and therefore whether their subjugation was permissible. Francisco de Vitoria is commonly seen as one of the most progressive members of this group because of his insistence that natives were human beings capable of making rational and moral decisions.[13] Yet, while "appearing to promote notions of equality and reciprocity between the Indians and the Spanish," Vitoria used this innate equality of the Indians to justify Spanish conquest over native populations.[14]

If natives were to be considered as equals, they were also to be subjected to the same rules that governed the relationship between Europeans. Indian resistance was seen to violate these rules. Anghie explains:

> Vitoria's apparently innocuous enunciation of a right to "travel" and "sojourn" extends finally to the creation of a comprehensive, indeed inescapable system of norms which are inevitably violated by the Indians. For example, Vitoria asserts that "to keep certain people out of the city or province as being enemies, or to expel them when already there, are acts of war." Thus any Indian attempt to resist Spanish penetration would amount to an act of war, which would justify Spanish retaliation. Each encounter between the Spanish and the Indians therefore entitles the Spanish to "defend" themselves against Indian aggression and, in doing so, continuously expand Spanish territory.[15]

Even if Vitoria insisted that Indians were human, then, he also believed that they engaged in inhumane acts against which their victims needed to be protected.

Conquest was also grounded in cultural difference. As Anghie explains, for Vitoria, "the Indian is very different from the Spaniard because the Indian's specific social and cultural practices are at variance from the practices required by the universal norms—which in effect are Spanish practices," and it is through these "universal norms" that "the Spanish acquire an extraordinarily powerful right of intervention and may act on behalf of the people seen as victims of Indian rituals."[16] This notion that certain cultural practices of indigenous peoples need to be condemned continues to appear in the discussion of the application of human rights to indigenous peoples. I outline it in chapter 4, using Elizabeth Povinelli's terminology of the "invisible asterisk."[17]

Using a variety of justifications, including those posited by Vitoria, the Spanish engaged in a long, brutal period of invasion and occupation of territory that involved destruction of civilizations such as those of the Incas and Aztecs as well as enslavement of indigenous people for labor, often in mining, cargo transportation, and agriculture. According to Anthony Pagden, this type of conquest was unique to the Spaniards:

> Only the Spanish settlers formally styled themselves conquerors, *conquistadores*, and only the native-born Spanish settlers (*criollos*) would, in the end, ground their claims to independence primarily upon their association with an aristocracy of conquest. An empire of this kind had to be an empire based upon people, defeated subjects who could be transformed into a pliant labour force. In America, only the Spaniards, and to a somewhat lesser degree the Portuguese, had found peoples in sufficient numbers whom they were able to overrun in this way.[18]

In contrast, he notes, "both the English and the French were . . . driven either to exclude the Native Americans from their colonies, or to incorporate them as trading partners."[19] Pagden argues that the British and French entered the Americas with the idea of following the model of the Spaniards, but that the lack of largely populated indigenous areas in the more northern region created different types of resistance and economic possibilities. Thus, the British and French turned to justifications for claiming territory rather than people.

While Patricia Seed agrees that the British focused on land and the Spanish and Portuguese on people and their labor, she contends that their approaches were attributable not simply to "demographic and ecological accidents of historic encounters," but to varying "cultural traditions about valuing, transferring, and allocating riches [that] emerged in Europe long before the colonists' quest for riches in the Americas."[20] Those different traditions facilitated different justifications for and modes of colonization: "Nomads could lose their land under English rules, and idolaters and pagans could be deprived of their rights to minerals and labor under Iberian conventions."[21]

Regardless of the source of their focus, the British, and to a certain extent the French, ended up relying on the doctrine of *terra nullius*. In this doctrine, lands that were not put to active use—generally agricultural use—were seen as empty, belonging to no one. Thus, the first person who put the land to use could properly claim title over it. The British therefore did not see themselves as engaged in conquest, but only in the improvement of land. For Pagden, an argument based on conquest, "even supposing that it had been historically sustainable," would have had little traction "in a political culture such as Britain which, because it had itself been the creation of the Norman Conquest of 1066, was committed to the 'continuity theory' of constitutional law in which the legal and political institutions of the conquered are deemed to survive a conquest."[22]

In contrast, the Spanish did not generally resort to terra nullius to justify their conquest, in part because it would have been difficult to maintain that lands were unoccupied, particularly in the cases of large parts of Peru and Mexico.[23] Moreover, the Spanish and Portuguese had already articulated justifications for discovery even before arriving in the Americas.[24] Robert Miller argues that Portugal had revised the doctrine of discovery in the context of justifications for colonizing the Canary Islands in the middle of the fifteenth century, basing it not "on the infidel's lack of dominion or natural rights, but instead . . . on the perceived need to protect natives from the oppression of others and lead them to civilization and conversion under papal guidance."[25]

There were times when the British and French were also unable to justify their occupation of land under the doctrine of terra nullius. Pagden explains that "in instances in which in those places where the Native Americans had proved to be too powerful to displace easily both the English and the French had, until the late nineteenth century, to rely upon land purchase or treaty."[26] Indeed, British law eventually recognized Indian territorial rights, and set forth procedures for making treaties.[27] In part because of the fraudulent nature of many private land sales between Indians and non-Indians, the Royal Proclamation of 1763 declared that all acquisition of land would need to be by treaty, thereby granting the state a monopoly on the acquisition of indigenous lands.[28]

Seed reminds us that the term "treaty" did not principally refer to agreements between nations (as opposed to contracts between individuals or other legal persons) until the mid-seventeenth century, with the Peace of Westphalia. When the requirement that treaties—rather than ordinary sales contracts—be used to convey property claimed by Native

Americans, it was clear that treaty referred to a state-tribal agreement. Indeed, the requirement was in response to battles among Englishmen (and sometimes Dutch colonizers) over who had properly purchased land. At that point, "colonial and then national officials at the end of the eighteenth century insisted upon the transfer of land through centrally written and authorized agreements, which they called *treaties*."[29]

Thus, the approaches to conquest by colonial powers often had as much, if not more, to do with their claims to territory vis-à-vis each other as they did with any claims against indigenous peoples. Miller explains: "On one esoteric level, Discovery was a legal principle designed only to control the European nations. Clearly, however, the native peoples and nations felt most heavily its onerous burdens."[30] For Seed, "the treaty purchases" not only granted the most secure legal title under English law, they "enable[d] public officials to dispense new land grants and put an end to ceaseless squabbles among colonists."[31]

Even after the Royal Proclamation of 1763, it would be hard to label many agreements or treaties as consensual. Indeed, Indians often had a different idea from the colonists as to what they had agreed to. Colonists might have made oral promises to Indians that they would reserve the right to occupy and use certain land, for example, but the written "agreement" might then strip them of any such right.[32] Still, that the English and later the Canadian and U.S. governments saw Indians as capable of entering into treaties for sale of land suggests that the colonial and postcolonial governments acknowledged both indigenous rights to land and their standing in international law. As Michael Banton explains in contrasting treaty making in Canada and the United States with the process of conquest in Latin America: "No leader of an indigenous group [in Latin America] can borrow the words of a Canadian counterpart . . . 'we have lived up to our side of the treaties . . . To us a treaty is an international document signed by two nations.' "[33]

This use of treaties has long provided the basis for an argument that indigenous tribes are subjects of international law. Indeed, most international indigenous advocacy calls for recognition of treaty rights, where applicable. The World Council of Indigenous Peoples, for example, has called upon the United Nations to "recognize the treaties that Indigenous Nations around the world have signed as binding under International Law,"[34] and Article 37 of the un Declaration calls for the enforcement of such agreements. Juxtaposing these potential uses of international law with international legal doctrine that long excluded or facilitated the exploitation of indigenous peoples, Thornberry refers to the development of international law in the context of indigenous peoples as constituting "ambiguous discourses."[35] Robert Williams is less optimistic, seeing international legal discourse as having "effectively dismissed" indigenous peoples: "Indigenous territories were regarded as vacant and appropriable by a 'civilized' Western state. Indigenous peoples did not possess internationally recognizable rights of self-determination. They were, as one early 20th century Western international tribunal noted, simply 'not a legal unit of international law.' "[36]

If British colonial law permitted displacement by settlers and the separation of indigenous peoples from them, Spanish colonial law was forced to find a way for indigenous and nonindigenous people to coexist. Indian tribute, or *alcabala*, for example, was meant to be paid to the crown, but it needed to be collected by *encomenderos*, the conquistadors to whom the crown gave rights to use indigenous labor. As *criollo* resistance to the Spanish crown increased, this triangulation presented an increasingly significant obstacle to Spanish control.

At least in much of Latin America, formal colonial laws often protected indigenous land and traditions, though for a price. As Angel Oquendo puts it: "During the colonial period, *Indiano* law often strove to protect autochthonous communities and to defend them from exploitation. It took pains to preserve their customs, traditions, and social structures, provided they accepted the empire's sovereignty claim and embraced its religion."[37] Oquendo might be overstating here the extent to which colonial law "took pains," while understating the contradiction between preserving "customs, traditions, and social structures" and embracing the empire's religion. Still, he recognizes that the formal law was mostly disregarded: "Obviously, this well-intentioned effort was unsuccessful. The imperial emissaries inexorably devastated tribes, as well as entire civilizations. With this experience, the Latin American gap between legal norm and reality was born."[38] Other scholars, of course, have disputed that the effort was "well-intentioned." Seed has argued, for example, that the maintenance of differences in custom (from requiring that indigenous people dress distinctively to forbidding them to ride horses) helped maintain "colonial domination" in Spanish America.[39]

In any event, laws enacted during the colonial period continue to play a role in contemporary indigenous movements in Latin America, sometimes serving the same function as treaties for indigenous peoples colonized by the British. In some instances, it is not so much that there is a gap between law and reality as that, over time, the law has changed. In other words, the formal law today is sometimes not as protective of indigenous land and custom as it was in the colonial period.

Joanne Rappaport illustrates how such a pattern has produced the fetishization of law in the indigenous community of Cumbal in southern Colombia.[40] She discusses, in particular, how the Cumbales today often articulate their land claims using Deed 228, a colonial law that defined the boundaries of indigenous lands. Yet they often confuse that law with Law 89, a law passed in 1890 that, ironically, called for the eventual privatization of communal land holdings, or *resguardos*.[41] They therefore base their land rights claims on a colonial law vastly altered by subsequent historical contexts.

While some indigenous groups might continue to use colonial laws to assert their claims, others make clear that these laws do not represent indigenous perspectives or needs. The World Council of Indigenous Peoples (WCIP), for example, maintains that "through the use of their colonial legal systems the colonizers imposed their own concepts of Indian Rights."[42] The WCIP has therefore held as its goal to elucidate and put into legal practice "an Indigenous interpretation of what 'land rights, international agreements and treaties, land reform and systems of tenure' means to us." Its members seek to stymie "colonial efforts to force us to adopt their views," not validate those efforts by attempting to readjust colonial laws.[43] While colonial laws have continued to present both pathways and obstacles to indigenous rights claims, so too has a new layer of legality arising out of the nation-states born in the late eighteenth and early nineteenth centuries.

Post-colonial Law and Policy

With independence of the United States and Canada from Britain and France and of most of Latin America from Spain and Portugal, the nineteenth century saw a reforging of relationships between indigenous peoples and the nation-state. The United States and Canada essentially continued the justifications for land control begun by the British, expanding, for example, the number of treaties they entered into with indigenous tribes. Post-independence legal issues regarding indigenous lands were largely preoccupied with issues of federalism and the extent to which indigenous groups fit into the state or federal systems (or neither or both). Newly formed states in Latin America made a more significant break from Spain and Portugal than the United States and Canada did from Britain and France. Indigenous peoples were an important part of that break, with many criollos imagining that indigenous peoples would be liberated in the new nation. As will be discussed below, this attempted liberation had unintended negative consequences, including the loss of protection for communally owned lands.

THE UNITED STATES, CANADA, AND FEDERALISM

As we have seen, treaties played an important role in British and former British colonies for colonial, and sometimes post-colonial, acquisition of indigenous lands. Such agreements were particularly prevalent in the United States and Canada.[44] In both those countries, however, the legal treatment of indigenous peoples after independence eventually became intertwined with questions about the rights of states and individuals versus those of the federal government.[45]

One important way in which this issue played out was through a series of U.S. Supreme Court cases in the 1820s and 1830s involving the Piankishaw and the Cherokee tribes.[46] In what is often referred to as "the Marshall Trilogy," because the decisions were authored by Chief Justice John Marshall the Court reasserted federal sovereignty over Indian land. It did so in different circumstances, against claims by both individuals and states.

In the first case in the trilogy, *Johnson v. M'Intosh*,[47] the Court ruled that federal ownership based on "discovery and conquest" was valid in spite of an individual claim of title based on purchase from the tribe. Chief Justice Marshall wrote that colonial "discovery" had vested property rights in the crown, and that those rights had transferred to the U.S. federal government at independence. Thus, claims of land purchase were illegitimate because indigenous peoples had no assignable property rights. In the third case, Chief Justice Marshall questioned the foundation of that holding, but nevertheless legitimized conquest. He found the basis of European colonial land rights to be conquest and war, plus possession, thus recognizing that indigenous peoples had held some prior property rights, but concluding that the land had been taken legitimately by the federal government.[48]

These cases had an impact on the understanding of treaties entered into between the U.S. government and Indian tribes. Even though the cases acknowledged the possibility of a treaty between the federal government and Indian tribes by recognizing that the Cherokee had some pre-colonial rights, they made it clear that possession of land did not constitute jurisdiction or territory comparable to that of sovereign nations. The second case in the trilogy, *Cherokee Nation v. Georgia*, most specifically addressed this issue, as it was there that the Court found Indian tribes to be "domestic dependent nations." Although the specific issue in the case was whether the Cherokee could sue on their own behalf in federal court or needed to be represented by the federal government, the Court opted for the second position by specifically rejecting the argument that the Cherokee nation could be treated in the same way as a sovereign state, at least under the U.S. Constitution.[49]

Despite, or perhaps due to, the Marshall Trilogy, the concept of the federal government's "trust responsibility"—considered a duty owed to "domestic dependent nations"—has evolved over time. In fact, it has been used by indigenous rights advocates and the government alike to articulate the duties that the federal government owes to tribes. Sometimes the source for the responsibility is located in Indian sovereignty and treaties. The Midwest Alliance of Sovereign Tribes, for example, includes the following in its definition of trust responsibility:

> Between 1787 and 1871, the U.S. and Indian tribes signed hundreds of treaties. In nearly every one of these treaties, tribes gave up lands in return for goods, money and other resources that were promised by the U.S. government. When the U.S. took Indian land and Indian resources, it made binding legal agreements that tribes would exercise sovereign authority within their reservation boundaries and be funded into perpetuity by the federal government.[50]

The federal government has not entirely disagreed. The Clinton administration's Department of Justice even found the basis of sovereignty in *Cherokee Nation v. Georgia*, putting a positive spin on the language about domestic dependent nations: "From its earliest days, the United States has recognized the sovereign status of Indian tribes as domestic dependent nations. Our Constitution recognizes Indian sovereignty by classing Indian treaties among the 'supreme law of the land,' and establishes Indian affairs as a unique area of federal concern."[51]

The Bush administration deleted the above language from its own policy statement (which remained in effect during the Obama administration as of December 2009), but kept the statement that the Department of Justice "acknowledges the federal trust responsibility arising from Indian treaties, statutes, executive orders, and the historical relations between the United States and Indian tribes. In a broad sense, the trust responsibility relates to the United States' unique legal and political relationship with Indian tribes."[52] At the same time, the statement makes clear (as had that under the Clinton administration as well) that Congress has plenary power over Indian affairs, a position that the Supreme Court has continually reinforced since its first articulation in the Marshall Trilogy. Thus, though according to the Department of Justice, "tribes retain important sovereign powers over their members and their territory," those powers are "subject to the plenary power of Congress."[53] In this telling, any Indian retention of sovereignty would be a gift from Congress (by virtue of a decision on its part not to assert its power), not an entitlement.

Though Canada has a significantly different experience from the United States in terms of colonization and independence, the two countries' approaches to Indian rights in the nineteenth century were fairly similar. When the British Parliament passed the Constitution Act of 1867, distributing legislative authority between federal and provincial governments, legislative jurisdiction over "Indians, and Lands reserved for the Indians" was granted to Parliament.[54] Debates ensued over the years about the extent of federal versus provincial authority over Indian affairs, but, according to Patrick Macklem, "Parliament and provincial legislatures accept without question a hierarchical relationship of sovereign and subject between the Canadian state and Aboriginal people."[55]

Canadian indigenous proprietary interests were also significantly undermined in the nineteenth and most of the twentieth century, primarily through judicial decisions. Macklem has argued that the judicial suggestion that "Aboriginal prior occupancy might not generate independently enforceable interests with respect to land served as a legal backdrop for almost a century of relations between the Crown and Aboriginal peoples, shaping expectations of governments, corporations, citizens, and other legal actors."[56] He contends that the resulting exploitation led to the need for constitutional protection for indigenous land titles as well as for culture and self-government.

Canadian legislative and judicial action with regard to property and territory went hand in hand with a general devaluation of indigenous culture and a desire to assimilate as many Indians as possible. In 1867, for example, the Canadian Parliament passed a law calling for the voluntary enfranchisement of Indian men of good character. The act was amended to make enfranchisement compulsory for Indian men with higher education.[57] Similar impulses explained the creation of residential schools for Indian children, begun in 1880 and lasting nearly a hundred years. With the federal Indian Act in 1920, all aboriginal children were required to attend residential schools for at least ten months of the year.[58] This type of assimilation, then, depended upon formal disparate treatment.

While the Canadian government had appealed to a "special relationship" with Indians in order to exercise considerable discretionary power over aboriginal lands since independence, it was not until 1984 that the Canadian government began to clarify its obligations to indigenous peoples. It was that year that the landmark Canadian Supreme Court decision in *Guerin v. The Queen*, in an opinion delivered by Justice Dickson, defined the legal relationship of the Crown to Canadian Indians as a fiduciary one.[59] This relationship entails, among other things, the duty of the Canadian government to give priority to indigenous land titles over other, conflicting claims and infringing legislation. At the same time, *Guerin* affirms the long-held position that, while crucial decisions about land ought to be made in the interest of indigenous peoples, they will be made by the Canadian government.[60] This fiduciary duty thus in many ways resembles the U.S. doctrine of trust responsibility, and it is based on similar ideas of paternalism.[61] Since the *Guerin* decision, it too has become a tool for many indigenous peoples who seek to hold the Canadian government accountable.[62]

LATIN AMERICA

In general, Spanish Americans in Latin America were much more antagonistic toward the policies of former colonial powers than were Anglo-Americans. Both mestizo and criollo identity were crucial to post-independence Latin America, and with that came a new attitude toward indigenous peoples.

Unlike in the United States and Canada, there was no history of treaties between indigenous peoples and either the Spanish crown or settlers, and there was thus no basis for even considering the separate collective international personality of indigenous peoples. Nevertheless, a focus on liberal rights was present from the beginning of the move for independence from Spain. As Oquendo puts it:

> Independence brought a new rhetoric to indigenous affairs. The constitutions and the codes of this period celebrated the liberal spirit that had inspired the secessionist insurrection . . . Evoking French revolutionary ideology, the constitutions informed these people that the republican family would welcome them as individuals, but not as members of their respective groups.[63]

Oquendo offers a common view that liberal ideology was not followed with regard to indigenous peoples, as "once again, deeds lagged far behind words. Indigenous citizens never fully enjoyed the freedoms they were promised. The authorities invariably disregarded both the letter and the spirit of the law."[64]

Yet a strong argument can be made that liberalism was part of the problem. Oquendo asserts as much through his acknowledgment that Indians were welcomed as individuals but not as group members, and in discussing the work of Hans Gundermann: "Gundermann explains how the notion of citizenship initially penetrated into these territories by seeking to suppress difference. The state accordingly overlaid formal equality upon colonial stratification. Consequently, it sought not to subjugate, but rather to assimilate these communities."[65]

In much of South America, Simón Bolívar sought to bring indigenous people into the state's fold through a number of his liberal decrees and proclamations aimed at ending the vestiges of the corporatist colonial years. Bolívar was troubled in particular by the prevalence of exploitative, coerced labor, and he believed that negotiations over wages and terms of work should require free and formal legal contracts between Indians and prospective employers. This rule should apply to governmental and private employers, as well as priests.[66] Bolívar consistently linked problems of labor exploitation to indigenous people's need for land, often assuming that satisfying the latter would eliminate the former.[67] The central concern for him was thus that "the majority of Indians have had no opportunity to enjoy land ownership,"[68] by which he meant ownership in the sense of private property. Remedying this deprivation meant that much land that had long been collectively owned (or at least used) by indigenous communities would be divided and given to individual Indian families.[69] In Peru, for example, he granted individual Indians alienable title over lands they had worked under colonial rule. He also abolished the Indian tribute for a few years, early on in his reign.

John Lynch argues that Bolívar's Indian decrees "were limited in scope and misguided in intent," and made Indians more vulnerable: "To give them land without capital, equipment and protection was to invite them to become indebted to more powerful landowners, to surrender their land in payment, and to end up in debt peonage."[70] For Lynch, these perhaps unintended consequences of Bolívar's policies stemmed from his failure to understand fully the issues facing indigenous peoples.[71] "The humanitarian instincts of the revolution were not themselves beneficial to the Andean communities,"[72] he concludes. Discussing Bolívar's legacy, Lynch explains:

> The liberals of post-independence regarded the Indians as an obstacle to national development and believed that the autonomy they had inherited from the colonial regime should be ended by integrating them into the nation. In Colombia and Peru the new legislators sought to destroy corporate entities in order to release Indian lands and mobilize Indian labour.[73]

Thus, formal equality worked against Indians, as they were left in a situation of relative powerlessness vis-à-vis their neighbors, portending their future impoverishment: "Their community lands were left without protection and eventually became one of the victims of land concentration."[74]

Newly formed states eventually responded to the widespread confiscation of communal lands that resulted from the liberalization project. According to Seed, "virtually everywhere in Spanish-speaking America, restoring communal native ownership grew increasingly popular in the final decades of the nineteenth century, and by the start of the twentieth century traditional Indian ownership of surface land was restored throughout most of the former Ibero-Americas."[75] The reference to surface land is significant, as it provided an important limitation to indigenous rights: the dominant population retained most mineral rights.

As the nineteenth century came to a close, state policies toward indigenous peoples had begun to embody formal inequality. While missionaries continued to attempt to assimilate indigenous peoples spiritually—sometimes under an explicit government mandate—states were distinguishing them politically. In yet another demonstration of the ideology of tutelage and trusteeship, the political distinctions were often meant to be temporary, with the idea of protecting Indians while they were in the process of becoming civilized. Indians were given the status of minors, for example, in a number of countries. In Colombia, one such country, Law 89 of 1890 stated that "the general legislation of the Republic shall not apply to savages who are being brought to civilized life by the missions."[76] The law specifically addressed how "savages in the process of being reduced to civilized life should be governed," and codified the existence of the resguardo system, even while limiting its power.[77]

Rappaport explains that "although the original intent of Law 89 was the *cultural* integration of indigenous peoples . . . it ultimately defines the Indian as a *legal* rather than a cultural being."[78] Much as with the trust responsibility in the United States, the legal status came with state responsibility to the Indians. It also delineated land for use, if not ownership. And, much as with the trust responsibility, Law 89—as previously discussed—is invoked by indigenous advocates today to support claims of autonomy.[79]

If in the nineteenth century, cultural integrationism and legal separatism worked side by side to accommodate what were considered to be the evolutionary needs of indigenous peoples (as well as of states), the twentieth century saw a change. Through the ideology of *indigenismo*, policies throughout the region began to give at least rhetorical weight to indigenous cultural identity, even while attempting to integrate indigenous peoples into the economic and political life of the state.

Twentieth-Century Latin American Indigenismo

As the twentieth century began to unfold, many Latin American state policies began to move toward a new type of integration, including economic integration, at least in theory. Alan Knight explains, in the context of Mexico, that the "old policy of coercive integration" was "as an official ideology . . . bankrupt after 1910; as a matter of daily practice it lived on lustily."[80] The "old policy" to which he refers was replaced with indigenismo, a reform agenda based on an ideology that recognized, even valorized, an Indian past as providing important ingredients for new mestizo societies. Although the shift might appear subtle today, Knight explains that indigenismo was seen in its early years as a significant departure from its precursors. The old form of integration came inevitably "at the expense of the Indians' pre-existing culture," while the new form intended to be "planned, enlightened, and respectful of that culture: Indian economic and intellectual development could proceed . . . 'without this, of course, signifying the annihilation of the original [Indian] culture.' "[81]

Again, at least in principle, one of the distinctions between the old and the new could be found in their approaches to race. Specifically, in postrevolutionary Mexico—where the ideology largely took shape—*indigenistas* explicitly rejected the racist, Spencerian evolutionism of those thinkers who had provided intellectual support for the 1876–1911 dictatorship of Porfirio Díaz. Rather than seeing Indian "misery" as the outcome of biologically rooted inferiority, they saw it as stemming from poverty and lack of economic integration.[82] As one indigenista explained in 1941, "it is wrong . . . to believe that the problem is racial, when in reality it is economic, it is social, it is cultural, it is governmental."[83]

In *Race and Ethnicity in Latin America*, Peter Wade explains the ideology of indigenismo in a broader context:

> From the 1920s, the indian became a prime symbol of national identity in countries such as Mexico and Peru: both countries created government departments for indigenous affairs, while Peru recognised the 'indigenous community' as a legal entity and Mexico created academic institutions dedicated to the study of indigenous peoples. In Brazil, an agency was set up in 1910 for the 'protection of the Indians.' This, in broad terms was the ideology of indigenismo. This term covers a variety of perspectives, but the central notion was that indians need special recognition and that special values attached to them. Very often, it was a question of exotic and romantic symbolism, based more on the glorification of the pre-Columbian indian ancestry of the nation than on respect for contemporary indian populations. Thus, the reality was often one of continued discrimination and exploitation. In addition, the future was generally envisioned as being integrated and mestizo in colour.[84]

Although integration was the ultimate aim, what the integrated society would look like was still open to question. Wade describes, for example, a radical (and less accepted) version of indigenismo that "wed[ded] socialism and indigenismo and model[ed] the future nation on the supposedly socialist aspects of ancient Andean indian culture."[85] Rather than call for explicit indigenous recognition, this version aimed to support a socialist worldview that it argued was inherent to indigenous thought.

For Wade, "whatever the variety . . . the point remains that indians were often seen as a special category, needy of the specific attention of intellectuals, the state and the Church."[86] Wade's inclusion of intellectuals and the church is significant. Indigenismo was an ideology, which means that it had to be perpetuated through civil society as well as formal state policy.

Indigenismo spread to the regional level as well. Indeed, it formed the basis of a regional international institution that is still in existence today, the Instituto Indigenista Interamericano, or (to use the official translation of its name) the Inter-American Indian Institute. The institute was authorized by a 1940 convention and entered into force a year later with the ratifications of Ecuador, El Salvador, Honduras, Mexico, Paraguay, and the United States; most other states in the region signed in the ensuing years. The participating governments focused on the "Indian Problem" in the Americas, pledging "to cooperate with one another, on a basis of mutual respect for the inherent rights of each to exercise absolute liberty in solving the 'Indian Problem' in America, by means of periodical meetings, by means of an Inter-American Indian Institute and of National Indian Institutes."[87]

The Mexican anthropologist Manuel Gamio, who many see as the father of indigenismo, was chosen in 1942 as the first director of the Inter-American Indian Institute, and he served in that position until his death in 1960. Although indigenismo is generally criticized today by indigenous rights advocates, the institute continues to be seen as a viable vehicle for indigenous rights. Indeed, one activist in the United States, Rudolph Ryser, has recently faulted the U.S. government for not living up to its financial as well as other obligations under the treaty. He describes the convention as having been promoted by social scientists in Mexico and the United States, and designed by President Cárdenas of Mexico and John Collier, head of the U.S. Bureau of Indian Affairs. According to Ryser, "they wanted to promote the development of education, health, and agricultural projects and revitalize Indian arts and crafts throughout the western hemisphere."[88]

Bonfil Batalla identifies three essential elements of indigenista policies from their ascent in 1940s Latin America through their dissolution in the 1980s: "These policies must be protective, because the Indian is understood 'as an economically and socially weak individual.' They must tend towards the full incorporation of the indigenous in the national life of each country, and must, simultaneously, guarantee the permanence and encourage the development of those aspects of the Indian culture that are 'positive.' "[89]

His third element—the retention of those aspects of indigenous culture that are seen as desirable—adds an important dimension, and helps explain the way in which the ideology worked both to accept and reject indigenous culture. It accepted those parts it saw as "positive," as something worth embracing for the national heritage. The other parts, presumably, did not need to be salvaged.

As we will see, indigenismo was reflected in the International Labor Organization (ILO) during the same period. Moreover, some of the tensions in the ideology, including over the value to be placed on different aspects of indigenous culture, continue to surface in contemporary human rights debates—as we will see, for example, in arguments that individual rights ought to trump certain collective rights of indigenous peoples. As discussed in the next section, an earlier incarnation of that perspective was rejected by the American Anthropological Association as early as 1947.

INTERNATIONAL LEGAL MODELS IN THE MID-TWENTIETH CENTURY

Two streams of international legal discourse began to dominate the world stage in the 1940s: self-determination and human rights. Although they had earlier roots, they were both enshrined in the UN Charter of 1945. Subsequent debates about decolonization challenged and further developed both of these two streams. Would human rights or self-determination for colonial Africa, for example, mean independence and statehood? If so, how would one draw the map of Africa? And what authority would new states have to dictate their own lives, free from interference from their former colonial powers?

While these issues played out directly in the context of colonial Africa, they also reflected different approaches toward the treatment of indigenous peoples geographically located inside settler states. Whether these indigenous groups would follow the road to statehood, find some other form of autonomy within those states, or demand individual or collective rights was a question that would need to be addressed later by indigenous rights advocates.

I thus consider the development of these two models to foreshadow the legal and political strategies considered by indigenous groups when they began to organize around a pan-indigenist identity in the 1970s. First, however, I consider the work of the ILO, the only international institution at the time to attend directly to indigenous peoples. Its 1957 convention pursued economic integration and, along with at least some versions of indigenismo in Latin America, provides an important backdrop against which indigenous peoples eventually organized.

Although the remainder of the chapter steps away from the Americas, it does so with an eye toward the roles that the models of integration, self-determination, and the right to culture played in subsequent arguments by indigenous peoples throughout the region.

*Economic Integration: International Labor
Organization Convention 107*

The International Labor Organization was the first intergovernmental organization to address directly the political and economic disempowerment of indigenous peoples. The organization was established in 1919, and its work on indigenous peoples began in the 1920s with its preparation of the Forced Labor Convention (eventually adopted in 1930), which aimed to prevent the imposition of compulsory labor on native populations. Such a focus fit relatively easily and obviously into the ILO's mandate.[90] It also fit within the structures of colonialism in existence at the time. Luis Rodríguez-Piñero has argued that the ILO was formed with the aim of "disciplining the exploitation of the 'indigenous' workforce in the colonies":[91] "From its very inception," he contends, "the organization considered 'native labour' according to notions of trusteeship prevailing in the international law of the time in its relation with non-European societies."[92]

By the 1950s, however, the ILO became concerned with the failure of indigenous peoples to integrate into their national populations. This failure had social and economic effects, on indigenous peoples as well as on the nation-states they inhabited. In 1957, the ILO drafted Convention 107, Concerning the Protection and Integration of Indigenous and Other Tribal and Semi-Tribal Populations in Independent Countries (ILO 107). According to Douglas Sanders, the convention saw "indigenous populations as 'less advanced' than other sectors of national society. They were seen as archaic lumps in the body politic, in need of modernization and integration."[93]

Although most of the convention was aimed at measures to integrate indigenous peoples, it did not explicitly call for their assimilation. In fact, an often overlooked provision is Article 4, which calls for "due account" to be "taken of the cultural and religious values and of the forms of social control existing among these populations"[94] and "the danger involved in disrupting the values and institutions of the said populations."[95] Moreover, it recognized indigenous peoples' right to collective lands they had traditionally occupied.[96]

That said, a new economic and social order was clearly imagined, and eventually—it was thought—indigenous peoples would not require extra attention to their cultures or traditions. Nor would they need special protections provided by the convention.[97] The convention aimed to "mitigat[e] the difficulties experienced by these populations in adjusting themselves to new conditions of life and work."[98] Similarly, it made land rights subject to the "interest of national economic development or . . . the health of the said populations."[99]

The scope of the population reached by the convention was broad, referring to "tribal" as well as "semi-tribal" populations. The latter included those "in the process of losing their tribal characteristics."[100] The reference to "tribal" and "semi-tribal," rather than simply to "indigenous" populations, resulted from pressure from African and Asian states. As Russell Barsh explains, these states "regarded their analogous problems . . . as 'tribal' rather than 'indigenous' . . . That is, the Convention had as its objects 'tribal' groups that were segregated culturally or legally from national society whether or not this had arisen from the historical circumstances of colonization."[101]

In the 1970s, pan-indigenous movements began to reject the convention. From their vantage point, it represented a perpetuation of the civilizing mission because of its support for conventional models of industrialized economic development and its explicit attempt to integrate indigenous peoples into those models. The movements viewed the convention as assimilationist, both culturally and economically. In the context of Latin America, it was considered by many to be a reflection of indigenismo. Some of these views can be summarized by Rodríguez-Piñero's more recent criticism of official ILO history for "overlook[ing] the fact that the organization's historical interest in the fate of 'indigenous workers' was colonial in nature."[102]

The ILO eventually revisited its approach, and in 1989 it produced Convention 169, Concerning Indigenous and Tribal Peoples in Independent Countries (ILO 169). As I discuss in chapter 4, that convention largely approaches indigenous rights from a cultural rights perspective.

Self-Determination and Decolonization

Today it is common to distinguish between internal and external forms of self-determination. While the latter suggests the right to statehood or secession, the former provides for various autonomy regimes that fall short of that paradigm.[103] Because both forms of self-determination (and a number of variations on them) have been called upon by indigenous rights advocates at various times, I briefly trace their development here.

Both internal and external self-determination have precursors in the period between the two world wars. In particular, members of the League of Nations agreed to make the granting of certain rights to ethnic minorities within their states a precondition for entry into the League.[104] As Nathaniel Berman notes, these minority protections included "not only equal civil rights under law for all, but also certain provisions for cultural, educational, and linguistic autonomy for members of minority groups."[105] Moreover, the League of Nations oversaw in limited cases the creation and use of plebiscites to determine the state to which certain communities would belong. Such plebiscites were prescribed, for example, in those border regions of new nation-states where a large proportion of the local population was identified with a nationality other than that of the state administering the territory.[106] While not allowing them to form their own state, and thus falling short of what we today consider to be external self-determination, plebiscites at least granted these communities some control over the contours of nation-state boundaries by permitting them to choose the state that would administer control over them.

In addition, the covenant of the League of Nations created a mandate system that was meant to facilitate decolonization for some territories and ensure the development of others under the ongoing tutelage of their colonizers.[107] Though the term "self-determination" was not included in the covenant's language, whether a territory was designated as A, B, or C determined the extent of its autonomy, including the possibility of eventual statehood under the system.

In 1934, the Montevideo Convention on the Rights and Duties of States entered into force. While also not using the term "self-determination," the convention defines what constitutes a state, essentially setting the bar for external self-determination claims. In Article 1, it provides that a state is an entity possessing "(a) a permanent population; (b) a defined territory; (c) government; and (d) capacity to enter into relations with the other states."[108] This meaning continues to define international legal personality with regard to statehood today.

When the UN Charter was drafted in 1945, it included two references to "self-determination." Article 1 states that one of the purposes of the UN is "to develop friendly relations among nations based on respect for the principle of equal rights and self-determination of peoples." Article 55 includes roughly the same language, aiming for the "creation of conditions of stability and well-being which are necessary for peaceful and friendly relations among nations based on respect for the principle of equal rights and self-determination of peoples."

Much has been made of this language, and its meaning for those who would later claim self-determination. To whom did self-determination apply, and what did the term signify in terms of autonomy and statehood?

With regard to the first question, Frederic Kirgis notes that while "the drafters did not bother to define self-determination or to identify who the 'peoples'" to whom self-determination applied were, "the Soviet Foreign Minister referred to the idea as 'equality and the self-determination of nations.' He seemed to view the beneficiaries to be the populations of colonies and the populations of territories then under League of Nations Mandates."[109] Kirgis contends, however, that "there is evidence . . . that a broader definition of 'peoples' was intended," referring to discussion of a memorandum by the UN Secretariat defining peoples for the purpose of Articles 1 and 55 as "groups of human beings who may, or may not, comprise states or nations."[110]

In terms of the second question on the implications of self-determination, the charter did not address minority rights or indigenous rights. It did, however, specifically focus on colonies and territories, setting up something akin to the League of Nation's mandate system through its establishment of a Trusteeship Council. The council assumed a slow but eventual decolonization of all trust territories.[111] In the meantime, Chapter XI of the charter required member states that continued to administer territories "to develop self-government . . . and to assist [the inhabitants] in the progressive development of their free political institutions."[112]

As the UN moved forward with its decolonization process, the question resurfaced about who would be entitled to self-determination. The UN General Assembly established a Fourth Committee, also referred to as the Decolonization Committee, with the goal of progressing more quickly than the Trusteeship Council.[113] In this context, disagreements occurred over the extent to which self-determination would apply to instances other than overseas colonization. In 1952, for example, the Belgian delegate argued for a broad application of Chapter XI, contending that the needs of underdeveloped ethnic groups extended well beyond those living in the eight states that had admitted to be "administering states" under its provisions. He was opposed by the delegates from the Soviet Union and from Latin American states, the latter of whom insisted that indigenous groups in their countries were integrated politically, rather than "non-self-governing." Barsh attributes the claims of Latin American states to the "blue water" thesis: "The Latin states suggested that overseas possessions be distinguished carefully from internal fusions of indigenous and immigrant populations, otherwise no state in the world would be immune from dismemberment."[114]

In 1960, the General Assembly adopted the Declaration on the Granting of Independence to Colonial Countries, which—though only a declaration—considered self-determination a right: "All peoples have the right to self-determination; by virtue of that right they freely determine their political status and freely pursue their economic, social and cultural development."[115] That language was repeated six years later in both human rights covenants, and eventually in the UN Declaration on the Rights of Indigenous Peoples, which specifically made it applicable to "indigenous peoples."[116]

When passing the Declaration on the Granting of Independence, the

General Assembly was not specifically thinking of indigenous groups, at least not in the sense that the term is most commonly used now. As André Frankovits notes: "The drafters . . . seriously limited their definition of the right to self-determination . . . [to] prevent any definition of self-determination that is not based on the gaining of independence by former colonies of the European powers and to exclude any other definition. It also shifts the focus away from the rights of peoples and communities to the rights of government."[117] Thus, as the earlier debate over the "blue water" thesis suggests, the General Assembly was very aware of the ongoing possible disruption to the nation-state system that could be caused by a broad application of self-determination. Thus, it limited the instances in which self-determination might be recognized: "Any attempt aimed at the partial or total disruption of the national unity and the territorial integrity of a country is incompatible with the purposes and principles of the Charter of the United Nations."[118]

Similar limitations were included in subsequent documents as well, such as the 1970 Declaration on Principles of International Law Concerning Friendly Relations and Cooperation among States in Accordance with the Charter of the United Nations, which includes the following provision:

Nothing in the foregoing paragraphs shall be construed as authorizing or encouraging any action which would dismember or impair, totally or in part, the territorial integrity or political unity of sovereign and independent States conducting themselves in compliance with the principle of equal rights and self-determination of peoples as described above and thus possessed of a government representing the whole people belonging to the territory without distinction as to race, creed or colour.[119]

The first part of this paragraph, as we will see in chapter 3, would later be invoked by states who opposed the right of external self-determination for indigenous peoples. The second part has been interpreted to provide an opening that may be useful to indigenous peoples and others claiming self-determination on the basis of a nondemocratic national political system.

If an understanding of self-determination as external was dominant during the period of decolonization (and did not include indigenous peoples), by the time the international human rights covenants entered into force in 1976, this view of it was beginning to change. According to

Alexandra Xanthaki, the covenants included both internal and external understandings of self-determination as a human right, but "gradually . . . there was a shift in international documents and legal literature towards the internal aspect of self-determination."[120] By the mid-1990s, she argues, self-determination had undergone a "dynamic transformation" from a right to statehood to a limited human right, as European states in particular "wanted to ensure that although they appeared to defend the right to self-determination, they clearly discouraged secession."[121] At the very least, "the meaning of self-determination has evolved considerably to include, apart from independence, integration or association with another state, democratic governance, participation and autonomy."[122] The consequences of this evolution will be discussed in subsequent chapters.

Human Rights and Cultural Relativism

If self-determination in the early years after the UN Charter was adopted seemed to apply only to territories (and not to groups within states or territories), we might think—from today's vantage point—that human rights would have provided some protection for indigenous peoples and minority groups. Yet the human rights model was seen as limited in its applicability to these groups from its inception, in large part because of its focus on what were considered individual and universal rights. Indigenous rights advocates were thus skeptical for many years of the utility of the human rights model to their cause.

The UN Charter recognized human rights, but the meaning of international human rights only began to be fleshed out in the 1948 Universal Declaration of Human Rights (UDHR)[123] and in subsequent covenants. As the declaration was being drafted, issues regarding indigenous peoples were not explicitly on the table. According to a contemporary fact sheet put out by the UN High Commissioner for Human Rights, "indigenous peoples' representatives made sporadic appeals" to the UN in its early days, but "there was no specific reaction."[124] The government of Bolivia asked in 1948 for a subcommission to study indigenous groups, but its request, a later UN report on indigenous rights noted, "was soon transformed into a proposal for a study of the situation of indigenous populations, and finally became a resolution for assistance and study which was not translated into practical measures except for the eradication of the chewing of coca leaf in Bolivia and Peru."[125]

Significant consideration was given early on to the question of whether to include minority rights. Advocates for ethnic minorities, particularly those within European states in the period after the Second World War, sought to claim a right to culture during the drafting of the UDHR. Robust claims for cultural rights for minorities were denied, however,[126] in favor of language saying that "everyone" has a right to culture.[127] The proposed minority-rights language was rejected for a variety of reasons, including political alliances during the cold war and the failure of the League of Nations and its minority protection regime.[128] In addition, many representatives of Latin American states opposed the inclusion of strong minority protection language in the UDHR, arguing that minority issues were regionally based.[129] Their skepticism about the applicability of minority rights to Latin America is reflected in the fact that neither the 1948 American Declaration of the Rights and Duties of Man nor its 1969 American Convention on Human Rights included a clause on minorities.

In 1966, minority rights were finally included in an international human rights instrument, the International Covenant on Civil and Political Rights (ICCPR).[130] Article 27 of that document guarantees: "In those States in which ethnic, religious or linguistic minorities exist, persons belonging to such minorities shall not be denied the right, in community with the other members of their group, to enjoy their own culture, to profess and practice their own religion, or to use their own language." This language was not an obvious fit for indigenous groups, however. Latin American states, for example, saw the clause as applying primarily to Europe, and generally denied its relevance to their own societies.[131] For their part, indigenous rights advocates—at least until the 1980s—were also uncertain about the utility of rights like those in Article 27, wary as they were of equating minorities with indigenous peoples and of using human rights language to make their claims.

In fact, indigenous advocates had long been skeptical of human rights. If human rights are "a product of modern, post-Enlightenment, liberal secular humanism . . . elevat[ing] the individual to the point that the group is forgotten,"[132] they would seem not only to conflict with, but also to threaten, indigenous culture. Or put another way, to the extent that human rights are inseparable from the civilizing mission of colonial days or the globalizing or liberalizing mission of neocolonialism, they would seem to offer little (other than a site of resistance) to those whose aim is to reject assimilation. How, then, could human rights be used to protect or promote indigenous rights?

This idea that human rights might conflict with indigenous rights is exemplified in the 1947 Statement on Human Rights by the American Anthropological Association (AAA).[133] The statement was written partly in response to an invitation by the United Nations Educational, Scientific and Cultural Organization (UNESCO), which had requested from a number of individuals and organizations an expression of views on the formulation of a declaration of human rights.[134] The Executive Board of the AAA submitted a document that was primarily authored by a well-known Boasian, Melville Herskovits.[135] Written at a time when colonialism was still commonplace and largely justified by a belief that colonized peoples were biologically inferior, the statement was antiracist and anticolonialist, even while skeptical of human rights. It is often seen as a prototypical statement of American cultural relativism, and it is therefore considered to have been in opposition to universal human rights.

The statement begins by saying that equally important as respect for the individual is "respect for the cultures of differing human groups."[136] It then sets forth three propositions that it sees as dictated by the "study of human psychology and culture . . . in terms of existing knowledge":[137] first, "the individual realizes his personality through his culture, hence respect for individual differences entails a respect for cultural differences";[138] second, "respect for differences between cultures is validated by the scientific fact that no technique of qualitatively evaluating cultures has been discovered";[139] and third, "standards and values are relative to the culture from which they derive so that any attempt to formulate postulates that grow out of the beliefs or moral codes of one culture must to that extent detract from the applicability of any Declaration of Human Rights to mankind as a whole."[140] The last sentence of the document supports the three propositions: "Only when a statement of the right of men to live in terms of their own traditions is incorporated into the proposed Declaration, then, can the next step of defining the rights and duties of human groups as regards each other be set upon the firm foundation of the present-day scientific knowledge of Man."[141]

As this last sentence underscores, the AAA did not argue against the idea of any declaration on human rights. Rather, it suggested that such a declaration must attend to differences among cultures. A declaration based on only one culture (Western culture), the third postulate suggests, would not be universal and would be inapplicable to "mankind as a whole." Thus, for the AAA in 1947, a declaration on human rights that failed to take into account the extent to which cultures varied in their values and norms would simply perpetuate the "white man's burden" assumed under missionary practices and colonialism.[142] In this view, human rights constituted a modernizing move that would threaten the culture of indigenous groups by imposing apparently universal values on their ways of life. Anthropologists argued in favor of the protection of such culture.

To be sure, those advocating for human rights in 1947 were not thinking of such rights as a means to limit the cultural expression of indigenous peoples. But American anthropologists, as well as many others among the individuals and groups who wrote to UNESCO during this time, pointed to the ways in which a declaration on universal human rights was indeed a Western construct. In this sense, the issue was not unique to those concerned specifically with indigenous peoples.

Mahatma Gandhi wrote, for example, in a statement that is often seen as representing a Hindu perspective, and emphasized the concept of duty over right:

> I learned from my illiterate but wise mother that all rights have to be deserved and preserved from duty well done. Thus the very right to live accrues to us only when we do the duty of citizenship to the world. From this one fundamental statement, perhaps it is easy enough to define the duties of Man and Women and correlate every right to some corresponding duty to be first performed. Every other right can be shown to be a usurpation hardly worth fighting for.[143]

I think it is fair to conclude that neither Gandhi nor the AAA succeeded in their calls for what they considered non-Western approaches to the declaration. Nevertheless, some seeds for the right to culture had been planted. Much of the rest of this book follows their growth.

THE FOURTH WORLD MOVEMENT AND *PANINDIANISMO*

In the 1970s, indigenous advocacy across tribal, national, and even regional lines began to emerge. Chapter 1 described the political and legal models available to these advocates at the time; integration, decolonization or self-determination, and human rights had all made their way into various international and national legal documents. While integrationism was the model that had been most specifically applied in the context of indigenous peoples (through ILO 107), self-determination and human rights frameworks had also begun to permeate the international scene, both doctrinally and discursively.

As the past few decades have unfolded, indigenous rights advocates have opposed integrationism and have, at different times, seized upon the other two models. The debates over the UN Declaration on the Rights of Indigenous Peoples discussed in the introduction to this book demonstrate how the self-determination model continues to vie for political and legal recognition. Nevertheless, human rights has become the dominant rubric for pursuing indigenous rights. The human rights model that has been advanced by and on behalf of indigenous peoples, however, is distinguishable from the universal human rights critiqued by the American Anthropological Association in 1947. Rather, as chapter 4 will demonstrate, a strategy focused on the right to culture has prevailed.

This chapter explores various strands of indigenous advocacy that emerged in the 1970s, before the UN had created institutions or procedures to specifically attend to indigenous issues. In doing so, the chapter focuses, though not exclusively, on movements in the Americas. It aims to understand the thought and legal and geopolitical situation in and by which indigenous movements began to organize across tribal and national affiliations as they—perhaps unknowingly—prepared themselves for international institutional participation in the 1980s and 1990s. In this chapter, I pursue the comparison begun in chapter 1, by considering similarities and differences between advocacy in the former British colonies in North America and that in the former Spanish colonies in Latin America. Again, I mean to offer only a sampling, not a comprehensive history or account, of the range of advocacy from those regions.

In the 1970s, indigenous movements across the Americas—and around the world, for that matter—shared a strong opposition to the integrationist and assimilationist policies of states represented in part in ILO 107. Because human rights discourse was largely still not in their purview for reasons discussed in chapter 1, indigenous groups and their proponents most commonly employed models of decolonization, self-determination, and autonomy in their advocacy. In Canada and the United States, advocates seized upon the language of decolonization and self-determination, the latter often including references to Indian treaties. In Latin America, the term "autonomy" tended to have more salience, with a focus on the preservation or recovery of culture.

Even if tribes in Canada and the United States did not always use self-determination language to claim a right to statehood, they did frequently call for the enforcement of treaties that Indian nations had entered into with former colonial powers and with settlers. The existence of those treaties provided a means by which Indian nations could claim territorial control of land and resources. As detailed in chapter 1 in relationship to Patricia Seed's work, indigenous peoples in Latin America tended not to rely on such arguments. Instead, they typically focused on the need for cultural, if not physical or territorial, distinction.

There were, of course, also significant overlaps in the advocacy movements that took place in North America and Latin America, particularly in their critiques of assimilationist policies and in their pan-indigenous politics. Yet I suggest that the differences in the emphasis in these streams of advocacy became significant in ensuing decades, even portending the different positions taken by countries in these regions on the self-determination language in the UN Declaration. While Canada and the United States were among the very few countries (along with two other former British colonies) to oppose the declaration, Peru was the main sponsor of a crucial revised draft resolution presented to the Third Committee in 2006.[1] Mexico played an instrumental role in brokering the last-minute deal that led to the adoption of the UN Declaration in 2007, and all but one Latin American state voted in favor of its passage.[2] I believe this general acceptance of the self-determination language by Latin American states reflects, at least partly, the lack of a threat of secession or claim to statehood by most of the region's indigenous groups.

Policies affecting indigenous peoples throughout the Americas in the 1970s were influenced significantly by the cold war. Indigenous rights advocacy and alliances among indigenous groups equally reflected cold war tensions, often vis-à-vis the states in which they resided. As capitalist and communist industrial states attempted to divide the world in two, a number of states—most of them newly decolonized—began to make clear their disinterest in aligning with either side. Considering themselves the Third World, many of these states organized themselves into what came to be called the nonaligned movement. Their lack of industrialized development formed a part of their identity, as did a critique of their dependence on First and Second World economies.

During roughly the same time period, a scholarly movement evolved in Latin America around "dependency theory."[3] *Dependistas*, as they often called themselves, argued not only that the Third World was dependent on the First, but that the reverse was also true; the First World in fact relied upon the impoverishment of the Third World. As André Gunder Frank, a well-known dependency theorist, explained in the late 1960s, "these capitalist contradictions and the historical development of the capitalist system have generated underdevelopment in the peripheral satellites whose economic surplus was expropriated, while generating economic development in the metropolitan centers which appropriate that surplus."[4]

Dependency theory largely emerged as a challenge to modernization theory, which held that industrialization and economic growth were key to the progress of the developing world. For dependistas, the capitalist system propelled by the First World actively recreated and reinforced wealth disparities and Third World dependence. Fernando Cardoso and Enzo Faletto characterized the relationship between the First and Third

Worlds as one of interdependence, writing that "the very existence of an economic 'periphery' cannot be understood without reference to the economic drive of advanced capitalist economies, which were responsible for the formation of a capitalist periphery and for the integration of traditional noncapitalist economies into the world market."[5]

States in the Third World were the site of many cold war struggles, and—particularly in the period immediately following decolonization—their arguments against dependence and in favor of self-determination and control over natural resources both reflected and formed an important part of their politics of nonalignment. Yet, from the perspective of some indigenous groups in the global North, Third World states had at least obtained formal recognition of their right to independence, which distinguished them from those nations that continued to find themselves politically and economically dependent upon existing states. This difference was noted by indigenous peoples who, especially in former British colonies, often described themselves as belonging to the Fourth World.

THE FOURTH WORLD MOVEMENT:
INDIGENOUS ADVOCACY IN NORTH AMERICA

Although the term "Fourth World" has been employed to represent a variety of movements and situations since the 1970s (it is sometimes now used, for example, to refer to the poorest of states), I focus on one of its earliest uses, in the context of indigenous advocacy in North America. In 1974, George Manuel, a chief of the Shuswap tribe and soon to become chair of the Union of British Columbia Indian Chiefs (from 1979 to 1981), published *The Fourth World: An Indian Reality* (with Michael Posluns). In this book, told in the voice of Manuel, Manuel identifies the Fourth World as comprised of the "indigenous peoples descended from a country's aboriginal population and who today are completely or partly deprived of the right to their own territories and its riches."[6]

As we will see in the following section, groups in Latin America began to organize in the 1970s around anti-assimilationist and pan-indigenous cultural identity. The Fourth World position shared many of their concerns, but called attention to the geopolitical situation in which indigenous peoples found themselves. The site for comparison for those who took a Fourth World approach was the Third World. In addition, Fourth World struggles were largely aimed at self-determination. As Richard

Griggs explained in 1992, "the Fourth World nation is engaged in a struggle to maintain or gain some degree of sovereignty over [its] national homeland."[7]

Indigenous Identity

For Manuel, the Fourth World—or the "Aboriginal World," as he sometimes referred to it—was distinguished economically and culturally, as well as politically, from the Third World. He argued:

> The distinction between the Third World and the Aboriginal World is at present political, but will eventually be seen as religious and economic. The Third World is emerging at this time primarily because it is rapidly learning to adapt its life-style to Western technology; it reacts to Western political concepts; and it uses racial issues to pivot its expanding influence between the super-powers, gathering concessions from both sides while struggling to imitate them.[8]

Thus, the Third World and Fourth World could not be easily aligned.

The Fourth World idea was developed—and continues to be used—mostly by indigenous groups and their advocates in the global North (including Australia and New Zealand), the same groups that have remained ardently in favor of a strong form of self-determination that includes the possibility of statehood. From the vantage point of these indigenous peoples in the 1970s, the Third World seemed to be on the path of independence in a way that had not been made available to the Fourth World, despite similarities of conquest. For Griggs, "a convenient shorthand for the Fourth World would be internationally unrecognized nations. These are the 5,000 to 6,000 nations representing a third of the world's population whose descendants maintain a distinct political culture within the states which claim their territories."[9]

Fourth World thought distinguished the effects of colonialism on the Third and Fourth Worlds, and even sought to make the global South accountable for its denial of the self-determination of its indigenous peoples. George Tinker, an academic and a member of the Osage Nation located in the United States, describes the purpose of the term "Fourth World" as drawing attention to the fact of indigenous peoples' being "oppressed by both the powerful nations and the so-called developing nations."[10] He continues:

We share with our Third World relatives the hunger, poverty and repression that have been the continuing common experience of those overpowered by the expansionism of European adventurers and their missionaries five hundred years ago. What distinguishes us from them are deeper, more hidden, but no less deadly effects of colonialism, which impact our distinct cultures in dramatically different ways.[11]

Of course, Tinker's own reference to "Third World relatives" in the above statement is ambiguous, as the place of indigenous peoples within the Third World is unclear.

Fourth World thought was often seen to revolve around a particular indigenous vision of the cosmos. Tinker argues that the distinguishing effects of colonialism in the Third and Fourth Worlds "are especially felt in the indigenous spiritual experience, and our struggle for liberation is within the context of this distinctive spirituality."[12] Manuel agrees that indigenous peoples might have a way of relating to the earth that is different from much of the rest of the world. That approach, however, seems to be due as much to their resistance to economic pressures to change as it is to any distinct, inherent cultural trait. For Manuel, the Fourth World has "lacked the political muscle to emerge [because] it is without economic power; it rejects Western political techniques; it is unable to comprehend Western technology unless it can be used to extend and enhance traditional life forms; and it finds its strength above and beyond Western ideas of historical process."[13]

In any event, the Fourth World claim is not that all indigenous peoples are necessarily cut from the same cultural cloth, but that they all experience a similar relationship with the other worlds. As Noel Dyck explained in the 1980s, "the notion of a 'Fourth World' . . . might most usefully be envisioned as comprising not so much discreet groups of people or specified aboriginal societies as complex political, economic and ideological *relations* between modern nation-states and a distinctive category of people."[14]

Similarly, the Fourth World movement has never been simply about indigenous peoples in the global North, including Australia and New Zealand. As Griggs's estimate of 5,000 to 6,000 indigenous nations makes clear, those who discuss the Fourth World generally claim to be talking about indigenous peoples throughout the world. Yet the bulk of the research and activism using the title remains in the global North, as that is where the early organization took place.

In October 1975, Manuel convened the first worldwide conference of indigenous peoples in British Columbia, Canada—an assembly that led to the formation of the World Council of Indigenous Peoples, of which Manuel was the first president.[15] The council's work has continued through the Center for World Indigenous Peoples, which maintains the Fourth World Documentation Project and the *Fourth World Journal*. All but one member of the center's Board of Directors are from tribes in North America (including one from Hawaii), although its monitoring and documentation projects span the globe.

For the most part, the term "Fourth World" and much of its ideology have not resonated with indigenous rights activists outside the global North.[16] At least with regard to Latin America, one explanation can be traced to the first meeting of the World Council of Indigenous Peoples. Douglas Sanders describes how, paradoxically, delegates from North America and Europe often received their government's financial and even political support to organize and attend the meeting, while those from Latin America attended at significant political risk. For Sanders, "the divisions in the conference were clearly along those [regional] lines. The Sami, the North American Indians, the Maoris and the Australian Aborigines could understand each other's situation quite easily," but "the political tension within which Indian organizations functioned in Latin America was difficult for the other delegates to appreciate."[17] The reverse was also true. Just as differences in access to political opportunities and material resources "seem to explain why the initiative for the World Council came from North America and Europe, though the crisis area for indigenous people is clearly in the hinterland of Latin America,"[18] they also hint at why political priorities of different groups varied by region.

The Importance of Statehood

In the 1970s, many tribes in Canada and the United States began to assert claims for external self-determination, or independent statehood. In 1974, for example, the First International Indian Treaty Council issued its Declaration of Continuing Independence, calling for the enforcement of previous treaties signed by the United States and the establishment of diplomatic relations between the council and the U.S. Department of State.[19] The declaration rejected "all executive orders, legislative acts and judicial decisions of the United States related to Native Nations since 1871, when the United States unilaterally suspended treaty-making relations with the Native Nations."[20] Asserting a strong notion of self-determination, the council further allied itself "with the colonized Puerto Rican People in their struggle for Independence from the same United States of America."[21]

These assertions of indigenous independence in North America can be traced back to the mid-1960s. During that time, self-determination became the primary demand of indigenous activists in the United States, in large part in opposition to proposed U.S. legislation called "termination." Much as with some of Bolívar's liberal reforms in Latin American countries after independence, there was an attempt in the United States to create formal equality for Indians. Formal equality, however, would have meant termination of the trust status for Indians, as well as of special government services for them. Christopher Riggs explains: "Indian communities on such trust lands were not subject to state jurisdiction. If the federal government removed the trust status, tribal laws would be null and void. In addition, Indian lands would become subject to state taxes . . . In other words, termination was a means of assimilating or 'de-tribalizing' Indians."[22]

Debates over the definition of self-determination in the United States came to a head in 1967. In that year, over sixty tribes convened in Santa Fe, New Mexico, at the National Congress of American Indians (NCAI) to oppose the Indian Resources Development Bill, a termination bill put forward by Secretary of the Interior Stewart Udall. In that meeting, according to the Indian activist and scholar Vine Deloria Jr., "delegates drew up a plan for 'self-determination' for Indian tribes, a phrase that was to echo through the minority groups three years later and catch the fancy of social-movement sloganeers."[23] The NCAI successfully blocked the bill. For Riggs, "the proposal's defeat marked an important moment in the development of self-determination. Not only had the Indian peoples blocked a bill they opposed, but the controversy also provided a chance for Native Americans to clarify the meaning of self-determination and to lay the groundwork for expanded self-determination in the future."[24] Riggs describes the NCAI's vision of self-determination as having "three core components: preservation of treaty rights, consultation on policy changes, and economic self-sufficiency. Most important was protection of tribal sovereignty through treaty rights and the trust status of Indian lands."[25]

For American Indians, then, the trust status had already become central to their independence claims. At least within the U.S., it would guarantee that they were seen as separate and "special." As discussed in chapter 1, some would later use the trust responsibility to put a positive spin even on the U.S. Supreme Court's 1831 decision in *Cherokee Nation v. Georgia*, considering them "domestic dependent nations." At the time, though, activists focused on the term "nation," and believed that the United States was obligated to them as a result of the treaties they had entered into long ago. Discussing the Native American movement from the 1960s through the 1980s, Deloria explains that "the idea that Indian problems are some exotic form of domestic disturbance will simply not hold water in view of the persistent attitude of Indians that they have superior rights to national existence which the United States must respect."[26] Treaties, he insists, were not simply "real-estate contracts."[27]

Many indigenous groups in Canada simultaneously made strong claims for territorial sovereignty. In 1969, Prime Minister Pierre Trudeau of Canada and Minister of Indian Affairs Jean Chretien released a paper on Indian policy that caused indigenous organizations from across Canada to mobilize to contest its strongly assimilationist goals. The Union of British Columbia Indian Chiefs (UBCIC) formed in response to what it called "the White Paper," which it labeled a "blueprint for assimilating Canada's First Peoples."[28] The Indian Association of Alberta responded with a "Red Paper,"[29] while the UBCIC issued a declaration known as the "Brown Paper."

The UBCIC Declaration denounced Canada's claims to lands historically occupied by indigenous groups, and asserted Indian control over natural resources within their territories. It did so by giving significance to treaties — or, more precisely, to the absence of treaties by which native peoples had extinguished their preexisting rights to territory. Specifically, the Brown Paper reads:

> We, the Native People of the Tribes of British Columbia, have never reached any agreement or Treaty with the Governments of Canada and British Columbia concerning the occupation, settlement, sovereignty, and jurisdiction over our Native Lands, and . . . such Native Title and Aboriginal Rights have never been extinguished, purchased, or

acquired by treaty, agreement or by any other means by the Government of Canada and the Government of British Columbia . . . We, the Native People of the Tribes of British Columbia, hereby declare and affirm our inalienable rights of Native Title and Aboriginal Rights to: the land, the minerals, the trees, the lakes, the rivers, the streams, the seas, and other resources of our Native land. We declare that our Native Title and Aboriginal Rights have existed from time immemorial, exists at the present time, and shall exist for all future time.[30]

The Brown Paper's claims rested on the need to respect both territorial integrity and land rights within Canada, as well as Native peoples' "inalienable and Aboriginal Rights to self-government within [their] respective Tribal Territorial Boundaries." It thus called for the governments of Canada and British Columbia to enter into tripartite negotiations over compensation for those "lands that have been unjustly, arbitrarily, and capriciously taken from Indian Reserves."[31]

Land was therefore central to indigenous claims for self-determination in the 1970s. For indigenous peoples in North America, land and territory had long been the object of conquest and, when possible, the subject of negotiation. Indigenous activists often invoked the treaties, or absence thereof, as a means of reasserting not only their sovereign identity, but also their jurisdictional and material control over territory.

PANINDIANISMO: INDIGENOUS ADVOCACY IN LATIN AMERICA

While control over land is today at the heart of many indigenous struggles in Latin America, it played a different role there in the 1970s than it did in North America. In Latin America, the exploitation of indigenous peoples' labor on the land they often continued to occupy represented lost traditions and culture. Thus, panindianismo developed in Latin America— across both tribal and state boundaries—in direct response to the assimilationist and integrationist tendencies of indigenismo (including that represented by ILO 107, discussed in chapter 1).

Like the Fourth World movement, this pan-indigenist advocacy rejected the hegemony of Western over indigenous thought, and aimed to recover indigenous relations to the natural and material world. Yet, panindianismo rarely used the terms "self-determination" or "decolonization." Instead, it focused and insisted on a unique indigenous culture that needed to be salvaged or, in some cases, revitalized. It relied on a sense of commonality among Indians throughout the region, if not the world. As Guillermo Bonfil Batalla explains, panindianismo "postulates that a single Indian civilization exists in America."[32]

Although differentiation between Indians and non-Indians might have originated with the sixteenth-century missionaries and settlers who identified indigenous cultures as backward, indigenous advocates in the 1970s took a different tack. They self-consciously attempted to reclaim and revalue practices that had previously been viewed in a derogatory light. While in the past, missionaries and settlers had tried to save indigenous peoples from many traditional practices—by putting an end to such practices—indigenous advocates now actively sought to protect some of those traditions that had survived. This approach to the revitalization of culture and reclaiming of indigenous identity, I believe, set the stage for the focus on the right to culture (as opposed to strong claims to self-determination) that we see in Latin America in subsequent decades.

The emphasis on culture in indigenous advocacy was supported, if not launched, by Latin American anthropologists in a 1971 meeting in Barbados (Barbados I) on the situation of indigenous peoples in Latin America. The meeting has been both criticized for its complete lack of indigenous representation and revered for its rebuke of states, missionaries, and anthropologists for their assimilationist and integrationist approaches to Indians. Alison Brysk sees the meeting as seminal, contending that "the transnational movement formally began in 1971 with the Barbados Conference of dissident anthropologists, who pledged to promote indigenous self-determination and enter politics to save endangered cultures," and noting that later, "broad-based indigenist advocacy groups such as Cultural Survival were founded in the United States and Europe."[33]

The Declaration of Barbados includes the term "self-determination," but it does so in the context of highlighting the responsibilities of multi-ethnic states. It does not directly challenge nation-state boundaries. Instead, its focus is much more on culture than on the type of independence being discussed in North America around the same time. The first numbered clause of the declaration, for example, calls upon states to guarantee "to all the Indian populations by virtue of their ethnic distinction, the right to be and to remain themselves, living according to their own customs and moral order, free to develop their own culture."[34]

I would argue that this focus on culture accords with Seed's account of the differences in British and Spanish colonialism discussed in chapter 1. Stefano Varese has, however, provided a different explanation for the lack of emphasis on strong self-determination in Latin America. "Until the Mayan rebellion of Chiapas in 1994," he contends, "the issue of indigenous people's sovereignty was unspeakable in Latin America. The terms sovereignty, autonomy, and self-determination when referred to Indian people could barely be whispered by anthropologists and indigenous intellectuals for they feared being accused of possessing subversive views."[35] He notes a shift in discourse that took place only "after more than two years of public debate in Mexico and in the world throughout the Internet." When Varese was writing, in 1997, he saw the shift as relatively new, leading him to conclude "that the concepts of indigenous people's sovereignty and ethnic rights to self-determination and autonomy have, albeit reluctantly, become part of the accepted general political discourse."[36]

Even if Varese's explanation for the late rise of the term "self-determination" is correct, I believe that the concept, even when it emerged in Latin America, was infused with the emphasis on culture and pan-indigeneity that had begun the movement and influenced it for two more decades. That said, as I will discuss more fully in chapter 3, I also would contend that there might have been more of an emphasis on autonomy in Latin America before 1994 than Varese admits.

The remainder of this chapter uses various statements and summaries of indigenous advocacy during the 1970s and early 1980s to sketch some of the basic positions attributed to panindianismo. While these positions sometimes seem overly simplistic, such oversimplification was arguably a part of the discourse itself and the political project it represented. Alcida Ramos, for instance, discusses the solidarity produced among and between indigenous groups and advocates in Brazil over their opposition to a 1978 bill meant to "emancipate" the Indians. Referring to indigenous rights advocacy in the late 1970s and early 1980s, she explains that "the need to rally support for indigenous rights from various quarters of public opinion produced a sort of international *lingua franca* of indigenism where subtleties were deleted and messy political games pasteurized."[37]

At the same time, indigenous rights advocates insisted that there were differences among indigenous groups that settlers failed to recognize. Bonfil Batalla explains: "The category of the *indio* [Indian] is supraethnic, which is to say, it neither makes reference to nor takes into account the diversity of peoples that are lumped together under the label *indio*, because the same definition (the concept of *indio*) departs from the contrast with the non-*indio* and this distinction is the only thing that matters, what gives sense to being *indio*."[38] Thus, the initial classification of *indio* was meant also to define and be defined in relationship to what was seen as its opposite. Differences among Indians would be suppressed in the process.

When, in 1981, Bonfil Batalla collected declarations and statements from various indigenous and pan-indigenous groups and thinkers throughout the Americas, he identified a number of characteristics and aims of what was then contemporary "Indian political thought." They included "the denial of the West" (which, importantly, was seen to include Marxist and socialist thought); "*panindianismo*: the affirmation of a civilization"; "the recovery of history"; "revaluation of indigenous cultures"; and an understanding of "nature and society" in which "man *is* nature; he neither dominates nor pretends to dominate."[39] Among concrete demands were recognition of indigenous ethnicity and culture, and the denouncement of the "folklorization" of such culture. Indigenous groups criticized the commodification of indigenous art, the use of indigenous areas as tourist attractions, the "banalization" of indigenous music, dances, and ceremonies ("in distorted interpretations") for non-Indian, public consumption, and the "defense and recuperation of land" for economic exploitation and penetration.[40]

Indigenous groups also organized to oppose the assimilationist policies of various governments. In Brazil, Ramos points to the "federal government's threat to 'emancipate' the Indians" in 1978 as sparking the beginning of what was then the contemporary movement: "What that meant was to legally declare them non-Indians and thus exempt the state from the duty of protecting them as well as their traditions and their lands."[41] Others organized specifically against a paternalistic indigenismo, calling for direct participation in the government. In Mexico, for example, indigenous activists in the 1970s made it clear that they did not desire "an *indigenista* policy that would be paternalistic and protective . . . We wish to be treated as equals and given more direct participation in all the nation's programs."[42]

Of course, there was no monolithic pan-indigenist thought. Real disagreements existed, even at local levels, about the extent to which indigenous demands should be culturally distinct. Other divisions existed, though perhaps less visibly, over what should be the ultimate aim of indigenous peoples vis-à-vis the states in which they lived. Some of these differences in perspective could be attributed to the percentages of indigenous peoples living in a particular state, and to the conditions under which they lived.

Contrasts among the needs and demands of various indigenous groups were articulated in a declaration from Barbados II, a 1977 symposium on indigenous peoples organized by the World Council of Churches and held in Barbados, this time with the participation of indigenous peoples.[43] The differences identified in the document do not necessarily correspond to state boundaries. But they are nevertheless helpful in seeing how the numbers and situation of indigenous peoples within a particular state might affect the advocacy within and toward that state.

The Barbados II declaration identifies three situations of indigenous peoples in the Americas. It first discusses indigenous groups that were able to protect their "cultural schemes," but only due to the fact that they "had remained relatively isolated." The negative consequence of this isolation is that these groups faced threats to their collective survival. Second, the declaration identifies a circumstance in which indigenous groups were able to conserve their cultures without being isolated, but under the domination of "the capitalist system," which denied them control over their resources. Third, it considers a "sector of the population that had been de-Indianized by integrationist forces." The declaration sees the recuperation of identity (of "its own self, its own culture") as this last group's most immediate need.[44] According to the declaration, these three situations faced by various indigenous groups have left "our people" (again, the hemisphere's indigenous peoples described as one) divided.[45]

As indigenous and pan-indigenous movements developed during this period, the differences that emerged in their approaches were at least partially foreshadowed by this categorization in the Barbados II declaration. I consider below how some of these distinctions played out in the perspectives of various movements in Latin America toward indigenous (versus *campesino*, or peasant) identity and toward the importance of statehood for indigenous peoples.

Indigenous versus Campesino Identity

Cold war politics formed an important backdrop to pan-indigenous movements in Latin America in the 1970s. As Marxism gained influence in the region, the role of indigenous peoples in class struggles was contested. Many Marxist thinkers attempted to address indigenous peoples' issues by viewing them primarily through a Marxist lens of class. At the same time, however, they often saw indigenous peoples' oppression as a product not only of their class position, but also of the cultural distinctiveness presumed to be inherent in indigenous identity. Rodolfo Stavenhagen notes, for example, that Marxist thinkers saw indigenous peoples as "the most exploited and backward element of the working class, lacking in class consciousness precisely because of their community-centered world outlook."[46] Marxists saw indigenous peoples' distinct language, dress, communal and family structures, and religion as facilitating their exploitation by separating them from mestizos and keeping them in "forced and servile labor arrangements, such as peonage [that] prevented [them] from joining forces with the revolutionary proletariat in the class struggle."[47]

Meanwhile, pan-indigenist leaders went about the work of organizing indigenous communities, while trying to discern where (if at all) they should position themselves within the activities of larger social movements. Some favored prioritizing the protection of indigenous cultures. These leaders often viewed radical peasant unions with mistrust, concerned that they would impose "a class identity that should be realized at the expense—and not by way—of one's ethnic identity, that is, alienation [from indigeneity] for liberation."[48] Other leaders chose to align with communist, worker, or campesino movements, and had varying degrees of success in keeping on the agenda issues that uniquely affect indigenous peoples. In this sense, much indigenous advocacy in Latin America was influenced by at least some of the same geopolitical considerations of the Fourth World movement.

Recall Bonfil Batalla's contention that the anti-occidental tendency within panindianismo rejected Marxism and socialism along with capitalism. Fausto Reinaga, a Bolivian indigenous intellectual and the founder of the Partido Indio de Bolivia, was one of those who articulated this position most clearly. In his seminal 1969 work, *La revolución india*, Reinaga explained that "campesino" is a Western construct, referring to "a social class subject to wage-labor, exploited by a territorial bourgeoisie." This construct could not apply to Bolivia, "where nothing like the territorial or rural bourgeoisie exists; the Indian is not a wage-laborer . . . The Indian is not a social class." Instead, "the Indian is a race, a people, an oppressed Nation."[49] In short, for Reinaga, "the Indian cannot, and does not have to be the 'campesino' of 'white' society; the Indian must be a *free man*, in 'his' free society."[50]

In Bolivia, it was particularly important for many indigenous rights activists to reject the identity that the 1952 revolution had thrust upon all Bolivians—that of mestizo and worker. A 1975 statement by one group of indigenous activists in Bolivia explained:

> When the masters enslaved us in the *haciendas* [large, rural estates], they treated us as *indios*; after losing the *latifundios* [large, corporate land holdings] they treat us like campesinos. With these facts before us, we declare, with insistence: Why should they call us campesinos? They should continue to call us *indios*.[51]

Another group argued that Marxism, while useful for some, would only weaken their struggle for an indigenous nation-state.[52]

In some cases, however, indigenous leaders' criticisms of Marxist strategies contained attempts to reclaim as indigenous a "true" campesino identity or a "true" communist ideology. The Peruvian indigenist activist Guillermo Carnero Hoke, for example, identified the objective of the Movimiento Indio Peruano as a "return to the true path of social evolution, departing from primitive communism and reject[ing], forever, the nightmare of slavery, feudalism, and capitalism."[53] In 1973, the Manifiesto de Tiawanacu—a manifesto inspired in part by Reinaga, and integrating and asserting the views and agendas of multiple organizations in Bolivia that use the term "campesino" in their name—called for a return to an "authentic" campesino organization.[54] Continuing to reject the Western notion of "campesino," the manifesto nevertheless reappropriates the term. Radical indigenist leaders from Andean Bolivia similarly aimed to reclaim socialism in a scathing 1971 statement against a national labor federation. The leaders turned their critique of what they saw as the influence of "foreign communism" into a statement on the autochthonous socialist essence of Indians. Indigenous leadership, the statement says, could return to its people "the noblest socialist system which lies latent in each Indian heart, and which has been the source of inspiration for all of those peoples that today preach socialism as though it is something novel."[55]

In other cases, Latin American indigenous leaders saw the peasant and unionist struggles as their own, openly aligning with non-indigenous campesino movements and claiming campesino identities. Colombia's Consejo Regional Indígena del Cauca (CRIC), for example, was born in the context of rural labor struggles, and initially described itself as "an organization managed by indigenous campesinos."[56] Although CRIC's platform included defending indigenous history, language, and customs, the organization saw no conflict in allying itself in the early 1970s with the broader peasant movement in Colombia.[57] Indeed, this alliance helped CRIC outgrow its original regional focus, with its membership and plans of action increasingly evincing an "affirmation of a multi-ethnic indigenous movement."[58] CRIC, however, did not hide the fact that its fight was "not only the struggle of a half million indigenous campesinos, but of all the exploited campesinos of Colombia."[59]

As CRIC grew and became increasingly committed to defending indigenous cultural practices and strengthening indigenous community-level organizations, tensions with the radical campesino movement emerged. It soon became clear that the latter was threatened by CRIC's evolving priorities and believed that a focus on indigenous culture detracted from the campesino class struggle. CRIC issued a statement that attempted to break down the emerging dichotomy between indigenous people and the rural proletariat: "We put on record that we indigenous make up part of the campesino movement but that, because of our own characteristics such as our internal organization, our language, our customs, etc., we have the right to our particular organization, which should be respected."[60]

By 1977, however, CRIC had broken from the peasant movement organization into which it had hoped to incorporate an indigenist agenda, complaining that the organization "was ignoring indigenous concerns and was attracted to the Indian struggle for purely propagandistic reasons."[61] Indigenous leaders also seemed concerned that the national peasant organization had become increasingly dominated by Maoism.[62] A few years later, continuing with its insistence that the left attend to indigenous concerns, CRIC publicly denounced the leftist guerrilla organization, Fuerzas Armadas Revolucionarias de Colombia (FARC), because it was "not prepared to accept [indigenous] autonomy."[63]

The Importance of Statehood

Somewhat surprisingly, given the ensuing and ongoing debates surrounding the use of terms like "peoples" and "self-determination" in the international legal arena, pan-indigenist movements in Latin America in the 1970s, as already suggested, did not seem particularly focused on the question of statehood. Unlike many Indian tribes in North America, they had never entered into treaties with the colonial powers and were therefore lacking in agreements that would form a basis for claims to external self-determination, or independent statehood.

Embedded in different regional statements and declarations were varying assumptions about desired arrangements between indigenous groups and the state, but the differences were mostly regional and were not the subject of much debate within the movements. The various models that emerged in the 1970s, however, have appeared again in contemporary discussions. Thus, I briefly describe them here.

Three principal examples of state-indigenous relations emerge from Bonfil Batalla's collection of statements: Bolivia, Colombia, and Mexico. While these examples do not include any groups making secessionist claims, they do include the attempts of Bolivian activists to transform the Bolivian state into an indigenous one, and various expressions of autonomy and governmental control by activists in Colombia and Mexico. The differences in the situations of Bolivia and the others can be summed up in a statement by the Commission on Indianist Ideology and Philosophy presented in 1980, at the First Congress of the Indian Council of South America (CISA):

> When the Indian people constitute a majority, its first aim will be to take power . . . When the Indian people is a minority, it should achieve autonomy, conserving for itself the right to decide its first action alongside the popular sectors, but without compromising its independence or cultural identity.[64]

The same document also claims an Indianist (and explicitly not an indigenist) philosophy that "advocates the political self-determination and the economic self-management of our peoples."[65] Again, for reasons I have already speculated about, the use of the term "self-determination" here is exceptional; "autonomy," even for CISA, as I discuss below, is the preferred term.

In Bolivia, where indigenous peoples are estimated to comprise more than half of the population, the movement of the 1970s was pan-indigenist. Leaders of the Aymara, Quechua, and other indigenous groups who were a part of the radical wing of the coalition that authored the 1973 Manifesto de Tiawanacu also formed the Movimiento Indio "Tupaj Katari" (MITKA), calling for a Bolivian state under indigenous control.[66] They referred to the new state as Kollasuyo, the name for the territory under the Inca Empire. MITKA made clear that it was not simply a "party" or "faction." Instead, it asserted that it "is the political vanguard of the Indian people of Kollasuyo and an autochthonous, autonomous and self-managing organism of Indian essence and presence; it is anti-imperialist, anti-Western and antiracist."[67] This essentialist indigenous state would thus be guided by what it saw as indigenous ideals. More specifically, indigenous peoples would direct a communal society "where man would be valued for his human condition and not for the color of his skin, for his attitude in front of collective society and not for his individual interests." They would create a society in which "the only ones with privileges would be the children, elders and invalids." Moreover, "misery, poverty, malnutrition, infant mortality and their causes would be eliminated," and "the natural riches and all the means of work would be collective property."[68]

Even though MITKA's political plan might sound similar to other pro-campesino visions of the time, recall that Bolivian indigenous activists considered that the latter were unable to attend to the needs of indigenous peoples. It was central to these activists' vision that indigenous peoples direct and control the state. However, direction and control were specifically tied not so much to precolonial rights as to the preservation of a way of being and knowing.

In Colombia, where indigenous peoples made up around 3 percent of the population, the goals of the indigenous movements were quite different. Even though they saw themselves as participating in the larger class struggle, they had few aspirations with regard to indigenous power in national government. They called for control over their traditional lands and preservation of their histories, customs, and languages. CRIC's seven-point program emphasized these issues, and included as one of its points that indigenous peoples should no longer pay rent for the lands on which they lived.[69] Although CRIC did not argue for secession or statehood, it insisted on this autonomy within any federal or national system that might exist. Recall that CRIC broke from the larger peasant movement on the ground that the latter did not respect indigenous autonomy. These calls for autonomy and control over land were not seen as minimal by the state. In fact, when indigenous activists from across Latin America met for Barbados II, those from Colombia were seen as having risked their lives to attend.[70]

Indigenous movements in Mexico in the 1970s offer a third approach to state-indigenous relations. While not constituting a majority as in Bolivia, Mexico's indigenous population is significantly larger than that of Colombia.[71] Despite a nonmajority status, one Mexican indigenous movement used the term "self-determination," and specifically called for authority over "all that configures our personality as a nation."[72] At the same time, however, these indigenous activists made clear that they "accept the positive things that [Mexican] nationality offers."[73] Indigenous peoples favored a Marxist revolution in Mexico, but they believed that a complete and successful revolution would require both indigenous autonomy, or self-determination (in this nonstatehood sense), and the guarantee of equality and other rights included in the constitution for all citizens.[74]

Despite these differences in approaches to state-indigenous relationships, pan-indigenous movements expanded as indigenous peoples recognized the strength they gained by organizing together. CISA concluded its second congress, held in 1983, with a statement asserting the need "to acquire again, to value and defend our culture as a model of a collective and community life and organisation" and "to acquire again our territorial and cultural unity as nations of ancestral origin, putting into second place the frontiers between the present countries which were put there by outsiders, dividing and confronting our peoples against each other."[75] Although CISA did not call for creating new borders around indigenous identity, it specifically included in its demands the autonomy that was a part of the philosophy it expressed at its first congress. The final document affirmed the "struggle for autonomy, respect for one's own culture and forms of life, and for national liberation in alliance with the forces of the people."[76] Yet, it seemed to assume that such liberation would come within the current nation-state structure, as it called "for all countries to recognise their plurinational, multicultural and multilinguistic character, where Creoles and Mestizos would be one more nationality, and under an alliance of nations to forge truly democratic governments, getting rid of all hegemony and imperialism."[77]

Regardless whether they experienced a real sense of need or entitlement for strong self-determination, when indigenous groups in North America and Latin America met, they generally left the door open for indigenous communities to seek as much self-determination as desired. At this moment in the development of indigenous advocacy, it seemed more important for indigenous groups to be able to assert their independence and difference from the state than to focus on their similarities with each other. Still, as described in part II of this book, assertions of an indigenous cosmovision that respects land and the environment began to develop in the 1980s, and those assertions have continued to affect the articulation of rights claims made by and on behalf of indigenous peoples throughout the world.

As the 1980s began, the formation of regional movements in both the global North and South came to have increasing international appeal. They were also fueled by growing international interaction, which eventually led to further alliances and activism. Some of this activity began in the 1970s with, for example, the Barbados conferences and the founding of Cultural Survival, discussed above. But these meetings were only the beginning of what has become nearly four decades of international and regional legal and political advocacy, concentrated in debates over the UN Declaration, a new ILO convention, and the applicability to indigenous peoples of human rights instruments such as the International Covenant on Civil and Political Rights, the International Convention on the Elimination of All Forms of Racial Discrimination, and the American Convention on Human Rights. Chapters 3 and 4 will explore the development of the two principal streams of thought that I have described in this chapter—self-determination in the North, and cultural distinctiveness in the South—as they play themselves out in the framing of claims in these international legal contexts.

International Institutions and Indigenous Advocacy since 1980

SELF-DETERMINATION CLAIMS

From the time that ILO 107 came into force in 1959 until the early 1980s, the International Labor Organization acted as the primary international organization with responsibility for indigenous issues.[1] As discussed in chapters 1 and 2, ILO 107 was rejected as assimilationist by indigenous groups throughout the hemisphere in the 1970s. It was particularly critiqued by those in the South.

In the 1980s, indigenous advocates began to turn to the larger international and legal political realm to address indigenous issues. Although the ILO continued to be a focus of attention, and a new ILO convention began to be discussed, another forum emerged that included the direct participation of indigenous groups: the Working Group on Indigenous Populations (Working Group, or WGIP), established in 1982 by the United Nations Subcommission on Prevention of Discrimination and Protection of Minorities. The Working Group, composed of representatives of states and indigenous groups, was assigned the task of drafting a declaration on the rights of indigenous peoples. It took eleven meetings before the Working Group released a draft. Much of this chapter follows those meetings, tracing in particular the discourse and debate around self-determination.

The Working Group was not the subcommission's first attempt to address indigenous issues. A decade earlier, in 1971, the subcommission had authorized a study on indigenous populations. That study was gradually published over the course of many years, Its final part—which includes its conclusions, proposals, and recommendations—was not released until 1983, a year after the establishment of the Working Group.[2] The study is often referred to as the Cobo Report because it was submitted by José Martinez Cobo, the special rapporteur. Commentators and activists hold different opinions about how widely available the Cobo Report was before its official release, and about whether, to the extent it was available, it made useful contributions.[3] With or without the Cobo Report's influence, commentators tend to agree that the Working Group was, at least in principle, institutionally innovative for its inclusion and even encouragement of indigenous participation.

The Working Group also followed the first international NGO conference on indigenous issues—specifically on indigenous peoples and discrimination in the Americas—which was held in Geneva in 1977. In 1981, another NGO conference in Geneva considered indigenous peoples and land rights. According to the UN, these meetings, along with the Cobo Report, which was "then nearing completion, influenced developments which led to the establishment in 1982 of the United Nations Working Group on Indigenous Populations."[4]

These international institutional processes both built upon and facilitated transnational and transregional indigenous organization. As Lee Swepston explained more than twenty years ago: "Once events began moving at the international level . . . [indigenous and tribal peoples'] slow movement towards international co-operation with each other was catalysed and they began to formulate their own positions."[5] The Working Group provided one forum for such co-operation, but there were others as well.

As the Working Group began to meet in the 1980s with the goal of proposing a draft UN Declaration, the self-determination issue loomed large. Indigenous groups and activists were as a whole in agreement that the declaration should include the term "self-determination." They differed significantly, however, in the meaning they attributed to it.

Those in favor of the strong self-determination position, which dominated indigenous voices during the first few years of the Working Group, insisted on leaving open the possibility for at least some indigenous groups to achieve statehood. During that time, many activists saw the declaration as a means to continue the process of decolonization. Not surprisingly, a number of states opposed the term "self-determination" from the beginning, often in reaction to these strong claims.

Other indigenous groups and activists, as well as many state representatives, supported the use of the term "self-determination," but as an indigenous right accruing within the context of existing, internationally recognized borders. This position was often expressed through the use of the word "autonomy," referring to various types of independence and territorial and jurisdictional claims. These approaches to autonomy were of course recognized as legitimate by those who took the strong position as well, given that they did not believe that secession was appropriate for every indigenous group. Some states, however, opposed nearly any kind of self-determination talk, expressing fears similar to those that drove later debates around the final UN Declaration: these states were concerned that any use of the term might embolden those who sought a right to independence and statehood.

During the years of debating the draft of the declaration, there were many discussions over whether and how to define the term "indigenous." The Cobo Report offered the following working definition:

> Indigenous communities, peoples and nations are those which, having a historical continuity with pre-invasion and pre-colonial societies that developed on their territories, consider themselves distinct from other sectors of the societies now prevailing in those territories, or parts of them. They form at present non-dominant sectors of society and are determined to preserve, develop and transmit to future generations their ancestral territories, and their ethnic identity, as the basis of their continued existence as peoples, in accordance with their own cultural patterns, social institutions and legal systems.[6]

While some believed that this language should be included in the declaration, and others pursued a different description of the meaning of indigenous peoples, no official draft of the declaration ever contained a definition of the term.[7] Because the absence of a definition suggested an expansive view of who is included in the declaration's scope, most of the discussion centered on the question of what substantive rights would be granted to those who were identified as indigenous. If an uncertain number of groups might claim those rights, states had an increased interest in limiting the rights that might be claimed. Thus, for most states, the right to self-determination either had to be excluded or narrowly defined.

Along with a refusal to define indigenous peoples often comes an understanding—implicit or explicit—that individuals and groups should have the right to define themselves as indigenous. ILO 169, which essentially replaced ILO 107, states that "self-identification as indigenous or tribal shall be regarded as a fundamental criterion for determining the groups to which the provisions of this Convention apply."[8] Self-identification is not, of course, the sole criterion offered. This provision follows those stating that the convention applies to tribal and indigenous groups who retain some form of cultural, social, or economic distinctiveness.[9] Unlike the UN Declaration, ILO 169 does not include the term "self-determination," suggesting that perhaps the stakes are not as high for being regarded as indigenous or tribal when self-determination is not on the table.

Such fundamental uncertainties in international rights instruments motivated Jeff J. Corntassel and Thomas Hopkins Primeau to urge in a 1995 article that indigenous activists attain "terminological precision" in the UN declaration.[10] According to the authors, the UN's proclamation of 1993 as the International Year of the World's Indigenous People coupled with the 1992 Columbian quincentennial to supply "an ideal backdrop" for evaluating the indigenous movement's past and future exigencies. Corntassel and Primeau argue that advocates must clearly define the term "indigenous," as well as abandon the terms "right of self-determination" and "sovereignty,"[11] and assert that permitting self-identification as a key criterion of indigeneity while including an unspecified right to self-determination is an unacceptable combination for many states. The authors maintain that defining "indigenous" is both complicated and necessary: "We do not prescribe this task lightly." Noting the difficulty in particular of distinguishing "indigenous populations from ethnic, linguistic or religious minorities," they contend nevertheless that "one must attempt to allay the fears of the states which attend Working Group meetings and ultimately vote on the passage of the Draft Declaration in the General Assembly."[12]

While ILO 169 comes closest of the international legal instruments to setting guidelines for categorizing a group as indigenous, none contains a precise definition of the term "indigenous." Similarly, none defines "self-determination" or "culture" (and not all even include those terms). As we saw in the introduction with regard to the UN Declaration's treatment of self-determination, however, the instruments often set parameters for the meanings of these terms in a variety of ways. Various ideas about indigeneity, of course, are presumed throughout the documents and in their interpretation and application, which I discuss at length in part II.

My research suggests that, as in the 1970s, there existed in the 1980s and 1990s a rough correlation in the Americas between arguments for self-determination in the global North and for cultural rights in the global South. The Working Group, at least in the 1980s, reflected a strong self-determination position—in part, I would argue, because indigenous groups in Latin America participated very little in international indigenous advocacy during that time. They were restricted in their ability to travel to international meetings, largely due to extreme economic and political hardship. While attention was paid in at least some circumstances to the violence suffered by indigenous peoples in Latin America, including threats of genocide, the situations were generally presented by outsiders. In many instances, indigenous peoples in Latin America only began to emerge as political actors and subjects within their national (state) frames in the late 1980s and early 1990s, with the official end of armed conflict and dictatorship and the subsequent advent of multicultural constitutions in the region.[13] As chapter 1 indicated, by then the stage had long been set for indigenous rights to be considered in cultural terms.

As will become clear in the ensuing chapters, the correspondence of indigenous movements in the North with self-determination and those in the South with cultural rights is not absolute. Different models have been proposed and tried in different places, such as in Nicaragua's experimentation with autonomous, quasi-independent territory. Such results would be expected from the cross-fertilization of ideas that took place as indigenous advocacy became more internationalized. Alison Brysk explains in the context of Latin America:

> These new movements and networks launched a series of national and transnational campaigns as the 1980's unfolded. In Ecuador they fought oil companies in the jungle and marched for civil rights in the highlands. In Brazil tribal groups resisted colonists' incursions and World Bank projects. Bolivian intellectuals revived Inca traditions and took over peasant unions, whose members later contested coca eradica-

tion. The Miskitos of Nicaragua struggled with the Sandinista government for local self-rule, using international weapons ranging from human rights inspections by the Organization of American States to North American guns. Throughout the hemisphere, indigenous peoples turned the 1992 quincentenary into a year-long series of protests, public education, and coalition-building.[14]

While I would argue that the majority of those movements relied on a right to culture to make their varied claims, as I discuss more fully below, self-determination discourse was certainly present in at least some of them.

When Bernadette Kelly Roy and Gudmundur Alfredsson published a review of indigenous rights literature in 1987 (focused on literature in English, and therefore largely from the global North), self-determination strains of advocacy—which generally included the possibility of secession or statehood—were prominent, if not dominant. Self-determination claims continued to be asserted despite and even against a human rights model that was beginning to make headway. Roy and Alfredsson wrote at the time that an "area of concern to many commentators is the shift away from the basic self-determination issues to a potential role for international human rights law in the prevention of discrimination and protection of indigenous peoples."[15] Discussing difficulties identified with the human rights approach, including its focus on the individual rather than the group and its failure to address the political rights of self-determination, Roy and Alfredsson concluded that "it should come as no surprise when many indigenous leaders speak in terms of decolonization or self-determination and eschew human rights."[16] Douglas Sanders had concurred, but with even a broader understanding of human rights in mind: "The framework of human rights and minority rights seems unable to deal with the issues of a distinctive land base or of collective political rights. For these reasons indigenous leaders speak in terms of decolonization and self-determination."[17]

Over time, however, many advocates all but abandoned their commitment to a strong form of self-determination. A weaker version—one removed from the framework of statehood and often articulated as autonomy—remains alive today. The remainder of this chapter considers the different ways that the term "self-determination" has been used in indigenous rights advocacy, particularly in discussions in the Working Group in the 1980s and 1990s. Some indigenous groups, primarily in the former British colonies, long insisted on keeping open the possibility of external self-determination, in the commonly accepted international legal sense of statehood, for at least some indigenous groups. A number of states worried that the use of the term by advocates and in legal documents might be used to make such claims.

Many activists and scholars, however, have been quick to point out that the majority of indigenous groups, even if they favor leaving open the option of statehood for some, do not themselves propose such a possibility, or even consider it feasible. Thus, they tend to argue for certain forms of autonomy within a multicultural or even a multinational state, which is often referred to as internal self-determination. Meanwhile, others contend that the existing regime of states itself must be altered in order for that type of self-determination to be possible.

As I argue in this chapter and chapter 4, the self-determination strategy has for the most part given way to models based on human rights, particularly the human right to culture. Yet I believe that the ongoing resonance of the term "self-determination" serves to pose some remaining resistance to, or at least imbue with more substance, the human rights model that has in many ways prevailed.

SELF-DETERMINATION AS A RIGHT
TO SECESSION OR STATEHOOD

Leading up to the first Working Group meeting in 1982, indigenous advocates began to revisit the debate over the "blue water" thesis that, as discussed in chapter 1, had taken place in the early days of decolonization. Many advocates used decolonization as the model for indigenous liberation, arguing that indigenous groups constituted independent states under the Montevideo Convention of 1933[18] or "peoples" under the United Nations Charter. As Chris Tennant explains, the international law claim "is not that some international body *should* recognize indigenous peoples' right to self-determination, but that indigenous peoples *always have had* the right to self-determination, that indigenous peoples are already 'separate sovereign nations.'"[19] Such a claim asserts that indigenous peoples meet traditional international law requirements for statehood because they have a "permanent population, defined territory, effective government and capacity to enter into foreign relations."[20]

Articulations of this position can be found in early international meetings before the Working Group was established. The 1977 International NGO Conference on Discrimination against Indigenous Populations in the Americas, for example, produced a document that emphasized maintaining the possibility of statehood for at least some indigenous groups. That document, the Draft Declaration of Principles for the Defense of the Indigenous Nations and Peoples of the Western Hemisphere, imagines indigenous nations as potential subjects of international law, with both the responsibilities and rights that would stem from that status. Among the document's main principles are:

1. *Recognition of Indigenous Nations*: Indigenous people shall be accorded recognition as nations and proper subjects of international law, provided the people concerned desire to be recognized as a nation and meet the fundamental requirement of nationhood . . .

2. *Subjects of International Law*: Indigenous groups not meeting the requirements of nationhood are hereby declared to be subjects of international law and are entitled to the protection of this Declaration, provided they are identifiable groups having bonds of language, heritage, tradition, or other common identity . . .

4. *Accordance of Independence*: Indigenous nations or groups shall be accorded such degree of independence as they may desire in accordance with international law.

While this declaration operates within international legal doctrine on the requirements of statehood, it also leaves open a number of possibilities for various forms of autonomy. As will be discussed later in this chapter, they include those claims centered on treaties, jurisdiction, territory, and culture.[21]

Decolonization Model

In 1981, another international NGO conference was convened, this time on Indigenous Peoples and the Land. There, a number of delegates focused on decolonization and independence. Indeed, indigenous calls for independence appealed to and attracted the attention of other groups that had for some time been claiming the right to statehood. Roxanne Dunbar-Ortiz identifies as "a striking aspect" of the conference that it included "the active participation of several national liberation organizations, including the Palestine Liberation Organization (PLO) and the Southwest Africa People's Organization (SWAPO)."[22] She notes that these groups took an interest in the conference not only for its thematic commissions focused on land reform and systems of tenure (in general), but also for its attention to other themes, such as the nuclear arms buildup.[23] In any case, the presence of national liberation and guerrilla groups not necessarily identified as indigenous seems to have been accepted. They contributed to the conference's final declaration, which includes a strong articulation of self-determination and was accepted unanimously by the participants.[24]

It is thus not surprising that, when the Working Group was formed in 1982, many early discussions and debates focused on the unfinished business of decolonization. Russel Barsh describes a moment at the Working Group's first meeting in which a representative from the Mi'kmaq tribe (whose members live in southeastern Canada and northeastern United States) argued that "those peoples we call indigenous are nothing more than colonized peoples who were missed by the great wave of global decolonization following the second world war . . . particularly where independence was granted, not to the original inhabitants of a territory, but to an intrusive and alien group newly arrived."[25] Brazilian and U.S. delegates countered that "their" Indians were too integrated into society to operate as independent nations.[26]

Many of the arguments for statehood came from tribal activists in North America, who constituted the bulk of the NGOs that held consultative status when the Working Group first met. The World Council of Indigenous Peoples (WCIP), the Indian Law Resource Center, and the International Indian Treaty Council (IITC) all held consultative status and represented North American tribes. The Indian Council of South America (CISA) was the only Latin American group to hold such a position, although it represented a number of organizations from throughout the region. The Working Group almost immediately adopted rules that allowed any interested party to speak at its meetings. Nevertheless, the groups with consultative status generally played the largest roles in the hearings, and it is primarily their statements that have made their way into the Working Group's official record. I derive my sense of the different positions of the groups and what took place at the meetings from that official record, which unfortunately consists mostly of those statements that were written and entered into the record, and therefore undoubtedly omits many brief comments and reactions made at the meetings.

Early on, North American groups participating in the Working Group seemed to hang their long-term interests and liberation on a strong claim to self-determination. The Indian Law Resource Center, for example, presented at the first meeting a document entitled "Principles for Guiding the Deliberations of the Working Group on Indigenous Populations."[27] These principles include a provision stating: "Indigenous peoples qualify as peoples possessing a right of self-determination; hence, indigenous peoples have the right to self-determination, that is, to possess whatever degree of self-government in their territories the indigenous peoples may choose."[28] That sentence follows another one making clear the connection of this right to the decolonization process, asserting that some indigenous peoples are "under a domination which is both alien and colonial in nature."[29]

However strong that language might appear, Sanders suggests that it did not make as specific a claim of self-determination as had been suggested by an earlier document, the Draft International Covenant on the Rights of Indigenous Peoples, approved for discussion at the WCIP's General Assembly in Australia in 1981. That draft, which was ultimately tabled, contains language indicating a wide range of possibilities for the exercise of self-determination, including that indigenous peoples might "associate their territory and institutions with one or more states in a manner involving free association, regional autonomy, home rule or associate statehood as self-governing units. Indigenous People may freely determine to enter into such relationships and to alter those relationships that have been established."[30]

The statement by the Indian Law Resource Center to the Working Group by no means settled the matter. As the Working Group continued to debate and revise the draft over the ensuing years, the issue would not disappear. The equation of indigenous rights and decolonization by many activists influenced a number of the early meetings. In 1983, the IITC, based in San Francisco, submitted a statement to the Working Group on its position on self-determination: "Indigenous nations and peoples who so desire should be granted the full rights and obligations of external self-determination."[31] During the Working Group's third session, in 1984, the IITC and the Coalition of First Nations made a statement about the colonial condition and claims of Indians in North America:

> The colonization of the Indian Nations and their territories by the Anglo-Canadian settlers has resulted in the dispossession of the Indigenous Indian Nations of their territories and their domination by an alien society. The Indian Nations share a common legacy with the Third World of dispossession and foreign control of natural resources, colonization, underdevelopment and poverty. The Indian Nations in Upper North America, like the Third World, have been involved in a struggle to decolonize their relations with the settler governments and to secure a fair share of the lands that have been taken from them. The issues have come into focus in terms of Canadian independence negotiations with Britain and legislative initiatives to finally disperse the Indian Nations. Canada's constitutional and legislative initiatives are a lesson to other states with unresolved Indigenous Peoples' issues on how not to remove a colonial legacy of betrayal and bitterness.[32]

This statement resonates with the Fourth World ideology discussed in chapter 2.

Though there is little evidence of their participation in the Working Group meetings, some Native Hawaiians have begun over the past decade to use a different type of decolonization argument as a basis for challenging Hawaii's status as a state of the United States. In particular, they have appealed to the UN Special Committee on Decolonization to press for Hawaii's inclusion on the list of non-self-governing territories. They assert that the 1959 ballot in which Hawaiians voted for statehood was invalid because it did not allow for the full range of options for association that have since become accepted in international law. Specifically, Hawaiians were not given the option of independence.[33]

Indigenous groups from North America have not been the only ones to make strong claims for self-determination based on decolonization. The Free Papua Movement, for example, argued before the Working Group that the Dutch decolonization plan had been subsumed by Indonesia's claim over West Papua, preventing West Papua from completing the decolonization process. Representatives of the movement made clear the basis of their claim in international law:

The UN Charter, the 1948 Universal Declaration on Human Rights as well as the United Nations Declaration on the Granting of Independence to Colonial Countries and Peoples (1960) fully safeguard the rights of the people of non-self-governing territories, both as individuals and as nations. On the basis of these documents, the refusal of the Indonesian government to implement A PROPER AND COMPLETELY FREE ACT OF SELF-DETERMINATION in 1969 with UN participation, was an act that should be most strongly condemned because it FLAGRANTLY VIOLATES THE NOBLE principles upheld in those documents.[34]

This argument became a perennial one made by the Free Papua Movement during some of the early sessions of the Working Group. Many early meetings also heard claims to the right to secession by the East Timorese and the South Moluccans against Indonesia, as well as by the Naga against India.[35]

In 1985, a number of indigenous organizations met at the Palais de Nations in Geneva for a special assembly to work on the draft UN Declaration. The assembly included several large organizations from North America, as well as indigenous groups and organizations from Chile, Ecuador, Mexico, Peru, India, and Norway. The organizations agreed on a statement that includes the following paragraph:

> All indigenous nations and peoples have the right to self-determination, by virtue of which they have the right to whatever degree of autonomy or self-government they choose. This includes the right to freely determine their political status, freely pursue their own economic, social, religious and cultural development, and determine their own membership and / or citizenship, without external interference.[36]

Thus, while not many indigenous groups would ultimately claim such a strong version of determination for themselves, all agreed that the option should remain open to those who would choose it.

North America: Treaty Rights as Basis for Self-Determination

In their 1984 statement excerpted above, the IITC and the Coalition of First Nations compared their situation with that of the Third World, and called for independence from colonial powers. For many North American tribes, respect for treaties with those powers was central to their claims for self-determination under international law. The 1984 statement continued:

Aboriginal Rights as understood by our Indian People refer to our rights to self-government and lands as being inherent, derived from our people and supported by the land, not given to us or taken by conquest. Our treaties, where these were made, and various British proclamations recognized our original nationhood and sovereignty . . . These aboriginal and treaty rights were in the Anglo-Canadian colonial period after 1867 undermined by the unilateral imposition of a debilitating trusteeship system on the Indian Nations without their consent.[37]

Discussing the Working Group in 1991, Raidza Torres summarizes the strong self-determination position taken by indigenous groups in Canada with regard to the British crown's 1763 Proclamation: "Canada's indigenous groups argue that since they have not ceded sovereignty over their lands, these groups should be recognized as separate Indian nations with the power to rule themselves without intervention from Canada's national and provincial governments."[38]

This position about treaties and international law is reflected in a proposal for the draft UN Declaration adopted at a preparatory meeting of indigenous groups prior to the 1987 Working Group session. One paragraph of that proposed draft, for example, calls for "treaties and other agreements freely made with indigenous nations or peoples" to be "recognized and applied in the same manner and according to the same international laws and principles as treaties and agreements entered with other States."[39]

For some indigenous groups, treaties were an indication of what they had agreed to concede as well as what rights they had maintained for themselves. The Treaty Six Chiefs, representing a number of communities in present-day Canada who had entered into a treaty with the British crown in the nineteenth century,[40] explained in a document they submitted to the 1988 meeting of the Working Group that their sovereignty was "political," not "legal." For them, political sovereignty "describes a relationship between the government and the governed by which the later places themselves under and defers to the former's exercise of the powers of government by CONSENT."[41] Such a position would seem to soften the secessionist threat even while making it clear that failure to call for secession is due to political consent, not lack of legal right. In this case, it functions as at least an attempted mediation between two conflicting claims to sovereignty. That said, the competing claims are clear. As the

Treaty Six Chiefs explained in another part of the document: "The failure to resolve this question of Indigenous Treaty issues created a situation where the federal state of Canada claims sovereignty over all territory within its boundaries, while indigenous nations claim independent sovereignty over our territories. These competing claims of sovereignty only serves [sic] as a basis for future confrontations."[42]

In 1993, the Working Group concluded its final version of the draft UN Declaration. It did not formally adopt it, however, until its next meeting, in 1994. In the 1994 session, the Subcommission on Prevention of Discrimination and Protection of Minorities, to whom the draft was initially to be presented, asked for comments on the Working Group's final version, even while making it clear that no amendments would be accepted at that time.[43] Thus, much of the meeting was devoted to a general discussion of the draft. As I discuss further below, self-determination was one of the principal issues debated during that discussion. Some who favored the right to external self-determination continued to invoke treaty rights. The International Confederation of Autonomous Chapters of the American Indian Movement, for example, criticized statements by United States delegates at the meeting:

> Our frustration is that twice in yesterday's statement the U.S. called us populations, nine times it called us People (with no "s"), and four times called us tribes or tribal. We are not populations, people or tribes or bands. We are not gaggles of geese or packs of wild dogs. We are peoples and nations, a reality that is confirmed in the over 400 treaties signed between indigenous peoples and the U.S., and we are demanding our rightful exercise of self-determination.[44]

For this group, the term "peoples" was synonymous with a strong form of self-determination. Treaties served as evidence that indigenous peoples possessed recognized international legal personality.[45]

The UN Declaration that was ultimately adopted by the General Assembly in 2007 reflects an insistence on the ongoing commitment to treaty recognition, if somewhat removed from the right to self-determination. Article 37 reads:

> 1. Indigenous peoples have the right to the recognition, observance and enforcement of treaties, agreements and other constructive ar-

rangements concluded with States or their successors and to have States honour and respect such treaties, agreements and other constructive arrangements.

2. Nothing in this Declaration may be interpreted as diminishing or eliminating the rights of indigenous peoples contained in treaties, agreements and other constructive arrangements.

This provision was retained even after the African Group expressed "serious reservations" about the implications of the provision in its initial opposition to the General Assembly's adoption of the declaration. For the African Group, the provision seemed yet another example of the possible encroachment of indigenous rights on state sovereignty: "The right of recognition, observance and enforcement of treaties is the responsibility of the state."[46]

Latin America: Majority Indigenous Populations as the Basis for Self-Determination

If Latin American indigenous groups could not make claims to self-determination based on treaty rights, some could nevertheless make an argument that was unavailable to any indigenous group in North America. In some instances, indigenous peoples constituted the majority of the population. Rather than calling for secession, these groups were in a position to claim the right to control the state in which they lived as a matter of popular sovereignty or majoritarian rule.

In 1985, for example, the author of much of the Cobo Report, Augusto Willemsen Diaz, publicly stated that he believed that a "full right to self-determination"[47] would apply in circumstances in which indigenous peoples comprised a majority of the population. Although his example appears to have been Guatemala, the situation is similar to that which I considered in the context of Bolivia in chapter 2. Political participation, not secession, would provide the substance for the right.

For the most part, however, the Working Group devoted little attention to self-determination with regard to indigenous groups in Latin America. Early meetings of the group covered some situations in Latin America, but with a focus of assuring the continued existence of certain threatened indigenous communities. Self-determination might have seemed a luxury—even a dangerous one—in Guatemala, for example, where the

Working Group concentrated on the urgent condemnation of genocide against indigenous peoples, which needed to be stopped immediately.[48]

Governmental Response: Reinforcing the Equation
of Self-Determination and Statehood

As discussed in ensuing sections of this chapter, even many of the indigenous groups and organizations that favored the language of self-determination did not necessarily equate the term with independence or statehood in Working Group sessions. Nevertheless, many governments either opposed the term altogether or called for defining it strictly, precisely to avoid such equation. As described in the introduction, the former position dictated much of the opposition by the United States, Canada, Australia, and New Zealand to the final UN Declaration. These governments opposed any use of the term for fear that it would be used by indigenous groups to claim full independence.

Concerns about this potentially broad sweep of the term were in fact expressed by states from the beginning, including in international forums outside the Working Group. The Inter-American Commission on Human Rights, for example, addressed the issue of applying self-determination to indigenous peoples in 1983 with regard to one group in Latin America that claimed self-determination, the Miskito Indians in Nicaragua. One of the Miskito's advocates, Armstrong Wiggins of the Indian Law Resource Center, identified the Indian peoples of Nicaragua as evincing the qualities of states: "The right to self-determination applies to all peoples, including the Indian population of Nicaragua, which possesses territory with defined borders, a permanent population, a government and the capacity to establish external relations."[49] In rejecting that argument, the commission's response was indicative of the position that many states would take during Working Group meetings in ensuing years. That is, the commission recognized that international law recognizes the right of self-determination of peoples, but insisted that "this does not mean . . . that it recognizes the right to self-determination of any ethnic group as such."[50]

In its analysis of the Miskito claim, the commission referred back to debates in the UN General Assembly's Third Committee in 1952, noting:

> Several states held the opinion that recognition of the right to self-determination of minorities would promote subversion and would

finally lead to separation. Consequently, it was agreed that self-determination should be harmonized with the other principles of equality under the law, sovereignty, territorial integrity and political independence that are set forth in the Charter of the United Nations.[51]

This position was echoed by many states during Working Group meetings as well.

By 1988, significant state opposition to the inclusion of the right to self-determination without specific limitation was clear. The first chair of the Working Group, Asbjørn Eide, has noted with regard to the early Working Group meetings:

> Government observers pointed out that the right to self-determination was viewed, in current international legal instruments, primarily in the context of decolonisation and could therefore not be applied to the Indigenous populations. It was widely held that it would be more practical to examine different current and possible self-government arrangements rather than to clarify the meaning and application of "self-determination."[52]

The "blue water" thesis was once again being invoked.

Some states deployed language from the 1970 UN Declaration on Principles of International Law Concerning Friendly Relations and Cooperation among States in Accordance with the Charter of the United Nations (Friendly Relations Declaration), which I first considered in chapter 1. According to Rudolph Ryser, states at the Working Group in 1988 were "circling the wagons against a perceived threat from colonized nations" by invoking this phrase from the declaration: "Nothing in the foregoing paragraphs shall be construed as authorizing or encouraging any action which would dismember or impair, totally or in part, the territorial integrity or political unity of sovereign and independent states . . ."[53] The ellipsis is necessary here because, as discussed in chapter 1 and again below, states were omitting the exception that follows: the right only adheres to states "conducting themselves in compliance with the principle of equal rights and self-determination of peoples as described above and thus possessed of a government representing the whole people belonging to the territory without distinction as to race, creed or colour." Ryser criticized state use of the declaration for another reason, complaining that "state observer delegations seem increasingly interested in closing off discussions on the self-determination of indigenous nations. Instead of free and open-minded dialogue, some delegations seem eager to hide behind a U.N. declaration contrived by states to deny nations their right to self-determination."[54]

In 1993, as the Working Group tried to finalize a draft of the UN Declaration, the stakes were high. This Working Group meeting pulled together delegations from more than 60 states and 125 indigenous groups. Writing after the session ended, Ryser describes what had been "a vigorous debate over key words and phrases to be contained in the Declaration on the Rights of Indigenous Peoples slated soon to go before the UN General Assembly for final adoption."[55] Ryser may have overestimated the likelihood of final adoption, but he seems to have accurately captured many of the tensions in the meeting, which would continue to animate debates on indigenous rights for years to come. For him, the issues at stake were:

—whether treaties between indigenous nations and states' governments will have the force of international law,

—whether states' governments may violate the rights of nations and avoid international scrutiny or sanctions,

—whether nations will have the actual rather than the implied right to self-determination, self-government and the right to exercise sovereignty over their territories, and

—whether nations will enjoy the same rights to freely choose their political, economic, social and cultural future without external interference in the same way as other peoples in the world have the guaranteed right under international law.[56]

Ryser's bias toward a strong form of self-determination was echoed by other indigenous representatives as well.

Many states again responded with the same language from the 1970 Friendly Relations Declaration that they had turned to in 1988. Maivân Lâm, speaking to the Working Group, argued that the Friendly Relations Declaration was inapplicable to the question of indigenous peoples' right to self-determination:

There is thus, Madam Chairperson, no instrument of international law that specifically prohibits the recognition of the full right of self-determination of Indigenous Peoples . . . The Declaration on Friendly

Relations and Cooperation among States, for example, prohibits a state from infringing the territorial integrity of another. It does not, and could not, without gutting the democratic political process itself, prohibit peoples who live within a state from modifying the latter's structures, or even boundaries as need be. Witness the separation of Bangladesh from Pakistan.[57]

Like Ryser, Lâm did not rely on the limited exception in the Friendly Relations Declaration. For her, indigenous peoples were entitled to self-determination regardless of the state in which they currently lived. She urged the Working Group not to allow any of the compromises on the language that states proposed.

The more insistent that some indigenous rights advocates were that self-determination included the possibility of secession, of course, the more states tried to limit it. The Swedish government stated at the same meeting, for example:

> It is important that we recognize in this context, as we have in others, that the concept [of self-determination], as used in international law, must not be blurred. It is therefore necessary to find another term in the declaration, or to introduce an explanatory definition such as that included in ILO Convention No. 169, which provides that "The use of the term 'peoples' in this Convention shall not be construed as having any implications as regards the rights which may attach to the term under international law."[58]

The United States concurred:

> Self-determination is generally understood to mean the right to establish a sovereign and independent state under international law. Self-determination, however, can be achieved through arrangements other than independence. The United States could not accept the inclusion of self-determination as applying specifically to indigenous groups if it implies or permits full independence generally recognized under international law.[59]

Somewhat ironically, the positions of the Swedish and U.S. governments reinforced the view that, under international law, self-determination allows for the possibility of secession.

SELF-DETERMINATION AS AUTONOMY
WITHIN THE STATE

As seen in the introduction, the UN Declaration, when finally adopted in 2007, both recognized and limited self-determination, essentially excluding the right to external self-determination. The seeds of that compromise can be seen years earlier in the proceedings of the Working Group meetings, where exclusion of the term "self-determination" was a deal breaker for indigenous peoples, as was its significant limitation by states. A less strong form of self-determination, one focused on autonomy within the state, both contributed to and emerged from a compromise first seen in the Working Group's 1993 draft.

Article 3 of the 1993 draft is identical to the text of the final declaration: "Indigenous peoples have the right to self-determination. By virtue of that right they freely determine their political status and freely pursue their economic, social and cultural development." On the fourth day of the 1993 Working Group session, it was made clear that the provision would be included in the draft. When the chair then announced that the Working Group experts had agreed on the language, Lâm reports that "the chamber exploded in ovation."[60] She notes that even those indigenous groups (such as those from Asia) that had not originally sought self-determination language supported it in the end.

The decision by the Working Group was celebrated by indigenous groups, in part because they had succeeded in rejecting a different version of Article 3 and an explanatory note proposed by Erica-Irene Daes, then the chair. The explanatory note, as Daes has since summarized it, would have stated that the declaration was aimed at "strengthen[ing] States to make them truly representative, democratic, liberal and inclusive" rather than "focusing on the right to form new States."[61] Through the proposed note, Daes made clear her general—though not unqualified—opposition to the right to secession, stating that "the preferred course of action, in every case except the most extreme ones, is to encourage the State in question to share power democratically with all groups, under a constitutional formula that guarantees that the Government is 'effectively representative.' "[62] Daes's qualification explicitly followed the exception found in the Friendly Relations Declaration. After quoting from the full paragraph often relied upon by states, the proposed note explained: "This requirement continues unless the national political system becomes so exclusive and non-democratic that it no longer can be said to be 'representing the whole people.' "[63]

Daes believed at the time that her explanatory note was essential to the adoption of the draft because Article 3 constituted the most significant obstacle for states. In a piece published in 2001, she elaborates:

Through all these years, governments have remained skeptical on the right to self-determination of indigenous peoples . . . [A] majority of governments has continued to express *fear and uncertainty* about self-determination, in particular about Article 3 of the Draft Declaration. This fear and uncertainty by the governments on this important and multifarious point has been the main factor delaying the completion of the elaboration of the draft Declaration as a whole at the level of the *ad hoc* Working Group of the Commission.[64]

Yet it appears that in 1993, the Working Group moved forward with the Article 3 language without the explanatory note.[65]

Lâm argues that when the draft version containing the celebrated Article 3 was finally completed, it contained another provision that could be read to limit that self-determination. Its language was more subtle than that proposed by some states from the Friendly Relations Declaration. While not emphasizing territorial integrity, the new provision made clear a focus on internal self-determination. Article 31 of the draft reads:

Indigenous peoples, as a specific form of exercising their right to self-determination, have the right to autonomy or self-government in matters relating to their internal and local affairs, including culture, religion, education, information, media, health, housing, employment, social welfare, economic activities, land and resources management, environment and entry by non-members, as well as ways and means for financing these autonomous functions.

By the time the final UN Declaration was passed in 2007, this language had been altered and moved to Articles 4 and 5, where it could be seen as further elaboration on the right to self-determination set forth in Article 3. Yet in 1994, when comments but not amendments were permitted with regard to the draft, Lâm notes that a number of indigenous rights advocates criticized Article 31 because it "might lead some states to read the

Draft Declaration to mean that autonomy was the prescribed expression of self-determination for indigenous peoples."[66]

By 2007, of course, the controversial and limiting Article 46, which I discussed in the introduction, was already included. States would therefore not need to rely solely upon the autonomy language. Recall that Article 46 states that the UN Declaration shall not be "construed as authorizing or encouraging any action which would dismember or impair, totally or in part the territorial integrity or political unity of sovereign and independent States." That language is, absent the ellipsis, an exact replica of that found in the 1970 Friendly Relations Declaration; the states that had been attempting to include it since 1988 had finally succeeded.

The willingness of indigenous representatives to accept Article 46 to assure the passage of the UN Declaration suggests that the strong meaning of self-determination had much less currency in 2007 than had been the case in the 1980s and early 1990s. That so few indigenous groups continue to articulate external self-determination arguments makes the insistence of so many states on the inclusion of Article 46 even more puzzling. The same language, had it not been rejected, would presumably have pacified, if not satisfied, even the United States government in 1993.

That positions of states would change over time, of course, is not surprising. The Bush administration representatives at the UN were more skeptical of granting rights to indigenous peoples—however stated—through international law than were the Clinton administration's representatives in 1993. Similarly, the representative of Australia's Labor government in 1993 noted that, since 1991, Australia had made clear its support of the term "self-determination," believing "that the principles of territorial integrity of states is sufficiently enshrined internationally that a reference to self-determination in the Draft Declaration would not imply a right of secession."[67] Later, the Australian government pulled away from support of the right to self-determination, voting against the declaration in 2007, notwithstanding the inclusion of Article 46. The return of the Labor Party to power shortly after that vote signaled yet another change, as the new government came out in support of the declaration.[68]

More surprising, I think, is that the positions of advocates have changed so substantially. While in 2007, indigenous groups continued to insist on the inclusion of the right to self-determination, the term had taken on a different hue: it no longer included the right to secession. In some ways, of course, the understanding of self-determination as internal was not new. Many indigenous groups had sought precisely this sort of autonomy for themselves from the beginning. The Cobo Report suggests a preference for internal over external self-determination for most groups. After concluding that human rights standards are inadequate for the protection of indigenous peoples, the report contends that "self-determination, in its many forms, must be recognized as the basic precondition for the enjoyment by indigenous peoples of their fundamental rights and the determination of their own future."[69] Although, as mentioned earlier, it acknowledges exceptional circumstances in which secession might be appropriate, for the most part it distances itself from the strong self-determination claim. For the report, self-determination "constitutes the exercise of free choice by indigenous peoples who must, to a large extent, create the specific content of this principle . . . which [does] not necessarily include the right to secede . . . This right may in fact be expressed in various forms of autonomy within the State."[70]

The Working Group's report on the first session in 1982 suggests that many indigenous organizations largely concurred:

> The representatives of several organizations stressed the importance of self-determination . . . It was emphasized that self-determination did not necessarily equate to separatism. In connection with self-determination, other specific rights were also stressed: the right to land and to the mineral resources it contained; the right to develop their own culture and education; the right to enjoy religious and political rights and to be consulted and to participate in the national development processes.[71]

The key seems to be choice:

> It was suggested that the situation varied from group to group, from country to country, and that the question of self-determination was varied in content and approach, leaving a kaleidoscope of positions in between, including the mere participation in decisions concerning their status in the country where the indigenous lived, through self-government arrangements establishing different forms of autonomy within the State.[72]

Thus, as with at least some of those peoples and territories achieving self-determination in the period between the world wars, and later during decolonization, indigenous peoples should be given the opportunity to decide for themselves what type of arrangement they would like to pursue with the state in which they currently live.[73]

Others opposed even offering a choice. Eide was a strong promoter of the application of human rights to indigenous populations. He resisted, however, a broad understanding of the right to secession and opposed its use in the context of indigenous advocacy. Lâm presents Eide's position, at least as articulated in a work published after he was no longer chair of the Working Group: "In his view, existing states are the proper guarantors of international law and order, whereas 'ethnonationalism, in its expansionist, exclusivist and secessionist modes,' represents one of the greatest threats to international peace and rights."[74]

In 1987, Russel Barsh explained that the focus on autonomy received growing interest in the 1980s because "as traditionally interpreted, at least, the right to self-determination may go too far in suggesting a choice between the existing state and the establishment of a new state."[75] In 1991, after the 1988 meeting of the Working Group, Raidza Torres observed that "only a small and extreme minority of indigenous groups demand independence" and that, because of political reality, "indigenous demands for self-determination usually stop short of seeking independence from the existing state, but instead ask for limited sovereignty (i.e., for the power to create and enforce laws without consulting with nonindigenous authorities)."[76] For Torres, independence is not only a nearly impossible goal to achieve, but it is also not in the best interest of most indigenous groups: "The lands that have been designated for natives are often lacking in economic resources. Furthermore, since many indigenous groups have become dependent on manufactured goods and have abandoned some of their subsistence economic activities, they may find it difficult to survive without aid or subsidies from the dominant state."[77]

Over a decade later, Ronald Niezen agrees that, due to lack of indigenous resources to pursue statehood, "concern over a global conflagration of indigenous secessionist movements is largely fanciful."[78] Indigenous peoples have not, however, given up on internal self-determination. For Niezen, "fully recognized rights of self-determination mean new forms of autonomy within states, the erection of new intra-state constitutional structures, and a shift toward formalized criteria and administration of citizenship within indigenous polities." He situates this definition in the context of decolonization, insisting that "it entails, in other words, an extension of the process of decolonization without the use of statehood as a method or manifestation of political autonomy."[79]

Whether for pragmatic or other reasons, demands for this form of self-determination—internal, autonomous, or semi-autonomous—were frequently made throughout the late 1980s into the 1990s, particularly by indigenous groups outside of North America. Of course, as Héctor Díaz Polanco observes, the term "autonomy" also has multiple meanings. He describes two principal understandings of the term. One "implies a situation of laissez-faire," indicating that there is "more or less broad permission for ethnic groups to tend to their own affairs or to retain their own customs."[80] This type of autonomy, he argues, ultimately relies on those in power to grant such permission, and is therefore quite limited. The second meaning of autonomy to which he refers is "a political-juridical regime, agreed upon and not merely granted, that implies the creation of a true political collectivity within the national society," which would include "a form of self-government for certain integrated communities that choose their authorities from among themselves, exercise legally attributed responsibilities, and have some minimal faculty for legislating their internal life and administering their affairs."[81]

Díaz Polanco urges against seeing self-determination and autonomy as separate options, suggesting that "instead, autonomy should be viewed as one way of exercising self-determination."[82] In the context of Latin America, he proposes a relatively strong form of autonomy, one in which territory is central, but culture is also key:

> In the Latin American case, we may expect the territorial principle to continue to be indispensable to the design of projects of autonomy, since territory, linked to natural and productive resources, to the environment, and even to sacred spaces, is a central demand among indigenous peoples. Nevertheless . . . [i]t is possible that cultural autonomy, at least a complementary formula, will prove more important for resolving complex ethnic-national issues than we can now imagine.[83]

The importance he places on territory, land, and culture resonates with some of the positions of panindianismo that we saw in chapter 2.

The focus on territory, land, and culture can also be seen in the contributions of many Latin American indigenous groups during the 1980s and 1990s—both to multicultural constitutions being drafted throughout the region and to the UN Working Group. Sometimes the interests were expressed in self-determination language, while at other times they could be found in human rights language—specifically, articulated as the human right to self-determination—as we will see in the next section.

CISA, the one South American indigenous group with consultative status before the Working Group, pursued a form of autonomy similar to the second meaning described by Díaz Polanco. Recall from chapter 2 the statement that the group issued during its second congress, urging that the frontiers between existing states be downplayed, in part by calling on states "to recognise their plurinational, multicultural and multilinguistic character."[84] Essentially, CISA called for a type of autonomy, at least in those states where indigenous peoples constituted a minority, in which mestizos and indigenous peoples alike would constitute separate and equal "nations" under one state. Such autonomy was the vehicle by which indigenous peoples would achieve respect for their culture.

Some indigenous groups and organizations made clear that they were not calling for statehood, even when using the term "self-determination." Because many of the groups that denied this strong claim to self-determination were from Latin America and did not begin to attend Working Group meetings until the late 1980s, their position was not often articulated in the Working Group's early years. Had Guatemalan Indians been able to attend early meetings, for example, either the tone of the Working Group or the advocacy of indigenous peoples in Guatemala—or both— might have been altered. At least initially, Guatemalan Indians would have been unlikely to call for a strong form of self-determination. What Torres wrote about them in 1991 would have been even more true in the early 1980s:

> Guatemalan Indians currently do not emphasize the right of self-determination as strongly as indigenous groups in other countries. In part, this is because they face the more immediate challenge of countering widespread murders by the government. In addition, because Indians form the majority of the Guatemalan population and because they are dispersed throughout the country, it is impractical to advance

the cause of a separate Indian state within Guatemala. The Guatemalan government is sensitive to any threats to the country's territorial integrity, especially given its struggle against leftist groups. Indian demands for substantial autonomy are perceived as threats to the state and are likely to result in more repressive policies.[85]

Recall that early discussions about Guatemalan indigenous peoples in the Working Group were aimed at condemning ethnocide and genocide.

The Mixe people of Oaxaca, Mexico, provide a different example. They issued their own declaration, "Fundamental Rights of the Indigenous Nations, Nationalities and Peoples of Indo-Latin America," which they presented at a regional conference in 1993 and then to the Working Group in 1994. They declared themselves to be "peoples" with their "own history, religion, culture, education, language and other fundamental characters of nations," but nevertheless stated that "the nation States must understand that the aspiration of our indigenous nations, nationalities and peoples is not to establish themselves as new States."[86]

The Mixe did not participate in a Working Group meeting until 1988. In 1989, they held a series of sessions with other indigenous groups in Mexico, as well as with anthropologists and human rights organizations, to discuss the proposed draft of the UN Declaration. In one such meeting, they heard from Gilberto López y Rivas, an anthropologist who, it turns out, was advising the government of Nicaragua on indigenous affairs (where the Miskito were demanding self-determination) and who later worked with the Zapatista Army. López y Rivas made clear his disagreement with the strong self-determination position taken by some indigenous groups in English-speaking North America. He distinguished between "free determination" and "self-determination," arguing that the former is broader and more applicable to the indigenous situation in Mexico. He went on to suggest that autonomy is a way to practice free determination, and that there are different forms of it. "Autonomy is not the same as separation," he observed: "The fight of the indigenous peoples is not separatist, although it offers space for the union and harmony of distinct peoples."[87] In this sense, he distinguished his position from that of the Indian Law Resource Center, whose focus on statehood, he believed, had a "disintegrating and prejudicial effect for indigenous populations of Latin America."[88]

Although some of the ideas expressed by López y Rivas can be found in the 1993 declaration by the Mixe, his statement should not be fully attributed to the group. His comments seem to have been aimed as much at the Miskito (and their allies in North America) as at North American indigenous groups in general. From 1980 to 1990, López y Rivas held the position of Advisor to the Nicaraguan Government on the Question of Indigeneity and Autonomy, and, in 1989, during the meeting of indigenous groups in Mexico, that government was still embroiled with the Miskito claim for independence. In his comments, López y Rivas offered the multiethnic and democratic government of Nicaragua as an example of the type of process that autonomy for indigenous peoples implies. At the same time, he called for an autonomy that is not simply cultural, but economic and political as well.[89] Finally, he suggested the need for territorial autonomy apart from land, given that not all indigenous people are campesinos.[90] These ideas, along with a call he made for constitutional reform, can be seen in the later Zapatista movement in Mexico.

Latin American indigenous groups (save perhaps the Miskito) were not alone in their pursuit of a nonseparatist form of self-determination. In 1988, for example, the Sami—who occupy land in Finland, Sweden, Norway, and Russia—made their first official statement to the Working Group. Although they emphasized that self-determination should be the principal theme of the draft of the UN Declaration, they tied their understanding of self-determination to the issue of territory, which "includes land of course, but also includes our distinct relationship to the land, waters and sea, as PEOPLES, and the full enjoyment of all resources within our boundaries."[91] For the Sami, the notion of well-being and cultural survival was tied to "economic well-being and often to economic survival."[92] Atle Grahl-Madsen, a professor at the University of Bergen who worked with the Sami Council, noted during the same Working Group meeting that the Sami model for autonomy is not secessionist, but grounded in social, cultural, and economic autonomy. The pursuit of this model, he noted, "might alleviate the fear of established governments that a recognition of the right to self-government of indigenous peoples might lead to the breaking up of the State or at least the map coming to look like a good Swiss cheese: full of holes."[93]

By the mid 1990s, after the draft of the UN Declaration had been finalized by the Working Group, I think it is fair to say that the insistence on leaving open the possibility for a right to external self-determination had largely disappeared. A move away from the focus on statehood could be attributed as much to the self-disciplining activities of the indigenous groups active in the Working Group as to direct pressure from above. Lâm argues:

> That indigenous peoples spent ten exhausting years at the WGIP commenting on every provision . . . clearly attests to their intention to maintain on-going associations with their encompassing states . . . Indigenous peoples paid close attention to the wording of all other 45 articles [in addition to Article 3] precisely because they understood, expected, and accepted that these would set the minimum standards for the behavior of states vis-à-vis their communities.[94]

Moreover, there is some evidence that those who argued too strongly for the right to secession were often disciplined by the Working Group. Bengt Karlsson, for example, reports: "An experienced Naga delegate told me that there were initially some controversies within the WGIP itself concerning their participation, because of their insistence on independence."[95] He observes, however, that the issue seems to have disappeared over the years: "As most of the later Naga statements focus on human rights violations and, towards the end of the 1990s, on the ongoing peace negotiations with the Indian government, one can assume that their participation later became less of a problem of the WGIP."[96]

By the late 1990s, while calls for the right to self-determination were still commonly made, it seems that most indigenous groups and advocates had attempted to reassure states that they used it to claim internal rather than external self-determination. Lâm points to a statement made by the aboriginal leader and activist Mick Dodson, director of the Indigenous Law Center at the University of New South Wales, making clear his support for international respect for the principles of territorial integrity and his belief that the secessionist version of self-determination was rarely taken up by indigenous peoples.[97]

James Anaya, currently the UN special rapporteur on the situation of human rights and fundamental freedoms of indigenous people, has long eschewed the distinction between internal and external self-determination, calling instead for dividing self-determination into "constitutive" and "ongoing" self-determination. Grounding each of these in human rights instruments, he argues that decolonization was a remedial measure to re-spond to violations of both types of self-determination in a particular moment. Maintaining that "in most cases in the post-colonial world . . . secession would most likely be a cure worse than the disease from the standpoint of all concerned,"[98] he warns against the application of constitu-tive self-determination in the indigenous context.

Anaya argues in favor of using the term "self-determination," but only in the "ongoing" sense, and he wants to make that meaning clear. He cites the 1983 decision of the Inter-American Commission on Human Rights regarding the Miskito as an endorsement of his understanding of the self-determination of indigenous groups, which is somewhat surprising given the commission's explicit statement that self-determination does not ap-ply to the Miskito Indians. For Anaya, the problem with the commission's decision, however, is its narrow view of self-determination—"effectively equating self-determination with decolonization procedures"—and not with its approach to indigenous rights.[99] The latter, which he sees in the commission's call for a new political order derived from consultation between the government and the Miskito, represents self-determination as it should be understood.[100]

Lâm criticizes Anaya's use of the term "self-determination" here, pre-cisely because she sees him equating it with autonomy.[101] While both Lâm and Anaya therefore agree that indigenous peoples are entitled to the right to self-determination, they give that right two very different, and often conflicting, meanings. As with most indigenous groups appearing before the Working Group during its many meetings, neither wants to abandon his or her definition of the term.

SELF-DETERMINATION AS A HUMAN RIGHT

A subtle shift took place in the debate over self-determination in the late 1980s and early 1990s. While early advocates for self-determination for indigenous peoples focused on the history of the colonization of indige-nous peoples, the Montevideo Convention, decolonization, and attributes of statehood shared by indigenous peoples, later advocates—particularly those who saw self-determination as autonomy within a state—began to reference human rights documents as the basis for indigenous peoples' right to self-determination.

Common Article 1 of the International Covenant on Civil and Political

Rights (ICCPR) and the International Covenant on Economic, Social and Cultural Rights recognizes the rights of peoples to self-determination. One might have thought that the Working Group would consider the applicability of this article to indigenous peoples, in much the way the debates over the "blue water" thesis addressed whether and how independence models of decolonization might apply to them. Yet, perhaps because of the focus of North American groups on treaty rights and a lack of general attention to the possibility of collective human rights, Working Group discussions in the 1980s rarely relied upon the right to self-determination in the covenants, though the covenants were sometimes listed alongside other applicable human rights instruments (such as the International Convention on the Elimination of All Forms of Racial Discrimination) and public international legal documents, including those on self-determination. Despite this lack of explicit discussion, the language of Article 1 of the two covenants was incorporated wholesale into Article 3 of both the 1993 draft and the final version of the UN Declaration.

By 1993 and 1994, when the draft of the UN Declaration was being finalized and formally submitted by the Working Group, the use of the language from the covenants had become important to advocates. The Cree, for example, made clear in their 1994 commentary on the draft that, although they had compromised on numerous issues, they did not see Article 3 as negotiable:

11. We insist upon the wording in article 3 of the text, and note that the technical review of the United Nations draft declaration on the rights of indigenous peoples prepared by the secretariat (E/CN.4/Sub.2/1994/2) notes that the text of article 3 is "precisely based on article 1, paragraph 1, of the two International Covenants."

12. The failure to fully apply the two International Covenants to the indigenous peoples would be prejudicial, and contrary to the principles of the universality and indivisibility of all human rights.[102]

The Cree were among a number of indigenous groups who, as I will explain in chapter 4, had attempted to bring collective indigenous claims of self-determination to the UN Human Rights Committee under Article 1 of the ICCPR, using the individual complaint procedure set up by the covenant's First Optional Protocol. The Human Rights Committee had ruled the Article 1 claims inadmissible (on the ground that the protocol permitted only individual—not collective—claims). The Cree might well have seen the inclusion of the self-determination language in the UN Declaration as eventually providing an alternative forum for the claims, or even supporting future admissibility of Article 1 petitions under the protocol.

Those indigenous rights advocates who began to invoke self-determination as a human right often did so alongside other uses of self-determination. The 1993 Mixe declaration discussed earlier, for example, which makes clear its lack of demand for statehood, reaffirms in its preamble that "the right of self-determination is a human right of peoples, as an absolute pre-requisite for the enjoyment of all other internationally recognized human rights."[103] It does so even as it later equates self-determination and autonomy. Even Lâm, with her strong claim for a self-determination that permits the possibility of secession, has invoked the self-determination provision of the covenants.[104]

But reliance on the covenants proved to be a double-edged sword. The Dutch government, for example, used them to argue against a strong self-determination position in its 1993 statement that generally supported the draft of the UN Declaration. The government explained:

> The premise underlying article 1 of the International Covenant on Civil and Political Rights (ICCPR) and of the International Covenant on Economic, Cultural and Social Rights (ICECSR) is that all peoples have a right to internal self-determination in order that they might preserve and develop their social, economic, and cultural identities. However, this right does not include the right to secede from existing sovereign States: indigenous peoples do not have a right to external self-determination.[105]

The same statement suggested reservations about the recognition of collective human rights, and reinforced the Human Rights Committee's decisions on the inadmissibility of claims brought under Article 1 of the ICCPR.[106]

Perhaps the strongest proponent of self-determination as a human right has been James Anaya. Although, as previously discussed, he continues to use the language of self-determination, he argues that it is a "foundational principle" to be elaborated on by other norms such as nondiscrimination, cultural integrity, the right to land and development, and autonomy. When he discusses such elaborations, however, he refers primarily to human rights instruments and the decisions that have interpreted them.[107] Thus, I see Anaya as representative of a legal, political, and discursive shift away from calls for external—and sometimes even internal—calls for self-determination, and toward an invocation of indigenous rights that, while sometimes articulated in self-determination terms, is supported and reinforced by human rights. It is that move on which I focus in chapter 4, although in contexts in which the term "self-determination" is generally not invoked as a basis for the claims.

Before turning to that shift, I would like to pause for a moment here at the intersection between self-determination and human rights. What does it mean for self-determination to be a human right, as opposed to a right to the political power seen as accompanying statehood? In a chapter titled "A Critique of the State-Centered Approach to Self-Determination," Lâm identifies what she calls a "fascinating detail":

> Indigenous peoples typically assert their political rights, which they encapsulate under the rubric of self-determination, not by invoking power (past, present, or imminent control of territory and population), which international law typically associates with statehood, but by evoking need (physical and cultural survival), which international law typically associates with human rights. In this regard, indigenous peoples are creating a provocative connection between two international law domains that have hitherto been conceptually segregated.[108]

Lâm suggests that the connection between those domains "remains to be explored." I intend for this chapter—with its focus on arguments for indigenous rights based on statehood and self-determination—and the ensuing chapter's consideration of arguments based on human rights to culture and property to participate in such an exploration.

HUMAN RIGHT TO CULTURE CLAIMS

Although the current status of international law does not allow the view that the ethnic groups of the Atlantic zone of Nicaragua have a right to political autonomy and self-determination, special legal protection is recognized for the use of their language, the observance of their religion, and in general, all those aspects related to the preservation of their cultural identity. To this should be added the aspects linked to productive organization, which includes, among other things, the issue of the ancestral and communal lands.—INTER-AMERICAN COMMISSION ON HUMAN RIGHTS, REPORT ON THE HUMAN RIGHTS OF THE MISKITO IN NICARAGUA, 1983[1]

The ultimate issue at stake here is not self-determination as traditionally conceived under international law and state practice. It centers rather on the maintenance of cultural integrity. By eschewing the phrase "self-determination," states and indigenous groups can communicate more constructively concerning the issues that are truly of interest to indigenous groups: namely, autonomy, control over natural resources, environmental preservation of the homeland, education and language issues, and religious freedoms, all of which are fundamental to the maintenance of cultural identity and integrity.—JEFF CORNTASSEL AND THOMAS HOPKINS PRIMEAU, "INDIGENOUS 'SOVEREIGNTY' AND INTERNATIONAL LAW," 1995[2]

As discussed in chapter 1, human rights law was not initially an obvious forum for indigenous rights advocates. To the extent that the human rights regime was seen to stem from the normalizing and even civilizing impulses of Western individualism, it was considered a threat to indigenous culture. In the

1980s and 1990s, however, a number of indigenous rights advocates began to turn to human rights law as a site for legal and political struggle. Genocidal attacks on and indiscriminate killings of indigenous people were clearly prohibited by fundamental and broadly accepted human rights like the right to life. But the sources for claims for rights to heritage, land, autonomy, and development—particularly in their collective form—were more difficult to ground in the traditional human rights corpus. Rather than seeing culture and human rights in opposition, indigenous rights advocates began to call for a human right to culture to pursue these claims.

Indigenous rights advocates simultaneously softened their stance on self-determination and attempted to broaden the general, liberal model of human rights, to incorporate a collective right to culture and to allow for difference within an equality model. In 1990, the indigenous rights advocate James Anaya explicitly argued for the use of the right to culture over a sovereignty approach, locating its legal authority in the UN Charter, Article 27 of the ICCPR, the UN Convention against Genocide, and UNESCO's Declaration of the Principles of International Cultural Co-operation. Even though these documents were all at least two decades old at the time, Anaya identified in them an "emergent human right of cultural survival and flourishment."[3]

Tom Svensson, seeing the recognition of the right to culture in Article 27 of the ICCPR as a breakthrough for collective rights, agrees: "Cultural survival is not only a matter of culture *per se*. It can also be regarded as a human rights issue based on political rights and land rights."[4] Svensson makes explicit his attempt to mediate the apparently individual nature of human rights and the seemingly group nature of indigenous rights:

> If one assumes this connection between culture and human rights to be a significant legal property according to international law and uses it as a fruitful point of departure in attempts at clarification of human rights in general terms, the somewhat unnecessary debate between liberal and nonliberal positions and the controversy as to whether human rights are individual or collective might be settled.[5]

James Zion, through describing human rights as a Western enlightenment construct, also sees the value of a right to culture: "There are two general approaches to support these rights. One is to expand current international doctrines of the law of self-determination to Indian groups, and another is to give liberal construction to the concept of 'the right to culture.' "[6]

Since the early 1990s, the human right to culture approach has become the favored legal and political strategy for most indigenous advocates. Partly because international institutions and adjudicatory bodies have recognized the right to culture, legal self-determination claims in both their strong and weak forms have largely disappeared. Although arguments for the right to self-determination remain alive in certain forums, such as in debates about the UN Declaration, the human right to culture strategy has become the expected terrain upon which indigenous individuals and sometimes groups bring their legal claims.

That claims are brought under the right to culture does not necessarily mean that they have different political goals than those articulated under at least some versions of the right to self-determination. As we will see, the right to culture is often called upon to make claims to land and territory, various forms of autonomy, and economic self-determination. Andrea Muehlebach, discussing the decisions and actions on indigenous rights by the UN Human Rights Committee, the ICCPR's monitoring body, notes that "the indigenous argumentative logic of culture as material and territorialized practice has been evoked in order to let the right of self-determination slip back into the debate implicitly."[7] Corntassel and Primeau argue that some of the strongest proponents of self-determination in fact strive to "preserve 'cultural integrity,' "[8] and they therefore call for making that aim clear rather than using the terms "self-determination" and "sovereignty." These latter terms, they believe, "cloud the issue of indigenous rights when it is unclear whether [they reflect] the traditional international law interpretation, the notion of cultural integrity or another competing definition."[9]

Although I focus here on the relatively broad acceptance of the applicability of human rights to indigenous rights, I want to make clear that the right to culture, particularly when articulated as a collective right, often makes claims that are rejected or tempered by states and international organizations. During the 1993 Working Group meeting, for example, both the Swedish and United States governments resisted the draft UN Declaration's inclusion of collective rights because of the impact that collective rights might have on individual rights.[10] I return to this and related concerns later in this chapter, under the discussion of the invisible asterisk.

This chapter considers in broad terms the acceptance, growth, and potential limitations and possibilities of the human right to culture model. It considers the reports and decisions of Inter-American Court of Human Rights and the Inter-American Commission on Human Rights. It also moves beyond the Americas, as much of the development of the model has taken place in other contexts, such as the ILO, the Human Rights Committee, and the UN Committee on the Elimination of Racial Discrimination (CERD). I begin by returning to the discussion I started in chapter 1 about the American Anthropological Association (AAA), to understand some of the theoretical and political bases for the assertion of a right to culture.

THEORETICAL UNDERPINNINGS: THE AMERICAN ANTHROPOLOGICAL ASSOCIATION IN THE 1990s

In 1999, more than fifty years after the AAA's 1947 statement expressing significant skepticism about the idea of a universal and individual model of human rights then being considered by the UN, the association issued a new declaration, this time in favor of human rights. The declaration was drafted and promoted by the AAA Committee for Human Rights, formed in 1995 by a group of anthropologists within the AAA. That committee grew out of the Commission for Human Rights, which the AAA established in 1992 to "develop concrete recommendations for the operation of a permanent Committee for Human Rights and to bring those recommendations to the Executive Board at the 1995 Annual Meeting."[11]

While pursuing many of the same substantive positions and commitments as the 1947 statement, the 1999 declaration represented a move from skepticism toward acceptance of human rights discourse. Human rights law and discourse, particularly through the human right to culture, was now seen as capable of facilitating—rather than hindering—those substantive pursuits.

For the AAA Committee for Human Rights, the human right to culture became a means to attempt to mediate the tension between human rights and culture. While the right to culture did not originate with the AAA, I believe the association's shift in attitude is representative of the broader trend to use the right to culture as a basis for the human rights claims of indigenous peoples.

At least as early as 1971, anthropologists had shown an interest in using cultural rights on behalf of indigenous peoples. A manifestation of this interest can be found in the 1971 Declaration of Barbados, produced at Barbados I, the seminal meeting of nonindigenous but "dissident anthropologists" that I discussed in chapter 2. That declaration calls upon states to recognize the cultural rights of indigenous peoples, including "the right to be and to remain themselves, living according to their own customs and moral order, free to develop their own culture."[12] In fact, it contends that states should "exempt [indigenous peoples] from compliance with those obligations that jeopardise their cultural integrity."[13] Importantly, the Declaration of Barbados places the right to culture within a larger political, historical, social, and economic context, and calls upon multi-cultural states to guarantee indigenous communities' rights to territory and to governance within those territories.[14]

When the AAA Committee for Human Rights formed, it deliberately situated itself inside rather than outside human rights discourse. The anthropologists involved continued to emphasize respect for culture consistent with parts of the Declaration of Barbados, even through favorable mention of the discipline's early understandings of cultural relativism that had "been developed by Boas, Benedict, Mead and others as an attempt to instill respect for variability and especially to defend indigenous peoples from ethnocide and genocide."[15] They also believed, however, that the relativism expressed in the 1947 statement had hampered the ability of anthropologists to participate in human rights debates.

In a 1993 article exploring reasons why anthropologists are rarely involved in human rights advocacy, Ellen Messer cites "the 'burden' of cultural relativism," explaining that the 1947 statement "rejected the notion of universal human rights."[16] The 1995 annual report of the AAA Commission for Human Rights echoes this sentiment: "Cultural relativism is a major factor which has severely retarded anthropological involvement in human rights since the Executive Board's 1947 statement."[17] Thus, early on the group made clear that it saw its work on human rights as a "complete turn around from the 1947 stance."[18]

In promoting the human right to culture, the AAA commission and committee strove to take advantage of a vehicle that appeared to provide a promising way to promote the rights of indigenous peoples. Because indigenous rights have become "legitimate demands within the international legal framework" over the past forty-five years, Messer explains, "the acceptance and advocacy of the human rights legal framework by anthropologists [is] an important means of protecting indigenous cultures and interests."[19]

That said, by focusing much of its human rights work on the right to culture, the AAA human rights bodies have posed an important challenge to both individual and universal conceptions of human rights. As the guidelines for the AAA Human Rights Committee explains, "many existing human rights NGOs focus on individual rights, and they treat violations of civil and political rights to the exclusion of economic, social, and cultural rights and indigenous and environmental rights."[20] The preamble to the 1999 declaration states that the committee's interventions require "expanding the definition of human rights to include areas not necessarily addressed by international law. These areas include collective as well as individual rights, cultural, social, and economic development, and a clean and safe environment."[21]

Continuing its sympathy for at least some relativist arguments, the committee expresses an understanding of human rights that is not only collective, but is also focused on respect for difference and is skeptical of universal claims. The 1999 declaration, for example, states:

> As a professional organization of anthropologists, the AAA has long been, and should continue to be concerned whenever human difference is made the basis for a denial of basic human rights, where "human" is understood in its full range of cultural, social, linguistic, psychological, and biological senses.
>
> Thus the AAA founds its approach on anthropological principles of respect for concrete human differences, both collective and individual, rather than the abstract legal uniformity of Western tradition.[22]

Terence Turner reads into similar language in an earlier statement by the AAA Commission on Human Rights something akin to a right to culture: "While difference is explicitly cited in this statement only as an invalid basis for denying rights, rather than a positive principle of right in itself, the implication is that the right to difference may constitute a positive, transcultural basis of human rights."[23]

Ultimately, I contend, the right to culture has been incapable of fully mediating the tension represented by this dual commitment to cultural difference and to the human rights regime. While the 1971 Declaration of

Barbados calls upon states to except indigenous peoples from legal obligations that threaten their cultural integrity, many of the international instruments used by indigenous rights advocates have taken a different approach, exempting from protection those expressions of cultural integrity that conflict with other human rights. While this latter position—the invocation of an invisible asterisk—responds to the tension at one level, it does not put it to rest. Indeed, the struggle between culture and human rights animates the development of the substance of the right to culture.

DEVELOPING AND EMBRACING THE
RIGHT TO CULTURE IN LAW

As early as the 1980s, a number of international institutional bodies began to interpret legal instruments to include the right to culture, and to see that right as applicable to indigenous people. In doing so, these bodies have both responded to and participated in the development of legal strategies based on the human right to culture. This section considers the doctrinal work of these bodies as it has developed over the past two decades, and the underlying international legal instruments with which they engage.

Specifically, I describe below the methods by which ILO 169, the ICCPR, the International Convention on the Elimination of All Forms of Racial Discrimination, the American Declaration of the Rights and Duties of Man, and the American Convention on Human Rights have been drafted and interpreted to protect indigenous culture under a human rights model. In doing so, I examine the extent to which the rejection of the right to self-determination has influenced the instruments, as well as the means by which they have attempted to respond to tensions between individual and collective rights, and between equal and special rights.

ILO 169: The Rejection of Assimilation and
Self-Determination for Cultural Rights

Between 1986 and 1989, the International Labor Organization worked on revising ILO 107. As discussed in chapters 1 and 2, most activists and scholars had already rejected that convention. They saw it as a perpetuation of the civilizing mission, not only because of its explicit attempt to integrate indigenous peoples, but also because of its support for basic models of industrialized economic development—into which it hoped to integrate them. In 1987, recounting the discussion at the first ILO meeting to consider revision of the convention, Russel Barsh described how ILO 107's integration focus had come "to be associated with 'destruction and absorption,' or even, in the words of UNESCO's observer . . . 'ethnocide [which] is a gross violation of human rights.' "[24]

In 1989, the ILO adopted the successor convention, ILO 169, noting in the preamble that its new international standards are meant to "remov[e] the assimilationist orientation of the earlier standards." The convention has been ratified by twenty countries, over two-thirds of which are in Latin America and the Caribbean.[25] While closed to new signatories, ILO 107 remains in effect for seventeen countries that have ratified it but not ILO 169, and ILO 107 has been interpreted in many ways to conform to ILO 169.[26] These two conventions comprise the only major binding international legal instruments that specifically focus on the rights of indigenous peoples.

ILO 169 foregrounds culture and recognizes collective rights, requiring that "the social, cultural, religious and spiritual values and practices of these peoples shall be recognized and protected, and due account shall be taken of the nature of the problems which face them both as groups and individuals."[27] It recognizes "rights of ownership and possession of the peoples concerned over the lands which they traditionally occupy,"[28] and it calls upon governments to "respect the special importance for the cultures and spiritual values of the peoples concerned of their relationship with the lands or territories . . . which they occupy or otherwise use, and in particular the collective aspects of this relationship."[29]

As discussed in chapter 3, most instruments have intentionally eschewed defining indigenous peoples, but perhaps ILO 169 comes closest to offering a definition. The convention concerns "tribal" as well as "indigenous" peoples, and largely identifies them based on culture. Thus, ILO 169 applies to "tribal peoples in independent countries whose social, cultural and economic conditions distinguish them from other sections of the national community and whose status is regulated wholly or partially by their own customs or traditions or special laws or regulations"[30] and to "peoples in independent countries who are regarded as indigenous on account of their descent from the populations which inhabited the country or [surrounding region] at the time of conquest or colonization or the establishment of present state boundaries and who . . . retain some or all of their own social, economic, cultural and political institutions."[31] In addition, "self identification" is a "fundamental criterion for determining the group to which the provisions of [the] Convention apply."[32]

Notwithstanding this specificity, the ILO's official guide to the convention insists that "the Convention does not strictly **define** who are indigenous and tribal peoples but rather describes the peoples it aims to protect."[33] The guide considers individuals as well as groups, and it notes that there is an objective as well as a subjective component to the convention's coverage. The collectivity must objectively meet the requirements in the convention, but it must also subjectively identify itself as indigenous or tribal. Individuals must both subjectively identify with the group and be considered (presumably objectively) as a part of it by the collectivity.[34]

Self-identification would seem to be a way to narrow the scope of the convention, as those who self-identify as tribal or indigenous would presumably be a subset of those who meet the general criteria. Yet the provision has been deployed by many groups for the purpose of insisting that they, not the state or other populations in the state, have the right to determine whether they are indigenous or tribal. At times, the "objective" criteria drop out of the picture. In a context in which being indigenous or tribal increasingly leads to rights, many groups would like to be considered indigenous or tribal. They often treat self-identification as the sole criterion for inclusion, and they are often supported by scholars and advocates in this view.[35]

While today indigenous rights advocates often deploy ILO 169 to argue for the right to culture and for collective rights—and many groups attempt to fit within its ambit—the convention was in fact criticized on two primary grounds by many indigenous advocates at the time of its passage. First, indigenous peoples were not permitted to participate directly in ILO conference discussions on the draft. Second, the document did not include the term "self-determination."

The first concern was largely about process. The ILO is comprised of representatives of governments, employers' organizations, and trade unions. Each sent delegations to the committee established to revise the convention. While some indigenous peoples participated as representatives of trade unions and, on rare occasions, indigenous people were permitted to make brief statements to the committee, the process did not provide a formal mechanism for direct indigenous participation.[36] Even those who were permitted to make comments directly to the committee made clear that they did not consider their presence a satisfactory substitute for a more systematic forum for participation. As Leonard Crate, the representative of the International Organisation of Indigenous Resource Development stated: "We did not come here to be passive observers while diplomats, labour leaders and executives decided what to do with us. We did not come here to give your deliberations our tacit approval by our presence."[37]

That indigenous peoples might be precluded from participating fully in the process of drafting ILO 169 is somewhat ironic, given that the convention includes provisions requiring government consultation with indigenous peoples prior to the enactment of development projects that might affect their traditional lands. While these provisions, found in Articles 6 and 7 of the convention, are often relied on by indigenous communities today, Article 7 was criticized from the beginning by some indigenous groups for not requiring indigenous consent (as opposed to consultation),[38] an issue I return to in some detail in chapter 7.

The second major point of contention manifested itself in debates over whether the convention would include the term "peoples" instead of either "people" or "populations," the latter of which was used in ILO 107.[39] Indigenous participants' insistence on the term "peoples" blocked the convention's adoption at one point, leading to two years of negotiation and an eventual compromise, after which the term was finally included. Were there any doubts whether "peoples" might suggest anything akin to the right to secession or sovereignty, the convention puts it to rest with Article 1(3), a provision similar to Article 46 of the UN Declaration: "The use of the term *peoples* in this Convention shall not be construed as having any implications as regards the rights which might attach under international law."[40] The inclusion of this provision was in line with what Lee Swepston, a longtime ILO official and supporter of ILO 169, predicted two years before the convention's passage: "It may be expected that the revised Convention will deal with mechanisms of protection of the rights of these peoples, rather than with such broad questions as self-determination; this kind of question must be left to the United Nations."[41]

The explicit rejection of self-determination as recognized in international law received a negative response from many indigenous advocates. As one commentator noted at the time:

> The indigenous peoples' representatives were furious that, of all the peoples of the world, they alone should be cut off from enjoying the same rights as other peoples as defined under international law. Cristobal Naikiai, a Shuar Indian from Ecuador and Vice-president of the Coordinator of Indigenous Organisations of the Amazon Basin, likened the process at the International Labour Conference to the infamous conference in the 16th century when the church in Spain had debated on whether Indian people had souls or not.[42]

Crate asked the committee: "What is the difference between our claim and the claim of oppressed colonial peoples who want to live in their homelands?"[43] Sharon Venne, a Cree from the Treaty Six territory in western Canada and a representative of the International Work Group for Indigenous Affairs, stated that "it is unfair and racially discriminatory to limit our rights as peoples under international law."[44]

Crate also asserted indigenous self-determination on the basis of treaties, complaining that state representatives denied that they had entered into treaties with indigenous peoples, and were taking advantage of the process to "rewrite history": "Treaties, they say, can only be entered into between States and intergovernmental organizations. Two or three hundred years after the treaties were signed with our people, which provided the basis in international law for the establishment of their States, they have decided that no treaties were signed at all."[45]

Of the three recorded statements given by indigenous groups at the 1989 conference leading up to the adoption of ILO 169, two were those mentioned by Crate and Venne, both from Canada. Asunción Ontiveros Yulquila, from the Indian Council of South America, made the third statement. He was also critical of the convention, though more hopeful about it. He complained about the process, and questioned the basis of states' rights to "deny [indigenous peoples] the use of natural resources of the surface and subsurface" as well as "food, education, and housing appropriate to our cultures at our workplaces."[46] He discussed the usurpation of territory and government, but he did not mention or allude to treaties or to Article 1(3). I do not think this difference in criticisms is incidental. North American indigenous groups continued to push a strong self-determination line, while the Latin American organization seemed more open to the possibilities of rights based on culture within existing states, as long as those rights included land and territory.

I consider the adoption of ILO 169 as both representative of and central to the move to protect indigenous rights under a human rights framework, particularly through the right to culture. Even though the ILO's procedure for adopting the convention precluded the collection of the rich diversity of perspectives from indigenous peoples that were making their way into the UN Working Group around the same time, it still offered a sense of which provisions were essential to indigenous advocates. While many of those advocates were initially unsatisfied with ILO 169, the memory of that dissatisfaction seems to have faded.

In Latin America, ILO 169 has been invoked by a large number of groups claiming indigenous or tribal identity, from the Zapatistas in Mexico to Afro-descendant communities in Colombia and the Mapuche in southern Argentina.[47] It is heard throughout the region in public discourse as well as in legal claims. The latter include challenges brought under domestic and international legal bodies, which frequently refer to the convention and the binding nature of its signatories' commitments.

Indigenous peoples' direct engagement with the ILO has affirmed, clarified, and strengthened the application of the convention, particularly on issues of political empowerment, land and territorial rights, and development. The engagement has happened partially through complaints— known as "representations"—addressed to the ILO's governing body by labor organizations acting in support of indigenous peoples.[48]

Decisions resulting from representations concerning ILO 169 have dealt with several issues of land and territory, including the extent to which the two can be differentiated, decision-making powers over them, and their centrality to indigenous peoples' continued social and cultural existence. While not presuming to know "whether individual or collective ownership is most appropriate for indigenous or tribal peoples in a given situation," the ILO's governing body asserts that it is equally outside a state's competence to make such a decision.[49]

The ILO has also continued to insist on indigenous peoples' rights over land that they use and occupy, even in the absence of collective title. A decision on a representation filed against the state of Guatemala, for example, notes that it is inconsistent with ILO 169 to refer to any lands traditionally occupied by indigenous communities as being "occupied illegally." The decision then affirms that possession of an official land title is not a necessary prerequisite for communities to hold rights to consultation,[50] noting that the convention requires consultations any time natural resources on lands that indigenous and tribal peoples "occupy or otherwise use" stand to be exploited.[51]

Outside of the ILO's official grievance process, a number of indigenous and tribal groups have made relatively far-reaching political and economic claims citing ILO 169. In Chiapas, for example, a group of human rights activists began a project called Project 169 (Proyecto 169), with the aim of mobilizing around the convention and bringing legal complaints—as part of the group's larger objective of training indigenous people to use national and international human rights law to seek redress within the context of the Mexican justice system and society.[52] So powerful are both the rhetorical and legal deployments of ILO 169 that some communities comprised of what might be considered formerly indigenous people have begun to reconstruct their identities around a framework of indigenous rights. Shannon Speed has described one such community, known as Nicolás Ruiz. At the close of the 1990s, after having joined with other Zapatista communities in demanding local autonomy, the community began describing itself as indigenous and reinterpreting some of its communal traditions as stemming from indigeneity.[53] According to Speed, Nicolás Ruiz relied in part on ILO 169's self-identification criteria to "claim the national and international rights which pertain to them based on [their indigenous] status."[54]

It is somewhat ironic that a convention put together by the International Labor Organization has played such a significant role in the Zapatista cause. In the 1990s, the Zapatista movement self-consciously attempted to alter the discourse of left movements in Mexico by making indigenous peoples central to a discussion that had previously focused on struggles about class, largely in the context of peasant labor. Yet ILO 169 provided a vehicle for asserting indigenous identity to attack the Mexican government's concession to and promotion of neoliberal policies, most notably through the North American Free Trade Agreement (NAFTA). Not by accident did the Zapatista uprising begin on January 1, 1994, the day that NAFTA went into effect.[55] As I argue in part II, however, the assertion of cultural identity might, in the end, fit quite comfortably with that same neoliberalism.

The Zapatistas articulate a stronger form of autonomy than most indigenous groups in Latin America. I use their example here simply to show how even a convention drafted to focus largely on cultural rights, explicitly rejecting the terms "self-determination" and "autonomy," has been taken advantage of by a movement centered around autonomy (if within a multicultural state). Other communities in Latin America—both indigenous and Afro-descendant—have used the convention similarly. In fact, the Constitutional Court of Colombia has stated that ILO 169 "concerns the autonomy of indigenous communities to recognize the aspiration of those peoples to assume control of their own institutions and ways of life, as well as their economic and social development, maintaining and fortifying their identities, language and religion."[56] This decision, written with regard to indigenous communities, is now being used by advocates for Afro-descendants who are bringing a claim under the Colombian constitution for collective property rights. I discuss their claim in detail in chapter 9.

The Right to Culture under Article 27 of the ICCPR

After all the work and preparation that went into drafting and adopting the UDHR, it did not immediately become the basis for a binding international treaty, as many had anticipated it would. Due in large part to cold war debates over the importance of civil and political rights versus economic and social rights, the UN's members eventually agreed that human rights should be divided into two separate instruments. The resulting treaties were the ICCPR and the International Covenant on Economic, Social and Cultural Rights (ICESCR). While the title of the latter suggests that it protects the right to culture, it was the language and enforcement mechanisms of the ICCPR that eventually caught the attention of indigenous rights advocates. That instrument came into force in 1976 and has been ratified by 165 states.

While the UDHR and the ICESCR grant "everyone" the right to culture, the ICCPR is more specific. Article 27 reads: "In those states in which ethnic, religious or linguistic minorities exist, persons belonging to such minorities shall not be denied the right, in community with the other members of their group, to enjoy their own culture, to profess and practice their own religion, or to use their own language." As discussed in chapter 1, when the provision was drafted, "ethnic, religious or linguistic minority" did not necessarily refer to indigenous peoples.[57] Moreover, according to Anaya, many indigenous rights advocates have avoided equating indigenous rights with minority rights "in their attempts to establish indigenous peoples within a separate regime with greater legal entitlements."[58] Over time, however, indigenous advocates began to use the provision with some success.

The Human Rights Committee has primarily interpreted Article 27 through its adjudication of complaints brought under its Optional Protocol, which permits nonstate parties to bring claims against states that have ratified the protocol. The first Article 27 complaints that the committee considered with regard to indigenous rights were brought by individual indigenous people who contended that, as a result of membership rules created or condoned by the state, they had been denied full membership rights in the indigenous group to which they belonged. Ironically, then, the avenue for eventual group protection to the right to culture would be found in challenges to restrictions or limitations on individual rights to culture. The first two cases in which the committee applied Article 27 to indigenous claims illustrate its early approach toward the individual right to culture: *Lovelace v. Canada*[59] and *Kitok v. Sweden*.[60]

In 1977, shortly after the ICCPR entered into force, Sandra Lovelace, born a Maliseet Indian, brought a complaint against Canada because, after marrying a non-Indian man, she had lost her tribal status under Canada's Indian Act. Much of her claim centered on gender discrimination and unequal treatment, because Indian men who married non-Indian women were entitled to keep their tribal status. She also argued that Canada had failed to protect her right to culture, guaranteed by Article 27 of the ICCPR.

The Human Rights Committee considered the case in 1981. It chose not to address the gender discrimination claim, basing its decision on a finding that the Indian Act, which Canada claimed was in line with indigenous custom, violated Lovelace's right "to access to her native culture and language 'in community with the other members' of her group."[61] The decision notes that states could limit this individual right to culture, but only with restrictions that could be shown to have a "reasonable and objective justification and be consistent with the other provisions of the Covenant."[62]

Seven years later, the committee decided a complaint brought by Ivan Kitok, who—though ethnically Sami—was not entitled to the full rights granted to reindeer-herding Sami communities because he had lost full membership in his village. He claimed that the Swedish government was responsible for his exclusion because it permitted the village to operate as a "closed shop," and had entered into an agreement with the Sami over membership rules designed to decrease reindeer herding. The committee admitted his case under Article 27 (although, as described below, he also brought it initially under Article 1's recognition of the right of self-determination), but it ultimately decided against him because it appeared that, notwithstanding the membership rules, he had been permitted to engage in some reindeer herding.

In *Kitok*, the Human Rights Committee appears to recognize that, had it found in Kitok's favor, it might have compromised the group's right to culture and even to make important decisions regarding membership. This recognition is partly manifested in an addition to the language in *Lovelace* as to when the state might properly restrict an individual's right to culture. The committee explains in *Kitok* that the state may do so not only when it has a "reasonable and objective justification," but also when it is "necessary for the continued viability and welfare of the minority as a whole."[63] Thus, the committee suggests that individual rights might not necessarily or always trump communal rights.

Over time, Article 27 came to be used by indigenous peoples to make land claims. Indeed, as Martin Scheinin, a member of the Human Rights Committee, noted in 2004, "somewhat paradoxically, the ICCPR which is a human rights treaty with neither a property clause nor a land rights clause—nor, to that matter, any explicit reference to 'indigenousness,' has become one of the main tools in positive human rights treaty law for indigenous peoples' land rights claims."[64] In 1994, the committee issued General Comment 23, which elaborates its understanding of Article 27. The committee makes clear not only that the provision applies to indigenous peoples, but "that culture manifests itself in many forms, including a particular way of life associated with the use of land resources, especially in the case of indigenous peoples. That right may include such traditional activities as fishing or hunting and the right to live in reserves protected by law."[65] In line with ILO 169, the committee further observes that "the enjoyment of those rights may require . . . measures to ensure the effective participation of members of minority communities in decisions which affect them."[66] Thus, in principle at least, General Comment 23 both represents and reinforces an understanding that the right to culture includes the right to live on (if not to own) traditional lands and to use them for sustainable purposes. The committee's Concluding Observations on states' reports have reinforced that position.[67]

Subsequent decisions of the committee under the Optional Protocol have further elaborated the meanings of Article 27 and General Comment 23, stating, for example, that "economic activities may come within the ambit of Article 27, if they are an essential element of the culture of an ethnic community."[68] Importantly, however, the Committee does not see that culture as static, noting that Article 27 "does not only protect traditional means of livelihood" but can cover practices of those traditional means that deploy technological advances.[69]

Despite much elaboration of the right to culture, even in the context of land rights and consultation, Scheinin identifies only one case—*Lubicon Lake Band v. Canada*[70]—in which the committee found that a state violated Article 27 by using land in a way that interfered with the economy and life of the indigenous community. He pins this result on what he earlier pointed out as a paradox: ultimately, "the weakness of ICCPR Article 27 as a basis for indigenous land rights lies in the absence of any reference to the right of property in Article 27 or elsewhere in the ICCPR . . . Article 27 would give support to indigenous title to land only in cases where it is proven that no other arrangement will meet this test."[71]

Of course, it could be argued that the right to self-determination in the ICCPR would essentially grant rights to property and territory, perhaps even in a way that would conflict with the committee's interpretation of the individual right to culture. Recall that Article 1 of the covenant states: "All peoples have the right of self-determination. By virtue of that right they freely determine their political status and freely pursue their economic, social and cultural development." The Human Rights Committee has been reluctant to apply Article 1 to indigenous claims, particularly under the Optional Protocol. This result could well be the dark side of both the protocol's innovation in allowing individual complaints against states and of its assimilation of indigenous peoples into the minorities protected under Article 27. As Patrick Thornberry notes, in the drafting of the ICCPR, "peoples were clearly to be distinguished from . . . 'minorities.' "[72]

The Human Rights Committee has largely maintained the distinction between Article 1's right to self-determination and Article 27's right to culture, if indirectly, in a variety of ways. First, General Comment 23, while making clear that Article 27 applies to members of indigenous communities and might even support "a way of life which is closely associated with territory and use of resources," also states that the right to culture is not meant to threaten territorial integrity: "The enjoyment of the rights to which Article 27 relates does not prejudice the sovereignty and territorial integrity of a State party."[73]

Second, a number of indigenous rights claims have been brought to the committee under the Optional Protocol using Article 1. Beginning with *Kitok*, the committee has denied admissibility of these claims under that article.[74] In the *Lubicon Lake Band* case, the committee *sua sponte* applied Article 27 after denying the applicability of Article 1. The committee determined that the question whether the band constituted a people was not before it because the claim had been brought by the band's chief— who, as an individual, "could not claim under the Optional Protocol to be a victim of a violation of the right of self-determination."[75] General Comment 23, after explaining that some people have confused Article 1 and Article 27, has since enshrined this limitation:

> The Covenant draws a distinction between the right to self-determination and the rights protected under article 27. The former is expressed to be a right belonging to peoples and is dealt with in a separate part (Part I) of the Covenant. Self-determination is not a right cognizable under the Optional Protocol. Article 27, on the other hand, relates to rights conferred on individuals as such . . . [and] is cognizable under the Optional Protocol.[76]

Subsequent decisions by the committee have affirmed the position that, as a collective right, Article 1 may not be the basis of claims under the Optional Protocol.[77]

The committee has not, however, completely read self-determination out of the covenant, even in the context of the Optional Protocol. Though it has not expounded upon it significantly, the committee has acknowledged that Article 1 might at times aid in the interpretation of other articles, "in particular article 27."[78] In its Concluding Observations regarding states' reports, the committee has occasionally reminded states of their obligation to report on their implementation of Article 1, but has done little more than that.[79]

I hope to have demonstrated here how the interpretation of the ICCPR is both representative of, and has participated, in the move away from self-determination and toward the right to culture for the protection of indigenous peoples. At the same time, I do not mean to suggest that the right to culture in Article 27 has not been invoked and interpreted in ways that have significant implications for groups and the meaning of group rights, and even for what some would term self-determination. Scheinin argues, for example, that the committee's test for determining whether "modern" development may justify interference with indigenous culture contains two components he sees as constitutive of self-determination: *"meaningful consultation* of the affected indigenous or minority community and securing the *sustainability* of its traditional or otherwise distinctive way of life."[80] He continues by noting how that test has been interpreted in the context of Article 27.

For my thesis, it is significant that even the committee's decisions that relate to indigenous groups (as opposed to individuals) emerge from the doctrinal interpretation of the right to culture. The substance of that right differs significantly from claims that were often made under the rubric of self-determination, in part because the right was first recognized as an individual right that in effect favored indigenous individuals over claims or potential claims by their communities. In some instances, the committee relied on an explicit suppression of the right to self-determination and on a distinction between it and the individual right to culture. I will consider more fully in part II some dark sides to the eventual turn to culture in which these decisions play an important role.

Special Rights and the International Convention on Racial Discrimination

In 1965, the United Nations General Assembly unanimously approved the International Convention on the Elimination of All Forms of Racial Discrimination (ICERD). The convention entered into force in 1969; 173 states have ratified it. Like the ICCPR, the ICERD created a committee to oversee its implementation. The Committee on the Elimination of Racial Discrimination (CERD) reviews periodic reports required of all ratifying states. The convention also contains a provision, Article 14, that functions much like the Optional Protocol of the ICCPR, although as of the end of 2009 there had been no decisions regarding indigenous rights.[81]

Since 1994, the CERD has also included "early warning and urgent procedures" as part of its regular agenda, which applies to all state parties.[82] It has at times applied these measures to indigenous rights disputes. In 2006, in a case concerning the rights of the Western Shoshone in the United States, the CERD called upon the United States to freeze any planned action with regard to the privatization or use of the land that the Shoshone claimed as their ancestral lands, until "final decision or settlement is reached on the status, use and occupation of Western Shoshone ancestral lands in accordance with due process of law and the State party's obligations under the Convention."[83]

The ICERD focuses on guaranteeing racial equality. For reasons that resonate with those offered by indigenous rights advocates who were skeptical about using human rights to advance their cause, advocates did not initially consider the ICERD as a promising tool for the promotion of indigenous rights. In 1983, Douglas Sanders expressed the concern that the convention would not only fail to support indigenous claims for "special rights," like those to autonomy, it might even threaten them.[84] Anaya has echoed that perspective more recently, noting how the views of many changed after the CERD's response to the Western Shoshone case: "Two decades ago, when the UN first began seriously considering Indigenous issues, there was a tendency among advocates, and I would count myself among them, to stay away from this Convention, and to regard it as not really speaking to native issues."[85] In the U.S. context, he explains, advocates were concerned that Native Americans might be viewed as "holding the same rights as other citizens, but no more."[86]

Indigenous advocates were not alone in their underestimation of the applicability of the ICERD to indigenous peoples; states also often failed to see the connection. Michael Banton discusses how most Latin American states supported the convention, but saw it as aimed narrowly at apartheid.[87] Most of those same states therefore reported to the committee in the 1970s and 1980s that no racial discrimination existed in their countries, without even considering their treatment of indigenous peoples.[88]

As early as the 1970s, the CERD began to ask a number of Latin American states about their policies toward their indigenous populations, including whether they were following a policy of assimilation or were instead protecting culture.[89] By 1996, Banton concluded—based on interactions of Latin American states with the CERD and other international legal bodies—that international human rights norms "have had an increasing and positive influence upon the policies of Latin America states affecting indigenous peoples."[90] He suggested that indigenous groups and individuals in Latin America take advantage of the "international cultural capital built up by the human rights movement" to bring petitions under the mechanism provided by Article 14 of the ICERD,[91] which is not limited to individual complaints.[92] Even without such petitions, the CERD has increasingly attended to indigenous rights through other mechanisms.

In 1997, the CERD issued its own General Recommendation 23, making clear its view that the ICERD has always applied to indigenous peoples "and that all appropriate means must be taken to combat and eliminate such discrimination."[93] In this General Recommendation as well as in its responses to states' reports, the CERD has primarily focused on culture and land when assessing states' treatments of their indigenous populations. It has essentially adopted a right to culture by maintaining that nondiscrimination requires the protection of culture. Again discussing the result in the Western Shoshone case, Anaya lauds the CERD for its understanding of equality, which "values difference and sees equality not just in terms of the individual within a presumably homogenous society, but also sees the individual as part of a group, part of a cultural group, and values that cultural group. This vision of equality considers equality as encompassing cultural integrity as well as individual integrity."[94] For Anaya, this vision of equality comports with that long pursued by indigenous peoples.[95]

The CERD's General Recommendation 23 fleshes out the role of indigenous culture and the need for states to protect it. It calls on states to recognize what I refer to in part II as indigenous culture as heritage, land, and development. With regard to heritage, states should "recognize and respect indigenous distinct culture, history, language and way of life as an enrichment of the State's cultural identity and to promote its preservation," and "ensure that indigenous communities can exercise their rights to practise and revitalize their cultural traditions and customs and to preserve and to practise their languages."[96] As for land, the recommendation instructs states "to recognize and protect the rights of indigenous peoples to own, develop, control and use their communal lands, territories and resources."[97] Concerning indigenous development, it calls on states to "provide indigenous peoples with conditions allowing for a sustainable economic and social development compatible with their cultural characteristics."[98] More generally, it requires that states obtain the informed consent of indigenous peoples before engaging in activities affecting their "rights and interests."[99] This requirement of consent, rather than simply of consultation as in ILO 169, is an issue I discuss in some detail in chapter 7.

In its Concluding Observations on reports by states, the CERD often considers the extent to which General Recommendation 23 is followed, sometimes by connecting the question of land to culture, and sometimes by invoking the ICERD's Article 5, which guarantees the right to property without discrimination.[100] It also encourages state parties to participate in other international bodies or ratify other treaties, such as ILO 169. In its 2000 response to Finland's report, for example, the CERD considered some of the same questions regarding Sami rights to reindeer herding and to be consulted on development projects that the Human Rights Committee had considered under Article 27 of the ICCPR. The CERD's Concluding Observations invoke ILO 169:

> The Committee regrets that the question of land ownership of the Sami has not yet been resolved and that Finland has not acceded to Convention (No. 169) . . . Furthermore, it expresses its concern about activities authorized by State bodies in Sami reindeer-breeding areas which may threaten Sami culture and their traditional way of life.[101]

The CERD has not shied away from the importance it places on the ratification of ILO 169, even in its reports on countries where the issue of indigenous status is highly controversial, such as India,[102] or on countries that claim that the convention is inconsistent with domestic legislation.[103]

More recently, the CERD has been promoting the UN Declaration on the Rights of Indigenous Peoples as a "guide" for the protection of indigenous rights, even with regard to the four states that voted against its passage. In 2007, for example, it chastised the Canadian government for its "change in position" vis-à-vis the UN Declaration, especially given "the positive contributions made and the support given" in the recent past. The CERD recommended that the Canadian government "support the immediate adoption" of the declaration.[104] In May 2008, the CERD used the UN Declaration in its Concluding Observations on the United States to evaluate "reports relating to activities, such as nuclear testing, toxic and dangerous waste storage, mining or logging, carried out or planned in areas of spiritual and cultural significance to Native Americans."[105] Although the Concluding Observations cite ICERD provisions (such as those on equal rights to property and culture), they also call upon the United States "to recognize the right of Native Americans to participate in decisions affecting them, and consult and cooperate in good faith with the indigenous peoples concerned before adopting and implementing any activity in areas of spiritual and cultural significance to Native Americans."[106] They recommend "that the declaration be used as a guide to interpret the State party's obligations under the Convention relating to indigenous peoples," even while "noting the position of the State party" regarding its adoption.[107]

The ICERD does not contain the terms "self-determination" or "autonomy," and these terms are also absent from General Recommendation 23. Yet the year before it issued that recommendation specific to indigenous peoples, the CERD adopted General Recommendation 21 on the right to self-determination, which makes clear a distinction between internal and external self-determination. While the committee distances itself from the latter, and uses international law to do so, it supports the former—"the rights of all peoples to pursue freely their economic, social and cultural development without outside interference."[108] General Comment 21 never uses the term "indigenous," however, and situates itself as responding to those "ethnic or religious groups or minorities" that "refer to the right of self-determination as a basis for an alleged right to secession."[109]

In much the way that Scheinin sees hope for a commitment to self-determination in the Human Rights Committee's decisions, Anaya uses General Recommendation 21 to contend that the CERD has incorporated a notion of self-determination.[110] To the extent that the recommendation represents the CERD's commitment to self-determination, however, I would contend that it embodies a relatively weak notion of it (in line with that generally supported by Anaya, as discussed in chapter 3). That is, I read the CERD's support of internal self-determination to be roughly equivalent to the rights to culture and participation it already outlines in General Comment 23—which, to be fair, encompass a thicker conception of culture than what we see in most other forums.

I do not mean to suggest that "self-determination" is a term that is never heard or considered in relationship to the CERD. Even if it rarely makes it into Concluding Observations or Annual Reports, the term is occasionally invoked during meetings with states. Given that the CERD seems to be the international organization most intent at the moment on interpreting the UN Declaration on the Rights of Indigenous Peoples, future reports might well provide a lens for viewing whether and how the debates about self-determination that animated the declaration's passage will continue to resonate.

Property and Culture under the Inter-American System of Human Rights

In 2000, the Inter-American Commission on Human Rights, an autonomous organ of the Organization of American States (OAS), published a report expressing the need for an American Declaration on the Rights of Indigenous Peoples.[111] The report's introduction was written by Carlos Ayala, then the commission's immediate past president, who had also been its special rapporteur on the rights of indigenous peoples. The introduction considers the two primary human rights instruments in the region—the 1948 American Declaration of the Rights and Duties of Man, to which all member states of the OAS have in principle agreed, and the 1969 American Convention on Human Rights, which applies to those states that have signed it.[112] The report concludes that those instruments, along with the jurisprudence resulting from the bodies designed to implement them—the Inter-American Commission, with regard to both instruments, and the Inter-American Court of Human Rights, in the case of the American Convention[113]—are inadequate to protect fully the rights of indigenous peoples.

In his introduction to the report, Ayala echoes many concerns expressed about the ICERD in the 1980s and the UDHR in the 1940s, concerning whether universal or "equal" rights would or even could assist indigenous peoples in their rights struggles. In particular, he asserts that the "approach to the rights of indigenous peoples via the concepts of 'minorities' or 'prohibition on discrimination,' while the only mechanism in some cases, is incomplete and reductionist, and therefore inadequate." He contrasts the American instruments on human rights with the ICCPR, noting that the latter, even if it "is not yet specifically tailored to" indigenous peoples, includes a right to culture.[114] The report supports the drafting of an American Declaration on the Rights of Indigenous Peoples because, unlike the current instruments in the inter-American system, it would embody "the legal principle that individual and collective rights are not opposed but, rather, are part of the principle of full and effective enjoyment of human rights."[115]

As of the end of 2009, the states of the Americas still had not agreed on the text of a declaration on the rights of indigenous peoples. The Inter-American Commission and Court have nevertheless attempted to mediate the difficulties identified in the 2000 report, both by using the prohibition on discrimination and the right to property to allow for special measures to protect indigenous culture, and by seeing collective rights—at least with regard to land—as a part of that culture. They have also extended the protection to some Afro-descendant groups that they see as fitting within ILO 169's "tribal" categorization.

Although much of this jurisprudence is relatively recent, I believe the stage was set for it even before the commission's report. The report reviews the commission's and court's jurisprudence on indigenous rights from 1970 to 1999, which was already beginning to include cultural and collective rights.[116] The report primarily considers culture in two areas: reparations and land.[117] The latter category is most important, I believe, to see how the court and commission have struggled to find a way to protect culture and to grant special rights in the process through a right to property. I therefore discuss its development in some detail below. Because the reparations cases demonstrate a general willingness of the court and commission to attend to issues of culture in their interpretation of other rights, I discuss them briefly first.

REPARATIONS CASES

Since the early 1990s, the Inter-American Court has deployed cultural definitions of family and custom to determine both who is entitled to receive reparations and which harms are eligible for such compensation. In *Aloeboetoe v. Suriname*, the earliest such case, the court determined that the polygamous custom of the "tribal" community of which the victims were a member, the Maroon community of Saramaka, meant that reparations assigned to spouses would be equally divided among each victim's wives.[118] This case is often cited as an example of the court's jurisprudence respecting culture and local custom.[119] I would like to call particular attention, however, to two aspects of the court's analysis. First, the court made clear that Suriname had not attempted to apply its family law to the Saramaka people, so that the court felt compelled to consider customary law authoritative.[120] Second, the court nevertheless placed important limits on its deference to customary law, an issue I return to in the final section of this chapter.

The consideration of culture for the purposes of determining who constitutes a family member entitled to reparations continued with the court's decision nearly a decade later in *Bámaca Valásquez v. Guatemala*. In that case, involving the death of an indigenous guerrilla leader who had been married to the American lawyer Jennifer Harbury, the court determined that reparations could be divided among Harbury and the victim's father and sisters in Guatemala because, in the Mam culture, the victim— as elder son—would be presumed to contribute to their sustenance.[121] As in *Aloeboetoe*, only the distribution—not the amount—of reparations was affected.

The court has also used culture to consider the nature of the harm for which redress is sought. In *Bámaca Velásquez v. Guatemala*, for example, the court found that the deceased's next of kin suffered "profound anguish" with regard to his forced disappearance and lack of knowledge of his whereabouts.[122] It accepted the commission's description of the harm, in which it had found that the lack of a proper burial is particularly damaging in the Mayan culture "due to the fundamental importance of its culture and the active relationship that unites the living and the dead."[123] In a later case involving the Plan de Sanchez massacre in Guatemala, the court ruled that the special cultural impact on victims be taken into account in determining nonpecuniary damages, including that the victims were unable to bury their next of kin appropriately and that there was a "cultural vacuum" caused by the death of women and elders who are the "oral transmitters of the Maya-Achí culture."[124]

The court has primarily made these decisions through factual analyses, not by recognizing a right to culture per se. Furthermore, in some instances the interpretation of culture has not been as expansive as the commission (which had represented the victims before the court) had advocated. I think the cases nevertheless represent successful advocacy to bring culture into cases that at first glance seemed to be solely about basic violations of civil and political rights. In this sense, they bear some resemblance to the origin of what I categorize as land and property cases below.

LAND AND PROPERTY

The majority of indigenous cases brought to the commission and court have concerned access to and occupation of land. In early cases, indigenous communities and their advocates did not necessarily seek a right to control or collectively own the land they occupied, but they often sought redress for civil and political human rights violations resulting from state efforts—or state complicity in private efforts—to remove them from those lands. Over time, the claims began to be conceived of and considered as cultural rights claims, with the commission and court at first importing the right to culture from the ICCPR. Eventually, the inter-American system settled on its own rubric for protecting culture: the right to property.

The American Convention on Human Rights was the second international or regional human rights treaty to recognize the right to property.[125] The right is set forth in Article 21: "Everyone has the right to the use and enjoyment of his property." Although it is immediately followed by a limitation—that "the law may subordinate such use and enjoyment to the interest of society"—it also requires just compensation for a taking of property. This article and the American Declaration's slightly different articulation of the right have been interpreted by a number of cases involving indigenous land claims.[126]

Although the right to property was also included in the UDHR, which acknowledges the "right to own property alone as well as in association with others,"[127] it was too controversial to be included in either the ICCPR or the ICESCR.[128] As Theo van Banning has explained, the right to property is a contentious issue for human rights advocates because "human rights are correctly perceived as an instrument for the defence of the vulnerable. Property rights have to the contrary often been perceived as an instrument to protect the rich and the powerful."[129] He believes the end of the cold war in 1989 made the right to property an increasingly likely instrument for the protection of vulnerable groups.

Of the international institutions that include the right to property in their mandate, the Inter-American Commission and Court have created the most extensive jurisprudence on collective property. In particular, they have used the right to property as the basis for the recognition of collective land rights for indigenous and certain Afro-descendant groups in the Americas. Their stated goal in doing so is generally to preserve culture.

EARLY INDIGENOUS CASES AND THE ROLE OF LAND CONFLICT. The first two indigenous cases, brought to the commission in the early 1970s, involved the Guahibo in Colombia and the Tribu Aché in Paraguay. Although both claims had their roots in historical and contemporary struggles over land, as Shelton Davis points out, the commission's decisions eluded the land conflicts.[130] They also, for the most part, failed to discuss culture. Thus, these cases represent the first stage of cases that present and view property claims through the lens of civil and political rights.

The Guahibo complaint, sent to the commission by the secretary general of the Latin American Peasants Federation in Caracas, listed various acts of persecution, torture, and illegal imprisonment of the Guahibo, which it claimed that the Colombian government both engaged in and permitted in the Planas region of the country.[131] The complaint attempted to draw attention to land issues, however, by including an open letter by a group of Colombian anthropologists and sociologists who condemned the vast inequality of land distribution that "had already created a social imbalance in the power relationships which favored all kinds of outrages, including plundering, eviction from land by harassment and even the attempt by the strong to achieve the total extermination of the weak."[132]

The Colombian government's defense was that it was engaged in "a state of irregular war," or a "racial Cold War." At one point, according to Davis, it seemed that the commission would accept the defense. Instead, though, it sought further information from the Colombian government, noting possible violations of the right to life, liberty, and personal security; the right to equality before the law; and the right to protection from arbitrary arrest under the American Declaration.[133] Davis contends that neither the government in its defense nor the commission in its response "seriously addressed the land issues underlying the Planas incidents" that had been included with the original complaint.[134]

In the end, the commission received information from Colombia, expressed its "satisfaction for the loyal and frank form [in which] the government had provided the requested facts," and decided to "archive" the complaint without prejudice to either side.[135] Despite this result and the commission's initial framing of the issues, the commission's 2000 report refers to its resolution in this case (without much specificity) under both the right to property and collective rights.[136] Only hindsight can account for such an interpretation.

The commission's next case on indigenous issues regarded the Tribu Aché-Guayaki Indians of Eastern Paraguay. The commission acted quickly this time, issuing a communication shortly after the complaint was filed that denounced the persecution of the tribe, "along with the murder of a number of Indians, the sale of children, the withholding of medical attention and medicines during epidemics, mistreatment and torture, inhuman working conditions, and acts aimed at destroying their culture."[137] The concern about destruction of culture soon dropped out of the picture. Even though the Paraguayan government never formally responded to the commission's request for information, the commission provisionally adopted a decision that, reminiscent of the indigenismo of the period, essentially accepted that the government's actions were "aimed at promoting assimilation and providing protection" rather than at "eliminating the Aché Indians."[138] It then expressed concern about the abuses of the Aché by private individuals, the status of Aché children, and certain working conditions. In its final resolution in 1977, the commission found numerous violations of civil and political—as well as economic and social—rights, from the right to life to the right to leisure time, but again did not address the claimed destruction of culture.[139]

Davis notes that the "critical land tenure situation faced by the Aché," which he convincingly demonstrates formed the basis of much of the oppression, was also essentially absent from the commission's consideration. He attributes the commission's actions in this and the Guahibo case to "its lack of historical and anthropological understanding of the complex relations that exist between indigenous land rights and other aspects of indigenous culture, such as native ecological adaptations, family and social organization, health, psychological well-being and religious beliefs."[140]

IMPORTING THE RIGHT TO CULTURE. Davis also applies his conclusion about the commission's failure to grasp the connection between land and culture to the third South American indigenous case it decided, involving a complaint against Brazil for its treatment of the Yanomami. I would contend, however, that the Yanonami case and an earlier case involving the Miskito in Nicaragua represent a significant shift in the commission's approach to indigenous cases. Specifically, the commission viewed both cases through the lens of the right to culture, explicitly incorporating Article 27 of the ICCPR.

In the early 1980s, conflicts arose between Miskito Indians and the Sandinista government, in large part over the government's new agrarian reform program. The Miskito believed the program failed to take into account Indian ownership of many lands to be redistributed under the program. The Miskito argued before the commission that they should be guaranteed the right to the natural resources of the territory and, as I discussed in chapter 3, the right to self-determination.

Even though the commission rejected the Miskito claim to self-determination, it recognized that individual rights would not do justice to the tribe's claims. The commission found the basis for the rights of individual group members under the American Convention on Human Rights, but used Article 27 of the ICCPR, to which Nicaragua was also a party, as the basis for Miskito entitlement to "special protection" as an ethnic group. The protection of minorities, the commission noted, "although also based on the principles of equal treatment of all peoples, requires a positive action: a concrete service is offered to a minority group."[141] The commission concluded that "special legal protection is recognized for the use of their language, the observance of their religion, and in general, all those aspects related to the preservation of their cultural identity . . . which includes, among other things, the issue of the ancestral and communal lands."[142]

While the commission's focus in the Miskito case was on the right to culture, it also recognized, for the first time and with little fanfare, the application of the right to property to indigenous claims. It considered two arguments made by the Miskito using the right to property—the right to possess ancestral lands and the right to avoid the "destruction of the homes, crops, livestock and other belongings of the Miskitos in the course of the compulsory relocation to new settlements."[143] It found that there had been a violation in the second sense,[144] although it did not analyze the right to property or even include it in its concluding list of the rights that had been violated.

When the commission considered the Yanomami case against Brazil (in *Coulter et al. v. Brazil*) two years later in 1985, the issue of self-determination was not even before it. The commission focused again on the special protection for the culture of ethnic groups found in Article 27 of the ICCPR.[145] It also noted that the OAS had "established, as an action of priority . . . the preservation and strengthening of the cultural heritage of these ethnic groups and the struggle against the discrimination that invalidates their members' potential as human beings through the destruction of their cultural identity and individuality as indigenous peoples."[146] Finally, it considered a connection between land and culture, in its recognition that the building of a highway had "proceed[ed] to displace the Indians from their ancestral lands, with all the negative consequences for their culture, traditions, and costumes."[147]

In its conclusion, the commission found that there had been a violation of the declaration's right to life, liberty, and personal security; the right to residence and movement; and the right to the preservation of health and to well-being.[148] Although the complainants had brought the claim under the right to property as well, unlike with the Miskito case, the commission did not address the issue.

Despite this omission, Anaya and the 2000 commission report read the Yanomami case as an application of the right to collective property to indigenous peoples.[149] Hindsight might again be responsible for the report's—and Anaya's, this time—reading of the case. Interpreted in this way, the decisions foreshadow future case law (which both Anaya and the commission helped develop). In particular, the new millennium brought a series of decisions from both the commission and the court that formally connected the right to property with culture, and found the basis of the nexus in the American Convention and the American Declaration.

DEVELOPING THE RIGHT TO PROPERTY AS A VEHICLE FOR CULTURE. In 2001, in a case against Nicaragua, the Inter-American Court decided its first case on indigenous land rights. The commission brought the case to the court on behalf of the Awas Tingni, who had complained of the state's grant of timber concessions on what it claimed were the group's traditional lands. The commission appears not to have invoked Article 27 of the ICCPR, despite its use of the provision in its own decisions, and the court did not consider it. Rather, the court self-consciously and explicitly used the right to property, not only to find a violation, but also as a vehicle to protect the right to culture (essentially eliminating the need for the separate right). In part, it did so by focusing on the right to collective property, which it claimed accorded with the culture of the Awas Tingni.

The court's decision shows that it sees itself as pushing the envelope by applying the right to property to communal land rights. "Through an evolutionary interpretation of international instruments for the protection of human rights," it notes, "article 21 of the Convention protects the right to property in a sense which includes, among others, the rights of members of the indigenous communities within the framework of communal property."[150] For the court, indigenous "communitarian tradition" requires a particular conception of property and land ownership which, in turn, is necessary for the reproduction of culture:

> Indigenous groups, by the fact of their very existence, have the right to live freely in their own territory; the close ties of indigenous people with the land must be recognized and understood as the fundamental basis of their cultures, their spiritual life, their integrity, and their economic survival. For indigenous communities, relations to the land are not merely a matter of possession and production but a material and spiritual element which they must fully enjoy, even to preserve their cultural legacy and transmit it to future generations.[151]

The court has since followed this reasoning to protect the right to property, with the explicit aim of facilitating indigenous culture.

The 2007 decision of *Saramaka People v. Suriname* provides a review of the court's development of the right to property, and also extends it to the Maroon community of Saramaka that had first come to its attention in *Aloeboetoe* in the early 1970s. In reviewing its own jurisprudence in *Awas Tingni* and subsequent cases, the court suggests the extent to which the protection of culture is accepted as the justification for its application of the right to property, both collective and individual, to indigenous and tribal peoples. It notes that it "has consistently held that 'the close ties the members of indigenous communities have with their traditional lands and the natural resources associated with their culture thereof, as well as the incorporeal elements deriving there from, must be secured under Article 21.' "[152]

Even though the court seems to have connected land to culture quite successfully under Article 21, it continues to bring in support for that position from other international and domestic obligations that states have undertaken. In cases preceding *Saramaka*, for example, the court had referred to ILO 169.[153] Presumably because Suriname had not signed that convention, however, the court's decision in *Saramaka* returns to Article 27 of the ICCPR and uses the right to culture embodied there to secure the right.

In *Saramaka*, the court also, for the first time, discusses the ICESCR in the context of indigenous rights. In something of a stretch (based on one sentence of the Economic, Social and Cultural Committee in a country report), the court invokes common Article 1 of the two covenants (regarding self-determination) to conclude that Article 21 calls "for the right of members of indigenous and tribal communities to freely determine and enjoy their own social, cultural and economic development, which includes the right to enjoy their particular spiritual relationship with the territory they have traditionally used and occupied."[154] Though the mention of self-determination is provocative here, the protection of culture would seem to remain the goal.

Returning to Special versus Equal Treatment

As discussed earlier, the commission articulated early on an understanding of human rights that not only permits, but sometimes even requires, special measures for particular groups. The court, however, did not tackle the issue of special versus equal rights squarely until *Saramaka*, when—among other arguments—Suriname asserted that "legislation providing for 'special treatment' for indigenous and tribal groups raises questions of State sovereignty and discrimination with regard to the rest of the population."[155] Responding that it has "already stated that special measures are necessary in order to ensure [the survival of indigenous and tribal groups] in accordance with their traditions and customs,"[156] the court claims to follow its previous decisions that have held "that members of indigenous and tribal communities require special measures that guarantee the full exercise of their rights, particularly with regards to their enjoyment of property rights, in order to safeguard their physical and cultural survival."[157] While the court cites specific paragraphs in previous cases for support, in fact the paragraphs to which it refers say nothing about special measures or special treatment. They merely discuss how indigenous and tribal peoples have a special relationship with the land.

In effect, the court has for the first time explicitly adopted an understanding of human rights that reconciles special treatment with equality. Its next sentence acknowledges that "other sources of international law have similarly declared that such special measures are necessary."[158] There its citations to the commission, the ICERD, and the European Court of Human Rights are more on point than those to its own case law.

The Inter-American Court has thus now secured indigenous rights to culture through both the right to property and through general non-discrimination provisions. It continues to do so, in part, through reliance on international and regional law outside the convention. The court will almost certainly be called upon to elaborate upon its reference to economic self-determination, a matter I will return to in chapter 7.

LIMITING THE RIGHT TO CULTURE:
THE INVISIBLE ASTERISK

The focus on the human right to culture, regardless where one finds its legislative or jurisprudential roots, has functioned to move much of the indigenous rights discourse to a new terrain and, for the most part, to defer the questions of self-determination and autonomy. Yet, as both advocates and skeptics of the right have begun to confront new sets of questions around the relationship between universal human rights discourse and the right to culture, the shadows of earlier debates are apparent. Even some of the strongest advocates of the right to culture have proposed, or at least accepted, restraints on that right. Those restraints generally find their source in the language of human rights.

I use Elizabeth Povinelli's reference to an "invisible asterisk" to discuss this not-so-invisible circumscription. As Povinelli explains in the context of the state's purported deference to indigenous customary law in Australia: "an invisible asterisk, a proviso, hovers above every enunciation of indigenous customary law: '(provided [they] . . . are not so repugnant).' "[159] This language of repugnance is a part of the colonial legacy, according to Leon Sheleff, who writes that "the word 'repugnant' was the term used almost exclusively to indicate the standard for determining non-compliance, with the values of western culture being used as the yardstick, and so the provision is referred to in the literature as the repugnancy clause."[160] Sheleff proceeds to demonstrate the ethnocentrism on which this clause was based and through which legal pluralism was permitted, noting that the clause was not presented "merely, or even mainly, as being some sort of compromise between conflicting value-systems and their normative rulings, but as being an expression of minimum standards being applied as a qualification to the toleration being accorded (by recognition) to the basically unacceptable norms of 'backward' communities."[161]

The "minimum standards" that today act to qualify tolerance for indigenous customs are often articulated through the discourse of human rights to counteract or temper the right to culture. As I suggested early in this chapter, the right to culture does not mediate the tension between universal human rights and cultural particularities, but rather defers it to another stage. The asterisk—visible or not—generally limits the right to culture at the moment that a cultural practice violates "universal," often individual, human rights. This asterisk has been enshrined in most of the institutional sites I have discussed in this chapter.

The 1999 declaration by the American Anthropological Association's Committee for Human Rights offers one example of the context in which the asterisk might appear. The declaration at first provides a fairly broad and fluid reading of a right to culture: "People and groups have a generic right to realize their capacity for culture, and to produce, reproduce and change the conditions and forms of their physical, personal and social existence."[162] The use of the term "people and groups" rather than "peoples and groups" or "individuals and groups" is curious. It would seem to recognize both individual and collective rights, denying the tension between the two. The end of the sentence, however, shies away from the broad call for the right to difference. The right to culture is protected "so long as such activities do not diminish the same capacities of others."[163] The limitation taps into individual, liberal rights discourse (the limit on tolerance is intolerance), but does not make it clear whose rights or which rights would trump in the event of conflict. At least in principle, group rights could prevail in the conflict.

The possibility of group rights prevailing over individual rights, or the right to culture trumping otherwise traditionally accepted human rights norms, is less likely in the international legal institutions I have considered in this chapter, despite a general agreement that international law protects the right to culture and, in some instances, customary law. ILO 169, for example, after several articles setting forth indigenous peoples' right to culture, attaches a proviso in an article dealing with indigenous custom. It grants indigenous peoples "the right to retain their own customs and institutions, where these are not incompatible with fundamental rights defined by the national legal system and with internationally recognised human rights."[164]

Albeit in a different setting, this provision of ILO 169 resonates with Susan Muller Okin's controversial argument regarding female members of a "more patriarchal minority culture in the context of a less patriarchal majority culture": "They *might* be much better off if the culture into which they were born were either to become extinct (so that its members would become integrated into the less sexist surrounding culture) or, preferably, to be encouraged to alter itself so as to reinforce the equality of women."[165] In this latter case, for Okin, as in ILO 169, the entire culture would not be seen as unworthy of protection—only those aspects of it that violate "universally accepted" human rights (or women's rights at least, for Okin), which can seemingly be disaggregated from the right to culture. For those who criticize ILO 169 for its refusal to grant indigenous self-determination, this proviso constitutes an example of such a refusal; it highlights the distinction between self-determination and the recognition of culture based on human rights.[166]

The UN Human Rights Committee has tackled a similar conflict with regard to Article 27's right to culture, making clear that the protection of culture does not prevail over other rights guaranteed by the ICCPR. In the committee's General Comment on the article, it states: "The Committee observes that none of the rights protected under article 27 of the Covenant may be legitimately exercised in a manner or to an extent inconsistent with the other provisions of the Covenant."[167] It makes clear that provisions of the covenant prohibiting discrimination (2.1 and 26) should permit positive measures to protect the right to culture, but only when "aimed at correcting conditions which prevent or impair the enjoyment of the rights guaranteed under article 27" and are "based on reasonable and objective criteria."[168] Otherwise, these provisions should not yield to the right to culture. Rather, "such positive measures must respect the provisions of articles 2.1 and 26 of the Covenant both as regards the treatment between different minorities and the treatment between the persons belonging to them and the remaining part of the population."[169]

The Inter-American Court's treatment of polygamy in *Aloeboetoe* provides an example of the asterisk in action. After determining that customary law, not Surinamese family law, effectively operates among the Saramaka people, the court decides to "take Saramaka custom into account . . . to the degree that it does not contradict the American Convention." Then, relying on the nondiscrimination provision of the convention, it concludes: "Hence, in referring to 'ascendants,' the court shall make no distinction as to sex, even if that might be contrary to Saramaka custom."[170]

The proposed American Declaration on the Rights of Indigenous Peoples is presumably intent on requiring that indigenous peoples not be permitted to discriminate based on sex. Article VII of the 2009 version includes language agreed upon in 2006: "Indigenous women have the right to the recognition, protection, and enjoyment of all human rights and fundamental freedoms provided for in international law, free of all forms of discrimination."[171] Article XXXII reinforces this position: "All the rights and freedoms recognized in the present Declaration are guaranteed equally to indigenous women and men."[172]

Finally, even the UN Declaration on the Rights of Indigenous Peoples has not escaped this issue. Article 46 not only limits self-determination but contains other limitations as well. Paragraph 2 reads: "In the exercise of the rights enunciated in the present Declaration, human rights and fundamental freedoms of all shall be respected. The exercise of the rights set forth in this Declaration shall be subject only to such limitations as are determined by law and in accordance with international human rights obligations." Paragraph 3 notes: "The provisions set forth in this Declaration shall be interpreted in accordance with the principles of justice, democracy, respect for human rights, equality, non-discrimination, good governance and good faith."[173] What these terms mean, of course, is unclear. And, as with the other instruments, provisions like this one are tautological: if the collective right to culture is a part of human rights, democracy, equality, etc., then there is little here to resolve competing claims. It is unclear whether this provision constitutes an acknowledgment or a denial of conflict at the international level.

Many of the invocations of the invisible asterisk arise in the context of women and gender equality. But, as Aída Hernández Castillo argues in her discussion of indigenous jurisdiction in Mexico, such expressed concerns often appear hypocritical: "Academics and politicians who had never be-

fore written or spoken a word about the gender inequalities which indigenous women suffer were suddenly worried by the way in which recognizing indigenous normative systems . . . could tread on their human
rights."[174] What might initially seem to be a contemporary instance of
what Gayatri Spivak has famously analyzed as "white men . . . saving
brown women from brown men,"[175] Hernández Castillo argues, in fact
provides a way to limit the autonomy of indigenous communities by
either "declaring that indigenous authorities' decisions must be validated
through courts and judges," or withholding recognition of their jurisdiction in toto.[176]

If Hernández Castillo's research is any indication, indigenous people
themselves (especially women) do not generally deny that their traditional norms and institutions should be contested and revised, but believe
that the contestation should take place through an internal process. More
specifically, "indigenous women do not reject their culture in the name of
equality; they claim the right to a culture of their own while at the same
time struggling to build more equal relations within the family, the community, and organizations."[177] As we shall see in part II, while powerful nonindigenous entities might be able to insist on being able to "pick
and choose" which parts of indigenous heritage shall be valorized and
preserved, indigenous communities themselves are rarely afforded such
liberty. The invisible asterisk functions to make that decision in their
stead. As such, it reappears in some form in every understanding of culture I describe in part II, from culture as heritage to culture as land or as
development.

Human Rights and the Uses of Culture in
Indigenous Rights Advocacy

[We are determined] to restore the use for the highest of occasions of the totemic symbols and values that represent the personality of the indigenous nation of Kollasuyo: the flag, the staff, the condor, the *pututu*, the poncho, the *lluch'u*, etc.—CONCLUSIONS OF THE FIRST HISTORICAL POLITICAL CONGRESS OF THE INDIAN MOVEMENT TUPAJ KATARI, 1978[1]

Indigenous and nonindigenous peoples alike have long discussed the distinct ways in which indigenous peoples see and relate to the world. In the early 1970s, as we saw in chapter 2, indigenous movements often articulated the need to protect this vision of the cosmos and its material inspirations and manifestations. The quotation above from a press release of the Bolivian indigenous movement offers one such example. To the extent that they have argued for the protection of indigenous heritage—including both material and intangible items that reflect their understanding of indigenous culture—indigenous rights advocates have been relatively successful in the international institutional arena, as well as at the nation-state level. Chapter 4 offered examples of a variety of such successes on the international plane.

At least in principle, heritage is something that states and their nonindigenous citizens often express a desire to protect. As Ronald Niezen explains:

The moral persuasiveness of indigenous peoples' claims to recognition derives not just from local grievances, but ultimately from a near-universal perception of cultural loss and nostalgia as well. It derives from a public that looks to timeless ways of life as a source of personal or civilizational improvement. It draws upon those who may have nothing to do with indigenous communities or international agencies, but who nevertheless feel strong stirrings of sympathy for those who represent a lost time of unhurried simplicity.[2]

Thus, perhaps the most commonly invoked and accepted meaning of culture in the context of indigenous rights is that culture is comprised of the practices, knowledge, and ways of seeing and relating to the world (cosmovision) of those societies that predated the settlers, primarily in the so-called New World.[3] In this usage, culture is often something to be preserved, much like a museum piece or a scarce natural resource. This notion of culture coincides with that of some anthropologists from the early twentieth century on, who sought to preserve indigenous societies as laboratories for studies of the premodern.[4] Cultural survival is key, but culture is something that indigenous peoples have (or had); it is not necessarily what or who they are.

Although what Niezen refers to as a "near-universal perception of cultural loss and nostalgia"[5] has led to a variety of international, regional, and domestic protections, it has its dark sides as well. At times, the cultural heritage becomes revered over, and disembodied from, the very peoples associated with it. The cultural heritage itself and what is seen as the values it holds become the objects of protection. They become commodified. Niezen continues:

> The indigenous peoples movement derives much of its energy and cultural creativity from those admirers who do not belong by birth to an indigenous community and who do not pursue a subsistence-based way of life. These individuals, nevertheless, often feel a deep sympathy for the values embodied by these communities and lifestyles. The products of indigenous self-discovery cannot, therefore, be entirely separated from a wide base of inter-cultural consumers. They are also interwoven with transnational relationships of organizational and cultural collaboration based upon broadly shared anti-modernist sentiments.[6]

States and regional and international organizations also often trade on these sentiments. What is considered the cultural heritage of a state's or region's original inhabitants might be treated as the property and identity of the state. Indeed, this perspective was central to the ideology of indigenismo discussed in chapter 1.

That heritage can be alienated from the groups from which it is seen to emanate provides the basis for another possibly unintended consequence of this understanding of culture. It permits states and even international institutions to pick and choose the parts of the heritage they believe are worth protecting, and to suppress those of which they do not approve. These influential actors thereby attach the invisible asterisk discussed in previous chapters to their application of cultural protection.

Of the various understandings of culture I explore in this book, heritage makes the least demand on states. It asks states to be tolerant, but it also enables them both to appropriate and to accommodate heritage without attending to the underlying economic, social, and political inequalities of which indigenous peoples generally bear the brunt.

Questions about "who owns native culture" have been considered extensively in the literature on intellectual property.[7] Those discussions, however, tend to focus mostly on the private appropriation of native culture for profit. I do not revisit those debates here. Rather, I consider the ways that "cultural heritage" is defined, protected, used, and sometimes appropriated by international organizations and states, as well as by indigenous rights and other (such as environmental) activists.

I discuss below two ways in which culture as heritage manifests itself. The first is as intangible cultural heritage, as defined and pursued by the United Nations Educational, Scientific and Cultural Organization (UNESCO). Even when aimed at protecting the underlying cultural and social practices of a given custodial community, the approach generally functions to separate the heritage from the source of its production. The second is through an understanding of an indigenous cosmovision, or way of seeing and relating to the world. This cosmovision has a material basis in land. The first is the least threatening notion of culture I will consider in this part of the book, and it does not necessarily require the second. The second sees land as intimately connected to, and the material basis for, the first. As such, it often calls for the protection of land, sometimes for the use of indigenous groups (to continue to pursue their culture), but just as often for preservation's sake, as something that should be maintained for the benefit of humanity. While chapter 6 will consider the protection of land as real property, the present chapter explores the implications for the centrality of land to an indigenous cosmovision.

CULTURE AS INTANGIBLE HERITAGE

Perhaps the best and most contemporary statement of this understanding of culture is found in UNESCO's 2003 Convention for the Safeguarding of the Intangible Cultural Heritage (Convention on Intangible Cultural Heritage) which, as of December 2009, had 118 state parties. Although extremely abstract in most parts, the convention protects as manifestations of intangible cultural heritage "oral traditions and expressions, including language as a vehicle of the intangible cultural heritage," "performing arts," "social practices, rituals and festive events," "knowledge and practices concerning nature and the universe," and "traditional craftsmanship."[8]

In the preamble, the convention "recognizes that communities, in particular indigenous communities, groups and, in some cases, individuals, play an important role in the production, safeguarding, maintenance and re-creation of the intangible cultural heritage, thus helping to enrich cultural diversity and human creativity." Moreover, one of the stated purposes of the convention is to "ensure respect for the intangible cultural heritage of the communities, groups and individuals concerned."[9] Yet the primary duty of each state under the convention is to "draw up, in a manner geared to its own situation, one or more inventories of the intangible cultural heritage present in its territory" and to keep the inventories updated.[10] Although states are encouraged to put together the inventories with "the participation of communities, groups and relevant nongovernmental organizations,"[11] communities are not given any right to contest the inventory or submit their own. And, of course, the convention is silent as to ownership. The focus is on preserving the things of production, not guaranteeing them for the people(s) who produce them.

The convention does not pay specific attention to indigenous peoples. When they are mentioned, they are only one source of intangible heritage. Yet the convention's approach to them in many ways echoes that of a 1997 UNESCO publication titled "Protection of the Heritage of Indigenous People" (known as the Daes Report). Authored by Erica-Irene Daes, the publication describes indigenous heritage as "includ[ing] all of those things which contemporary international law regards as the creative production of human thought and craftsmanship, such as songs, music, dances, literature, artworks, scientific research and knowledge."[12]

Neither the Daes Report nor the Convention on Intangible Cultural Heritage suggests that the heritage comes from nowhere. And, to a certain extent, both leave the decision whether to safeguard (by sharing) the heritage up to those who possess it. No one—including indigenous communities—has a duty to cooperate with states in creating the inventories under the convention. And the Daes Report, at least in its introduction, arguably recognizes indigenous ownership of the heritage, considering heritage as "everything that belongs to the distinct identity of a people and which is theirs to share, if they wish."[13]

As I discuss below, however, other aspects of both the convention and the report belie the suggestion of indigenous peoples' control over and ownership of their heritage. The goal of each is to bring the heritage to the awareness of the public, if not to place it in the public domain. While communities might not have a duty to cooperate with states, neither are states required to obtain the permission of individuals or groups to include in inventories what the states identify as their intangible heritage. Moreover, if indigenous peoples choose not to share their heritage by at least identifying it as a part of their culture, they risk having it appropriated by others.

CULTURE AS COSMOVISION BASED IN LAND

Indigenous peoples are commonly thought to have a special relationship to nature—to land, sea, and sky—which suggests a different worldview from that commonly found in the industrialized world. As the Convention on Intangible Cultural Heritage's protection of "knowledge and practices concerning nature and the universe" demonstrates, that cosmovision is thought to be worth safeguarding. Sometimes the cosmovision is considered to be like a rare artifact that is valuable in its own right. At other times, it appears to have the power to save the earth from environmental destruction.

Most descriptions of an indigenous cosmovision see its material basis as located in land. Because, as we saw in chapter 4, indigenous claims to land constitute the majority of indigenous legal and political demands, the inclusion of land as a cultural right to be protected potentially adds substantive bite to the intangible heritage conception.

The Daes Report articulates the centrality of land to the cosmovision by explaining that "indigenous peoples regard all products of the human mind and heart as interrelated, and as flowing from the same source: the relationship between the people and their land, their kinship with other living creatures that share the land and with the spiritual world."[14] This kinship is assumed in most indigenous rights advocacy, and it is often asserted by indigenous peoples themselves as a basis for recognition of their cultural difference.[15]

In 1993, Maori claimants in New Zealand put forth a strong statement of this view in proceedings before the UN Human Rights Committee over the impact of outside commercial ventures on their traditional fishing rights: "The taonga [group of treasured possessions] endures through fluctuations in the occupation of tribal areas and the possession of resources over periods of time, blending into one, the whole of the land, waters, sky, animals, plants and the cosmos itself, a holistic body encompassing living and non-living elements."[16] The American Indian theologian George Tinker puts it more succinctly, but with no less force: "Indigenous peoples experience their very personhood in terms of their relationship to the land."[17]

The relationship is often stated in ecological terms, suggesting that indigenous peoples have a special key to unlocking environmental knowledge. Deborah McGregor explains:

> [Indigenous Knowledge] is not just about knowledge about relationships with Creation or the natural world; it is the relationship itself. It is about being in the relationships with Creation; it is about realizing one's vision and purpose and assuming responsibilities accordingly. Indigenous Knowledge, then, is fundamentally related to environmental or ecological knowledge.[18]

David Choquehuanca Céspedes, speaking on behalf of the Bolivian government, used a similar idea in a statement he made to the UN Permanent Forum on Indigenous Issues in 2006:

> Brothers and sisters, in order to save the world and the planet from this threat against Life, it is up to us as the original indigenous populations

and first nations, representatives of ancestral peoples and cultures, to offer to the world the values of our culture—The Culture of Life—which is based on giving and receiving, in complementarity, in the common good, the system of mutual support, unfolding the capacities of man and nature without destroying it, and raising the level of consensus, always putting us in agreement, so that no one oppresses anyone else.[19]

To the extent that indigenous peoples (and their advocates) argue that they have an authentic understanding of the environment and community, their positions resonate with some of the indigenous positions from the 1970s that I discussed in chapter 2.

While the implications for such a cosmovision might be disputed, that indigenous peoples have a special cosmovision connected to nature is a relatively uncontroversial political claim. When in 1984, for example, the third session of the Working Group was unable to make much headway on the chosen topic for the meeting—land rights—it agreed nevertheless to follow language from the 1978 World Conference to Combat Racism, which had recognized "the special relationship of indigenous peoples to their land."[20] A 2001 UN Report notes the centrality of the assumption in its introduction: "The relationship with the land and all living things is at the core of indigenous societies."[21] It adds: "Indigenous peoples have a distinctive and profound spiritual and material relationship with their lands and with the air, waters, coastal sea, ice, flora, fauna and other resources."[22]

At times, mention of this special relationship foregrounds a discussion of territory and ownership, which I discuss in chapter 6 as culture as grounded in land. At other times, it is used to argue for indigenous participation in matters of the earth. The 1992 Rio Declaration on Environment and Development, for example, states: "Indigenous people and their communities and other local communities have a vital role in environmental management and development because of their knowledge and traditional practices. States should recognize and duly support their identity, culture and interests and enable their effective participation in the achievement of sustainable development."[23] I consider this issue more fully in the next two chapters. For the purpose of this chapter, I use the term "culture as heritage" to refer to the stream of indigenous rights advocacy that focuses on maintaining and even propagating indigenous ideas and worldviews.

At one level, the understanding of culture as heritage in the context of indigenous advocacy is essentialist, at times even biologically so, as heritage is seen as something that indigenous peoples—and only indigenous peoples—possess. At another, it idealizes (or at least seeks to preserve) a pre-industrial and preglobal view of the world that even the ancestors of settler societies are thought to have possessed. Whether the aim is to protect the former or the latter has significant material consequences for the lives of contemporary indigenous peoples. If the former, the ownership of heritage remains with indigenous peoples. If the latter, they are alienated from it. The question of ownership is also related to one of autonomy and decision making. Who has the right to determine which parts of the heritage are worthy of protection?

Although indigenous groups have had some success in pursuing protection of cultural heritage and in attracting many nonindigenous people to their cause, they have not acquired the type of self-determination or autonomy that indigenous movements have sought since at least the 1970s. Rather, as the following sections illuminate, more often than not, some aspects of both indigenismo and colonialism have reproduced themselves within this frame.

The Invisible Asterisk

Chapter 4 discussed Elizabeth Povinelli's term "invisible asterisk" in considering the ways that different human rights instruments and the jurisprudence interpreting them contain a proviso on the general grant of cultural rights. As with the instruments discussed there, the Convention on Intangible Cultural Heritage also contains a caveat: not all intangible culture is worth preserving. Rather, the convention applies only to those practices that are "compatible with existing international human rights instruments, as well as with the requirements of mutual respect among communities, groups and individuals, and of sustainable development."[24] As in earlier contexts, this provision recognizes that the right to culture might not mediate the potential conflict between human rights and respect for diverse cultures after all. It also provides yet another avenue for states and regional and international organizations to oppose or fail to protect those parts of indigenous culture that appear uncivilized.

The convention does not offer examples of potential conflicts.[25] In fact, policies based on intangible heritage or cosmovision are unlikely to need to invoke the invisible asterisk, because they generally do not require the state to make significant political power-sharing arrangements. Indeed, to the extent that intangible heritage contains a relatively thin concept of culture (dress, festivals, art, and the like), it falls well short of constituting a threat to the neoliberal, multicultural state. Still, the asterisk's existence has a disciplinary effect. As Charles Hale elaborates through the case of Guatemala, in some contexts there appear to be "built-in limits" to indigenous cultural and political demands that constitute certain Indians (and manifestations of indigeneity) as "permitted" and others as "prohibited." Attempts to transgress the boundaries of "neoliberal multiculturalism" end in indigenous activists either being "nudg[ed] . . . back inside the line," or "isolated and dismissed."[26]

Of course, certain elements of indigenous peoples' relationship to nature have long been condemned, seen as primitive and in need of taming or conquering. Indeed, the natural, far from forming the basis of culture, was once considered antithetical to it. As Astrid Ulloa reminds us, discussing two different images of the native:

> The first is associated with medieval empirical notions about environmental determinism that fed the descriptions of the Colonies in which the tropics did not allow for the flourishing of culture and, as a result, its inhabitants had an almost animal-like degree of closeness to nature. The second idea tended towards the moral improvement through the disciplines and activities that proclaim the necessity of moral and social reconstruction of the natives of America.[27]

The asterisk functions to keep this animalized primitive at bay.

Alienable Heritage

As already mentioned, the Daes Report suggests at least at one point that the heritage to be protected belongs to indigenous communities, in the sense that they can share it if they wish. That document also sees indigenous control over access to territory as "the most critical and effective means for the protection of indigenous peoples' heritage."[28]

In general, however, cultural heritage is separated from the very indigenous peoples from whom it is thought to emanate. Often indigenous peoples are not expected or even permitted to have private ownership over their heritage, especially because they are thought not to have a concept of private property. Instead, the heritage is usually considered to be in the public domain.

Both the Daes Report and the Convention on Intangible Cultural Heritage, for example, refer favorably to the 1966 UNESCO Declaration on the Principles of International Cultural Co-operation. That declaration presents a view of the purposes of protecting heritage that is still widely held today, which is that cultures should be protected for the good of humanity. Article 1 states:

> 1. Each culture has a dignity and value which must be respected and reserved. 2. Every people has the right and duty to develop its culture. 3. In their rich variety and diversity, and in the reciprocal influences they exert on one another, *all cultures form part of the common heritage belonging to all mankind.*[29]

In this declaration, then, people not only have a right but a duty to develop their culture, the ownership of which is public. The Daes Report comes close to offering a biological mandate for protecting heritage when it states that "cultural diversity is essential to the adaptability and creativity of the human species as a whole."[30] The protection of the heritage of any given community might be important for that community's perpetuation, but the survival of the human race would seem to depend upon the maintenance of cultures of many different communities.

Robert Albro has discussed UNESCO's treatment of heritage as the management of diversity as a "potentially nonrenewable resource." Discussing the ways that both the Convention on Intangible Cultural Heritage and the Convention on the Protection of the Diversity of Cultural Contents and Artistic Expressions require states to list and count cultural content to be safeguarded, he notes: "In practice diversity becomes a kind of *inventory* of cultural 'content' that is potentially extractable from any context, to be copied, appropriated, traded or recirculated. Diversity turns into a question of *access* to the cultural public domain."[31]

The aim of some environmentalists to borrow what they see as an indigenous cosmovision for everyday use provides one example of how cultural heritage might be alienated from indigenous peoples: real indigenous peoples might have a natural kinship with the land, but it would seem to be transmittable. The 1987 report of the World Commission on Environment and Development (known as the Brundtland Commission), *Our Common Future*, contends that indigenous understandings about development and environment could and should be used to help the world.[32] As we will see in chapter 7, this report represented a significant shift in thinking about ecology, development, and the role of local communities. Similar ideas prevailed several years later during the Rio Conference on the Environment and Development, as discussed above.

Julian Burger both invokes the utility of indigenous knowledge and makes nonindigenous interest explicit in his argument for opposing certain development projects on traditional native lands: "If damaged for indigenous peoples, the land is eventually made barren for all."[33] Burger ultimately calls for a stronger conception of culture than simply the heritage concept because—much as we saw in a number of cases in chapter 4 and will explore more fully in chapter 6—he sees the land as essential to the continuation of indigenous peoples' culture. Nevertheless, the "eventually" part of his prognosis suggests that there will be a period "after" indigenous occupation of land, or that the land in some sense already belongs to everyone.

It is understandable that advocates for indigenous peoples as well as for other causes, such as the environment or sustainable development, would invoke the special knowledge of indigenous peoples in these ways. It might well make sense to present nonindigenous people with an incentive to protect indigenous culture. If everyone's future is at stake, nonindigenous people might pay closer attention. As Laura Graham and Beth Conklin observe: "The Kayapo leader Payakan entered millions of American homes on the cover of Parade magazine with the plea, 'Help me to save lives—ours and yours.' The idea of commonality between first- and fourth-world peoples appeals to a large, transnational audience, in part because it resonates with multiple Western cultural trends."[34]

Moreover, indigenous peoples sometimes benefit from and even exploit some of these representations. Conklin, for example, has discussed some of the national and international successes of indigenous advocacy on behalf of Brazilian and Amazonian tribal members that have resulted from what she terms the "greening of indigenous advocacy," or alliances between environmental activists and indigenous rights advocates.[35] Ironically, she points out, the same indigenous advocates who had begun to wear Western-style clothing to participate in local politics would wear traditional dress in international meetings, at media events, and during political activism so as to "resonate with the ideology and aesthetic sensibilities of their environmentalist allies."[36] Those images are infused with representations of naturalness, as "part of a Western aesthetic vocabulary out of which Amazonian activists constructed public images that turned notions of primitivism, authenticity and environmentalism to the advantage of indigenous advocacy."[37]

Even in their political activism, however, some indigenous leaders have rejected the use of essentialism to pursue their claims. According to Alcida Ramos: "Whereas 'playing Indian' has been a very effective way to claim their rights and air their grievances, indigenous leaders are increasingly favoring other tactics of empowerment, either rejecting altogether the appeal to essentialization, or invoking cultural primordialities not as bastions of incommensurable otherness, but as an affirmation of equality within a regime of legitimate differences."[38] With their unique (non-essential) understanding of culture, she claims, indigenous peoples are teaching nonindigenous people and anthropologists "how to critically absorb and reshape ideas."[39]

Ramos might be a bit optimistic about the extent to which the idea of culture is being critically reshaped, or the extent to which such reshaping has penetrated modern consumption of indigeneity. Indeed, the understanding of culture as heritage fits nicely with state efforts to display, some might even say to commodify, native cultures. Such displays perform the multicultural sensitivity—even if not the nature—of the state, sometimes serving to suppress deeper political divides.

The 2000 Sydney Olympics, for example, although fraught with internal debates in Australia about who would represent the country, seemingly allowed for the performance of harmony in its opening ceremonies. Beyond multiculturalism and difference, it provided all Australians with a certain national pride at the beauty of the customs and traditions of those indigenous to Australia. That beauty was rendered as a possession shared by the entire country. Unlike their settler ancestors, present-day Anglo-Australians are not only able to enjoy and attempt to preserve indigenous culture, they can claim it. In the process, of course, they can also legitimize their own presence.

A less contested, but equally dramatic, performance was produced two years later in Salt Lake City, as the apparently homogeneous (white and Mormon) state of Utah defied stereotypes by showing off its seemingly populous indigenous communities, smoothly blending the historical trajectories of American Indians and the United States. Jackie Hogan contends that—like Sydney's program, with its celebration of Australian aborigines—Salt Lake City's program was "on its surface . . . a broad endorsement of American cultural pluralism: the languages, costumes, music, and dance of the indigenous performers were presented as pleasurable and apolitical multicultural spectacle."[40] Nevertheless, Hogan points out that the program actually "staged a highly expurgated narrative of colonization." In the ceremony's final scenes, for example, "settlers of all backgrounds joined together in a rousing dance," so that even "the completion of the railroad that spanned the country from east to west" became a historical episode where "any competing interests [were] cast aside and all [performers or settlers were] united in a celebration of technological progress."[41]

I agree with Ramos that it would be a mistake to see the indigenous displays in these ceremonies as inauthentic or hopelessly essentialist, or to think that indigenous peoples were somehow duped into performing. Ramos explains:

> The act of performing culture is not necessarily an act of essentialism. It would not be appropriate, for instance, to call essentialist the enactment of a rite of passage for the internal purposes of a given society. But whenever cultural traits are displayed out of their specific cultural contexts, one has at least potentially an act of instrumentalization.[42]

Indigenous peoples, then, are caught in a bind: either they have their history and existence ignored, or they use the international stage for recognition.

However valuable this recognition might be—even to show the diversity of indigenous peoples themselves—the costumes and dances are what are remembered. What is lost in the display is that the numbers of indigenous people in both Australia and Utah are infinitesimally smaller than their presence in the ceremonies might suggest, that they are small as a result of conquest, and that—in great contrast to the beauty of their costumes—their lives are seriously impoverished. Moreover, even as Australia and the United States take pride in their indigenous heritage, they are notorious for their refusal to take serious responsibility for the ongoing effects of their conquest.

Of course, this type of indigenous display is not reserved exclusively for Olympic ceremonies or similar international stages. A number of people have criticized state appropriation or deployment of indigenous cultures in a variety of government-sponsored performances, such as in the use of female Indian dress in beauty pageants. Seeing this use as an example of modern-day indigenismo, Peter Wade argues that "if indian identity is constituted within the nation-state, the opposite is also true."[43] He explains that, on one hand, the ideology of indigenismo continues in the state's use of Indians "to confer uniqueness to Latin American national identities in a global world" and, on the other hand, the state continues to define itself against "disorder and savagery."[44]

Carol Hendrickson's work demonstrates how Guatemalan elites have manipulated the imagery of Maya descendants' culture in just this way. Traditional indigenous dress, or *traje*, is used strategically at the local and national levels as "a powerful means for expressing social unity and ignoring or . . . repairing tears in the social fabric."[45] But at the same time that it enters the national state imagery as a way "to celebrate *nuestra Guatemalidad*—'our Guatemala-ity' or 'Guatemala-ness,'"[46] traje continues to signify low status and limited opportunities when worn by an Indian in daily life. Further, because of its use in government-produced tourism literature, "*traje* is or is not laudable, beautiful, and unique . . . is or is not dirty, crude, and lower class according to how it suits the money making situation," leaving Indian culture to be "either glorified to turn a profit or debased to turn indigenous people into less-than-humans, good only for labor."[47] Responding to similar ambivalences, the Maori scholar Linda Smith writes: "It appalls us that the West can desire, extract, and claim ownership of our ways of knowing, our imagery, the things we create and produce, and then simultaneously reject the people who created and developed those ideas and seek to deny them further opportunities to be creators of their own culture and nations."[48]

This alienation of heritage thus works alongside the invisible asterisk to valorize, and even claim ownership of, certain aspects of the culture that the state finds appealing—as public display. In public performances, it is the state that chooses how to present the nation and its indigenous groups. As Charles Briggs asserts in the context of Venezuela in the 1990s:

> Institutions of the nation-state exert control over the representation of difference by sponsoring *espectáculos* (pageants), in which "representatives" of the different *etnias* (ethnic groups) engage in theatrical presentations of "their culture"; these events reflect the agendas and budgets of state and national ministries of culture and other bureaucratic entities.[49]

Thus, for some critics, state control problematically combines with a belief that culture can exist apart from the people. As one such critic has argued, "Indigenous Knowledge cannot be separated from the people who hold and practice it, nor can it be separated from land / environment / Creation."[50]

Povinelli, however, suggests that the relationship between the state that represents the Indians and the Indians themselves is more symbiotic than the cosmovision position suggests. "Real" indigenous people simply do not and cannot exist apart from national expectations of them. In *The Cunning of Recognition*, she discusses the role that aboriginal peoples play in the identity of the Australian nation:

> The nation looks not at but through contemporary Aboriginal faces, past where every Aboriginal and non-Aboriginal Australian meet, wanting the spirit of something promised there: "Tell us something we do not, cannot, know *from here*—what it was (you and we were) like before all this. What our best side looks like." In the moment before any particular answer, ears and eyes are transfixed by the potential of indigenous knowledge, by what might be unveiled, and by a more general possibility of experiencing the new, the ruptural, the truly transformative. This moment is filled with horror, anticipation, excitement. Of course no Aboriginal person can fulfill the desire, be truly positively alterior, nor if they could would they *make sense* to the institutional apparatuses necessary to their livelihood. This "first speaker, the one who disturbs the eternal silence of the universe" would in fact be experienced as stereotypically psychotic.[51]

This dissonance, she continues, affects contemporary aboriginal Australians: "For the entire span of their lives they heard their grandfather, grandmother, and mother publicly valued primarily for their traditional knowledge and role. Now they must be that impossible thing of national desire."[52]

Although critical theorists have long noted that the state and ethnic identity are mutually constituted, this disembodied notion of culture as heritage persists and appears in a variety of political positions. The perspective has some elements of what the anthropologist Jean Jackson calls "culture as possession." While discussing the three goals of indigenous advocates in Colombia—the first being to defend the land, the second to defend the people, and the third to defend the culture—she notes the separation of culture from land and people, asking:

> But what exactly is the meaning of [the] third goal, "to defend the culture"? As Handler (1988) has shown, culture so conceived is a thing to be possessed, a *thing* to defend. One "has" culture, an entity that can be lost, enriched, or stolen—in other words, a commodity, subject to all the processes to which any commodity is subject, a familiar notion in our late capitalist society. This notion of culture as a possession that can be alienated . . .[53]

Somewhat paradoxically, I would argue that culture is most like a commodity when it is seen to be owned by indigenous peoples. As the Daes Report states in its introduction, culture is theirs to share with whom they wish. Once the heritage becomes seen as belonging to all of humanity, however, it is taken out of the market and placed into the public domain. Commodified or not, it is nevertheless still a thing, largely alienated from the very people whose protection it is said to ensure.

Dependency Displacement

Although the alienation of heritage might be an unintended consequence of the recognition of indigenous culture as heritage, it is not wholly unexpected. As Conklin argues and Ramos acknowledges at some level, indigenous advocates have played a role in the valorization of indigenous culture and cosmovision, so as to make it attractive to nonindigenous people and entities. As I began to discuss in the introduction, they have engaged in "strategic essentialism."[54]

In their own critical assessment of the use of strategic essentialism in indigenous advocacy, Bartholomew Dean and Jerome Levi maintain that "in the absence of electoral clout, economic prowess, or military might, the 'symbolic capital' accompanying authentically performed cultural identities represents one of the most influential political resources available to indigenous peoples."[55] Although they then raise a number of cautionary flags with regard to strategic essentialism, this defense of it is a common one: we must turn to essentialism in the absence of political, economic, or military power. But what would be the strategy if there were not such an absence? Is a strategically essentialist idea of culture meant to be a means to such power, or a concession to (and displacement of a focus on) the lack of it?

I would like to revisit for a moment the idea that culture as heritage fits the neoliberal model well, both nationally and internationally. It is neither threatening to the promotion of economic and political decentralization nor dependent upon indigenous economic power. Indeed, it offers states and international institutions a way both to protect and share in the wealth of indigenous culture. As Dean and Levi acknowledge, drawing on Laura Graham's work, in the international arena, the worth of indigenous peoples "has all too often been predicated on 'symbols and images, and not real economic or political advantage.' "[56]

The symbolic / economic divide is sometimes reproduced in the different responses of states and international institutions to intangible and tangible cultural heritage. The latter is even more likely to be disembodied and placed in the public sphere than the former, although there are often disputes over which nonindigenous space it belongs in.

The Organization of American States has tried to define the scope of the protection of cultural heritage in its ongoing debates over the proposed American Declaration on the Rights of Indigenous Peoples. While there is near consensus that "cultural identity" should be protected, there is little agreement over what exactly such protection would entail. In 2007, the Working Group charged with preparing the draft agreed on a provision stating:

Indigenous people have the right to the recognition and respect for all their ways of life, world views, spirituality, uses and customs, norms and traditions, forms of social, economic and political organization, forms of transmission of knowledge, institutions, practices, beliefs, values, dress and languages, recognizing their inter-relationship as elaborated in this Declaration.[57]

Although this language refers to indigenous people, not peoples, the understanding of culture it projects is one of intangible heritage.

Perhaps the language regarding the protection of culture upon which the Working Group was unable to agree is more telling than that upon which it has agreed. Proposed Article XII (1) (which, as of December 2009, remains the proposed language) specifically discusses heritage: "Indigenous peoples have the right to their cultural integrity and to their historical and ancestral heritage, which are important for their collective continuity, and for their identity and that of their members and their States."[58] This language has been significantly watered down from the results of informal consultations that had been held at a previous meeting, which had included the following language:

> Indigenous peoples have the right to / rights pertaining to their own identity and cultural integrity and to their cultural heritage, both tangible and intangible, including historic and ancestral heritage; and to the protection, preservation, maintenance, and development of that cultural heritage for their collective continuity and that of their members and so as to pass on / and to transmit that heritage to future generations.[59]

It would thus appear that the attempt to break down the distinction between the protection of tangible and intangible heritage has been rejected.

Finally, there has been no agreement over the right to the restitution of tangible property. The 2007 meeting also rejected language informally agreed upon at a previous meeting that read:

> States shall provide reparation, including the right of restitution, whenever possible, of any cultural heritage of which indigenous peoples have been dispossessed without their free, prior, and informed consent. Should return not be possible, indigenous peoples shall have the right to fair and equitable compensation. States, in conjunction with indigenous peoples, shall establish effective mechanisms for that purpose.[60]

The newly proposed language—on which, importantly, there is still no agreement—avoids the word "repatriation," as well as any requirement that states and indigenous peoples work together to establish mechanisms for these actions. Rather, the proposed Article XII (2) simply states: "Indigenous peoples have the right to restitution of the property that is part of that heritage of which they may be dispossessed, or, when restitution is not possible, to fair and equitable compensation."[61]

This reluctance to recognize the rights of indigenous peoples to tangible heritage can be seen in other contexts as well, both relying upon and reproducing economic inequality. As with arguments for keeping the Parthenon Marbles (also known as the Elgin Marbles) and the beard of the Sphinx of Giza in the British Museum, it is contended that some cultural heritage is better protected if removed from the people whose ancestors are thought to have produced it. Thus, the latter's lack of material resources hurts, rather than helps, their cause.

Indigenous peoples are often left out of the picture altogether in disputes over the custody of tangible heritage. The Boston Museum of Fine Arts, for example, rejected demands by the Guatemalan government to return "looted" Mayan artifacts when, in the late 1990s it asserted in a letter sent to the Guatemalan Ministry of Culture that "through an examination of applicable law, we have found no basis for concluding that the Government of Guatemala has any claim to ownership of the objects."[62] The museum's primary argument was that the artifacts had entered the United States before the museum had agreed to international standards that would prohibit it from accepting them. But its letter also suggests that the Guatemalan state has no better claim to the artifacts than a nonprofit museum in the United States. One might indeed ask why a state that has been responsible for the massacre of a large part of its indigenous population should be entitled to the contents of the graves of those same people's ancestors. The state would no doubt proudly display and take advantage of the antiquities, but in much the way that Hendrickson describes the display of indigenous traje.

In June 2007 the *New York Times Magazine* featured a story on a dispute between the government of Peru and Yale University over relics from Machu Picchu that are housed at Yale's Peabody Museum. Peru sought repatriation of this very tangible heritage, and Yale resisted, claiming that it was better able to protect and study the collection. The magazine's cover reads: "The Reconquest: Should Yale have to return its Machu Picchu artifacts? And who in Peru would actually benefit if it does?"[63]

While the article explores the first question more directly than the second, the second raises the issue of how indigenous peoples in Peru would benefit from the return of the artifacts to the state.

As the story has continued to unfold, little attention has been paid to the impact on Peru's indigenous peoples of any resolution of the debate between Yale and Peru. At one point, it seemed that the parties had agreed on a compromise, expressed in a memorandum of understanding (MOU) that, according to a Yale press release, "recognized Peru's and Yale's shared interests in the history, stewardship and scholarship of the materials excavated by Hiram Bingham from Machu Picchu in 1912, and provided for joint activities, and the return of museum quality pieces, along with a substantial portion of study fragments to Peru for display and study under agreed conditions."[64] In December 2008, however, the agreement apparently fell through, as Peru filed suit against Yale in the United States Federal Court.[65]

In its complaint, Peru seeks not only to recover the artifacts, but to be compensated for Yale's unjust enrichment from (wrongful possession) of them, and to be awarded punitive damages for a number of claims alleging fraud. The complaint relies on a number of international legal instruments, including the 1970 UNESCO Convention on the Means of Prohibiting and Preventing the Illicit Import, Export and Transfer of Ownership of Cultural Property and the 1972 UNESCO Convention Concerning the Protection of the World Cultural and Natural Heritage.[66]

Yale seems to have a different understanding of the meaning of the UNESCO instruments. According to a statement from the university's Office of Public Affairs shortly after the complaint was filed, "Yale shares the premise that Machu Picchu belongs to humanity and that its monuments were properly declared a Cultural Patrimony of the World by UNESCO and, in this spirit, believes that the MOU represents a balanced and creative solution."[67] Here, Yale stands in for humanity, willing to share, but not hand over responsibility for the patrimony with Peru. The state of Peru stands as the descendant of those who built Machu Picchu, in a way that is reminiscent of twentieth-century indigenismo. In fact, when the former First Lady of Peru, Eliane Karp-Toledo (a French-born, Jewish, Stanford-trained anthropologist), spoke at Yale to call for the unconditional and immediate repatriation of all Inca artifacts held at the university, she wore a brightly colored, embroidered indigenous blouse.

If I have returned to the material here (and to dress), it is not by accident. International instruments dealing with tangible cultural heritage differ from those that deal with the intangible. Yet, as we have seen, both understandings of culture function at times to alienate indigenous peoples from their heritage. They also often separate heritage from place. If indigenous groups assert that certain development projects, for example, might encroach upon their land and therefore their culture, the heritage model provides states with a way out. Indigenous peoples can simply move or be moved, carrying with them their culture (including its memories and associations with the land or water it is moved from). Or the state or UNESCO can guard it. Such alienability is precisely what the conception of culture discussed in the next chapter—culture as grounded in land—opposes. As we shall see, however, strategies centered on that conception also carry their dark sides, and ultimately fail to address the very issues of economic development at which they are often aimed.

As in the Indianist phase of Brazilian literature, when nineteenth-century writers such as Jose de Alencar conjured up an Indian character that was to feed into the nationalist dream, the contemporary version of the friends of the Indians also portrays him with a generous dash of romanticism. In fact, he is required to display, if not redeeming exoticism, at least an invincible integrity of principles: die, if need be, as the hero of official indigenism, Marshall Rondon, would say but never surrender to greed over your lands, never succumb to the bribes of the powerful, never capitulate to corruption, always denounce injustice. The more stoic and resistant to temptation, the more deserving he will be of white solidarity. Co-option was not made for Indian use.—ALCIDA RITA RAMOS, "THE HYPERREAL INDIAN," 1994[1]

The cosmovision discussion in chapter 5 demonstrated that land is an integral part of the understanding of indigenous cultural identity that is expressed in indigenous rights advocacy. As a part of the exploration of culture as heritage, I considered the special knowledge of the land that indigenous peoples sometimes claim, and that others often assert on their behalf. With culture as heritage, however, the knowledge was mostly disconnected from the very people who were thought to possess it. In the present chapter, I turn to a conception of culture in which historical occupation or use of particular land or territory is seen as the very basis of indigenous cultural identity.

Until relatively recently, the discussion of land rights based on indigeneity has been largely dominated by debates about what community or group is thought to be the first to occupy a given piece of land. This understanding of indigeneity, concerned primarily with a group's original relationship to the land, often bypasses questions of culture (The relationship is simple in theory, if not in practice: those who were first are, by definition, indigenous and should have authority over the land that they have always inhabited.) Of course, that relationship assumes that those who originally inhabited the land continue to reside on it; thus, there is a focus on ancestrality. This literal understanding of indigeneity has underwritten a lot of criticisms of special rights for indigenous peoples. Why should any group have an ongoing right to property just because it arrived first?

With the rise and relative success of the right to culture argument, indigenous rights advocates have come to depend less on the claim that a group was the first to occupy land, and more on the assertion that a group has customs and traditions related to a particular piece of land. Indeed, this latter argument can be seen in many of the successful claims for land discussed in chapter 4. Recall, in particular, that the decisions of the Inter-American Commission and Court often consider real property as essential to the preservation and practice of culture.

While an emphasis on the connection between land and culture opens up the possibility of land rights for groups that might not be able to demonstrate that they were the first to occupy the property, those rights are often limited, as we saw in chapter 4 as well. International law, for example, permits states to maintain subsurface, or mineral, rights to property. Additionally, lands that are available to indigenous groups for title or use are generally those that belong to the state or are not occupied by nonindigenous individuals or groups. Thus, indigenous groups have no right to unsettle the title of settler groups on the land (though states may, at their discretion and within domestic and international law, choose to expropriate the property). Finally, the lands are generally limited to non-urban areas. Noting that a majority of indigenous peoples in many countries live in urban areas, Michael Brown comments that it is a "curious feature of cultural-rights approaches . . . that their portrayal of native societies bears only a faint resemblance to the way indigenous peoples actually live."[2] Of course, while the majority of indigenous people in many other countries continue to live in rural areas, there is in general a growing trend of migration to urban areas.

Even with these limitations, indigenous land claims challenge neo-liberalism more than claims based on cultural heritage. If nothing else, they challenge the neoliberal preference for individual over collective property. When land is protected as part of the culture, indigenous peoples are generally recognized as having collective rights over the territory that is designated as belonging to them. While this view of culture might make more demands on the state than does the model of culture as heritage, as I will discuss at some length in chapter 7, it fits comfortably with the objective of bringing a human face to capitalist development that we often see in today's post–Washington Consensus.

As with culture as heritage, the conception of culture as land has its dark sides. The invisible asterisk reappears, and inalienability leads to undervaluation of land and restraints on development. Class biases are once again obscured.

CULTURE AS GROUNDED IN LAND USE

Culture as land both grounds and embodies culture as heritage. It suggests that lands traditionally occupied by indigenous peoples have done more than aid in the production of unique knowledge. Indeed, continued occupation and use of land seems crucial to the reproduction of that knowledge. As such, indigenous peoples have responsibilities as well as rights, an issue I will turn to later in this chapter.

This stronger conception of culture—as grounded in land, and sometimes territory—takes seriously the material implications of a cosmovision centered on land, and belies a distinction between intellectual and real property. As the Daes Report puts it (in a culture as territory moment), "all of the aspects of heritage are interrelated and cannot be separated from the traditional territory of the people concerned."[3] The Charter of the Indigenous and Tribal Peoples of the Tropical Forests similarly describes the significance of land as more than, but inclusive of, the material: "Our territories and forests are to us more than an economic resource. For us, they are life itself and have an integral and spiritual value for our communities. They are fundamental to our social, cultural, spiritual, economic and political survival as distinct peoples."[4]

(This conception of culture sees indigenous peoples as key to the protection of lands.) Hence, it is often used to argue that indigenous peoples must be permitted to stay on—perhaps even control, if not own—their traditional territories because the land (and the peoples) both hold and carry forth the heritage. This view is expressed in the Human Rights

Committee's General Comment on Article 27 of the ICCPR, protecting the right to culture. That comment, as discussed in chapter 4, "observes that culture manifests itself in many forms, including a particular way of life associated with the use of land resources, especially in the case of indigenous peoples. That right may include such traditional activities as fishing or hunting and the right to live in reserves protected by law."[5]

This approach to culture is also used to argue for indigenous control of territory in order to protect the land in accordance with an environmentally friendly cosmovision. Such an argument is based on an assumption that real Indians care about the land in traditional and sustainable ways, and are therefore its proper guardians.

Sometimes the cosmovision is thought to be so strong that even many years of forced assimilation could not extinguish it. Julian Burger, for example, after describing indigenous loss of identity, states that, nevertheless, "the most important distinguishing feature of indigenous peoples is their shared respect for the land—Mother Earth."[6] This view, he contends, is represented by the International Indian Treaty Council's description of the "great love and respect for the sacred quality of the land which has given birth to and nourished the cultures of indigenous peoples. These peoples are the guardians of their lands which over the centuries have become inextricably bound up with their culture, spirits, their identity and survival. Without the land bases, their cultures will not survive."[7] Indeed, contemporary indigenous peoples are as likely to promote this view as anyone else. Citing statements by indigenous peoples, James Anaya claims that there is a wide acceptance of "indigenous peoples' articulated ideas of communal stewardship over land and a deeply felt spiritual and emotional nexus with the earth and its fruits."[8]

At times, the description of and emphasis on this cosmovision might sound overly essentialist, monolithic, or separated from the everyday life of many indigenous peoples. Yet, in many ways that parallel the discussion of the performance of culture as heritage in chapter 5, it is a deliberate but not inauthentic strategy. That the cosmovision continues to resonate with indigenous advocates and many of their audiences is apparent in some of the strategies and results of indigenous advocacy.

In fact, the strategy centered on culture as requiring traditional usage of land has been relatively successful. It has been incorporated into a number of international legal instruments and their interpretation. ILO

169, for example, requires signatory states to "respect the special importance for the cultures and spiritual values of the peoples concerned of their relationship with the lands or territories . . . which they occupy or use."[9] A similar provision can be found in Article 25 of the UN Declaration on the Rights of Indigenous Peoples: "Indigenous peoples have the right to maintain and strengthen their distinctive spiritual relationship with their traditionally owned or otherwise occupied and used lands, territories, waters and coastal seas and other resources and to uphold their responsibilities to future generations in this regard."[10]

Although an acknowledgment of a "spiritual relationship" to the land would seem to suggest a need for occupation of that land, in fact this provision in the UN Declaration was weakened from the 1993 draft of the UN Declaration submitted by the Working Group, of which Article 25 read: "Indigenous peoples have the right to maintain and strengthen their distinctive *spiritual and material* relationship with the lands."[11] Indeed, this provision of the draft became contentious at one point, with Australia and others arguing for the replacement of "spiritual and material" with the term "special." According to Andrea Muehlebach, this change was attempted because "certain types of recognition can and would be construed as necessitating certain obligations. The denial of the spirituality and materiality of a people's relationship to land, then, is indicative of the rights that states are ready to grant."[12] The apparent compromise to include "spiritual" but not "material" in the final declaration keeps the relationship at an intangible level, but nevertheless implies that, for indigenous peoples to practice their religion (or culture), land might be required.

For the most part, however, the understanding of land as culture goes beyond an implied relationship to land use and occupation. Asbjørn Eide draws the connection in this way: "Many of the cultural practices of Indigenous populations are reflections of the way they use the natural resources around them. If their cultural rights are to be respected, this may imply also that their rights to land and other natural resources may have to be respected and protected so that they can continue their way of life."[13] Although, as Eide acknowledges, this position is controversial, it is reflected in a number of international and regional institutions and documents. As discussed in chapter 4, the inter-American system for the protection of human rights has been the most specific about the connection between land and culture. In fact, by foregrounding the right to property as the chief vehicle for the preservation and practice of culture, it has reversed the more usual position that the right to culture requires guaranteeing land rights.

CULTURE AS GROUNDED IN COLLECTIVE OWNERSHIP

The understanding of culture as land generally envisions a communal conception of property. This communal model is often thought to be based in indigenous culture. The Inter-American Commission and Court have made this connection through their interpretation of customary international law as well as of American human rights documents.

I have discussed in detail the jurisprudence of these bodies in chapter 4, but I want to return here to the role that collective rights has played in that jurisprudence, beginning with the 2001 Inter-American Court's decision in *Awas Tingni v. Nicaragua*.[14] There, the court determined that Nicaragua's grant of a logging concession on land used and occupied by an indigenous group violated the community's right to property as guaranteed in Article 21 of the American Convention on Human Rights. Article 21 is very general, stating simply that "everyone has the right to the use and enjoyment of his property." The court's decision interprets the provision in favor of the Awas Tingni community, using both customary international law and an understanding of the cultural importance of communal property for indigenous peoples. With regard to the latter, the decision reads: "Among indigenous communities, there is a communal tradition as demonstrated by the communal form of collective ownership of their lands, in the sense that ownership is not centered in the individual but rather in the group and in the community."[15]

The Inter-American Commission has similarly interpreted Article 23 of the American Declaration on the Rights and Duties of Man, which also recognizes the right to property. In another case about concessions, this time against the government of Belize with regard to timber and oil concessions it granted on lands occupied by descendants of the Maya, the commission's decision states:

> Among the developments arising from the advancement of indigenous human rights has been recognition that rights and freedoms are frequently exercised and enjoyed by indigenous communities in a collective manner, in the sense that they can only be properly ensured

through their guarantee to an indigenous community as a whole. The right to property has been recognized as one of the rights having such a collective aspect.[16]

The commission reinforces this and related conclusions by citing not only *Awas Tingni* and previous decisions by the commission, but also ILO 169's Article 13, which calls for governments to respect the "collective aspects" of indigenous relationships with their lands and territories.[17]

Calls for the recognition of culture as land at times border on claims of self-determination. Once a group is recognized as having control or ownership over a piece of land, it may also be granted some form of territorial jurisdiction over it. Chapter 3's exploration of various meanings of self-determination assumed that, if statehood or autonomy were sought or granted, territorial boundaries might be redefined. Thus, legal and political decisions about land analyzed under the right to culture or right to property might have significant implications for the right and scope of self-determination. In this sense, culture as grounded in land would appear to offer indigenous groups greater opportunities for material and jurisdictional control than would the culture as heritage approach.

DARK SIDES AND UNINTENDED CONSEQUENCES

If culture as grounded in land seems to imbue the right to culture with more teeth than culture as heritage does, the approach nevertheless produces its own potential dark sides and unintended consequences. First, it contains an invisible asterisk: the concept of culture as territory sometimes provides a tool for distinguishing those who are indigenous and deserving of protection from those who are not. That is, if real Indians care about the land, those who are seen not to care for it properly might be restricted in their uses of it, or denied rights to it altogether. Second, given that the object of protection is the land, its stewardship sometimes takes priority over the autonomy of indigenous peoples. In this sense, culture as land again becomes like culture as heritage—only this time, the land is protected as a noncommodity. States are permitted, in the public interest, to prohibit its alienation. Finally, these two dark sides work together to restrict long-term possibilities for indigenous groups' economic development, often displacing concerns for underlying economic disparities that cannot be attended to by basing land rights on culture.

The Invisible Asterisk: Land Use and Abuse

Alcida Ramos writes:

> It should be emphasized that there are fundamental differences be-
> tween NGOS concerned with indigenous peoples. For instance, environ-
> mental NGOS tend to regard the Indians from opposing viewpoints: one
> sees them as predators and therefore excludes them from ecologically
> protected areas, even at the cost of eviction. The other naturalizes the
> Indian, reducing him to yet another endangered species, or to the role
> of custodian of nature.[18]

What Ramos states about NGOS is often true of governments as well.
Consequently, indigenous peoples are given little flexibility with regard to
the use of their land. Because of their apparent special relationship to the
land, they are expected to be its protectors and guardians.

In some instances, states even prohibit indigenous groups from using
land in a manner that goes against what the state sees as the group's
purported attachment to it. The Canadian Supreme Court's 1997 decision
in *Delgamuukw v. British Columbia* is illustrative. After explicitly stating that
indigenous occupancy constitutes "a special bond between the group and
the land in question such that the land will be part of the definition of the
group's distinctive culture," the court turns to the "inherent limitation on
the uses to which the land, over which such title exists, may be put."[19] The
decision explains:

> For example, if occupation is established with reference to the use of
> the land as a hunting ground, then the group that successfully claims
> aboriginal title to that land may not use it in such a fashion as to
> destroy its value for such a use (e.g., by strip mining it). Similarly, if a
> group claims a special bond with the land because of its ceremonial or
> cultural significance, it may not use the land in such a way as to destroy
> that relationship (e.g., by developing it in such a way that the bond is
> destroyed, perhaps by turning it into a parking lot).[20]

A 2001 report by the UN Working Group on Indigenous Populations on
indigenous peoples and their relationship to land (UN Report on Relationship to Land) identifies Canada's position as an example of discriminatory

treatment against indigenous peoples with regard to land title, though it does not specifically recommend any change.[21]

For many groups, there are even more serious consequences to the pursuit of a political and legal strategy based on a special relationship to the land. When they do not behave toward the land in the idealized manner that has come to be expected of them, these groups might cease to be considered real Indians(The focus on occupation and use of land often leads to successful claims for those groups who have maintained existence on their ancestral lands for centuries.) But it misses the experiences of many groups that consider themselves, and are considered by others, to be indigenous—because of the language they speak, the traditions they practice, the ways and groups in which they live, their internal administrative functioning, or their local control—but who nevertheless live on land to which they have no proven ancestral, or possibly even cultural, ties. Such groups are often on land to which they were forcibly relocated, or that they have occupied as a result of dislocation from another area. They therefore do not necessarily have the knowledge or means to subsist in the ways that might be considered traditional. Martin Scheinin refers to such situations as "pathological."[22]

Diane Nelson attributes much of the difficulty that such groups have in claiming a right to land to the definition of indigenous peoples found in the Cobo Report. Recall from chapter 3 that the Cobo Report had offered a working definition of the term "indigenous." For Nelson, the definition's requirement that indigenous peoples exhibit "an historical continuity with pre-invasion and pre-colonial societies that developed on their territories"[23] is particularly problematic. She explains: "The claims to an identity before—anterior to—the law, which grounds the special claim to 'ancestral lands,' thus places indigenous peoples in the double bind that in order to sue for land they must be 'Indians' (or a tribe, or peoples), and to be 'Indian' they must have land."[24]

International instruments that have since considered indigenous peoples have refused to define the term "indigenous," though ILO 169 at least suggests a broader understanding of it than that provided by the Cobo Report.[25] Moreover, indigenous rights advocates have attempted, somewhat successfully, to move from a focus on ancestrality to one on culture. Muehlebach notes: "Territorial precedence has on the international level shifted by now from being a primary marker of what it means to be 'indigenous' to being only one of the possible variables mobilized when indigenousness is asserted."[26] Nevertheless, as chapter 4 demonstrated, those groups that have had the most success with land claims are those that currently occupy land and can show historical and cultural ties to it, suggesting that Nelson is right to consider the lasting impact of the Cobo Report's definition.

A relatively recent situation in Chiapas provides an example of the resonance of the dynamic identified by Nelson, as well as the one described by Ramos in the quotation at the beginning of this section. In particular, it illustrates how these dynamics play out in state policy, and in conflicts between some environmental groups and indigenous populations.

For several years, the Mexican government has threatened to dislocate, or "relocate," groups of indigenous peoples living in the Montes Azules Integral Biosphere Reserve in the heart of the jungle that is also the home to the Zapatista army. Much of Montes Azules is inside territory that the government ceded in 1972 to the Lacandones, the only group the government considers indigenous to the area. Although there is a dispute over whether the group that is today called "Los Lacandones" is in fact descended from the people that initially occupied the territory, or instead migrated there in the early eighteenth century from the Yucatan Peninsula, its presence in the area predates that of other contemporary groups by at least a hundred years.

Between 1820 and 1910, timber companies began to exploit what is now Montes Azules, bringing in large numbers of workers. Ranchers also moved to the area and brought with them Tseltales and Ch'oles, indigenous peoples living in the highlands, as indentured workers. Since then, there have been three primary waves of indigenous migration to the area. The first was in the mid-1950s, when Tsotsiles and Tojolabales as well as Tseltales and Ch'oles, in search of land on which to subsist, moved to the ranching areas where other Tseltales and Ch'oles were already present. In 1994, a second wave resulted from the displacement of populations by military and paramilitary violence after the Zapatista uprising. Finally, in 2000, just as the Mexican government was relocating certain groups outside of the reserve, others began to move in.

Those who entered after 2000 have been under the greatest threat of expulsion. One group that received a number of threats from both the government and the Lacandones calls itself "8 de febrero," in honor of the day that its members arrived, in 2002. In response to a threat in February

2003, the group issued a press release declaring itself a base of support for the Zapatistas. Other groups followed suit, finding that this strategy at least delayed the otherwise seemingly imminent dislocation.

The primary reason given by the Mexican government for moving indigenous peoples out of the biosphere region was that they were destroying the environment through slash-and-burn agriculture and the use of harsh chemicals. Indeed, Mexico's environmental protection agency, the Procuraduría Federal de Protección al Ambiente (PROFEPA), was at the center of the attempts to relocate 8 de febrero and other non-Lacandon indigenous groups living in the region. Several international environmental NGOs, including Conservation International and the World Wildlife Fund, publicly supported the government's efforts, lending credence to the perception that the conflict was between the environment and Zapatista communities.

I traveled to the Montes Azules region in 2003 with members of the Red de Defensores Comunitarios por los Derechos Humanos (Network of Community Defenders for Human Rights), a local human rights NGO in Chiapas that was investigating the conflict. We met with the leaders of 8 de febrero, who explained the government's attempts to expel them and its offers to relocate them outside of the biosphere region. Neither these leaders nor those advocating on behalf of them and similar groups denied that they had used slash-and-burn techniques in working the land, but they argued that any damage done to the environment was minimal in comparison to that done by the military and by commercial activities.

Global Exchange, an international human rights NGO focusing on environmental and social justice, opposed the displacement, maintaining that indigenous peoples in the area were learning to use environmentally friendly forms of agriculture. As their press release at the time states:

> The communities we visited are cooperating in an important experiment to demonstrate a more sustainable way of living on the land. For eight or more years they have ceased using slash and burn agriculture and have ended the use of harmful chemicals. They seek international support to continue developing new organic methods of cultivation based on some of the most traditional means of caring for the land.[27]

The press release is carefully crafted, recognizing that there are "traditional means of caring for the land," but acknowledging that the groups might need to be taught sustainable ways of living on the land, based on such traditions. Many of the current residents in Montes Azules, the release continues, are descendants of people who had moved to the area (at the behest of previous governments) to escape the harsh working conditions of labor on landed estates in southern Mexico. In other words, the special relationship to land might be as much nurture as nature. One Mexican NGO responded by working with indigenous groups in Chiapas, as well as in Oaxaca, to teach them forms of sustainable development which, as we will see in chapter 7, are often attributed to indigenous origins and practices.

In Chiapas, no one denied that the individuals living on the biosphere lands are indigenous, primarily because they speak indigenous languages. Also, it seemed undisputed that they are entitled to some land. Yet the government's position suggests that, far from having a special relationship to the land, the communities had harmed it. Hence, there would be no reason not to move them to another area. Global Exchange responded by invoking the Mayan ancestry of those living on the land, and then using ILO 169 to make a claim based more on possession than on use of land. One paragraph of the press release, for example, reads:

> Indigenous people have the right to remain on their land and to farm their land in the ways that they see fit. They have an ethical claim to live on their land and work it in ways that support the earth. In addition, their presence on the land is legitimate under the provisions of the indigenous rights convention (Convention 169) of the UN International Labor Organization.[28]

Global Exchange also reasserted indigenous interest in preservation of the earth, ultimately concluding that "the biodiversity of Montes Azules will best be implemented by the indigenous peoples themselves."[29]

The Mexican government did not necessarily disagree with the position that indigenous peoples were in the best position to preserve Montes Azules. But it considered the Lacandones, in many ways the model Indians, to be the group that is indigenous to most of the land. In the 1940s, the Danish archeologist Frans Blom and his wife, the Swiss photographer Gertrudis Duby, began to study the Lacandones and then to advocate on their behalf. The Na Bolom Center, in San Cristobal de las Casas, built by Blom and Duby, presents a story of the area now called the Lacandon

Jungle (in which Montes Azules is situated) that suggests that the Lacandones are the true Indians of the region. When I visited the museum, I encountered no information on indigenous organizing. Rather, Blom and Duby are portrayed as the protectors of the culture and heritage of the group.

Today there are only about sixty Lacandon families. They live miles apart from each other and do not come close to occupying, even using, most of the 614,000 hectares they were deeded (in response to a request for 10,000 hectares) in 1972. The Lacandones have not participated in indigenous organization in Chiapas. For example, they are not members of the Indigenous Congress that was formed in 1974, the same year that the Lacandones granted a multi-year contract to a government-owned timber company to extract large quantities of wood. Advocates for indigenous groups threatened with expulsion began to make their own authenticity claims, arguing that the Lacandones are responsible for most of the environmental destruction done to the land because of these contracts, and also arguing that the Lacandones are not truly indigenous to the land.

A pamphlet written by the NGO Maderas del Pueblo del Sureste consistently refers to the Lacandones as "los caribes," arguing that all but two of the "true Lacandones" were killed by conquistadors. The other two, it claims, died in prison in Guatemala in 1712. Hence, those who are called Lacandones today, the authors insist, are descendants of the Yucatan Maya who moved to the region around 1700. They contend that this group has no greater right to the land than those who arrived in the 1950s and later. The title of the pamphlet, as written on the cover, is "A Brief History of the Community called 'Lacandona.'" The first page, or inside cover, continues in large letters "... Or How the Caribes Won the Lottery without Buying a Ticket."[30] Seen in this light, the threatened expulsions did not present a conflict between the environment and indigenous peoples, but among indigenous groups themselves. Yet all sides participated in a discussion about who has caused or is likely to cause further damage to the land, with the assumption that those who would harm the land cannot be indigenous to it.

In the years between 2003 and 2006, the Mexican government did not in fact expel any of the groups, although it continued to threaten to do so. In 2006, however, the secretary of agrarian reform concluded an agreement with the Lacandones to expropriate 17,200 hectares of land in exchange for

172 million pesos. The Mexican government did not set forth any plans for using the land; its primary aim, it claimed, was to solve disputes over land titles.[31] By paying the Lancandones, however, the government recognized and legitimized their legal title, and at the same time assumed power over decisions with regard to land usage. Although the deal had been in the works for some time, it was concluded only after the Lacandones blocked part of the federal highway to pressure the government to finalize the transaction. Within weeks of the agreement's conclusion, the Lacandones were asserting their ownership over other parts of Montes Azules, attempting—with the backing of the Secretary of Agrarian Reform—to dislocate five non-Lacandon communities. The inhabitants of these communities were among the first wave of those who had moved there over thirty years earlier.

Some of the non-Lacandon indigenous groups who had been negotiating with the government for permission to stay on the land and manage it in ecologically sensitive ways broke off those negotiations over these new attempts at dislocation. The organization representing these groups, the Asociación Rural de Interés Colectivo Independiente y Democrática (ARIC-ID), used an argument to oppose the government's attempts that is reminiscent of some of the disembodied heritage approaches we saw in the previous chapter. As part of the Lacandon Jungle, ARICID asserted, Montes Azules forms a significant part of the "patrimony of humanity and of all Mexicans, not only of a group of business persons and a group of indigenous people driven by the whims of the environmental sector."[32]

After non-Lacandon communities refused the small amount they were offered for relocation, the government took a new tack. In August 2007, the state public prosecutor's office acted on charges long asserted by the secretary of environment and natural resources and the Lacandones. With the help of the federal government, 200 troops were sent to dislocate the families on the basis that they were causing environmental destruction. The troops detained six heads of families, accusing them of environmental crimes, theft, and harm to others' property. Shortly after the relocation operation was completed, the Mexican daily *La Jornada* reported: "Lacandon Indians and personnel from Semarnat [secretary of environment and natural resources] went up the zone to destroy the houses and dwellings that the villagers constructed over three decades."[33]

The Mexican government is not alone in using its alignment with, and land grants to, certain indigenous groups as a means to respond to threats it believes are posed by other groups, both indigenous and non-indigenous. According to Jean Jackson, for example, the Colombian government granted land to Colombian indigenous groups in the 1990s as "an attempt to win hearts and minds in the government's fight against guerrillas and narcotics traffickers and to co-opt the country's Indian movement."[34] At the same time, the government situated itself to be able to claim that it was protecting the environment. Jackson explains:

> Clearly, the Colombian state perceives several advantages to responding this way to Indian rights organizing. The government wants to reduce violence and diminish the appeal of radical groups, especially in the Andes. In addition, the state is coming to see Indian communities as the best guardians of natural resources and has publicized the *resguardo* entitlement to gain favor in the international ecology movement.[35]

"Co-opted" or not, these indigenous groups have ended up with land legally granted to them by the state.

I do not want to suggest here that the assertion of a special cultural relationship between indigenous peoples and the earth is disingenuous on the part of any who make it, whether they be indigenous peoples, their advocates, international organizations, or even states. Nor do I deny that, used as a strategy, it has led to numerous successes. Rather, I hope to suggest that culture understood as grounded in land is a better fit for some than for others. As Beth Conklin has noted with regard to dress: "However positive their content, essentialist constructions of Indian identity constitute a 'legislation of authenticity' that can work against Indian interests, undermining the legitimacy of both native people who promote them and those who do not."[36]

If we were to follow Povinelli's analysis, of course, no group would actually fit the ideal. More than the matter of fit, I want to pursue the question whether it is because of a special relationship to land that indigenous peoples should have some type of possession over it. If, in the absence of fit, advocates would still pursue a claim, what would be its basis?

Inalienable Land

Most states treat indigenous land as inalienable. Much as indigenous heritage is seen as an integral part of the identity of many modern nation-states, these states often see indigenous land as part of the land of the nation. As such, they generally recognize what they deem to be indigenous land as a protected form of public land, set aside for the use of indigenous peoples. Recall, for example, chapter 1's discussion of the 1984 Canadian Supreme Court decision, *Guerin v. The Queen*, which recognizes the fiduciary responsibility of the Canadian government toward indigenous peoples. According to Patrick Macklem, the rationale for the Crown's fiduciary duty is "the vulnerability of Indian bands, which cannot sell or lease reserve land directly to third parties."[37] In short, Indians are unable to alienate the lands other than by surrendering them back to the Crown, an arrangement that is said to be in their interest as, among other things, it "facilitate[s] the Crown's ability to represent the Indians in dealings with third parties."[38] Proponents reason that, in this way, the government prevents indigenous peoples from being exploited or taken advantage of, even though the obvious flip side is that the government claims for itself the power to decide what is in the best interest of indigenous peoples.

Even when indigenous peoples are granted collective title to the land, a number of exclusions and restrictions adhere. In Latin America, for example, states nearly always maintain ownership of mineral and other subsurface resources, an issue I will turn to in chapter 7 in some detail. States also generally make communal land that is titled to indigenous groups inalienable and inseverable, and prohibit its use for collateral.[39] No international legal instrument prohibits these restrictions.

Of course, even private property owners cannot use land however they please. Most states retain the right to "take" property for public purposes (although they are required to provide "just compensation").[40] International legal instruments recognizing the right to property also permit such expropriation.[41] Even if property is in this sense merely a "bundle of rights,"[42] it would seem that indigenous peoples are given fewer sticks than most, despite their purported special relationship to land. The UN Report on Relationship to Land explains that "in many countries, particularly those of the British Commonwealth, exclusive use and occupancy of land from time immemorial gives rise to aboriginal title, a title that is good against all but the Sovereign, that is, the Government of the State." The report contrasts the way that aboriginal title is subject to the "illegitimate assumption of State power to extinguish such title" with "the legal protection and rights that, in most countries, protect the land and property of non-indigenous citizens, other individuals and corporations." The consequences, it contends, are significant: "This single fact probably accounts for the overwhelming majority of human rights problems affecting indigenous peoples."[43]

For many, the greatest value in owning property comes from the right to sell at least the parts of the bundle to which one can claim title. International law and indigenous advocates alike have been reluctant to claim that part. ILO 169 does leave open the possibility that a state might grant such a right, but certainly does not require it. States do not need to consider the right to alienation, but "the peoples concerned shall be consulted whenever [read: "if ever"] consideration is being given to their capacity to alienate their lands or otherwise transmit their rights outside their own community."[44]

The UN Report on Relationship to Land also falls short of calling for the right to alienation. In outlining discrimination that indigenous peoples suffer with regard to land title, it includes the prevention of alienation.[45] Yet, when it lists its recommendations, it does not call for a right to alienate. The closest it comes to suggesting such a recommendation is with a general statement that "special measures . . . must not deprive indigenous peoples of legal rights with respect to land and resources that other groups and individuals in the country enjoy."[46] No legal instrument, including the UN Declaration on the Rights of Indigenous Peoples, explicitly recognizes a right to alienation. To my knowledge, neither states nor indigenous groups have attempted to include such a right.

Certainly the inability to alienate property makes the property less valuable, in that it would be worthless on the open market, to indigenous peoples. And to the extent that indigenous lands are generally subject to sovereign decisions to appropriate the land, it seems an all-out power grab by the state. That, in these circumstances, the state could then alienate the land suggests that states, not indigenous peoples, are the ones with a special (legal) relationship to the land. That said, the state's power to appropriate the land without compensation is considered illegitimate.

Under ILO 169, if the state finds it absolutely necessary to move indigenous peoples off the land they occupy, for example, it must compensate them with other land or with money, the first being preferable.[47] The UN Declaration adds a requirement that there be "free, prior and informed consent" before land can be appropriated, recognizing the right of indigenous peoples "to redress, by means that can include restitution or, when this is not possible, just, fair and equitable compensation, for [their] lands, territories and resources" that "have been confiscated, taken, occupied, used or damaged without their free, prior and informed consent."[48]

The best argument for preventing alienation, in my mind, comes not from the fear of state appropriation but from the concern that private individuals or corporations will essentially create and profit from distress sales. If the land is held collectively, this result might be less likely, but historically we know that it has occurred. Hence, the idea of the trust responsibility in the United States is in part that it holds the land in trust, not just for present-day Indians, but for future generations (of indigenous and nonindigenous people alike, to the extent that the land is the medium by which culture is preserved). As discussed in chapter 1, the trust responsibility is not only paternalistic but tenuous, given that the United States continues to assert ownership over the land. Yet the trust status at least acknowledges the real lack of power and wealth of most Indian tribes and understands why a land sale might be attractive as a short-term solution, even if it goes against everything that is presumably believed about indigenous ways of thinking. At the same time, it fails to attend to the root of the problem, as it often leaves indigenous peoples deprived of an obvious means to produce income and often with the impossibility of sustaining themselves on lands where they settled only after their traditional lands were taken from them.

Understanding that at times more rights are not necessarily the way to liberation, particularly in a context of significant structural inequalities, indigenous rights advocates often oppose the right to land alienation, even for groups. If some indigenous groups were to alienate their land for short-term gains, indigenous culture and the number of individuals with indigenous identity could diminish significantly. Future generations of would-be Indians would have little possibility of participating in traditional life. They would essentially have been forced into assimilation by their ancestors, who did not themselves behave like Indians. Real Indians, as Ramos's quotation at the beginning of this chapter tells us, are thought to take care of and be responsible for the land; they do not use it to make a profit.

Indigenous rights advocates have often pursued the recognition of collective title, with the aims of preventing individual Indians from selling their land and of placing control over the land in the hands of the indigenous community rather than the government. Yet, while ILO 169 calls upon governments to respect "the collective aspects" of indigenous cultural and spiritual values in relationship to their land, no international instrument has recognized the collective property rights of indigenous peoples.[49] The jurisprudence of the Inter-American Court of Human Rights, discussed in chapter 4, has made the greatest strides with regard to such recognition.

Of course, collective title in and of itself would not respond to many of the concerns about alienation. Indeed, the principal concern of most indigenous rights advocates in this regard is to prevent alienation by individuals of property that should belong to the whole. If individuals could alienate property, the entire group could be seriously undermined by individuals who choose to opt out of it by selling their land.

If a state wanted to destroy a group's cohesion, granting land to indigenous people—not peoples—might be one way to do it. As a decision by the ILO Governing Body regarding a complaint against Peru observes:

> The ILO's experience with indigenous and tribal peoples has shown that when communally owned indigenous lands are divided and assigned to individuals or third parties, the exercise of their rights by indigenous communities tends to be weakened and [the communities] generally end up losing all or most of the lands, resulting in a general reduction of the resources that are available to indigenous peoples when they keep their lands in common.[50]

In fact, dividing collective property into individually owned parcels was part of the colonial strategy in many parts of the world. The "allotment and assimilation era" in the United States, for example, represented a deliberate attempt to civilize and Christianize Indians, and to dissolve tribal authority.[51] From the Americas to Africa, colonial powers dissolved collective indigenous property, imposed private property regimes, and maintained state control through a concept of public domain over those lands not granted to individuals.[52]

In Latin America, dissolution of property has long provided a method of undermining Indian communities, often under the auspices of liberal or modernizing reforms. Perhaps this history helps to explain why indigenous rights activists so quickly formed a committed opposition to Mexico's federal land reform of 1992, which granted individuals the right to lands previously held communally (*ejidos*). Ejidos were not exclusive to indigenous peoples, having been formed after the Mexican Revolution for the purpose of ensuring communal ownership and group maintenance of and production from land.[53] In largely indigenous areas, though, such as Chiapas and parts of Oaxaca, individual land ownership has undermined communal means of decision making that many deem essential to indigenous identity, as well as to indigenous economic and political power stemming from control over large areas of land.

Indigenous rights advocates are understandably ambivalent about alienation. Those who argue for maintaining the possibility of independence or statehood, or even strong forms of autonomy connected to specific territory, have a stake in maintaining the prohibition on alienation. If alienability of land were permitted, it would foreclose discussion of such arrangements now and in the future. At the same time, the prohibition comes from the state and expresses itself as a limitation on indigenous autonomy at both the group and individual level.

Dependency Displacement

As we have seen, the understanding of culture as grounded in land is limited in a number of ways. It has effectively been used to narrow the definition of indigenous peoples to those groups that, if they cannot demonstrate ancestral ties to the land, at least are able to show that their uses of the land are in accordance with their traditional culture. And it has accepted a limited bundle of rights that attach to those who are considered indigenous.

The right to culture as land thus functions to limit as much as to empower. Although the land that indigenous groups claim the right to use and occupy is often called their territory, it generally bears little resemblance to the types of autonomous jurisdictional territory that we saw called for in chapter 3. Even in states where indigenous groups are granted significant autonomy, the key word there is that the autonomy is *granted*. As Patrick Thornberry explains: "In terms of *lex lata* . . . self-determination is a right, autonomy is not; autonomy is essentially a gift by the state (grudgingly offered, ungratefully accepted) though it can be entrenched."[54] It is generally also limited (in comparison to the potential "flexibility and dynamism" of self-determination[55]) and subject to being taken away. The invisible asterisk is one constant reminder of that possibility.

The focus on culture as land often displaces an attention to the reasons why indigenous peoples are in need of land and resources. It could be said that the ILO's attempt through ILO 107 to assimilate indigenous people and make them a productive part of economic modernization at least recognized the extent to which they had long been deprived of economic resources. Arguments based on culture as land are implicitly and explicitly aimed at years of indigenous assimilation and displacement, and often recognize that neoliberal land reform policies have also functioned to destroy communal forms of ownership and weakened the ability of indigenous peoples to control their natural resources and maximize the productivity of the land. Yet the culture as land strategy has in some ways served to exclude indigenous peoples from many of the benefits of modernization.

The issue of alienability of land provides an example of how land rights based on culture might limit the possible economic arrangements available to indigenous people, thereby cementing their dependence on states and on a stagnant understanding of their culture and their role in protecting it. If indigenous peoples were to argue for the right to alienate their property, they would find themselves in a strategic dilemma. The moment they were to articulate a desire for the right, they would be seen as potentially using it—which, as mentioned above, would go against what is considered their cosmovision and thus undermine the authenticity of their claim. That is, they are largely dependent upon capitalist states for recognition of their right to culture, in which is embedded a precapitalist, communal, use-based understanding of land. If they aim to participate in the market with regard to land, they go against their culture, potentially losing their claim to indigenousness.

In Latin America ethnodevelopment of the native Indian populations means a complete reversal of government indigenista policies which have been followed up to now by most governments. A new, militant brand of Indian social movements has arisen which demands a reaffirmation of Indian cultural values and a revaluation of the position of Indians within the social structure.—RODOLFO STAVENHAGEN, "ETHNODEVELOPMENT: A NEGLECTED DIMENSION IN DEVELOPMENT THINKING," 1986[1]

The rise of indigenous identity in the 1970s brought, among other things, opposition to Western-style development. (As many indigenous peoples and their advocates attempted to put the brakes on modern development, and even to turn the clocks back in an effort to unearth indigenous "lost culture" and prevent its further demise, they began to consider alternative forms of development.) They found promise in what has come to be termed "ethnodevelopment," or development based on the traditional culture of indigenous groups. Their goal was not only to rescue culture from the modernization projects that threatened to erase it, but to provide the means by which indigenous peoples might sustain themselves and their cultures in the modern world.

Those pursuing the promise of indigenous development recognized that land alone is insufficient to ensure development. As George Manuel, the founder of the World Council of Indigenous Peoples, put it early on:

The racial myths that were created to justify the seizure of land will only be fully dispelled when we have received the legal recognition of our effective title to the lands that remain to us, and sufficient grants to compensate for what is lost that we can afford to develop what does remain. Only then will we be able to demonstrate that there is no conflict between wanting to live comfortably and wanting to develop within our own traditional framework.[2]

Efforts to combat racism, guarantee economic compensation, and protect land and heritage thus all play a role in this conception of development.

I have attempted to show throughout this book, and particularly in this part, how economic disparities have both driven and often been displaced by indigenous rights advocacy. If, as we saw in chapters 5 and 6, focuses on culture as heritage and culture as land tend to repress attention to disparities in access to wealth and resources, we might expect an understanding of culture as development to place these disparities at the center of the discussion. In its early stages, culture as development was explicitly aimed at addressing structural economic inequality. But, I contend, its economic aims have become less radical over time, in part because of the understanding of culture that it has privileged.

In much the same way that culture as heritage and culture as land often fit comfortably alongside neoliberalism, so too does culture as development. But culture as development also fits with—and has arguably both found a new home in and been transformed by—post-neoliberal market reforms aimed at development and environmental preservation. As such, I would place many of the arguments based on culture as development (including their own deployment of understandings of culture as heritage and land) alongside the post-neoliberal deployments of law and development reforms that Alvaro Santos and David Trubek have called the "third moment" in law and development theory.[3] Ethnodevelopment has therefore largely been transformed from a radical critique of state and international development policy in the 1970s to a less radical critique of (and sometimes an acquiescent bystander to) neoliberal reforms of the 1980s and 1990s. Today, it at times appears to be a sympathetic supplement to (and beneficiary of) what David Kennedy refers to as "chastened neoliberalism."[4] This last term denotes the explicit efforts of states to protect indigenous peoples (among others) from the excesses of neoliberalism by taking into account "the social" and expanding the notion of property.

Because both the threats and promises of development have loomed large throughout the story of indigenous rights advocacy and come to a head around ethnodevelopment, I dedicate a significant portion of this part of the book to that subject. The chapter begins by revisiting some of the history from chapter 1 to contextualize the rise and acceptance of ethnodevelopment models. Next, it considers multiple understandings of ethnodevelopment, tracing its trajectory from critique to entrance into the mainstream. It then turns to some of the dark sides of culture as development, including that—as with culture as heritage and culture as land—ethnodevelopment often relies on representations of identity and lifestyle that are, like much development, simply not sustainable.

I conclude this chapter and part II of the book by examining both the need for a focus on redistribution and the extent to which the cultural identity paradigm might have outlived its usefulness. The right to culture continues to have legal and rhetorical force, as the development models with which it often worked in tandem have begun to be replaced by new models that explicitly incorporate it. With that in mind, I consider some of the strategic dilemmas faced by indigenous rights advocates when they recognize that, though marginalized, indigenous peoples often are already economically modernized, and that the pressures to traditionalize come as much from a new global economic order as from indigenous peoples themselves.

CULTURE AND DEVELOPMENT IN OPPOSITION

Culture and development have long been linked. Western expansion was largely based on a perception of the inferiority of indigenous people, often pinned on their supposed backward, traditional, and communalist culture, as well as on their low levels of socioeconomic development. Lack of indigenous development was seen to obstruct not only the advancement of indigenous peoples, but Western society in general.[6] Military conquest, forced acculturation, and industrialization were all espoused as ways to civilize or modernize indigenous peoples. If indigenous peoples and their advocates were long skeptical of human rights discourse, as I discussed in part I, they were perhaps even more wary of development discourse.

Even when world opinion appeared to have moved away from at least an explicit goal of either conquest or forced acculturation of indigenous peoples, indigenous peoples' ways of life—their differences—continued to be seen as constituting a problem for economic development. As Rodolfo Stavenhagen explains: "Within the generally accepted framework of development as a unilinear progression along a series of necessary stages . . . [t]raditional values, which were considered to be inimical to progress, would have to be changed through modern education . . . and the bonds of the local community would have to be broken so that the outside world could penetrate and impart its bounties."[7]

Stavenhagen reiterates a dynamic we began to explore in chapter 2: those on otherwise opposite sides of the political spectrum often shared an interest in the assimilation of indigenous peoples. As early as the 1920s, for example, some Marxists saw indigenous peoples' desire to maintain their traditional cultural practices as a major factor in their position among the most oppressed peasants. At the same time, their "community-centered, traditional world outlook" was seen to detract from their capacity to become class conscious.[8] In the 1960s, dependency theorists saw "cultural specificity" as "in the interests of the bourgeoisie, or at least its more backward factions, within the framework of underdeveloped and dependent capitalism."[9]

As modern development took shape, states and the indigenous peoples residing in them faced new challenges. Indeed, Stavenhagen notes that the "indigenous problem was an economic problem to be solved by technological change, investments, cash crops, wage labor, profit maximization and the monetarization of the local subsistence economy."[10] Such solutions would ultimately improve Indians' quality of life and ensure that they were not a drain on the state's ability to move forward.[11] International development theory emerging in the 1950s and 1960s called upon states in all parts of the world to help manage indigenous peoples' resources, integrate them into the economy, and transform their social relations.

ILO 107 embodies this approach to development, stating in part that its intent is to "assure the protection of the populations concerned . . . and the improvement of their living and working conditions."[12] Despite the many criticisms of ILO 107, most experts would agree that—though its approach to indigenous development entailed assimilation—its ultimate objective was to provide greater prosperity for indigenous people. As Patrick Thornberry explains, the convention's "intentions appear to have been benign—under the influence of 'indigenist' perspectives rather than indigenous rights."[13]

During the 1970s, indigenous rights advocates increasingly took a critical view of even the seemingly benevolent forms of development, often coupled with a general critique of capitalism. Economic exploitation and cultural extermination were seen as inextricably linked. Some critics went so far as to identify capitalism as a form of "cultural genocide."[14] In the 1980s, Julian Burger argued that the economic impact of development projects served as a catalyst for cultural destruction:

> The displacement and environmental degradation brought about by mining, deforestation, dam-building or unsuitable large-scale farming, may cause hardship; but more importantly, they also sever the vital link between indigenous peoples and their environment. When indigenous peoples are separated from their land, the social and cultural cohesion of their communities is eroded.[15]

Economic development thus had a pernicious effect on culture.

Even when indigenous peoples were not forcibly removed from their land, capitalism required that they have a different relationship to it. Often transforming them into laborers, it alienated them from the work as well as the land. The 2001 UN Report on Relationship to Land explains, "National economic development schemes not only dispossess indigenous peoples of their lands, but also convert indigenous peoples into cheap labourers for industry, because the exploitation of the lands and the environmental degradation have deprived them of their livelihood."[16] The result was loss of indigenous culture—and land.[17]

In this telling, states did not set out to eliminate indigenous culture; they intended to increase development. To the extent that indigenous peoples were in the way, their loss of culture was collateral damage. As Stavenhagen explained in the mid-1980s, "within this functionalist-structuralist viewpoint of development, there is little place for the role of ethnic groups. They are dismissed as remnants of the past, as obstacles to modernization" for which "ethnic attachments would be considered as non-rational, traditional, even conservative."[18]

From another perspective, though, development policies are indicative of what many would today call "structural racism." Stavenhagen, who has used that term in relation to the situation of indigenous peoples,[19] argues that such "neglect" is "not an oversight, but a paradigmatic blindspot" with significant consequences for ethnic groups, particularly minority groups, around the world.[20] These consequences include ethnocide: "The policies of most Latin American governments regarding their own native Indian populations, which are known as *indigenismo* and are couched in the best of intentions and in developmental terminology, are ethnocidal in their content and their expected results."[21]

In any event, indigenous peoples and those involved in indigenous advocacy began to respond directly to development initiatives in the 1970s. As Mario Blaser, Harvey Feit, and Glenn McRae note in the introduction to their book, *In the Way of Development: Indigenous Peoples, Life Projects and Globalization*, it was then that governments launched "grand schemes of development affecting resources and Indigenous peoples in 'peripheral areas,' including, among others, agrarian reform, agricultural coloniza-tion, green revolution schemes, road building, dams, mining, oil exporta-tion and production."[22] Thus, they contend, "the proliferation of Indige-nous advocacy and Indigenous organizations closely matched the internal expansion of many nation-states."[23]

In the 1970s, indigenous peoples had available to them two potential strategies to combat the threat of development. As discussed in chapter 2, they could organize around class—perhaps allying with the Third World in its class-conscious, postcolonial struggles—or they could assert their indig-enous cultural identity. Just as culture-centered arguments prevailed over those based in self-determination in the late 1980s and early 1990s, the focus on cultural identity ultimately won out over class-conscious approaches in the context of development. Of course, as we have seen in previous chap-ters, the struggle between the approaches animated much of the move-ment, particularly in the 1970s and early 1980s, and the boundary between them was and continues to be challenged in a number of ways.

In the case of North America, those who identified with the Fourth World did not do so as much to reject class consciousness as to seek to ensure that their struggle did not become subsumed by cold war politics or other issues facing the Third World. Rudolph Ryser explains part of the impetus behind the assertion of Fourth World identity by George Manuel:

Seeing with his own eyes as he had through years of "political work," George concluded that the First World, Second World and the Third World would not come to the aid of his people. But he had made a profound discovery as a result of his travels to other parts of the world and his visits with other native peoples: "We share the same vision and the same experiences and we are alike in our traditional ways." He learned that the concepts of the "Sacred Four Directions" and the "Sacred Circle" were common to nearly all native peoples he had met.[24]

Thus, the assertion of indigenous identity through the concept of the Fourth World was, as Robin Wright explains, a means "to affirm a specifically indigenous identity as a viable and long-run strategy for liberation, equally viable but distinct from class consciousness."[25]

As discussed in chapter 2, many Latin American indigenous movements emerged out of intense debate over whether cultural identity (as opposed to class alone) was a legitimate basis of organization. Blaser, Feit, and McRae note that some indigenous peoples opted for class-based organizing when that was likely to further their development goals, and thus many founded or joined unions, cooperatives, and political parties active in agrarian reform and related struggles.[26] Such participation was one of many ways that indigenous peoples attempted to mediate the tension between class and cultural identity.

By the 1980s, the move to organize around indigenous identity was strong enough that it had begun to provoke a backlash. Stavenhagen described the opposition at the time:

If at the root of so many ethnic demands we find basic economic grievances, why are these not always expressed in class terms? If tribals or native American Indians or Blacks in the United States or Catholics in Ulster are economically underprivileged or exploited, should not the class struggle and organization along class lines be a better vehicle for political action than ethnic mobilization? This is indeed what some analysts maintain when they suggest that ethnic demands are either a clear-cut instance of 'false consciousness,' or else are simply the object of manipulation by self-interested elites, used to divert the attention of oppressed groups from their real (even if unperceived) class interests.[27]

Although Stavenhagen expresses sympathy for parts of the oppositional position he describes, he nevertheless insists that "it would be too simple to reduce ethnicity to class, just as it is equally simplistic to deny the class factor in so many forms of ethnic struggle." For him, "sometimes, indeed, class interests are better served through ethnopolitics than through social class organization."[28]

Indigenous peoples, of course, were not the only groups to turn to cultural identity. In fact, by the mid-1980s, states in the Third World were invoking a form of identity politics (the lack of which Manuel had bemoaned in the mid-1970s) to respond to technocratic approaches to development economics. As Stavenhagen pointed out then, "the Third World has rallied around the demand for respect of cultural identity, for a development process in harmony with cultural traditions."[29] The difficulty with the approach arose, according to Stavenhagen, because the dominant culture within the Third World is often the only one respected there. In other words, "When Latin Americans affirm, for instance, the primacy of their cultural values over those of materialistic Anglo-Saxon consumer culture . . . they frequently tend to show at the same time complete disregard for the cultural identity of the native Indian societies that inhabit their countries."[30]

CULTURE AS DEVELOPMENT: ETHNODEVELOPMENT

Andrew Gray describes development as "a two-edged sword which can both threaten and offer a future for indigenous peoples."[31] Focusing on the edge that might offer a future, indigenous rights advocates eventually began to appropriate development discourse. In particular, many called for alternative models of development based on the cultural specificities they identified with indigenous knowledge. They often argued for taking advantage of culture, resources, and sustainable attitudes toward the earth to permit indigenous groups to develop in culturally appropriate ways. Some initially hoped that, in the absence of Western-style industrialization, indigenous groups could return to traditional and sustainable livelihoods such as small-scale agriculture, whale hunting, reindeer herding, and fishing from natural habitats.

The use of culture to support indigenous development brings together the indigenous knowledge focus of heritage and the material focus of land. Combined, the two permit culture to flourish by promising to facilitate the economic well-being of indigenous groups while contesting the encroachment and the primacy of modern Western development. Terms for this approach vary. I use "ethnodevelopment" because it is perhaps the most commonly used term, and because it makes explicit the connection between culture and development. Other names for the concept include "development-with-identity," "alternative development," and "self-development."[32] In the indigenous context, "sustainable development" also generally refers to development wed to culture.

Ethnodevelopment has its roots in the 1970s, when indigenous rights advocates began to expose the clash between indigenous rights and modern development models. At that point, to the extent that states and international financial and development institutions responded to the criticism, they simply aimed to temper the impact of development on indigenous peoples. Nevertheless, according to Blaser, Feit, and McRae, the increasing awareness of the clash in the 1970s "helped to open a crack in the so-far solid confidence that progress justified almost everything."[33]

"The Crack": Inclusion of Ethnodevelopment in International Development

The 1970s "crack" that Blaser, Feit, and McRae identify ultimately "was widened with the consolidation in the 1980s of the transnational environmentalist movement," when "the idea that Indigenous peoples have the right to sustain their own life projects received new impetus."[34] The crack also coincided with critiques of neoliberalism, in which the environmental movement played but one part. In general, ethnodevelopment discourse contributed to critiques of neoliberalism by refusing, as Gray puts it, to see "the state and markets as the starting point for development."[35]

Both Gray and Arturo Escobar see as central to this period the 1987 publication of *Our Common Future*, the Brundtland Commission's report commissioned by the UN that, as discussed in chapter 5, connects indigenous peoples with the earth's sustainability because of the unique knowledge that indigenous peoples are thought to have (and often claim to have). This relationship is perhaps nowhere more evident in *Our Common Future* than where the report cites the president of the Native Council of Canada: "Indigenous peoples are the base of what I guess could be called the environmental security system. We are the gate-keepers of success or failure to husband our resources."[36] For Escobar, *Our Common Future* "launched to the world the strategy of sustainable development as the great alternative for the end of the century and the beginning of the next."[37] It attempted to "bring into place" the "new constructions of the social that allow nature's health to be preserved."[38]

The social has since joined the mainstream development discourse—in word, if not fully in deed—as can be seen in the work of international financial institutions. In the second half of the 1990s, for example, the World Bank and other international and regional financial institutions began to turn away from their doctrinaire commitment to neoliberalism, or what had been labeled the "Washington Consensus." This turn was perhaps most clearly manifested in the World Bank's Comprehensive Development Framework (CDF).[39] According to the Bank, the CDF recognized the "interdependence of all elements of development—social, structural, human, governance, environmental, macroeconomic, and financial."[40] More importantly, this interdependence required a shift "from donor-led development assistance strategies to the development of a country strategy led by a country itself, with vigorous participation of government at all levels, including representative institutions, civil society and the private sector, and with the support of multilateral and bilateral organizations."[41]

Since the inauguration of the World Bank's CDF, many documents and programs produced by international and regional financial institutions have highlighted the need to judge development projects not simply by traditional measures of growth, but by their attention to human and social dimensions.[42] A contemporary statement of this ideal can be seen in UN Secretary General Ban Ki-Moon's foreword to the 2008 report on the UN Millennium Development Goals (MDGS): "The MDGS encapsulate the development aspirations of the world as a whole. But they are not only development objectives; they encompass universally accepted human values and rights such as freedom from hunger, the right to basic education, the right to health and a responsibility to future generations."[43]

Even before the CDF was developed, however, efforts to temper the effects of neoliberalism appeared in the World Bank's operations. In 1991, for example, the Bank issued Operational Directive 4.20 (OD 4.20), which it derived in part from ILO 169.[44] The directive states:

> The Bank's broad objective towards indigenous people . . . is to ensure that the development process fosters full respect for their dignity, human rights, and cultural uniqueness. More specifically, the objective at the center of this directive is to ensure that indigenous peoples do not suffer adverse effects during the development process, particularly

from Bank-financed projects, and that they receive culturally compatible social and economic benefits.[45]

It also proclaims that the Bank's policy is that strategies for responding to issues related to indigenous peoples "must be based on the *informed participation* of the indigenous peoples themselves" and calls for, among other things, "incorporation of indigenous knowledge into project approaches."[46]

In the now extensive literature on neoliberalism and identity politics, some disagreement exists about whether identity politics and an eventual focus on human aspects of development constituted a challenge to neoliberalism, or was a conduit for it. The brief history presented above suggests that it was both. As Alvaro Santos and others maintain, the World Bank has no unitary position.[47] Charles Hale discusses how policymakers within the World Bank debated each other vigorously during the 1990s. Rather than a "pitched battle between proponents of incompatible principles: neoliberal modernization on the one hand and indigenous cultural rights on the other," those internal disagreements are more aptly described for Hale by what he terms "neoliberal multiculturalism."[48] As he explains, "proponents of the neoliberal doctrine pro-actively endorse a substantive, if limited, version of indigenous cultural rights, as a means to resolve their own problems and advance their own political agendas."[49]

The lack of unity might account for how Shelton Davis—who, as I noted in chapter 4, was critical of the Inter-American Commission's lack of attention to land and identity in the 1970s—could work on indigenous policy in the World Bank during the design and implementation of OD 4.20 in the early 1990s.[50] Of course, if Hale is right, it also suggests that the directive itself (even in principle) might not have been out of sync with neoliberalism.[51]

Many would contend that even within neoliberal regimes, indigenous peoples are able to find room for meaningful maneuvering. Nina Laurie, Robert Andolina, and Sarah Radcliffe argue that, "while neoliberalism is increasingly setting the social development agenda, in some contexts this occurs in ways that open up spaces for indigenous challenges to, and participation in, local and regional policy implementation."[52] Hale agrees but warns that those new spaces "come with clearly articulated limits," including having "the concessions and prohibitions of neoliberal multiculturalism [themselves] structure the spaces that cultural rights activists occupy."[53] Whether those spaces ultimately limit indigenous autonomy is a question I explore later in this chapter.

Ethnodevelopment in Human Rights Instruments

I discussed in chapter 5 some examples of how indigenous knowledge has been incorporated into international environmental instruments, such as the 1992 Rio Declaration on Environment and Development. In that document, the focus is less on indigenous peoples themselves and more on the ways in which their special knowledge might lead to sustainable development for all of humanity. One article of the declaration, for example, while calling upon states to support indigenous peoples' culture and identity and to enable their participation in development, does so based on their "vital role in environmental management and development because of their knowledge and traditional practices."[54]

Since the late 1980s, human rights documents and jurisprudence regarding indigenous rights also have begun to connect culture and development, although arguably with more of a focus on indigenous peoples for their own sake. Many documents and decisions have enshrined rights or interpretations of rights that sound much like ethnodevelopment. ILO 169, for example, makes culture central to its discussion of development, particularly with regard to vocational training, subsistence economic activity, and education.[55] Its Article 23(1) reads in part: "Handicrafts, rural and community-based industries, and subsistence economy and traditional activities of the peoples concerned, such as hunting, fishing, trapping and gathering, shall be recognised as important factors in the maintenance of their cultures and in their economic self-reliance and development." The article further calls on governments to "ensure that these activities are strengthened and promoted" and to include indigenous peoples in the process. The convention includes similar language in other provisions on training programs, education, and language, although some of those provisions are also aimed at providing skills that will allow indigenous peoples to "participate fully and on an equal footing . . . in the national community" as well as in their own.[56]

In the mid-1990s, the UN Human Rights Committee began to apply the right to culture directly to development, most prominently in two cases brought under the Optional Protocol of the ICCPR that I discussed in chapter 4. One case, brought by traditional Sami reindeer herders, challenged the Finnish government's plans to approve logging that would destroy forests used by the Sami for their traditional economic activities of hunting, fishing, and reindeer husbandry. The other, brought against New Zealand, considered the protection of the Maori's traditional fishing economy from the rapidly expanding fishing industry. In both cases, the committee affirmed that "economic activities may come within the ambit of article 27, if they are an essential element of the culture of an ethnic community."[57] At least in principle, the committee has even interpreted the right to culture to encompass more than development deployed in traditional ways. In fact, its decision in the Maori case regards Article 27 of the convention as a provision that "not only protect[s] traditional means of livelihood of minorities, but allows also for adaptation of those means to the modern way of life and ensuing technology."[58]

Other human rights instruments and institutions have also tied culture to development. For instance, the CERD's General Recommendation on indigenous peoples instructs states to "provide indigenous peoples with conditions allowing for a sustainable economic and social development compatible with their cultural characteristics."[59] The Inter-American Commission and Court have essentially linked development to land and culture through the right to property. In its 2007 decision concerning traditional land rights of the Saramaka in Suriname, which I considered in chapter 4, the Inter-American Court even referenced common Article 1 (on self-determination) of the ICCPR and the ICESCR to conclude that the right to property under the American Convention on Human Rights calls "for the right of members of indigenous and tribal communities to freely determine and enjoy their own social, cultural and economic development, which includes the right to enjoy their particular spiritual relationship with the territory they have traditionally used and occupied."[60]

Finally, the UN Declaration on the Rights of Indigenous Peoples both acknowledges the ways in which modern development has harmed indigenous peoples and calls for development in accordance with traditional practices. The preamble's sixth paragraph, for instance, which the UN Special Rapporteur James Anaya has called the declaration's "basic normative justification,"[61] asserts that "indigenous peoples have suffered from historic injustices as a result of, inter alia, their colonization and dispossession of their lands, territories and resources, thus preventing them from exercising, in particular, their right to development in accordance with their own needs and interests." One article supports ethnodevelopment (and perhaps more), allowing for the right of indigenous peoples "to engage freely in all their traditional and other economic activities."[62]

DARK SIDES

As with the other meanings of culture in the context of indigenous rights, culture as development has achieved relative success in terms of inclusion in international instruments and their interpretation. Moreover, the concept has been mainstreamed into many policies of international financial institutions, so that assistance to states by those institutions—and even free-market reforms at which the assistance is sometimes aimed—are, at least in principle, meant to take into account the needs and interests of indigenous peoples. Ethnodevelopment has appealed to environmentalists and has provided a rubric for considering and promoting sustainable means of development, often based on what are considered to be traditional indigenous understandings of and relationships to the land and the environment.

Culture as development has its dark sides as well. It often limits indigenous peoples' options for development as well as their autonomy over development decisions. If culture as heritage and land displaced an important focus on development, culture as development sometimes does the reverse. Particularly as ethnodevelopment has become mainstreamed, it has overlooked important analyses of heritage and land and the extent to which each is central to indigenous peoples' development struggles. It has also missed the degree to which background distributional inequalities continue to force indigenous peoples to make untenable decisions between development and identity.

Limitations on Development

Perhaps the most obvious critique of ethnodevelopment is that traditional modes of production and subsistence might no longer be feasible options for many of the world's indigenous peoples. This problem is particularly acute for indigenous peoples who have been displaced from their lands or territories. Even if they succeed in reclaiming such lands or are given new territory, it is often difficult—if not impossible—for them to sustain a community around development projects connected to traditional uses.

As William Partridge and Jorge Uquillas explain, "indigenous people have often been relegated to fragile or risk-prone areas in the Andes and Meso-america and due to poverty and inefficient land use practices, the land has been degraded."[63] Similar to the dark side examined in chapter 6 on land use and abuse, indigenous peoples are then often subject to criticism for their treatment of the land, sometimes resulting in the suggestion that they are not real Indians. Partridge and Uquillas are more forgiving than some. For them, "it is important to note that indigenous development strategies and daily practices are not always the best or most sustainable activity. Indigenous knowledge is wise, but not always perfect, just as western knowledge may be faulty."[64]

Even when there is no concern that the land has been degraded, indige-nous communities often struggle to find development projects that fit within a narrow vision of traditional production that is sometimes required for financial support. David Gow follows the development planning of four Nasa communities in the northern department of Cauca, in Colombia. Three have "wrestled with conflicting visions of development" after the communities' destruction by an earthquake in 1994.[65] The communities engaged in the process of planning in accordance with the 1991 Colombian constitution and subsequent legislation, which—while guaranteeing indig-enous peoples' control over their own development—requires that they produce detailed development plans.[66]

Claiming that they do not fit either the "modern" or the "traditional" side of the usual dichotomy, Gow refers to the communities as the "indig-enous inappropriate others in Cauca," meaning communities that "strad-dle both worlds, in a sense belonging to neither yet managing to survive in both."[67] Members of two of the communities explained that their communities were engaged in or aiming for a "solidarity economy," a term that in many ways corresponds to ethnodevelopment. According to Gow, a member of one community outlined "a system of subsistence production involving both reciprocity and redistribution."[68] A member of the other community, which had received a prize from the national gov-ernment for having the best development plan in the country, pointed out that the model involved communal undertakings in a "culturally em-bedded" economy.[69]

Gow contends that this model has not been successful. In one of the communities, for example, even those who support the solidarity economy point out that, while it may be sufficient to provide food and clothing, it is still incapable of providing needed education. In the other community, however, the concept of the solidarity economy has become central to Nasa identity, "in spite of all the empirical evidence to the contrary regarding the nonviability of the local economy."[70]

Noting that these economies are not viable, of course, is not meant as an indictment of the model's logic. Rather, it suggests that the model cannot succeed within the capitalist frame in which people and peoples, indigenous or not, are currently embroiled. This frame dominates the world that Escobar asserts is characterized by the reign of discourses and practices of development that have already "displaced indigenous communities, disrupted peoples' habitats and occupations, and forced many rural societies to increase pressure on the environment."[71]

Limitations on Autonomy

After discussing the nonviability of the local economy in northern Cauca, Gow observes that, "while there is a tendency to essentialize this 'traditional' economy, their development 'message' is clear: the desire to exert *some control* over their lopsided, impoverished local production and marketing system, and at the same time recover certain key social values already lost."[72] Similarly, in her study of Latin American Indian rights movements, Alison Brysk affirms that "cultural survival in the sense of the preservation of precontact, low-technology indigenous cultures is neither viable nor desired by most groups."[73] For her, the important question is "who manages the pace and content of development so that indigenous peoples can exercise self-determination."[74]

The promotion of ethnodevelopment—by indigenous peoples, their advocates, and even international law and institutions—often elides the larger question suggested by Gow and Brysk: Who ultimately has control over development? This question is implicated in at least two contexts. First, what kind of power do or should indigenous peoples have in terms of rejecting or consenting to development projects proposed by private industry or the state? Second, what type of control should they have over their own means of development? In other words, are they, as with the culture as land paradigm, limited to development that is consistent with the sustainability ideals that they and others have put forth?

In both contexts, international instruments have fallen short of granting indigenous peoples anything close to what would be required by a regime of autonomy or self-determination. That is, the development decisions of indigenous peoples are often subject either to government decision-making processes or to pressures about how they can and should live their lives. Laurie, Andolina, and Radcliffe reveal that "ethnodevelopment interprets culture and indigenous identity in ways that make it compatible with neoliberal social policy but potentially restrict indigenous agency, seeing indigenous culture mainly as a means of allocating resources and recognizing beneficiary groups in development projects."[75] What they refer to as "neoliberal social policy," I would contend, is even more central to the post-neoliberal or post–Washington Consensus era, in Kennedy's "chastened neoliberalism" that explicitly takes the social into consideration.

Astrid Ulloa explains that indigenous knowledge and deference to it seem to offer indigenous peoples the autonomy to manage their territories, but in a manner that "is subject to the inclusion of sustainable exploitation projects that make up part of western ideologies."[76] Recall from chapter 6 the attempts by NGOs to teach environmentally friendly farming practices to indigenous peoples living in the Montes Azules region in Chiapas. As indigenous peoples are told that their knowledge is respected, but that they must be taught how to use it, Ulloa sees "a double discourse that entails the permanence of paternalistic and colonialist logics."[77] More important, perhaps, indigenous peoples may have no interest in using the knowledge. As Gow notes in his discussion of the planning process of one of the communities he followed (one that did not articulate a vision of economic solidarity): "Organic farming and the recovery of local crops, particularly various tubers whose production had significantly declined, did not arouse much interest. These reflect a form of Andean nostalgia, felt more by the consultants than the participants."[78]

PRIOR CONSULTATION OR INFORMED CONSENT

Disagreements about the extent to which indigenous peoples should have the right to be consulted on, or even to veto, government decisions affecting indigenous lands have animated much of the drafting and interpretation of international legal instruments. The requirement of prior consultation was included in some early indigenous rights documents. In recent years, advocates have made some progress in pushing for a stronger right—to free, prior, and informed consent.

The issues of consultation and consent arise with regard to the use and ownership of both land and resources. As I discussed in chapter 6, subsurface and mineral rights have typically remained with the state in most Latin American countries, even when collective title to land is granted. International law has generally permitted that arrangement, though recent decisions by the Inter-American Court of Human Rights have begun to challenge it. In many instances, however, indigenous peoples do not possess title to the land, but are simply granted use or occupation rights. In those cases, states maintain the power to grant concessions with regard to natural resources, both above and below the surface. Debates over consultation are often about a state's power to grant such concessions, both with and without meaningful input from the indigenous communities who use the land.

ILO 169, for example, specifically protects the right of states to separate ownership of natural resources and land by allowing them to retain "ownership of mineral or sub-surface resources or rights to other resources pertaining to lands."[79] However, the convention also requires states to consult with the peoples living on the land prior to permitting resource exploitation, and sometimes to compensate them for damage resulting from the exploitation that is permitted:

> Governments shall establish or maintain procedures through which they shall consult these peoples, with a view to ascertaining whether and to what degree their interests would be prejudiced, before undertaking or permitting any programmes for the exploration or exploitation of such resources pertaining to their lands. The peoples concerned shall wherever possible participate in the benefits of such activities, and shall receive fair compensation for any damages which they may sustain as a result of such activities.[80]

More generally (and perhaps in tension with the above), the convention recognizes the right of indigenous peoples "to decide their own priorities for the process of development as it affects their lives, beliefs, institutions and spiritual well-being and the lands they occupy or otherwise use." It also gives them the right to "participate in the formulation, implementation and evaluation of plans and programmes for national and regional development which may affect them directly,"[81] and calls for studies on "the social, spiritual, cultural and environmental impact on them of planned development activities," the results of which "shall be considered as fundamental criteria for the implementation of these activities."[82]

While all of these provisions call for the involvement of indigenous peoples, they stop short of requiring that indigenous peoples themselves have control over the decisions in question. That said, as discussed in chapter 4, the consultation provisions have been relied upon by a number of indigenous rights advocates, partly because the convention itself makes it clear that, in general, the consultations it calls for should not be taken lightly. Rather, they "shall be undertaken, in good faith and in a form appropriate to the circumstances, with the objective of achieving agreement or consent to the proposed measures."[83]

The right to consultation has also taken hold, at least in principle, in the interpretation and application of international instruments. The Human Rights Committee, for example, has effectively read the right to consultation into Article 27 of the ICCPR, though often while finding that the state has met its duties in that regard. In the Maori case mentioned above, for example, the committee recognizes that whether Article 27's guarantees are met "depends on whether members of the minority in question have had the opportunity to participate in the decision-making process in relation to these measures."[84] It then finds against the complainants, a group of individual Maori who contended that the majority of Maori had opposed the settlement that resulted from the state's process, on the ground that the government had engaged in "a complicated process of consultation in order to secure broad Maori support to a nation-wide settlement and regulation of fishing activities."[85] Likewise, in a subsequent decision following a complaint filed by Sami reindeer breeders against Finland, the committee essentially defers to a consultation process in which the complainants "and other key stakeholder groups, were consulted in the evolution of the logging plans drawn up by the Forestry Service, and [in which] the plans were partially altered in response to criticisms from those quarters."[86]

While these Human Rights Committee decisions thus support a right to consultation, the consultation they demand is, at best, relatively weak. At worst, they illuminate how the fact of consultation might be used to legitimize seemingly foreordained state development policies. Anaya attributes the weak form of consultation applied in the case against Finland, as well as in another decision involving the Sami, at least partly to their lack of property rights over the land in question. "It is noteworthy," he remarks, "that in neither case did the Committee consider that the Sämi had property rights in the lands in question in addition to the cultural interests in those lands, in which case a more demanding duty of consultation would at least arguably have applied."[87]

In *Saramaka v. Suriname*, the Inter-American Court of Human Rights appears to have strengthened the right to consultation, even while failing to recognize the exclusive rights of the group to natural resources on its territory. In its decision, the court uses a cultural framework to reiterate that indigenous and tribal peoples are entitled to "the right to own the natural resources they have traditionally used within their territory for the same reasons that they have a right to own the land they have traditionally used and occupied for centuries. Without them, the very physical and cultural survival of such peoples is at stake."[88] The court then tempers what at first sounds like a far-ranging claim, even if restricted to natural resources that have been "traditionally used." After conceding "that all exploration and extraction activity in the Saramaka territory could affect, to a greater or lesser degree, the use and enjoyment of some natural resource traditionally used for the subsistence of the Saramakas," the court makes it clear "that Article 21 [recognizing the right to property] of the Convention should not be interpreted in a way that prevents the State from granting any type of concession for the exploration and extraction of natural resources within Saramaka territory."[89]

The Inter-American Court subsequently discusses the safeguards required of the state before engaging in large-scale development projects that involve the Saramaka lands. In short, "if the State wants to restrict, legitimately, the Saramakas' right to communal property, it must consult with the communities affected by the development or investment project planned within territories which they have traditionally occupied, reasonably share the benefits with them, and complete prior assessments of the environmental and social impact of the project."[90] It notes the Human Rights Committee's decision regarding the Maori, but suggests that more is demanded of states than what might appear there. It requires, for example, that the consultation be done in conformity with the traditions and customs of the group, and that it be conducted in good faith and in early stages of development.[91]

Of course, what constitutes good-faith and prior consultation has been

an ongoing subject of debate and litigation. Even when states have enforced—at least formally—the right to consultation, it is not clear that
such consultations have been enforced or led to any difference in outcome. The Colombian Constitutional Court, for example, has found prior
consultation, in both substance and form, to be a fundamental right of
indigenous peoples.[92] Yet, a recent report by the UN special rapporteur on
indigenous rights finds that the failure of prior consultation is a "persistent
problem" in Colombia, and faults the government for failing to demonstrate that its consultations have been carried out properly.[93]

Many indigenous rights advocates have thus begun to call for free,
prior, and informed consent rather than consultation. The *Saramaka* decision is again a victory in that it calls for just that, at least in certain
circumstances. Specifically, "regarding large-scale development or investment projects that would have a major impact within Saramaka territory,
the State has a duty, not only to consult with the Saramakas, but also to
obtain their free, prior, and informed consent, according to their customs
and traditions."[94] The court cites a report of the UN special rapporteur and
the CERD's Concluding Observations on Ecuador to support the injunction
that large-scale projects require consent. With regard to the latter, the
CERD observes that simply consulting indigenous communities before exploiting the subsoil resources of their traditional lands "falls short of
meeting the requirements set out in the Committee's general recommendation 23 on the rights of indigenous peoples. The Committee therefore
recommends that the prior informed consent of these communities be
sought."[95]

The *Saramaka* decision also cites the UN Declaration, then recently
passed, for its provisions on consent and consultation. The declaration calls
upon states to "consult and cooperate in good faith with the indigenous
peoples concerned . . . in order to obtain their free and informed consent
prior to the approval of any project affecting their lands or territories and
other resources, particularly in connection with the development, utilization or exploitation of mineral, water or other resources."[96] While the
inclusion of the consent language was one of the reasons given by Canada
for opposing the final version of the declaration—contending that it would
give indigenous peoples veto power over development projects[97]—the
right is in fact watered down from the 1993 draft originally submitted by the
Working Group. The first part of the same provision in the earlier draft

reads: "Indigenous peoples have the right to determine and develop priorities and strategies for the development or use of their lands, territories and other resources, including the right to require that States obtain their free and informed consent prior to the approval" of any such project.[98] Consent was required in the original version; it is arguably only the aim of consultation in the final version.[99] Nevertheless, the UN Declaration is seen to have "strengthened [the] case" of those who argue for consent as the standard.[100]

The World Bank has arguably strengthened its consultation requirements. In 2005, it replaced OD 4.20 with Operational Policy 4.10 (OP 4.10), which provides that, before agreeing to finance projects affecting indigenous peoples, "the Bank requires the borrower to engage in a process of free, prior, and informed consultation" that *results in broad community support to the project by the affected Indigenous Peoples.*" The latter language could be read to call for something close to consent, though the policy clarifies in a footnote that it does not "constitute a veto rights."[101]

Of course, the question remains whether states and institutions like the World Bank will take seriously the requirements for either prior consultation or consent. Critics have, for example, long pointed to the World Bank's lack of will to enforce its operational policies on these matters, leading to some skepticism about OP 4.10.[102]

Beyond the practical concern about enforcement are other worries. If, at the end of the day, consultation or consent is grounded in the protection of culture, that consultation or consent might be limited in terms of its ability to attend to economic inequalities and other forms of discrimination. As Ariel Dulitzky argues with regard to the *Saramaka* case:

> Although at the end the Court demanded in both scenarios prior consultation, shared benefits, and studies on environmental and social impact, the distinction of concessions to exploit natural resources depending on their traditional or nontraditional uses rather than on the economic, social, or political value of those natural resources, opens up the possibility of different levels of protections. This distinction is made exclusively as a consequence of protecting the territories based upon their cultural value and significance rather than considering the economic, political or anti-discriminatory aspects of these territorial claims.[103]

Moreover, even consent requirements assume that indigenous peoples are in a position to make meaningful choices. The next subsection discusses the ways in which such choices are significantly restricted.

CONTROL OVER INDIGENOUS DEVELOPMENT PROJECTS

Much of the previous section was concerned with the power that indigenous peoples have to respond to or participate in the national or regional development plans for the areas in which their traditional lands are located. But what about their own development, whether local, community-based initiatives or joint enterprises with entities involved in megadevelopment projects?

International legal documents, World Bank policies, and the laws of many states generally assume—partly as a result of the ethnodevelopment strategies pursued by indigenous peoples and environmentalists—that indigenous peoples will engage in eco-friendly development. Accordingly, they often provide for environmental protection of indigenous lands, at least against certain types of encroachment. In ILO 169, for instance, governments commit to "take measures, in co-operation with the peoples concerned, to protect and preserve the environment of the territories they inhabit."[104] Similarly, the UN Declaration stipulates that "indigenous peoples have the right to the conservation and protection of the environment and the productive capacity of their lands or territories and resources."[105]

These and similar provisions in domestic law, however, potentially put the brakes on forms of unsustainable development by indigenous peoples themselves. Once a particular territory is legally recognized as that of an indigenous community, governments often restrict the extent and ways in which the land can be used. At one level, such restrictions are a victory; indeed, they are precisely what many environmentalists and indigenous activists demanded, and were even the focal point of the alliance between those groups. Yet the restrictions sometimes come back to haunt indigenous peoples in many of the ways discussed in chapter 6. It is suspicious if indigenous groups attempt to engage in economic activities that are not sustainable, even if they have few other opportunities for development. Thus, both their self-identity claims and their autonomy are threatened.

At some level, the recent decision by the Inter-American Court in the *Saramaka* case and the concluding observations on Ecuador by the CERD that were cited in that case, resist such restrictions by recognizing the right of communities to share equitably in the benefits of major exploitation activities on their traditionally owned lands.[106] Paradoxically, they thus provide incentives for indigenous and tribal communities to consent to the same types of activities that have long been responsible for the destruction of their lands and resources, and for their inability to engage in ethnodevelopment.

A case involving the Skull Valley Band of Goshute Indians in Utah provides an example of the difficult choices indigenous communities sometimes face with regard to development. In the early 1990s, the band became engaged in an internal struggle over whether to accept an offer by Private Fuel Storage (PFS), a consortium of electric utility companies, to put a temporary nuclear waste storage site on its reservation. Although some members opposed the site as potentially endangering their land and well-being, the incentives for the tribe to enter into the agreement with PFS were significant. As David Keller, who has made the case the subject of a study for teaching ethics, noted in the *Salt Lake Tribune* in December 2002: "Presently, only 125 Skull Valley Goshute remain, and the 30 living on the reservation have virtually no economic opportunities. Thus it is no surprise that [tribal chairman Leon] Bear would be interested in reaping the benefits of the proposed $3 billion nuclear repository project."[107]

A number of Utah legislators and environmentalists argued against the contract, largely on the basis of environmental hazards. The governor of Utah at the time publicly stated his own concerns—with the risks of exposure and with the housing of nuclear waste not produced in Utah. He also worried that, despite that the contract was for a temporary site, the storage site might nevertheless become permanent.[108]

Goshutes who favored the plan, however, argued that U.S. federal law's recognition of Indian sovereignty trumped any environmental or state laws that might otherwise restrict the project. According to Keller, some Utah politicians responded to these arguments by describing "American Indian sovereignty as 'un-American.'" Keller reads it differently: "Taken in context, however, the plan appears to be very American: The Goshute are simply beating capitalists at our own game."[109]

Goshutes who opposed the contract urged the tribe to assert its sovereignty by refusing pressure to enter into the contract. For many, the very future of indigenous lands was at stake. Margene Bullcreek, a Goshute living near the proposed site, for example, led a grass-roots campaign against the contract, explaining that it "is not an economic salvation when in fact it might be the ruin of our land" and that "it's about being in harmony with our creator, and showing Him we do not wish to spoil His gift to us."[110] A number of other Indian tribes joined the opposition to the waste site on similar grounds, seeing the right to reject such sites as a manifestation of tribal sovereign power. The National Environmental Coalition of Native Americans, for example, mobilized to encourage tribes to pass laws establishing nuclear-free zones. Such laws would "offer a legal avenue for tribal governments to assert their sovereign rights to block unwanted nuclear facilities."[111]

When, in 2006—nearly a decade after the initial application was filed—the Nuclear Regulatory Commission granted the license to build the site, it appeared that those Goshutes who favored the plan had succeeded. In the end, however, the victory appears to have been short-lived; the Indians might not be permitted to be so capitalistic.

Several months after the license was granted, two agencies within the U.S. Department of Interior—the Bureau of Land Management (BLM) and the Bureau of Indian Affairs (BIA)—denied applications necessary to facilitate the construction. The BLM refused the right of way for a rail line requested by PFS, on the grounds that the line would cross a protected wilderness area and that the environmental impact statement had failed to consider the impact of moving nuclear waste from one site to another.[112] The BIA reversed its conditional approval of the agreement in 1997 on a variety of grounds.[113] The *New York Times* reported at the time (though before all the bases for denial had been stated) that "the Interior Department said that acting as a 'prudent' trustee of Indian lands, it could 'derive no confidence from the public record' that there would be someplace for the fuel ultimately to go."[114]

An association of members of the Skull Valley Band who opposed the facility petitioned, along with the State of Utah, for judicial review of the decision. In 2007, the Court of Appeals considering the case decided to hold it in abeyance because neither PFS nor the Skull Valley Band had formally challenged the denials by the BIA and the BLM, and it was "speculative whether the project will ever be able to proceed."[115]

It could of course be argued—and indeed was argued—that PFS was taking advantage both of the dire economic need of the Goshutes and of federal law, which it thought would give the Goshutes greater rights than nonsovereign entities to enter into such agreements. Still, attempts by the state and federal governments to limit the band's autonomy in this regard seem problematic.

Would international law support the right of Indian tribes to move forward with such an agreement? The UN Declaration specifically addresses hazardous waste storage on Indian lands. In fact, its provision on the issue is the only one that unequivocally grants indigenous peoples the power of the veto on development projects. Article 29, which names the right of indigenous peoples "to the conservation and protection of the environment and the productive capacity of their lands or territories and resources," also provides that "states shall take effective measures to ensure that no storage or disposal of hazardous materials shall take place in the lands or territories of indigenous peoples without their full, prior and informed consent."[116] The declaration remains silent, however, on whether states might altogether prohibit the use of indigenous lands for hazardous waste disposal, even if the indigenous peoples who occupy the lands attempt to enter into such an arrangement.

This dilemma is in many ways similar to that presented by alienation of land. Indigenous groups sometimes make different decisions from that made by the Goshute band, concluding that it might be better not to have the option to destroy their communal land arrangements or ecological well-being. But consent assumes they have a choice. As with consultation, it can be used to legitimize state decisions.

Land Displacement

As ethnodevelopment has become accepted, perhaps even expected, by international law and financial institutions, questions remain as to how it might be put into practice. What does the World Bank mean, for example, when it says it has agreed to "mainstream" ethnodevelopment in a particular policy or project? What role do indigenous heritage and land play in such mainstreaming?

Partridge and Uquillas contend that "the main condition for ethnodevelopment is secure land tenure."[117] At some level, the World Bank has agreed. The 1991 OD 4.20, for example, calls on the Bank to assist states in "establishing legal recognition of the customary or traditional land tenure systems of indigenous peoples."[118] Moreover, "where the traditional lands of indigenous peoples have been brought by law into the domain of the state and where it is inappropriate to convert traditional rights into those of legal ownership, alternative arrangements should be implemented to grant long-term, renewable rights of custodianship and use to indigenous peoples."[119] The World Bank's 2005 revision of that policy, OP 4.10, affirms these same basic tenets.[120] Although, as I have already suggested, both OD 4.20 and OP 4.10 are certainly subject to criticism on a number of grounds, the point I would like to make for the moment is that when discussing indigenous peoples specifically, the World Bank has directed itself to attend to the importance of indigenous land rights for development.

(That same attention, however, seems to be missing from the Bank's work on poverty reduction) According to Maarten H. J. van den Berg, in its assessment of poverty and the needs of indigenous peoples in Latin America, the Bank has largely divorced development from access to land. Focusing on the Bank's 1994 survey on poverty, entitled *Indigenous People and Poverty in Latin America*, van den Berg notes that, although it shows "pervasive and severe" poverty among the indigenous population and connects poverty to lack of "human capital," it merely proposes better and more education as the best means of alleviating poverty.[121]

While not denying the importance of education, van den Berg faults the survey for "ignor[ing] the highly unequal distribution of arable land in the region," despite the focus on land in the World Bank's own indigenous policy. The failure to consider unequal distribution of land, however, is not unique to this survey. According to van den Berg, "later work published by the World Bank and other major development agencies, notably the Inter-American Development Bank (IDB), utterly dismissed land reforms as a means to overcome poverty in Latin America."[122] In fact, the IDB, at least according to one of its consultants in 2000, has supported "more open and flexible land markets in the interest of poverty alleviation and agricultural efficiency—despite the fact that this can lead to some land concentration."[123] Van den Berg connects this position to the IDB's strong commitment to sustained economic growth as the "only 'path out of poverty' " and to its—and the World Bank's—promotion of "the cultivation of cut flowers and other so-called 'non traditional agricultural exports.' "[124]

Van den Berg discusses the focus of the World Bank's OD 4.20 on land in order to argue that the difficulty is not that the World Bank never sees land as important to indigenous policy, but that its poverty analysts have somehow missed its importance. Thus, his analysis demonstrates how a discussion of poverty elimination and development can displace issues of land, similar to the way I argued that a focus on culture as land can miss development. Given my earlier discussion about how the World Bank is not a monolithic entity, however, I am not as surprised about this result as van den Berg seems to be. As Santos explains in the context of rule of law projects, the Bank's "hodge-podge" approach "enables different and often conflicting projects to be pursued under the same agenda."[125] Unfortunately, just as such an approach can open space for creative and progressive thinking (for example, Shelton Davis's participation in the implementation of OD 4.20), it can also close it off.

Challenges to Identity, Reinforcement of Development

(As with culture as land, culture as development often depends upon and requires an ongoing link between economic activity and traditional means of livelihood.) In its contemporary incarnation, ethnodevelopment does not necessarily reject modernity, and—for the most part—international institutions have not held indigenous peoples who claim the right to development to premodern standards of subsistence. As mentioned earlier, for example, the Human Rights Committee has granted protection for modernized group activity, as long as the modernization is connected to a historically traditional way of life.

As discussed above with regard to consultation and consent, most indigenous rights advocates argue that indigenous peoples are entitled to control over their means of development. They contend that, rather than being consulted about development projects, their consent should be sought. In terms of their own development, with the possible exception of entering into agreements that are destructive of their land or the environment, control seems to be key. Partridge and Uquillas write: "The general consensus among indigenous leaders, advocates, scholars, and practitioners is that genuine development is an autonomous process representing a community's vision of its history, its values, and its future goals as it seeks for a better quality of life."[126] To these authors, ethnodevelopment means precisely "those processes which are defined by and controlled by the indigenous peoples themselves as they seek better lives for their communities in the face of increasing poverty and social disintegration."[127] In this vision, autonomy is paramount.

The question remains: What if indigenous groups want to engage in development activities that have nothing to do with traditional cultures? Or, to put it another way, if indigenous groups are entitled to autonomy, why should anyone outside the group have a say over how they choose to develop? I began to address this question above when I discussed economic arrangements with the nuclear waste industry. I want to study here a case that is more benign environmentally, but that still raises the issue of what or who is the subject of protection in indigenous rights advocacy. Is it the culture, the people, or the peoples?

With the passage of the Indian Gaming Regulatory Act (IGRA) in 1988, the United States attempted to regulate the indigenous high-stakes gaming industry that had begun to emerge in the late 1970s.[128] That act seems to support the view that, at least with regard to recognized tribes, economic development is more important than an insistence on a cultural tie to the form of subsistence. IGRA permits Indian tribes, within limits—including some determined by the state in which the tribe is located[129]—to run gaming operations as a means to facilitate economic development. Although it is thought that some games might actually be "traditional," thereby earning special protection,[130] the vast majority of profits from gaming are generated by casinos. Naomi Mezey has argued that IGRA has, somewhat paradoxically, functioned to assist in the creation or reclamation of indigenous identity for those tribes that are least cohesive or traditional, and in the demise of culture or cohesion in those tribes that are the most traditional.[131] Indeed, some tribes, like the Hopi and Navajo, have refused to take advantage of the act because of concerns over the assimilative effects of gaming, as well as religious objections to it. Other tribes have responded to these and other concerns, such as about economic feasibility, by operating off-reservation casinos on lands purchased for such purposes. In at least one case, tribes offered to cede potential claims to ancestral lands in exchange for the right to purchase such land.[132]

Jessica Cattelino has studied the impact of gaming on the Florida Seminole's ability "to maintain politically and culturally distinct values under new economic conditions."[133] In *High Stakes*, she considers the Seminole's strikingly successful casino industry in the context of decades of failed economic development projects that had sought to combat poverty, including those based on cultural tourism and the production of traditional crafts. When the tribe decided to sell tobacco in the mid-1970s, it used arguments about tribal sovereignty (in the U.S. sense of the word which, as I discussed in chapter 1, means that Native American sovereignty is subject to the plenary powers of Congress) to negotiate an agreement with the State of Florida to permit them to open the shops. Although the Seminole were heavily criticized by indigenous and nonindigenous people alike for "selling out," Cattelino seems to agree with Stephen Cornell and Joseph Kalt, who contend that "the key to economic development 'success' is not the form of economic activity but whether it is 'self-determined economic development' that is controlled by tribes."[134] Many of the issues raised with regard to selling tobacco followed the Seminole into their decisions to open casinos.

(With this example of gaming, I do not mean to suggest that the United States has recognized anything close to the type of autonomy that many indigenous groups claim. Rather, I simply aim to illustrate that the government has permitted, in some instances, economic development in ways that make little pretension to be connected to traditional ways of life. Nor do I want to suggest that all tribes have achieved economic success (in fact, most have not[135]), or even that economic success premised on a notion of sovereignty has not encountered many of the dark sides we have seen before. As Cattelino puts it: "Poverty symbolically structures indigeneity in the contemporary United States, making a 'rich Indian' an oxymoron to many—a signal of corruption, cultural loss, or values gone awry—and a threat to some."[136] Considering the historical friction between these dominant sociocultural conceptions of American Indians and those found in federal policy and endorsed by at least some members of the U.S. Supreme Court, Cattelino writes that "gaming brings into relief a double bind of tribal sovereignty: American Indians enjoy political autonomy under conditions of economic development, but indigenous economic power undermines their political status."[137]

I would like to focus here on the extent to which the goal of preserving cultural identity has been divorced from at least the legal justification for the economic activity. U.S. constitutional and federal statutory arrangements create a particular form of sovereignty—not independent statehood in the postcolonial sense and not based on a right to culture—that structure the relationship by which recognized American Indian tribes are not subject to state taxation and business regulations. They can therefore, as Cattelino explains, "enjoy competitive advantage in sectors including high-stakes gaming and the sale of highly taxed and regulated commodities, such as tobacco, alcohol, gasoline, and fireworks."[138]

Does the indigenous promise of development ultimately require the abandonment of the assertion of cultural identity? If so, at what cost?

Challenges to Development, Reinforcement of Identity

In the mid-1990s, the development paradigm began to be challenged from both the right and the left. Kennedy explains that as the center pursued a chastened neoliberalism, the right "increasingly . . . sense[d] that development may not be possible or appropriate" and used "a vocabulary of security and political realism . . . and cultural clash [to replace] development as a framework for discussing third world societies." "On the left," he continues, "one finds a parallel resistance to the cultural disruptions of economic development and enthusiasm for cultural and ecological preservation."[139] What was either an "absent" or a "rising counterpoint" position on the left (Kennedy leaves this question open) includes the following: "localism, antiglobalism, revival [of] dependency theory [and] import substitution, focus on distribution, fair trade [as] free trade's destiny."[140] This new left position both follows from and contrasts somewhat with the left critique during neoliberalism, which, for Kennedy, has been "largely absent."

Escobar's *Encountering Development* (1995), though principally a poststructuralist critique of development, is in many ways representative of this new left critique of the development paradigm. Escobar's book considers the history and trajectory of development discourse and its grip on the political imagination, before ending with a call to explore "alternatives to development" and to imagine a postdevelopment world.[141] Powerfully and convincingly critical of the then-recent mainstreaming of arguments for sustainable, or "alternative," development, Escobar insists: "To think about alternatives in the manner of sustainable development . . . is to remain within the same model of thought that produced development and kept it in place."[142]

In the conclusion to *Encountering Development*, entitled "Imagining a Postdevelopment Era," Escobar stresses the importance of a focus on cultural difference while drawing a distinction between alternative development and alternatives to development:

At the bottom of the investigation of alternatives lies the sheer fact of cultural difference. Cultural differences embody—for better or for worse, this is relevant to the politics of research and intervention— possibilities for transforming the politics of representation, that is, for transforming social life itself. Out of hybrid or minority cultural situations might emerge other ways of building economies, of dealing with basic needs, of coming together in social groups. The greatest political promise of minority cultures is their potential for resisting and subverting the axiomatic of capitalism and modernity in their hegemonic form.[143]

This conclusion can be read in part as a call to find living examples of postdevelopment alternatives, and Escobar and others have since written or identified ethnographies of minority cultures that appear to demonstrate such possibility for resistance. Escobar's 2008 *Territories of Difference*, which I discuss later in this chapter and rely on in some detail in chapter 8, offers one example.

I find surprising Escobar's discussion of the treatment and co-optation of sustainable development in the bulk of *Encountering Development*, on one hand, and his belief in the transformative promise of cultural difference in the conclusion, on the other hand. Much of my analysis above is meant to show the ways in which ethnodevelopment (based on a model of cultural difference) and sustainable development were in fact conflated, and were proposed and accepted by many as alternative forms of development, often as part of a deliberate strategy. Indigenous peoples and their advocates have participated greatly in this conflation, and they have—for the most part—based their claims for the right to development on the cosmovision reflected in their traditional practices and relationship to land. How one (sustainable development) would simply perpetuate modern development while the other (cultural difference as development) would provide a challenge to it is not altogether clear. In fact, a statement near the end of the penultimate chapter of *Encountering Development* rings true for me with regard to both:

Nothing has really changed at the level of the discourse, even if perhaps the conditions for its continued reproduction have been altered. "Development" continues to reverberate in the social imaginary of states, institutions, and communities, perhaps more so after the inclusion of women, peasants, and nature into its repertoire and imaginative geographies.[144]

This observation provides an apt critique of much that I have described thus far.

As Escobar and others have searched for evidence that capitalism and neoliberalism are subverted by local knowledge, they have often found that indigenous and minority cultures provide less of a challenge to those ideologies than might have been hoped. The surprise might not be that indigenous peoples, for example, engage in communal economic arrangements, but that they continue to see the need for capitalism and wage labor. Gaming might be the extreme example (although Indian gaming establishments are communally owned), but the prevalence of, or at least the desire for, hybrid economies over the past decade or so provides the more telling lesson.

Recall Gow's discussion of the community that followed the idea of economic solidarity but found the model insufficient to provide for more than its immediate needs. According to the former leader of the community, who was also an economics student, community members had found it necessary to participate in the market economy, for which they were not well prepared. They were day laborers, middlemen, and small businessmen. Although the former leader hoped for a "mixed economy, combining the better elements of both systems," he "predicted that all vestiges of this solidarity economy would disappear in the next decade."[145] Gow notes this leader's prescience, for the community "was in the process of modernizing, of accepting development discourse at face value."[146]

Similarly, Gray considers a disagreement among the Arakmbut over the building of a road across their territory in Peru. While most community members opposed the road, they did so because they feared that it would provide a means for colonists to enter their territory and exploit their resources. Others, however, pointed to the ways that the road might be useful for them, particularly for exporting produce. Seeing some points of agreement, Gray explains, "the Arakmbut are not opposed to development, only to those aspects which they cannot control and which threaten their communal resources."[147] They do want development (even though they do not have a word in their language for it) in order "to supplement their subsistence activities." They seek to develop not for the sake of growth, Gray insists, but to perpetuate "a form of reciprocity which could provide the means to make life easier."[148] The Arakmbut approach, as Gray sees it, is "both an alternative development and an alternative to development."[149]

Escobar himself has spent much of the past decade considering a social movement of Afro-descendants along Colombia's Pacific coast, a subject to which I devote chapter 8 of this book. His hope for the movement is articulated in the endnote to the penultimate paragraph of *Encountering Development*. In that paragraph, Escobar generally describes Third World groups whose strategies revolve around "the defense of cultural difference, not as a static but as a transformed and transformative force; and the valorization of economic needs and opportunities that are not strictly those of profit and the market."[150] The endnote explains that he is referencing "the organization of black communities in the Pacific Coast region of Colombia . . . Their social movement is framed by large-scale government plans for the 'sustainable development' of the region . . . capitalist pressures for control of the land . . . and a political opening for the defense of minority rights, territories and cultures."[151]

Thirteen years later, with the publication of *Territories of Difference*, a tour de force study of this same social movement, Escobar seems to have tempered his claims about the extent to which paradigms of development and modernity are circumvented by Afro-Colombian communities. At the same time, he places less emphasis on the need to provide alternatives to development. He instead rearticulates the idea of postdevelopment, noting that it "could be restated today in terms of the construction of forms of globality that, while engaging with modernity, are not necessarily modernizing or developmentalist, precisely because they are built from the colonial difference."[152] He encourages social movements, along with academics and policy makers who study them, to

> hold in tension three coexisting processes and political projects: *alternative development*, focused on food security, the satisfaction of basic needs, and the well-being of the population; *alternative modernities*, building on the countertendencies effected on development interventions by local groups and toward the contestation of global designs; and *alternatives to modernity*, as a more radical and visionary project of redefining and reconstructing local and regional worlds from the per-

spective of practices of cultural, economic and ecological difference, following a network logic in contexts of power.[153]

He then applies this analysis to several Afro-Colombian development and political projects in the Pacific region to emphasize that "alternative development, alternative modernities, and alternatives to modernity are partially conflicting but complementary projects."[154] In other words, he appears to see subversive potential even in the first two, not solely in the third.

In his chapter on capital, Escobar considers the possibility that some hybrid economic models or entrepreneurship using capital might even "be a tool against the capitalization of subjectivity," particularly if they are "place-based."[155] In considering the noncapitalist potential of communal shrimp farming by Afro-Colombians, for example, he notes: "It is a different subjectivity that utters the 'if they can do it, why can't we' without meaning that theirs is going to be a business of the same kind."[156] Escobar calls for an "antiessentialist view of the economy," because it "makes visible noncapitalist practices and leads to a rethinking of production from cultural and ecological perspectives."[157] That said, he adds a lengthy endnote discussing what would need to be further analyzed over a number of years with the shrimp farming examples he offers, to determine whether in fact they fit into the "noncapitalist" category.[158] It is a curious endnote, which belies the certainty expressed in the heading for the discussion: "Beyond Capital: Collective Shrimp Farming as Noncapitalist Practice."[159]

Escobar's appeal to keep alternative development and alternative modernities in tension with alternatives to modernity serves to leave open the question of the extent to which many place-based practices have subversive potential. Escobar considers a number of economic development projects throughout the book, and nearly always questions implicitly or explicitly whether they are evidence of radicalism or of cooptation. After discussing the role that small farmers—as opposed to large agro-business—play in oil palm cultivation in the Pacific coast region, for example, he asks (without answering) the following question: "How is one to gauge the completeness or incompleteness of capitalist development, avoiding the extreme of seeing capital everywhere without falling into the trap of seeing resistance everywhere?"[160]

What has been constant for Escobar is the importance of territory and place-based, localized politics in even imagining alternatives. In 1998, he used the declaration of principles that had emerged from the 1993 National Conference of Black Communities in Colombia to further explore the ethnocultural approach he saw as guiding the movement:

> This declaration of principles already suggested a particular reading of the socioeconomic and political situation of the Pacific Coast region as a strategic ethnic and ecological unit, with the concomitant emphasis placed on cultural difference and the defense of the territory. It underlies an ethnocultural approach based on the reconstruction of cultural difference as a means to lessening ecological, socioeconomic, and political forms of domination. For the ethnocultural process, the movement needs to be built on the basis of broad demands for territory, identity, autonomy, and the right to its own vision of development and the future. Similarly, ethnocultural activists espouse a view of blackness that goes well beyond issues of skin color and the racial aspects of identity.[161]

In the introduction to *Territories of Difference*, Escobar continues to explain the centrality of place to his analysis: "Black and Indigenous movements see the aim of their struggle as one of retaining control of their territory; it is not far-fetched to see these movements as expressions of ecological and cultural attachment to place."[162] For Afro-Colombian activists, he later puts it, "biodiversity equals territory plus culture."[163]

Control over development and over territory on which to exercise that control thus come together in Escobar's postdevelopment world (in both his current and former articulation of postdevelopment). But they combine with the assertion or reconstruction of cultural, or what he now prefers to call colonial, difference (which he has always insisted is not essentialist).

Why is the requirement of cultural difference—an ingredient that was largely missing from, or at least not emphasized in, the American Indian gaming story—so important for Escobar? In the early days at least, it seems that he saw the promise of Afro-Colombian and similar movements as much in their interaction with and critique of the biodiversity frame that had become mainstreamed in development discourse as in their potential critique of unfettered capitalism. As he noted in 1998 after a discussion of the many tensions already existing within the Afro-Colombian movement: "Despite its precariousness, its articulation of a link between culture, nature, and development constitutes an alternative political ecology framework for biodiversity discussions. The movement can be seen as an attempt to show that social life, work, nature, and culture can be organized differently than dominant models of culture and the economy mandate."[164]

In this telling, the end or chastening of neoliberalism would call for increased attention to cultural difference. Recall Kennedy's typology, in which localism and antiglobalism are two responses from the left to a chastened neoliberalism. If that characterization is correct, assertions of cultural identity—at least subaltern cultural identity (or colonial difference)—become even more important in the post–Washington Consensus era than before. But are these assertions sustainable? Might it be time for them also to be chastened?

Even antiessentialist thinkers like Escobar, I would argue, sometimes rely too much on the paradigm-shifting power of local, identity-based social movements and often overstate (or overdesire) their potential for resistance in a world in which their options are in fact quite limited. As I will discuss more fully in chapter 8, the Colombian government has used disagreements among and within black communities over appropriate means of development as a partial excuse for its failure to implement the specific development mechanisms included in a 1993 law that grants the communities the right to collective land title. As Escobar himself acknowledges in his latest book, the political ecology frame of the Afro-Colombian movement has been difficult to sustain in a state where, due to violence and ongoing neoliberal policies of development (among other things), "a crude form of capitalist modernity seems to have been entrenched once again."[165] Perhaps—whether intentionally or not—Escobar's recent work suggests that we have as much to learn from the difficulties of sustaining a vision or practice of ethnodevelopment as we do from its potential challenges to the center or right. Yet few have pursued that line.

If neoliberalism could tolerate and even thrive upon culture as heritage, perhaps the post–Washington Consensus era of development can adjust not only to cultural rights, but also to communal property and a certain (if limited) amount of territory and autonomy based on indigenous or indigenous-like identity. That is, the center (if not the right) can share with the left the (local and anti-global) idea that indigenous peoples are situated to be the stewards, not only of the environment but also of noncapitalist economies. Therein lies much of my concern: If the left puts its hope in the margins, relegating to the margins its challenges to the center, I fear it will keep the challenges marginalized. Not only does such a focus place a heavy burden on those situated at the margins, it facilitates the center's legitimization of its admittedly chastened neoliberal development or modernity enterprise, perhaps keeping at bay larger structural questions about the distribution of power and resources.

PART III

Indigenous Models in Other Contexts

THE CASE OF AFRO-COLOMBIANS

CULTURE AS HERITAGE, LAND, AND DEVELOPMENT

The apparent "invisibility" of black people in Colombia, for example, has not been due to a simple process of discrimination—indians have, if anything, suffered even greater discrimination—but due to the precise mode of their insertion into the structures of alterity. They have not been institutionalized as Others in the same way that indians have. Interestingly, however, there has been a relatively recent appearance of blacks on the public political stage in Colombia, Brazil and Nicaragua where constitutional measures recognise the special status of blacks. In some sense, this corresponds to a relocation of "blackness" in structures of alterity in ways that make it look increasingly like "indianness."—PETER WADE, *RACE AND ETHNICITY IN LATIN AMERICA*, 1997[1]

The purpose of this law is to recognize the right to collective property of the black communities that have been occupying *tierras baldías* [empty or unused land] in the river-side rural zones of the rivers of the Pacific Basin in accordance with their traditional practices of production . . . Likewise it has as its purpose to establish mechanisms for the protection of the cultural identity and the rights of the black communities of Colombia as an ethnic group and the fostering of their social and economic development, with the end of guaranteeing that these communities obtain a real position of equality of opportunities in relationship to the rest of Colombian society.—COLOMBIA, LAW 70, 1993[2]

In 1991, Colombia replaced its 1886 constitution, which had been the longest-lasting constitution in Latin America. The new constitution followed the trends of multiculturalism and decentralization that were taking hold in much of Latin

America—enumerating individual rights, guaranteeing collective rights for indigenous and Afro-descendant communities,[3] and moving centers of fiscal power from the national to the municipal level. This combination of neoliberal decentralization and pluricultural citizenship resulted, as Karl Offen notes, from "a wide constellation of internal and external forces, including bottom-up localized pressures for social change and top-down global pressures for political-economic reform."[4] The resulting new document broke from the ideology of indigenismo that had constructed politics in much of Latin America for decades. As Eduardo Restrepo explains, "the constitutional definition of the 'Colombian nationality' as pluriethnic and multicultural represents a break with respect to the nation-State model shaped in the political ideology of *mestizaje*, with the Hispanic-mestizo as the cultural paradigm necessary to the achievement of civilization, of progress."[5]

Two groups central to the new Colombian multicultural state were indigenous peoples and Afro-descendants. The latter were attended to in Transitory Article 55 (TA 55) of the new constitution. This article provided for the establishment of a special commission to study, "within the following two years," the situation of Afro-Colombians. The Colombian Congress was to use the commission's findings to pass "a law that recognizes the right to collective property of black communities that have been occupying *tierras baldías* in the river-side rural zones of the Pacific Basin according to their traditional production practices."[6] TA 55 also called for the ensuing law to "establish mechanisms for the protection of the cultural identity and the rights of these communities, and for the fostering of their economic and social development."[7]

The prescribed law was eventually drafted and adopted as Law 70 in August 1993. In 1996, the state issued the first collective land title under the new law's authority. By the end of 2007, it had issued 159 such titles in Colombia's Pacific region, covering more than 5.2 million hectares (nearly fifty percent of the region's land) and including over 63,000 families.[8]

Although it specifically mentions the Pacific region, TA 55 also states that the law "could apply to other zones of the country that present similar conditions."[9] As a result, a number of communities in the Atlantic department of Bolívar have applied for land titles, although, as of the end of 2008, none had received them. In chapter 9, I discuss some legal and political battles over the government's failure to grant titles under Law 70 in this region.

The Special Commission for Black Communities (Special Commission) was officially established by legal decree and given one year, beginning in August 1992, to "identify and propose mechanisms for the protection of the cultural identity and rights of the black communities" and to propose programs for their economic and social development.[10] The decree required that the commission include the minister of government or his delegate, as well as representatives of five named government institutions that work on development, territory, and culture,[11] ten specifically named delegates (academics, advocates, and members of Congress),[12] and three representatives from networks of Afro-Colombian communities and NGOS (referred to as consultative commissions) named in each of four departments in the Pacific region seen to be affected by the law: Chocó, Valle, Cauca, and Nariño.[13] NGOS were already organized in some areas, partly around ethnic identity and partly around campesino identity, and were in many instances actively opposing development projects they believed were threatening their use and occupation of land and their ways of life.[14]

During the drafting and implementation of Law 70, many Colombians, including many of African descent, became particularly aware of the category of "Afro-Colombian" as an ethnic group. Yet the discourse was not totally new. Restrepo explains:

If it is true that the emergence of the Afro-Colombian ethnic issue is situated at the intersection of national and international structural factors, it cannot be attributed only to such factors. At least since the 1960s, in some urban intellectual circles, the antecedents of the emergence of the Afro-Colombian ethnic question can be found, even though in those years the discourse was constructed from a racial claim founded in the common experience of slavery and economic and social marginality.[15]

Moreover, this process of identification and politics has been ongoing. Restrepo describes the view of Carlos Rosero, one of the founders of the Process of Black Communities (PCN), the largest network of Afro-descendant communities in Colombia:

According to Rosero, this alterity paradigm of the black community, of the *afrocolombianidad,* is still far from achieving clarity about many aspects; it is still subject to a distillation process, the results of which cannot be known with certainty. Therefore, from the perspective of the organizations that put their faith in this representation paradigm, Afro-Colombian ethnicity is a construction that, although it has permitted frontiers in negotiation with the State and in the constitution of a particular social movement, is still in the process of elaboration.[16]

Thus, Law 70 has played and continues to play a significant role in the understanding of Afro-Colombian identity, by those who claim that identity as well as by others.

As with the legal and policy frames regarding indigenous identity discussed in the first two parts of this book, the focus of Law 70 is on rural communities with communal land arrangements. Particularly since the late 1990s—even after a significant amount of the land in the Pacific region had been collectively titled to Afro-descendants—economic threats have combined with internal armed conflict to lead to massive displacement of the population to urban centers. Although the Afro-Colombian urban presence, including the increase that has occurred due to displacement, is essential to understanding the complex ways in which Afro-Colombians are situated in contemporary Colombia, it is beyond the scope of this chapter.[17] Rather, my concern here and in the next chapter is to consider the historical debates around Law 70, as well as contemporary challenges to the law's full implementation in the Pacific region and attempts to expand it to primarily rural areas in the Caribbean.

There has always been conflicting information about the exact size of the Afro-Colombian population. The government's 2005 census reports that 10.3 percent of Colombia's population is of African descent—just below 4.3 million individuals.[18] While this number is significantly higher than the 1.5 percent figure produced by the 1993 census, many Afro-Colombian and human rights organizations maintain that the population continues to be undercounted significantly.[19] For example, in their 2001 estimate, scholars at the Universidad del Valle, in Colombia, put the country's Afro-descendant population at 7,990,049 persons, or 18.6 percent of the national total.[20] Similarly, a 2005 World Bank report, titled "The Gap Matters," largely basing its assessment on the Universidad del Valle study, finds that 19.3 percent of Colombians are of African descent.[21] Challenges to the official census numbers are based on errors in reporting as well as on the difficulty of relying on self-identification in areas where "being black" is still strongly stigmatized.

During discussions about Law 70 in the Colombian Congress in 1993, the same year that the census produced the incredibly low estimate of the percentage of Afro-Colombians, Senator José Renán Trujillo García stated that 20 percent of the Colombian population was black.[22] While this number does not appear to have been contested, perhaps the national percentage was considered unimportant. The Special Commission had focused on the Pacific region, where no one doubted that Afro-Colombians constitute the vast majority of the population—between 80 percent and 100 percent in some of the region's municipal departments.[23] These Afro-Colombians, as Senator Trujillo García explained, live in an area "characterized by the extreme poverty of their population, by their great environmental riches and by a weak State presence."[24]

The country's African diaspora dates back to the early sixteenth century, when slaves were brought to what was then called Nueva Granada to work in industrial sectors, ranging from plantations and ranches to gold mines and commercial fishing boats. In some cases, those slaves who were able to escape from their captors or buy their freedom established fortified villages, called *palenques*, in and around coastal regions and rivers. Only one such palenque survives, Palenque de San Basilio, which I discuss later in this chapter. By the time slavery was abolished in 1851, Afro-Colombian communities were located throughout the Pacific coastal region; the Caribbean region of Magdalena, Bolivar, and lower Sinú; and the upper central Cauca Valley, including the northeastern Cauca and southwestern Valle del Cauca.

Whether slave or free, purely African or of mixed blood (or *casta*), those seen to possess black blood in Colombia and across the Spanish empire were, as María Elena Martínez points out, "more frequently and systematically construed as [having] a stain on a lineage."[25] A lack of what was considered purity of blood barred even financially successful colonial subjects from the priesthood, military, universities, and countless other avenues of social mobility and honor.[26]

While the context in which black heritage in Latin America was disparaged shifted legally after independence, the stigma remained. As Brooke

Larson has demonstrated, when Colombian elites constructed the new nation, they "'privileged' highland Indians as readily assimilable, and therefore civilizable."[27] By contrast, she notes, blackness proved to be "the most intractable 'problem of race.'"[28] Nevertheless, the nation's "civilizing project" ultimately "charted the pathway toward nationhood through the process of cultural and biological *mestizaje* and, eventually, through whiteness."[29] Such a dominant national narrative afforded Afro-Colombians little historical or popular visibility, discursively or otherwise.[30]

Thus, despite their presence in the country for centuries, Afro-Colombians were largely invisible to the Colombian state before 1991. As Elisabeth Cunin points out, invisibility does not connote lack of awareness, at least with regard to the state. Rather, it is, as Nina de Freidemann had put it, a "negation of the actuality and history of Africans and their descendants in America."[31]

The Pacific region came to the attention of the state in a new way when the timber industry began to enter parts of it in the 1950s. Offen notes that, "while railroads, roads and pipelines descended from the highlands," the Pacific region became home to "giant lumber enterprises representing both national and international capital [that] received large concessions" from the state.[32] Others also saw development potential, including the World Bank, which during this time "initiated its first mission to Colombia by introducing African oil palm plantations near Tumaco."[33] Over the ensuing years, and partly through the Agrarian Law of 1961, much of the area became available, either through concession or title, to individuals and corporations from outside the region. Some individual black families gained title at this time as well, but collective title to communities was rare, if existent.[34]

The relative isolation of black communities had facilitated the development of some traditions and cultures particular to Afro-Colombians, but the very existence of the communities was threatened in the 1980s, when timber, oil palm, mining, and shrimp harvesting businesses moved into the region in large numbers.[35] Afro-Colombian political strategies focused on responding to the economic threats in many ways that we saw in the indigenous context, particularly through the assertion of identity and cultural rights.

In his 2008 book *Territories of Difference*, which I began to discuss in chapter 7, Escobar's description of the development and philosophy of the Colombian black social movement concentrates primarily on the PCN, the above-mentioned largest organization of black communities in Colombia. Escobar points to what he considers a landmark meeting in 1995, which brought together indigenous and black communities and established guidelines for future negotiations between the groups and with the state. This meeting also precipitated the "theorization of the concept of territory according to the movement concept of *cosmovisión* (worldview) of local communities."[36] While Escobar focuses largely on the movement's elaboration of its philosophy after the passage of Law 70, I believe we can find the roots of much of that philosophy—as well as a sense of the way in which it was articulated in negotiation with the state—in the proceedings of the Special Commission leading up to the drafting of Law 70. Thus, I rely largely on the minutes of those meetings, as well as on some of the congressional debates about the legislation, in my reading of the uses of culture as heritage, land, and development.[37] I share Escobar's commitment to studying the language of the social movement itself, but I have attempted to capture it at a slightly earlier stage.[38]

Before analyzing these three meanings of culture that emerged in the drafting of Law 70, I will consider a particularly early discussion in the Special Commission's hearings about the similarities and differences in the history, situation, and needs of indigenous and black groups in Colombia.

THE APPLICATION OF INDIGENOUS MODEL
TO BLACK COMMUNITIES?

From the beginning of the process of recognizing and constructing identity through the design and deployment of Law 70, one question that frequently arose was what the relationship should be between the protection of Afro-descendant communities and that of indigenous communities. Prior to the 1991 Colombian constitution, the 1988 constitution of Brazil was the only constitution in Latin America to guarantee collective title to certain Afro-descendant communities. Its provision that the state grant title to "the remaining members of the *quilombo* communities who are occupying their lands,"[39] however, had not yet been used to grant title to any communities in Brazil.[40] Moreover, there is little evidence of transnational Afro-descendant coalitions working on land rights issues at this time.[41] Thus, in their struggles for land rights and recognition, Afro-

Colombians were more likely to align with, or at least attempt to learn from, indigenous communities in Colombia. Despite the many difficulties of indigenous models for the protection of land and culture discussed in parts I and II of this book, the models had resulted in land title—however precarious—for many indigenous groups in Colombia and throughout the rest of Latin America.

The claims and assumptions about indigenous peoples that supported their acquisition of collective land title clearly influenced the politics of Afro-descendants and their advocates leading up to the formulation of Law 70. Offen, relying in part on the work of others, contends that "in the late 1980s, the strategies of black leaders began to change in Colombia. As indigenous movements became 'green' and increasingly successful in reaching out to transnational NGOs, black leaders began to emulate their organizational strategies and aligned themselves politically."[42] He quotes Peter Wade for the proposition that "black leaders in the Pacific began to cultivate 'an "indian-like" identity in the eyes of the state.' "[43]

In discussions ranging from the historical and the anthropological to the jurisdictional, multiple presentations before the Special Commission considered the similarities and differences between Afro-descendants and indigenous peoples in Colombia. On one hand, advocates for Afro-descendant land rights claimed that Afro-Colombians "have suffered a historical process comparable and symmetrical to the indigenous communities, as in the loss of territory, ethnocide and cultural marginalization. As with indigenous peoples, they had their humanity destroyed by means of philosophical positions, both moral and ethical."[44] On the other hand, they noted differences in the situations of the two groups. Indigenous peoples, for example, live primarily in rural areas, whereas black communities generally live in villages but make their livelihood from rivers, seas and forests and from the cultivation of rural areas. Commissioner Zulia Mena explained this distinction, and described the rural-village relationships around which black communities were organized:

> The territory that the black communities have traditionally inhabited is a unity . . . [I]t has also been said that the territorial situation of the black communities cannot be equated with the situation of the indigenous communities, because basically the latter are located in the

rural zones . . . As to how the collective titling process of these territories should be done, several proposals have arisen from these communities. One of them is that this recognition should take into account the integrality of the black communities' territory within the rural-village relationship, which is characterized by semi-nomadism, multiplicity of residences, and which is based on an economy of complementary activities (traditional production practices) and multioptional activities.[45]

Importantly, the differences noted by advocates were meant to stimulate attention to the specific needs of Afro-Colombians, not to suggest that they were either more or less entitled than indigenous peoples.

Still, an issue that appeared a number of times in the discussions of the Special Commission—and one that persists to this day—is whether black communities, even with their different social structure, would eventually be recognized as having the same type of territorial rights as indigenous peoples. Commissioner Saturnino Moreno argued that they should be. According to the minutes of one meeting, Moreno "affirmed that the territorial problem of blacks and Indians is the same, in the sense that it is about ethnic minorities, traditionally marginalized, that need a territory to be able to develop their culture and tradition that differ from that of the rest of the Colombian people."[46] Dr. Héctor Riveros Serrato, the vice minister of government, disagreed. He argued that the constitution gave different recognition to the two groups: indigenous groups, not black communities, constituted Indigenous Territorial Entities (ETIs).[47] In fact, while black communities are referred to only in TA 55, indigenous communities are attended to in numerous articles of the constitution, including one on territorial entities, where they are granted certain rights to self-government equivalent to those granted "departments, districts and municipalities."[48] Commissioner Jaime Arocha used this difference to criticize the constitution for having created an "asymmetry in the territoriality" of Colombia's black and indigenous peoples "by denying the former certain territorial rights."[49]

While some advocates for Afro-Colombian rights have argued that Law 70 lays the framework for the creation of Afro-Colombian Territorial Entities (ETAS), they often fail to consider that indigenous communities themselves have yet to see the level of independence promised them by the constitution. Subsequent legislation—namely, the Organic Law of Territorial Ordering—makes indigenous *cabildos* (councils) responsible for the administration of justice in their territory and, in principle, puts them in charge of managing public funds allocated by the national government for public services. Yet, as of the end of 2009, it appeared that the government had not issued the implementing regulations needed to enact the law fully. Thus, as Offen had noted years earlier, "cabildo funds continue to be managed by local municipalities."[50]

Some advocates have been working to ensure that any implementing regulations promulgated for ETIs also establish ETAs, which would give black communities "the same political, administrative, and judicial powers *theoretically* enjoyed by indigenous resguardos."[51] Yet the vice minister's interpretation of the constitution seems to have prevailed, as few advocates consider that ETAs will ever be a political reality. That said, as I explore in chapter 9, some advocates have recently used a 2001 Constitutional Court sentence—finding ILO 169 to be applicable to Afro-Colombians[52]—to suggest more generally that black communities should be given rights equal to those of indigenous peoples.

Today, many Afro-Colombian communities and organizations continue to make strong territorial claims akin to those that are at least formally recognized for indigenous peoples. They do not primarily do so, however, to ensure the rights of Afro-Colombians vis-à-vis indigenous peoples, the latter of whom currently comprise only 5 percent of the population in the Pacific region.[53] That said, there are sporadic conflicts between indigenous and Afro-Colombian groups over land, and Law 70's regulations include special provisions for addressing these issues.[54]

Some argue that Law 70 has increased tensions or brought them to the fore, by requiring demarcation of territory in an exclusive—rather than a fluid, shared-use—manner, and that is almost certainly the case.[55] Yet, for the most part, the social movements have aligned themselves in their national political struggles, as already mentioned with regard to the PCN's 1995 landmark meeting, which brought together indigenous and black community leaders.

In fact, the number of indigenous resguardos (territorial entities) and their total area in hectares increased under the mass formalization of title in the Pacific region that was precipitated by Law 70. In addition to increasing the amount of collectively titled property for both Afro-descendants and indigenous peoples, Escobar contends that the new legal instruments for titling "fostered interethnic collaboration as well as collaboration between ethnic groups and the state . . . and enabled for a time the construction of an alternative imaginary of territoriality and development."[56]

THE MEANINGS OF CULTURE

The discussion leading up to the drafting of Law 70, the law itself, and subsequent debates about its successes and failures reproduce many of the themes and tensions that I have already discussed in this book in the context of indigenous rights. Not surprisingly, given that multiculturalism was a principal focus of the 1991 constitution, the law was worded so as to protect Afro-Colombian culture. While many of the discussions took place in that context, all three meanings of culture that we have seen thus far reappeared in Law 70: culture as heritage, culture as grounded in land, and culture as development.

Culture as Heritage

Throughout the creation of Law 70, the situation of Afro-Colombians was largely seen as an ethnic, not a racial, issue. The law itself defines "black community" as a "group of families of Afro-Colombian descent that possess their own culture, share a history and have their own traditions and customs within a rural-village relationship that reveals and conserves a consciousness about identity that distinguishes them from other ethnic groups."[57]

While the history and ongoing effects of slavery and the racial construction of Afro-Colombians were referred to in the discussions of the Special Commission and the need for Law 70, the commission deliberately focused on the future protection of the culture of Afro-Colombians. Nevertheless, there were times when advocates felt the need to remind government representatives of the distinctiveness of that culture. Abigail Serna, a representative from the consultative commission of the Chocó, complained during one meeting of the Special Commission: "Effectively there is only one commission, but within it there are two visions of life, two cultures: the Afro-Colombian culture and the dominant traditional culture in this country. This should be recognized in order to achieve results."[58]

At a formal level, there was agreement that Afro-Colombians were an ethnic group. What precisely characterized their culture, however, was the subject of much discussion. In part to address this question, the Special Commission created, among its several subcommissions, a Subcommission on Cultural Identity. Within the hearings of that body, community representatives and anthropologists often referred to the Afro-Colombian cosmovision.

The description of an Afro-Colombian cosmovision differed in many ways from that attributed to indigenous peoples. Most significantly, it was generally seen as having its roots in another continent—Africa. Pastor Murillo, who was an advisor to the Special Commission (and later became director of the Office of Black, Afro-Colombian, *Raizal* and *Palenquero* Communities within the Ministry of the Interior), spoke to the commissioners about Afro-Colombian identity. He discussed the context of slavery and exploitation, but he also asserted that Afro-Colombians have a particular way of seeing the world:

> The *afro* notion has for us much relevance, despite some anthropologists' ignorance of the historical convention that exists between Africa and our presence . . . [It is] clear that we are Americans, but it is also clear that we have an African ancestry, reflected not only in pigmentation, in color, but in our particular cosmovision and cultural manifestations.[59]

Because of years of oppression, many who testified before the commission explained, it was difficult to identify or describe the cosmovision in great detail. One person speaking to the subcommission "concluded that black communities have their own identity, resulting from an imposition, adaptation and transformation, which has not been able to be realized because the State has not recognized them."[60] Indeed, one of the purposes of Law 70 would seem to have been to facilitate the recognition and development of the cosmovision.

To the extent that a cosmovision was articulated, it was seen primarily in relationship to land. Commissioner Trífilo Viveros suggested, for example, that some of the features that distinguish Afro-Colombian culture are its religion and its "cosmovision of traditional medicine," both of which result from a clear view of and relationship with nature. Even though racism has prohibited anthropologists from spending much time understanding Afro-Colombian identity, Viveros continued, "it cannot be said that the black community does not love the land, since it forms a part of it and its coexistence in harmony with nature is evident."[61] Commissioner Silvio Garcés, for his part, spoke more generally, but also in more vivid terms than Viveros, as he referred to Afro-Colombian use of language. According to the meeting's minutes, "he signaled how communities have recreated the language and have adapted it to their own cosmovision, have expressed, through this, their relationship with nature, their relationship of affection, their sexuality, which has its own particularities."[62] Garcés then illustrated how Afro-Colombians' use of language embodies their connection to land by invoking the imagery captured by a poet from Chocó, Miguel Angel Alceno, whose poem "La Suyanza" compares the relationship to "the *'fever'* that a black man feels when he falls in love with a woman."[63]

Regardless of the extent to which they were willing or able to describe the cosmovision, advocates and government officials alike saw the need for cultural education. Because they recognized that many traditions and customs were unknown to, or denied or forgotten by, the vast majority of Colombians, even Afro-Colombians, they focused a number of provisions in Law 70 on ethno-education. Most of these provisions address education for Afro-Colombians, suggesting that education could be used to help develop and propagate the cosmovision. Article 34 states:

> Education for the black communities must take into account the environment, the productive process and the whole social and cultural life of these communities. As a consequence, the curricular programs will assure and reflect the respect and encouragement of their economic, natural, cultural and social patrimony, their artistic values, their means of expression and their religious beliefs.[64]

Other articles have a similar aim. Articles 32 and 35, for example, highlight the importance of ethno-education in maintaining Afro-Colombians' knowledge and ways of life in accordance with their history and culture.[65]

Ironically, the less developed articulation of the Afro-Colombian cosmovision, relative to that of indigenous peoples, would seem to permit the former to avoid some of the unintended consequences that plague the latter's use of heritage discourse. With the possible exception of the cosmovision's relationship to land, which I discuss below, Afro-Colombian heritage—unlike indigenous heritage—has not been appropriated by the Colombian nation for all to use or preserve. For the most part, neither the state nor its citizens who do not identify themselves as Afro-Colombian appear to have much interest in claiming Afro-descendant heritage.

Until very recently, for example, the National Museum of Colombia made only marginal references to Afro-Colombians in its permanent collection. And these references were far from glorifying Afro-Colombians.[66] After significant protests and lobbying in 2007, the museum agreed to sponsor and house a three-month exhibit in 2008. The exhibit, organized with the assistance of numerous black communities, focused on contemporary ceremonies to honor the dead in those communities and tied those ceremonies to contemporary political issues, such as war and displacement. It was titled *Velorios y santos vivos: Comunidades negras, afro-colombianas, raizales y palenqueras* (Wakes and Living Saints: Black, Afro-Colombians, *Raizales* and *Palenquero* Communities). The exhibit covered communities from both the Pacific and Caribbean regions of the country. Indeed, *raizales* is the name Afro-Colombians living in the Caribbean islands of San Andrés, Providencia, and Santa Catalina use for themselves, while *Palenqueros* is what Afro-Colombians from the Palenque de San Basilio call themselves.

The exhibit contained only a few artifacts from the black communities whose ceremonies it displayed. The objects included carved wooden pieces and musical instruments that resemble what one might find in parts of Africa. The exhibit also featured carvings and masks from Africa's Bantu-speaking areas, from where it is thought that many of the original Afro-descendants in Colombia were brought. These objects were donated to the museum in 1998 by two sociologists from Tulane University who had taught and worked in Colombia. The museum had never before displayed them as a means to offer a context for Colombia's Afro-descendant population. The exhibit, it seems, aimed to provide some sense of resonance between these pieces from Africa and today's Afro-Colombian population.

Even this recent exhibit, however, failed to draw a strong connection between the national heritage of Colombia and that of Afro-Colombians. It highlighted the death rituals as uniquely Afro-Colombian, although the ceremonies would be familiar to many Colombians not of African descent. Indeed, the Christian religion is central to the ceremonies themselves and the differences among them. That some communities are Baptist (in San Andrés) and others Catholic, for example, is used to highlight some of the distinctions among their approaches to death.

The exhibit could be seen as part of a larger effort, also enshrined in Law 70, to teach all Colombians about Afro-descendant culture. In addition to calling for support for ethno-education among Afro-Colombians, Law 70 outlines the need for the national education system to understand and spread "knowledge of the cultural practices of black communities and their roles in building Colombian history and culture."[67] It likewise promises that "the Ministry of Education will formulate and execute a policy of ethno-education for the black communities and create a pedagogical commission that will assess those policies with representatives of the communities."[68] Although there has been some implementation of regulations to provide ethno-education for Afro-Colombians,[69] as well as to improve Afro-Colombian access to universities through scholarships,[70] little appears to have been done to include Afro-Colombian history and culture in the national education system, particularly with regard to Afro-Colombians' role in the development of the nation.

The approach to black heritage in Colombia, then, differs significantly from the *mestizaje* approach to Indians. In the latter, the mix of ethnicities represents, as Wade puts it, "a symbol of a distinctive Latin American identity."[71] In contrast, in Latin America in general, "blacks were much less likely to be symbolized [as a special category] and were rarely held up as the symbols of a glorious heritage."[72]

Of course, unlike indigenous peoples, Afro-descendants did not predate early colonizers. That they were separated from their cultural and territorial roots, in fact, is sometimes used to argue against their ability to possess or transmit culture. As Senator Trujillo García put it during the congressional debate over the adoption of Law 70, anthropologists in the early twentieth century made an assumption that is still too common: "that those beings deprived of freedom, naked, hungry, lacking an intelligible language, could have anything to contribute to American acculturation other than their hands and muscles."[73] He continued:

It has been ignored that even a human being put in the most extreme situation of isolation, a stranger in his land, dispossessed of his culture, as long as he can remember, constitutes a cultural cell capable of creating ideas, providing himself with expressive means, forms and adequate tools to generate for himself or in association with others, the traditional values of the culture from which he proceeds.[74]

One possible exception to the state's lack of interest in recognizing— if not in appropriating—black culture in Colombia is Palenque de San Basilio. Located in the Atlantic region of the country, Palenque de San Basilio has about 3,500 inhabitants and is the only remaining walled community founded by slave refugees in Colombia in the seventeenth century. It has been designated by UNESCO as a "Masterpiece of the Oral and Intangible Heritage of Humanity" for its "cultural space" and "social practices." According to UNESCO's website:

> Of the many palenques that existed in former times, only the one of San Basilio has survived until the present day and developed into a unique cultural space . . . Central to the cultural space of Palenque de San Basilio is the language of palenquero, the only creole language in the Americas comprising a lexical Spanish basis with morpho-syntactic characteristics of African (Bantu) native languages. It constitutes a vital factor reinforcing social cohesion among community members.[75]

UNESCO asserts, however, that Palenque's "cultural space is threatened" by both market transformations and the country's enduring armed conflict. Further erosion of the community's traditions, it continues, occurs when villagers are outside Palenque. There they "are commonly subjected to racial discrimination and ethnic stereotyping leading to a denial of their cultural values."[76]

To the extent that Palenque continues to be seen as having a significant cultural heritage relevant to the national narrative of Colombia, it is exceptional. Moreover, as with the occasional recognition of black heritage in other parts of Latin America, cultural validation is often illusory. Wade argues:

> Only in Cuba and Brazil, with their very large black populations, was there a positive revaluation of blackness in some quarters, although, again, this tended to be integrationist in tone, with the emphasis on the emergence of a mixed society in which a black input was valued as long as it was under control. Even then, the trend was mainly literary, with little discernible impact on government policy.[77]

Others have pointed to the fact that such celebrations of heritage stand alongside modern-day neglect and structural racism.[78]

Culture as Grounded in Land

Law 70 is largely known for its facilitation of the granting of collective land rights to Afro-Colombians in the Pacific region. In doing so, it connects that land to culture. The law, for example, defines collective occupation by Afro-Colombians as "the historical and ancestral settling of the black communities on lands for their collective use, which constitute their habitat, and over which they today develop their traditional production practices."[79]

In addition to the Subcommission on Cultural Identity, the Special Commission created a Subcommission on Territory and Development. Early in the meetings of the subcommissions, Myriam Jimeno, who was working on the technical aspects of the law through the government's Institute of Anthropology, suggested that these subcommissions be combined, given that the "two are related and the objective is to amplify, not reduce, the theme."[80] Although her proposal failed, it indicates the extent to which, from the beginning, territory and culture could not be easily separated for many of the law's proponents.

Discussions on the importance of land to Afro-Colombian communities occurred throughout the sessions of the Special Commission. Even if the communities' cosmovision and its connection to land were not spelled out as clearly as in the indigenous context, the understanding that Afro-Colombian culture was grounded in land was widely held. A representative of Palenque de San Basilio described Afro-Colombian territory as "a body that includes [the Afro-Colombian's] own language, tradition and production."[81]

Murillo, the advisor to the Special Commission mentioned earlier, and Commissioner Mena focused on the extent to which Afro-Colombian land use was distinct from that of indigenous peoples and of other campesinos not of African descent because of the rural-village relationship discussed above. The two proposed that, because of this unique relationship, collective property rights should be granted to the "unity." After explaining that Afro-Colombians in the Pacific live in communities but cultivate land in rural areas and work in the natural areas of the rivers, sea, and forests, Mena maintained that all of these zones "should be granted collective title as a block, understanding the three levels."[82] Such a "global title,"

Murillo added, would "legitimately bring together uses and customs concerning the territorial rights of the black community."[83] Ultimately, the proposal by Murillo and Mena was rejected, as Law 70 specifically excludes from collective title "the urban areas of municipalities."[84]

Just as it was seen as the source of or reference for a preexisting Afro-Colombian culture, land was considered the basis for the recuperation and future development of that culture. Commissioner Mena, for example, explained that while "indigenous communities already have their *cabildos*, for black communities it is about reconstructing their own community authorities that have existed and exist and that are threatened by all external influence."[85] Nevaldo Perea, a representative of the Comprehensive Association of Small Farmers of the Atrato (ACIA), the most significant campesino organization in the Chocó, wrote to the Special Commision: "We have to demonstrate in the fight and the practice that black communities need a territory in order to be able to develop their own culture . . . It will be they [government officials] who are responsible if the future generation disappears because no people without territory can develop."[86] Jorge Perea, one of the commissioners on the Subcommission on Territory and Development, explained that the focus on territory is not "caprice," but instead "a rationality in the usage of resources, which is what finally allows that culture and people (*pueblo*) to reproduce."[87]

For many Afro-Colombian leaders, the protection of culture required collective property rights, as opposed merely to land use or tenancy. This understanding that collective property is sometimes necessary to maintain and foster cultural identity comports with the jurisprudence of the Inter-American Court of Human Rights discussed in chapter 4. As we saw there and in chapter 6, the reverse is often true: collective property is frequently seen as culturally dictated. Commissioner Jaime Arocha, for example, discussed the complexity of the history of the collective territory for Afro-Colombians and suggested that the conception of community property that should be applied was that of the black communities, and not that of the Institute of Geography.[88]

Ultimately, Law 70 began a process of permitting black communities to petition for collective property rights. That process has resulted in some of the same dark sides we examined for indigenous peoples with regard to culture as grounded in land. Law 70 explicitly places restrictions on the land that can be claimed as collective property, and on the ways in which it can be used once it is titled. These limitations reflect assumptions about Afro-Colombian ethnic identity and serve to distinguish those Afro-Colombians who have a recognized culture and ethnic identity from those who do not.

Law 70's restrictions on land use are connected to an exceedingly general understanding of Afro-Colombian culture and traditions that does not do justice to the Subcommission on Cultural Identity's interrogation of these concepts. In the application for collective title, for example, black communities must include information on, among other things, their "ethnohistorical antecedents" and their "traditional practices of production."[89] The regulations that set forth the process (found in *decretos*) do not add much specificity to the meaning of these terms. With regard to traditional production, for example, communities must describe "a) forms of individual and collective uses of natural resources; b) forms of work of members of the community; c) other forms of cultural use and appropriation of territory."[90]

Moreover, Law 70 and the decretos implementing it not only assume, but require, that black communities use the land in ecologically sustainable ways. Law 70 specifically states: "With regard to the surfaces and forests, the property will be used in accordance with its social and inherently ecological function."[91] This requirement might not have been considered onerous, given that during the meetings of the Special Commission, mention of Afro-Colombians' attention to ecological matters was made a number of times. For instance, Commissioner Viveros pointed to the ways that such attention on the part of black communities had aided in the building of the country: "From the historical point of view, we point to the presence of our ancestors who, since the year 1709, have been dominating the zone, working tirelessly for the acquisition of their food and, through the balanced exploitation of their resources, have contributed to the country in order to lift up the socio-economical level of it."[92] He later even maintained that "the black man and the indigenous are those who have the authority to sustain and balance the ecosystem."[93]

Commissioner Viveros's position was echoed by the minister of government, Fabio Villegas Ramirez, in his statements to Congress in support of the adoption of Law 70. One of the reasons for the law, Villegas claimed, was "the great environmental wealth" of the Pacific region. He noted that "the articles pertaining to the management of natural resources on the lands that would be given in collective form to black communities point to the necessity of protecting biodiversity, as a fundamental basis of the economic and social development of these communities and as a valuable resource for the country."[94] That collective ownership might have stemmed from an Afro-Colombian cosmovision seemed unimportant. Its significance lay in its ability to protect national resources for the entire country. To the extent that it was a part of Afro-Colombian heritage, that heritage was alienable.

Regardless, Law 70 took seriously the idea that Afro-Colombian communities had not just the authority, but the duty, to find or maintain ecological balance. The law points to the ecological fragility of the region and stipulates that those who receive collective title "will develop practices of conservation and management that are compatible with ecological conditions."[95] In this instance, however, it does not require or even assume that the inhabitants of the area already engage in such practices. Rather, it obliges them to "develop appropriate models of production such as agrosilviculture, agroforestry or other similar models, designing the ideal mechanisms for encouraging them and for discouraging unsustainable environmental practices."[96] Much like with the Chiapas example discussed in chapter 6, the Afro-Colombians must (re)learn sustainable traditions and practices.

In addition to granting Afro-Colombians environmental stewardship of titled lands (or requiring the same of them), Law 70 dictates that the land that is titled be "inalienable, inseverable, and unable to be used for collateral."[97] Given that one of the reasons Afro-Colombian communities and their advocates sought collective title was to provide a shield against the large development projects that were taking over the region, the inalienability and indivisible nature of the title was generally presumed to be desirable. Yet, at least for Commissioner Silvio Garcés, the issue needed to be discussed and addressed. Garcés pointed out in a meeting of the Special Commission that "an aspect that is not clear is the definition of the conditions in which these [communal] lands will be able to be alienated."[98] He considered that "the inalienable character of the lands that are won here would mean that the land movement in the Pacific would be immobilized from a commercial point of view,"[99] and ultimately he argued for such inalienability.

The restriction on alienability, however, comes with both the advantages and disadvantages discussed in the indigenous context. For instance, black communities have continued to claim their distinct history and culture, including a cosmovision connected to an environmentally sensitive understanding of the ecosystem. While this vision comports with Law 70 and its dual purpose of protecting collective title and the environment, it supports limiting land use to sustainable development considered consistent with Afro-Colombians' supposedly natural attachment to the land and water. As I discuss below, however, some communities resist such restrictions, questioning why they should be prevented from pursuing or benefiting from commercial uses of the land.

Culture as and against Development

As discussed above, at the time of the passage of Law 70, a significant amount of outside development was already beginning to take place in the Pacific region of Colombia. Law 70 responded by promoting participatory, sustainable development for black communities, including through credit and technical assistance. Culture and land played an important role in the understanding of development evinced in the law. One provision of Law 70, for example, states:

> The design, execution and coordination of social and economic development plans, programs and projects put forward by the government and the International Technical Cooperation for the benefit of the black communities which this law addresses, must be made with the participation of the representatives of such communities, with the purpose of responding to their particular needs, to the preservation of the environment, to the conservation and qualification of their traditional practices of production, to the eradication of poverty and to the respect and recognition of their social and cultural life. These plans, programs and projects will need to reflect the aspirations of the black communities with regard to development.[100]

Furthermore, the law commits the government to "encourage and finance research activities aimed at . . . the study of the realities and potentialities of black communities, in a manner that will facilitate their economic and social development."[101]

At the end of 2009, sixteen years after the passage of Law 70, the rather extensive provisions on development had yet to be implemented by the

Colombian government. A glance at the history and background of Law 70 demonstrates the ongoing controversial nature of these provisions.

As Law 70 was being debated, businesses engaged in timber, oil palm plantations, gold mining, and shrimp cultivation were expanding in the Pacific region of Colombia. The government was regularly granting concessions, even after the passage of the new constitution. Thus, many of the presentations made to the Special Commission, including those from peasant coalition groups containing indigenous and black community members, spoke about the need to halt outside development. As we saw with indigenous peoples in chapter 7, that development was seen as a threat to the sustainability of Afro-Colombian communities.

In hearings before the Subcommission on Territory and Development, Murillo contended that there was consensus among the participating organizations that TA 55's focus on traditional practices of production "contrasts with the model of development put forward by the Colombian state in the territory of the Pacific, [which] does not respond to the needs of the population."[102] Commissioner Silvio Garcés explained the attraction of the Pacific to transnational corporations, as well as the ensuing threat:

> The next century will be about the Pacific, and already the transnational companies and the groups with economic power inside and outside the country have their eyes set on the region, not only to appropriate the resources for themselves, but to lead its development. Development, if not done in concert with the communities, will end up generating an economy of colonies, such as those that lived in the region with the gold exploitation by foreign companies.[103]

Garcés was referring to the gold mining in the region that can be traced back to Spanish colonial times and that was the impetus for much of the slave trade in Colombia.[104]

In the early 1990s, gold mining continued to pose a threat to Afro-Colombian communities and was opposed by many. The Peasant Organization of the High Atrato, for example, presented a statement explaining that new mining technologies had a negative impact on both the environment and human beings. The group's representative pointed to effects on the communities' ability to maintain their traditional subsistence economies, in which "they have been exploiting natural resources in perfect harmony with nature, conserving the environment."[105] He explained that the new technologies for mining had destroyed the land's utility for agriculture through erosion, polluted the drinking water, and increased sediment in the river, making it difficult to navigate and reducing the fish population. Invoking provisions of the 1991 constitution that grant everyone the right to a clean environment, as well as TA 55, his organization called for suspension of the permits that had been granted since the constitution had taken effect.[106]

The Peasant Organization of the Lower Atrato (OCABA) and the Traditional Indigenous Authority of the Lower Atrato Region (CAMIZBA) sent a joint statement noting a contradiction between the government's creation of the Special Commission to facilitate titling of land for black communities and the government's grant of concessions to timber companies.[107] The organizations' statement "reject[ed] the concessions already in force and in process of being made to large timber companies," and named the companies and projects it aimed to stop.[108] Although many advocates and communities urged the suspension of these concessions, the state expressed a number of concerns about doing so. Commissioner Manuel Rodríguez, director of what was then called the National Institute of Natural Resources (INDERNA), explained that INDERNA opposed the suspension of all timber concessions, in part "because there are some black communities that live on that profit."[109] He did not offer evidence that the communities themselves had made this argument.

Most of the calls for halting outside development were combined with pleas for supporting development in accordance with the ecologically sustainable way of life that black communities were seen to have led traditionally. Ethnodevelopment was a concept that was in wide circulation by the early 1990s, and Afro-Colombian rights advocates deployed it often. The above statement by OCABA and CAMIZBA, for example, after calling for an end to timber concessions, "demand[ed] economic and social development in accordance with our culture, needs and interests."[110] Murillo noted that Afro-Colombian organizations agree that Afro-Colombians have a "distinct vision" and "particularities" that must be attended to in development planning.[111] He specifically called for a "model of ethnodevelopment, understood as the exercise of the social capacity that a people has to construct its future, taking advantage of its real and potential cultural resources, in agreement with a defined project conforming to its values and aspirations."[112]

As discussed in chapter 7, this appeal to ethnodevelopment coincided with at least some of the commitments and priorities of environmentalists that emerged in the late 1980s and early 1990s. It also fit with some priorities of the World Bank, international development agencies, and a number of private corporations. Although Escobar points to a 1983 plan by the Colombian state for the development of the "Pacific Coast" as the "invention of the Pacific as a 'developmentalizable' entity,"[113] Offen sees the early 1990s as the point at which the Pacific region of Colombia came to be identified and named. Offen attributes the identification to a sense of the region as one that embodied biodiversity: "Being one of the most biodiverse regions on the planet, the Pacific region of Colombia is courted by many projects seeking to demarcate its boundaries and assign them new meanings."[114]

Both Escobar and Offen attribute particular significance to the Plan Biopacífico (PBP), which began in 1992 and was thus under way when the Special Commission was discussing Law 70. The PBP was funded by $6 million from the World Bank's Global Environment Facility and $3 million from the Swiss government. Its stated primary objective was "to contribute to the consolidation of a new development strategy for the *Chocó Biogeográfico* based on the application of scientific knowledge and the identification of strategies for the management of biodiversity that guarantee its protection and sustainable utilization, and in a concerted fashion with local communities."[115] Escobar contends that, while the plan's commitment to local participation was more present in word than in deed, it was there. He explains: "More than in the mainstream biodiversity approaches favored by northern NGOs, PBP registered from the start the correlation between biological and cultural diversity, and the importance of taking into account traditional knowledge and practices."[116]

The PBP's budget, however, paled in comparison to the funds the Colombian government had received from the World Bank and the Inter-American Development Bank for Plan Pacífico, a project which, according to Escobar, "belonged to an era of planning that saw no need for serious negotiation with local people."[117] It was initially aimed at investing in large-scale infrastructure "to create the basis for regional capitalist development."[118] While the PBP received $6 million for its first three years, Plan Pacífico received $250 million for the same period. Escobar notes that, as a result "of internal critiques and pressure from external funders, subsequent versions of [Plan Pacífico] incorporated a more explicit environmental and conservation dimension," but the plan continued to operate with a "largely economistic orientation."[119]

Thus, the World Bank's own programs, including its funding of much of the titling under Law 70, embodied the tension between the stated goals of the PBP and Plan Pacífico (local participation in sustainable development versus large-scale capitalist development). The tension was reflected in the Colombian government's actions as well, particularly in what often appeared to be a Janus-faced approach to the establishment of Law 70. The ongoing granting of concessions during this time evinced a conflicted government—torn between, on one hand, its desire to accommodate the interests of large-scale modern development and, on the other hand, the benefit it could see in protecting biodiversity while at the same time providing formal land title to Afro-Colombians. It seemed to understand even then that delegating to these communities the responsibility for maintaining biodiversity might fit well with its neoliberal ambitions.

Roberto Franco, advisor to Commissioner Rodríguez of INDERNA, exemplified the government's conflicting positions. In October 1992, he defended the state's decision to grant a controversial timber concession called Balsa II, which included over 34,000 hectares of land that, according to Franco, were usable forests in areas where there was no evidence of settlement.[120] Only three months later, he suggested four "focuses of analysis" regarding the region's economic development that would seem incongruous with his defense of Balsa II. One entailed ensuring that large development projects "consider the environmental, cultural and social impact that they will cause with regard to the communities."[121] The other three involved developments to be pursued by the communities themselves, including ethnodevelopment and subsistence development in territories managed by the black communities.[122] Franco's shift in discourse, if nothing else, suggests that he understood the importance of at least giving lip service to the development needs of the communities, and of suggesting limitations on large development projects.

Those who drafted Law 70 also understood that development imperatives could not be separated from the aim to protect Afro-Colombian culture and land, and included a chapter on development in the law. Chapter VII of Law 70 requires that the state play an active role in the development of black communities. Article 58, for example, declares that "state funds for social investment will have an administrative unit for projects in order to support black communities in the processes of training, identification, formulation, execution and evaluation of projects."[123] Article 55 provides that "the Government will adapt credit and technical assistance programs to the particular socioeconomic and environmental conditions of the black communities."[124] Article 52, as I discuss further below, calls for financial programs to facilitate partnerships between black communities and other entities for the sustainable production and use of those communities' resources. Significantly, the provision permits the value of such resources to be used as a guarantee for credit.[125] Given that land titled under Law 70 cannot be used as collateral, any credit program that finds other forms of guaranteeing loans, such as that proposed in Article 52, would be key to providing meaningful prospects for development.

Chapter VII also pledges the state's support for sustainable development with participation by black communities. In particular, it stipulates that "the National Government will create a commission for the study of the formulation of a development plan for black communities."[126] That commission ultimately "will propose long-term policies and be the point of reference so that the policies of the National Development Plan respect the Nation's ethnic diversity and promote the sustainable development of these communities in agreement with their own vision."[127] In general, Chapter VII makes clear that sustainable development initiatives should occur with the input of black communities. Article 49, for example, insists that "the design, execution and coordination of social and economic development plans, programs and projects . . . must be made with the participation of the representatives of those communities."[128]

As mentioned earlier, although Law 70 was passed in 1993, the first collective title was not granted until December 1996. Since then, titling in the Pacific region has progressed steadily, nearly meeting its numerical goals. Yet many obstacles remain, a number of which are related to development. The continued expansion of agro-business, the rise in internal conflict in the region and the resulting displacement of black communities, and new or proposed legislation that essentially negates portions of Law 70 have been well documented.[129]

The PCN and other social movements have garnered some success in challenging legislation that contradicts the guarantees of Law 70. In 2008, they had a significant victory when the Constitutional Court struck down the 2006 General Forestry Law.[130] Many environmentalists, indigenous peoples, and black communities opposed the new law for a number of reasons, including that it reduced the total amount of reserved forest land and that it separated the rights to land from those to forest cover, thereby permitting forest cover to serve as collateral. This latter provision appears to be a way around Law 70's prohibition on using land for collateral and around similar provisions with regard to indigenous territory.[131] The successful challenge to the law argued in part that it violated ILO 169 and the Colombian constitution because the legislature had failed to engage affected Afro-Colombians and indigenous peoples in proper consultation before the drafting of the law. Given that nearly 65 percent of the territory collectively titled to black communities is located in legally designated forestland,[132] the decision—if taken seriously—should give Afro-Colombians a significant voice in determining what will be permitted on their land. Of course, we should not expect that Afro-Colombian communities will be more likely to speak with one voice on issues of land or forest use than the indigenous groups we considered in chapter 7. Thus proper consultation might shift the balance of power vis-à-vis the government and black communities, but it does not guarantee a particular outcome.

Notwithstanding this successful challenge to the Forestry Law, as mentioned earlier, important provisions of Law 70 affecting development remained to be implemented at the end of 2009. In particular, the government had not issued the regulations necessary for implementation of Chapters VII, IV (on the protection of natural resources and the environment), or V (on mining resources). In 2002, Colombia's National Planning Department (DNP) had called on multiple ministries and departments to work with Afro-Colombian representatives to put into effect regulations on these three key chapters of Law 70.[133] By 2008, the government had hired a group of experts to work on the issue. Although the designated parties had been meeting, they had not reached agreement. While it is difficult to find information on the precise sources of disagreement, my interviews with some of the officials and advocates involved in the process, along with my review of a few public statements and some proposed drafts of the regulations, suggest the following.

The PCN and other groups with which it is aligned have consistently called for "integrated regulations," meaning they do not want any one of the three chapters implemented independently of the others. I gather that this insistence is both because of the interrelatedness of the chapters— provisions on the environment and on development, for example—and to prevent a victory in one area from being taken away or tempered in another.

The Ministry of the Environment and Territorial Development issued a draft set of regulations in the summer of 2007. This draft represented part of the ministry's response to a meeting held earlier that year by a group of organizations from four regions in the Pacific that had convened to consider and propose necessary revisions.[134] The ministry claims to have incorporated changes as a result of recommendations from that meeting. With regard to Chapter VII, "references were made to the means of realizing economic and social rights, new lines of existing funds and the adoption of differential programs in favor of the development of black communities."[135] The following summer, there were two additional drafts, one integrated and another that covers only Chapter VII.

Both of the newest drafts support sustainable development projects, as they attempt to give meaning to Article 52 of Law 70, which calls in part for financial and credit programs for partnerships with private entities for sustainable projects. It appears that Afro-Colombians disagree over whether financing under the new regulations should be permitted to be used for agreements between communities and private companies involved in the production of oil palm.

As earlier parts of this section indicated, the issue of oil palm production has been present in discussions about the Pacific region since before the drafting of Law 70. In addition to expressing discontent over the numerous concessions that have been granted to those engaged in the agro-business, even since the passage of Law 70, many Afro-Colombian activists have long contended that oil palm has devastating effects on the land and on biodiversity. I think it is fair to say that, for the PCN and many others involved in the Afro-Colombian social movement, state support for the oil palm industry has long been considered the paradigmatic example of the state's lack of commitment to Law 70. That is, the continued expansion of oil palm in the region is often the target of the battles many Afro-Colombians wage, as exemplified by a headline description of a recent statement by the PCN and a group of communities in the Pacific region: "No to Palm, Yes to Territorial Rights and Life!"[136]

Some contend that the threat to rural Afro-Colombians is not from oil palm per se, but from the way in which the crop is cultivated.[137] As one human rights report explains the position:

> Some assert that the crop is "good business," but that the current practices of the industry exclude the local communities from its benefits, leaving them only to fill positions as low-paid, manual laborers. Indeed, if oil palm cultivation were to follow the guidelines of [prior consultation], ecological sustainability, and community participation outlined in [Law 70], perhaps it would have the potential to be a much-needed development tool for these communities.[138]

Of course, that position, while potentially favoring some oil palm production, contains significant caveats. Perhaps a more difficult issue is whether the state should implement regulations that would permit arrangements with private entities for the cultivation of oil palm (and other economic development arrangements) that are not necessarily sustainable, but that might lead to profit for the communities. What should the approach be of organizations, such as the PCN, that have led the way in promoting a vision of territory, culture, and biodiversity? How should economic development be defined and prioritized, particularly in those situations discussed in chapter 7, where sustainable development might no longer be an option?

In November 2008, the PCN and a number of black communities issued the "No to Palm" statement mentioned above, rejecting state palm initiatives and calling for the government to issue regulations for Chapters IV, V, and VII within three months. The document complained that integral regulations had yet to be implemented and that "racism, exclusion and institutionalized discrimination have not permitted the positive intervention of the state toward the aspirations" of Afro-Colombians in the Pacific.[139] It further pointed to the government's "desires to deepen environmental imbalances of our region [by] inserting large expanses of single crops like that of oil palm which together with coca are part of the greatest threats that our communities face."[140] The statement urged the government to support development that accords with "our ancestral practices of production, which are mining, fishing, agriculture, timber use, [and] traditional medicine, among others."[141]

Over fifteen years after the passage of Law 70, acceptable parameters for development initiatives and funding uses—particularly those regarding oil palm—remained unsettled, even among Afro-Colombians and their advocates. Both drafts of proposed regulations in circulation in late 2008 (integrated and not), include the following language:

> Black communities possessing the right of collective ownership . . . will be able to make contracts of association and / or collaboration with business owners of the national or international private sector, or with public or private entities of whatever nationality, for the development of projects. Equally, they will be able to share in the processing and commercialization of the production.[142]

Thus, both proposed versions of the regulations appear to give communities significant autonomy in dealing with private business.

This high level of negotiating latitude for Afro-Colombians, however, could conflict with their general obligation under Law 70 to adhere to sustainable development practices. Perhaps for this reason, the integrated draft provides that black communities have the "exclusive right of the use of forest resources in their collective territories" as long as their practices are "in observance of the guardianship norms of conservation and sustainable forest use."[143] In addition, any use by Afro-Colombians of natural resources and the environment on their collectively held lands under Law 70 should be in accordance with the lands' "inherent social and ecological function," which means "maintain[ing] their conditions of conservation and sustainability."[144]

These provisions in the integrated draft point to one of the critical reasons that many community leaders insist on integrated, rather than piecemeal, regulations: the integrated regulations set clear limitations on development initiatives that might otherwise appear to be permitted by regulations on development alone. Moreover, by agreeing to a single set of regulations, a settlement regarding development in one area, such as that related to forestry, would hold for other areas, thereby obviating the need for Afro-Colombian communities to negotiate each sphere of development separately.

DARK SIDES AND UNINTENDED CONSEQUENCES

In the above discussions of the three meanings of culture in Law 70— culture as heritage, as land, and as development—I have already explored some of their dark sides and unintended consequences. I have also considered how the consequences are similar to and different from those accompanying parallel uses of culture in indigenous rights advocacy. While some dark sides of heritage, paradoxically, have been largely avoided because the Colombian nation has not valorized or claimed its African heritage in the same way it has claimed its indigenous heritage, the consequences regarding land and development seem similar. Not having a preconceived cosmovision might have liberated black communities to the extent that it has given them more space to construct their own identities, but their championing of traditional practices of production and connection to land has turned out to be problematic for many whose options in terms of development are limited in ways similar to those discussed in chapter 7. The PCN's support for integrated regulations that not only provide for, but require, sustainable development are intended to ensure that certain forms of development are off the table. Thus, the struggles over the regulations hint at deep divides between communities (and governmental agencies) over how to prioritize biodiversity, territory, and various types of development.

Despite the pessimistic spin that can be put on this story, the struggle of Afro-Colombians in the Pacific has had appeal. Academics concerned with local knowledge, legal scholars and political scientists attentive to multicultural citizenship, and advocates for Afro-descendant and indigenous rights throughout Latin America have applauded the theoretical bases of the movement along with its successes, however limited those successes might be. They have not, however, paid adequate attention to the differences in interests and perspectives within and between Afro-Colombian communities.

The vagaries of Law 70's implementation in the Pacific region also resound strongly in Colombia's Caribbean region, even though they revolve around different issues, mainly related to the question of which communities are intended to be covered under the law. This book's concluding chapter therefore turns to a community in Colombia's Caribbean region that is struggling to be recognized under Law 70. It considers why, given all the disappointments, difficulties, and false starts that Afro-Colombians in the Pacific region have experienced, Law 70 would be the model their peers in the Caribbean region would turn to for land security and development.

AFRO-COLOMBIANS IN THE CARIBBEAN

The Islas del Rosario comprise an archipelago of over twenty-five islands off Colombia's Caribbean coastline. They form a national park and are also under the municipal jurisdiction of the district of Cartagena de Indias, in the department of Bolívar. In 1984, the Colombian Institute of Agrarian Reform (INCORA) concluded a process begun nearly twenty years earlier to declare the Islas *baldíos reservados de la nación*, a technical term that translates roughly to national unused, or uncultivated, reserved lands.[1] This designation stems from a 1912 law declaring that all Colombian islands in the Atlantic and Pacific oceans without an "organized population" were to be reserved to the nation and could not legally be sold.[2]

Isla Grande, the largest and most populated island in the archipelago, can be reached from the city of Cartagena in a tourist speedboat in an hour. Its current permanent population consists primarily of two groups: *blancos* (whites) and *nativos* (natives). The whites include some of Colombia's wealthiest citizens, who occupy private houses and hotels on the beaches. The natives are of African descent and primarily reside in the interior of the island, although some also live on other islands in the archipelago.

The natives from the Islas del Rosario have formed a community council in accordance with Law 70, the 1993 Colombian law discussed in chapter 8, which enacts the 1991 constitution's guarantee of the right to collective land title for certain Afro-descendant communities. The council was officially registered in 2005 by the mayor's office of Cartagena under the name of Orika.[3] In January 2006, the community applied for title under Law 70, indicating that its population at the time was 597, of which 99 percent was black and 1 percent was mestizo.[4] In 2008, the community claimed 723 members.[5]

While in most of Colombia the terms "mestizo" and "black"—or even "white" and "black"—are commonly used, different categories are deployed in the Caribbean, at least in the islands and along the coast near Cartagena. "White" refers to those we might call "white" or "mestizo" in other contexts. "Native" refers to Afro-descendants on the islands near Cartagena and, at times, in other coastal areas in the Caribbean part of Colombia. It is one of many categories that is a subset of or overlaps with "black" in the region.[6] Although there is some uncertainty about the origin of the term, "native" commonly appears today in newspaper coverage about, and even in official documents relating to, black communities whose members also self-identify as such. Even those who oppose the application of Law 70 to Isla Grande often describe community members as native. Thus, the term does not necessarily carry with it the legal or political significance that might be intended by at least some of those who use it in their claims for collective land rights.

In the case of Isla Grande, though they did not permanently settle there until relatively recently, self-identified natives trace their history to the arrival of slaves in nearby Barú in the 1600s. These slaves eventually purchased their freedom and subsisted by fishing, collecting fruit, and tending livestock in the Islas del Rosario, even if they did not live there full time.[7] Today the natives on Isla Grande have various jobs, including performing manual labor at the hotels and houses owned by whites. Others make their living by fishing; providing transport for natives to and from Cartagena and other islands in the area; and selling gas, water, and small grocery and pharmaceutical items to other natives. A number are also engaged in ecotourism, through native-owned and operated businesses or cooperatives. There is one school, which is located on Isla Grande and is funded by the district of Cartagena. It offers classes only through the ninth grade. Students who want to continue their education beyond that level must travel to Barú or Cartagena.

Javier Morales—or "Cuco," as he is known on the island—is a native who first came to Isla Grande forty-five years ago from Barú. He was eight years old at the time. Because he worked as a child and his family had few to no resources, he never learned to write—nor, he adds, even to ride a bicycle. More than twenty years ago, he and his wife moved to a four-hectare piece of property near the edge of the island. The property, called "Buena Esperanza" (good hope), is registered in the name of Garcés, a white man who rarely comes to the island and who has essentially given Cuco free reign to tend it. Cuco is raising his family on the property and, as one of the pioneers in the ecotourism business on the island, has constructed a restaurant and some small, ecofriendly guest facilities. In 2007, he charged the equivalent of around $70 a day for a simple, palm-thatched, one-room hut for two, with meals included. The price was a bargain on the island.

On the morning of March 22, 2007, nine police officers, several authorities from the Colombian Institute of Rural Development (INCODER, formerly INCORA), and a representative of the Ministry of the Environment arrived unannounced at Cuco's door with orders to evict him from the property. They left six or seven hours later with full stomachs (thanks to their prospective evictee's notorious hospitality) and after extended conversations with Cuco, community leaders, and over a hundred residents from elsewhere on the island. When the officials boarded the boat back to the mainland, the situation remained unresolved.

Although the police arrived with an eviction notice, INCODER's original aim seems to have been to pressure Garcés to sign a rental agreement with the state. In 2001, seventeen years after the Islas were designated as baldíos reservados, INCORA received orders to evict unlawful residents from the Islas del Rosario. Since then, INCORA (and now INCODER) has been involved in a process of "recuperating" the property on the island. Instead of simply evicting whites, it offered them an option that was partially made available by the 1912 law. That is, the whites could enter into rental contracts with the state for renewable terms of up to eight years, during which time they agreed to provide public access to the ocean and along the shore, and not to make improvements to the property without state permission. By the end of March 2007, INCODER had reached such an agreement with nearly 80 percent of the white occupants of the island,[8] and was serving eviction notices to many of those who had refused. Because Garcés had declined to enter into the rental contract, Cuco received an eviction notice.

I arrived on Isla Grande as part of a human rights delegation the day after the attempted eviction. Several community leaders came to meet with us at Cuco's restaurant. As we drank coffee in the open-air restaurant, we tried to get a grasp on what had happened the day before. The copy of Cartagena's morning newspaper we had brought with us contained a front-page mention of the events, and a quarter-page article inside with the headline *"Nativos impedieron diligencia: Desalojo chocó con problema ignorado"* ("Natives Obstructed the Law: Expulsion Clashed with an Unknown Problem"). The unknown, or perhaps unexpected, problem to which the newspaper referred was that the expulsion notice would directly displace or force an agreement between a black occupant and the state, and that the natives would turn out en masse to oppose the eviction order. In this sense, it would seem that Cuco's attempted eviction was an unforeseen side effect of the state's plan. There was little evidence at that time that INCODER was threatening to expel natives, although it was offering them a different type of contract to sign than that offered to whites. Natives were offered usufruct contracts, a legal arrangement generally made available to those with scarce resources, which would allow them to enjoy the land they currently occupy for a renewable term of eight years at no charge.

For native community leaders, however, the eviction order had much larger, and perhaps not so surprising, consequences. Recall that the community had applied for collective title in 2006. As a start, the community asked for approximately four hundred hectares, but it also seems to have left up to INCODER the decision about which portions of the islands were eligible for collective title.[9] INCODER had responded to the application with a letter stating that, because of the archipelago's designation as baldíos reservados de la nación, the island was in fact not constituted of tierras baldías—meaning empty or uncultivated lands—made available for collective title by Law 70.[10] INCODER's position was that it did not even have to consider the application. Cuco's attempted expulsion came at the same time that the community was formulating legal and political responses to INCODER. Thus, for a while, he was a cause célèbre of the community.

Eventually, Garcés transferred the land to Cuco, and Cuco entered into a usufruct contract with INCODER. Under the agreement, Cuco may use the land for eight years, though he is to pay rent for the businesses on the land (the restaurant and guest accommodations). As of August 2008, according to Cuco, INCODER had yet to attempt to collect the rental fee.

The resolution of Cuco's case, of course, did not address—and arguably harmed—Orika's claim for collective title. The community challenged INCODER's refusal to consider its application by filing a *tutela*—an action demanding protection of fundamental rights—under the Colombian constitution. The community lost in the lower courts, but the Constitutional Court used its discretion to consider the case.

———

Before venturing further into the story of the Islas del Rosario and other communities along the Atlantic coastline that have, without success, applied for collective land title under Law 70, I would like to step back to consider the aim of this chapter. As discussed in chapter 8, both TA 55—the 1991 constitution's provision regarding collective title for Afro-Colombian communities—and the 1993 Law 70 enacting that portion of the constitution refer primarily to the Pacific region. TA 55, however, makes clear that it also applies to "other areas of the country that present similar conditions."[11] Law 70 reads: "This law also will apply to zones that are unused, rural and riverine, which have been occupied by black communities that have traditional practices of production in other areas of the country and satisfy the requirements established in this law."[12]

Even with this acknowledgment, nearly all of the discussions in the Special Commission to draft the law and in Congress dealt with the Pacific basin area, where the great majority of tierras baldías could be found. As I noted at the end of chapter 8, the central question I would like to pose in the present chapter is why, given all the difficulties encountered by those in the Pacific region of Colombia with regard to Law 70—including large-scale displacements, violence, and the inability to engage in meaningful development projects—would communities along the Caribbean coast seek to be included in the law's coverage?

This question is made more pressing by the fact that, at least as of the end of 2008, no community along the Atlantic coast had yet been granted collective title and, in most cases, INCODER (or INCORA before it) had simply refused to consider applications from communities in that region. The community council of Orika seemed to be facing a particularly uphill battle, given that the 1912 law makes clear that the islands are baldíos reservados de la nación and, as such, cannot be sold. Moreover, 1995 legislation in further enactment of Law 70 specifically states that the law does not apply to "unused lands that constitute the territorial reserve of the state."[13] Other communities in the region face different obstacles to the application of Law 70, most notably that the lands must be tierras baldías (and not belong to private individuals), that they present conditions "similar" to those of recognized black communities in the Pacific basin (generally understood as being situated on the shore, whether of a river or a coast), and that the communities be engaged in traditional practices of production. Many communities, having been forcibly displaced from the lands they traditionally occupied, find themselves ill situated to meet these requirements.

Communities in the Caribbean nevertheless sometimes turn to Law 70, I would argue, in large part because they see few alternatives. They are often considered to be illegal occupants of the land on which they live, and their needs are generally ignored by the state. Many communities do not have electricity or running water. Recognition under Law 70 would, at least in principle, give them access to development assistance under Chapter VII of the law (assuming some resolution of the dispute over the regulations discussed in chapter 8). If nothing else, investment in infrastructure would be long-term, as the communities would have secure title to the land. Collective title would serve as a tool in their fight against the large development projects—primarily megatourism—that constantly threaten to encroach upon the areas where they live and upon their livelihood.

That said, there is in fact significant disagreement within communities over whether they should seek collective title under the law. Even in Palenque de San Basilio, the community most likely to succeed in an application for collective title—given its recognition as a UNESCO world heritage site, as discussed in chapter 8—residents are involved in a dispute over whether they should seek title under Law 70.

For black community leaders in the Caribbean region pushing for the application of Law 70, one advantage of collective title is that it removes pressure on individuals to transfer or sell the land they occupy (regardless whether they have legitimate title to it). Another advantage is that the title is inalienable, which precludes a community decision to transfer it. Those same advantages are disadvantages for community members who are interested in at least leaving open the possibility of selling the land they now occupy. Indeed, across the region, individuals and communities have decided to move, in return for an immediate influx of urgently needed cash. Even many of the natives on Isla Grande had earlier sold to whites much of the area that the latter occupy.[14]

——

Cuco eventually decided to sign the rental and usufruct contract with INCODER because, according to the tutela, he and his family could no longer tolerate living under the constant threat of dislocation. At the time the tutela was filed, however, Cuco was the only native to have signed an agreement with INCODER. Moreover, the tutela notes that his case is extraordinary because, unlike most other community members on the island, he was able to enter into a rental agreement because Garcés had ceded his rights to Cuco. A government lawyer I spoke with who was working on the case claimed that, if anything, the terms of the usufruct agreement are preferable because individuals do not have to pay rent on the land (though, as in Cuco's case, they can be charged for commercial use of it), but the tutela assumes that the rental agreement is more favorable than a contract of usufruct. For natives and their advocates, the crucial distinction is that most whites entering into rental agreements live on the island only part time and presumably have full and clear title to other properties off the island. The natives, in contrast, generally have no other property than that on which they live on the island.

Of course, those natives who favor collective title oppose signing any contract, whether of usufruct or rent. Both arrangements recognize the state, not the black community, as the lawful owner of the land. As discussed below, however, other pressures operate to cause some individuals to consider signing usufruct agreements. In particular, it is the only way currently available for natives to have a formal and secure (if only in the short term) relationship to the land.

Upon first glance, much of the disagreement between INCODER and the community council appears to be procedural. INCODER's position is that it does not even need to respond formally to the Law 70 application because, as discussed above, the land is not alienable under the 1912 law. In 2007, the minister of agriculture sought a consultative opinion from Colombia's administrative court[15] on the question of whether INCODER even has the power to consider Orika's application under Law 70. The court concluded that, while INCODER has the authority to adjudicate collective titles under the parameters of Law 70, it is not empowered to resolve collective property claims by black communities on baldíos reservados de la nación, such as the Islas del Rosario.[16] The decision invokes the 1912 law and its definition of lands reserved to the nation as including islands where there was no "organized population." That no one argues that such a population existed on the Islas del Rosario in 1912, the court contends, lends further support to the special status of the island, and its exclusion from Law 70.[17] Finally, the decision states that any usufruct contracts by INCODER with Afro-descendants living on Isla Grande are not in conflict with Law 70, and are therefore permissible.[18]

The administrative court's conclusion in essence reinforces the government's position, which the tutela before the Constitutional Court challenges. The tutela acknowledges a tension between the declaration of certain lands as baldíos reservados and the rights of black communities to apply for collective title. It argues, however, that the latter should take precedence as a fundamental constitutional right.[19] INCODER's failure even to consider the application for title, the tutela maintains, constitutes a violation of the community's fundamental right to petition as well as its rights to administrative due process—such as that of prior consultation.[20] Moreover, the tutela claims the community's fundamental rights to existence, cultural identity, cultural and social integrity, and autonomy are threatened by INCODER's actions.[21] It finds these fundamental rights in the Colombian constitution, as well as in the international human rights treaties in accordance with which the constitution—under the concept of the "block of constitutionality"—is to be interpreted.[22] The court itself, the tutela argues, has indicated that this block includes at least certain parts of ILO 169, such as the right to prior consultation.[23]

In terms of the applicability of Law 70 to the Islas del Rosario, two aspects of the tutela are particularly salient. First, perhaps because a tutela must assert a violation of fundamental rights, it does not specifically discuss the language in TA 55 about its applicability to "other areas of the country that present similar conditions" to the areas of the Pacific region that clearly fall under its ambit. TA 55 does not, by itself, constitute a fundamental right. At the same time, by not relying on TA 55, the tutela makes an argument that, if successful, might avoid the parsing of the language there and in its enactment in Law 70 and subsequent administrative decrees that interpret it. That language has in fact been used by

INCODER to determine that some communities in the area, particularly those that do not abut water, do not meet the requisite requirements. The tutela skirts consideration of this presumed limitation, in part by suggesting that international law (via the constitution) requires more than the constitutional and statutory language would suggest. It relies heavily on ILO 169's applicability to tribal peoples, and combines that with Constitutional Court jurisprudence on the rights of indigenous peoples to argue for strong constitutional rights for Afro-Colombian communities that do not necessarily depend on TA 55 or on Law 70's statutory implementation of it.

Second, the tutela uses the terms "autonomy" and "self-determination." In doing so, it again relies upon ILO 169 and the Constitutional Court's interpretation of that document, capitalizing on language in one particular decision regarding indigenous peoples in Colombia. The decision notes that ILO 169 "refers to the autonomy of indigenous communities to recognize the aspiration of these peoples to assume control of the proper institutions and forms of life, as well as their economic and social development, maintaining and strengthening their identities, languages and religions."[24] Recall from chapter 4 that ILO 169 does not include the term "autonomy." The Constitutional Court's decision thus provides an expansive interpretation of the convention here, in accordance with the court's recognized progressive jurisprudence in a number of areas.[25] The tutela urges the court to go even further, by interpreting the constitution—on the basis of ILO 169—to recognize as fundamental rights the autonomy and self-determination of black communities, and not only with regard to language, religion, and identity. Rather, the communities should be permitted "to determine their own destiny, defining the priorities of their development and their forms of life, as well as deciding the manner of executing them inside their territory."[26]

This section of the tutela is remarkable not only because of its reading of self-determination into ILO 169 and the constitution but because, until recently, the term has not often been employed by Afro-Colombians or in relationship to their Law 70 guarantees. The earliest example of its use that I have found is in the name of a group of community councils in the Pacific region of the Chocó. The name Consejos Comunitarios del Cacarica de Autodeterminación, Vida, Dignidad (Community Councils of the Cacarica of Self-determination, Life, Dignity, known as CAVIDA) was adopted by a group of black communities that had been displaced from the Cacarica River Basin by military and paramilitary threats and attacks in the late 1990s. One particularly brutal attack in 1997, called Operation Genesis, killed dozens of people and forced the displacement of several thousand others.[27] Though a claim under Law 70 conferred collective title of 103,024 hectares to the communities, their members have been able to settle on only a small portion of that land due to continued paramilitary presence and illegal oil palm operations.[28] In this context, "self-determination" takes on special meaning: communities know that being able to continue to live their lives with dignity necessarily entails being free from incursions, not necessarily by the state, but by paramilitaries and large agro-business.

The term "self-determination" has appeared in documents and demands of Afro-Colombian organizations since then, but only recently has it become a primary means of articulating their claims. Indeed, when interviewing and working with community leaders and advocates in 2007, I do not recall much use of the word "self-determination." But when I returned to Colombia for a few weeks in the summer of 2008, the term seemed to have taken hold. At least my experience in the Islas del Rosario was that some of the same community leaders who had talked about collective rights in 2007 now framed their concerns around self-determination. I am unsure whether the tutela was a reflection of or an impetus for this discursive shift there.

Afro-Colombian calls for self-determination are being voiced in other areas and contexts as well. In the summer of 2007, for example, Afro-Colombians came together with rural workers, indigenous peoples, and labor union members to issue a public declaration against the proposed free-trade agreement between Colombia and the United States. Their rallying cry was "For territory, dignity and self-determination: No to transnationals in our territories,"[29] again to oppose outside intervention by non-state actors. As with the case of contemporary deployments of the term "self-determination" in the context of indigenous rights, here the term is not meant to promote a right to secession or separation from the state. In fact, it is often asserted in a manner that is closely connected to cultural rights. As a representative of Palenque de San Basilio put it at a 2007 conference in Bogotá: "The primary cultural right is self-determination of peoples; without this self-determination, there are no cultural rights."[30]

Orika's case remained undecided at the end of 2009. The stakes for the case seem to be high, not just for that community but for other communities in the Caribbean region who have applied for collective title or might do so. On one hand, a loss for Orika—particularly one decided on the 1912 law—would apply to few of the other communities seeking title. On the other hand, were the Constitutional Court to find that even a limited concept of self-determination were to apply to Afro-Colombians, including those living in the Caribbean region, the decision's impact could be tremendous, at least in terms of sealing the shift in discourse. Of course, the court could also rule for the community on narrow grounds, finding only that it has the right to have its application for title considered, which would simply defer many of the issues for another day.

Despite its legal uniqueness, the situation of Orika is representative of many of the economic and social issues at play throughout Colombia's Caribbean region. Although Afro-Colombian communities there have only over the past decade begun to organize and identify themselves as culturally distinct, the prevalence of both direct and systemic discrimination based on race is undeniable. In the Department of Bolívar, where Cartagena and the Islas del Rosario are located, 66 percent of the population is black.[31] Cartagena is well known for its cosmopolitan appeal and world-class hotels and restaurants, and even for having been one of the main slave ports in Latin America. It is less known as one of Colombia's poorest cities. The poverty rate in the city exceeds 75 percent, while 25 percent of the population lacks basic necessities.[32] In general, the departments in the Caribbean region have some of the lowest economic development indicators in the nation. According to the UN Development Programme, the region has the highest levels of chronic malnutrition (14 percent) and food insecurity (52 percent) in the country. Five of the region's seven departments have a rate of infant mortality that is higher than the national average.[33]

When disparities of wealth are discussed within the district of Cartagena—and in Colombia more generally—their disproportionate impact on Afro-descendants is too often ignored. An April 22, 2007, Associated Press article titled "Poverty, Crime Cloud Cartagena's Tourism Hopes," for example, only makes one reference to race. It is somewhat veiled. Seemingly as a way to inform its readers that Afro-descendants live in the region, the article quotes a priest who runs the Afro-Caribbean Cultural Center.[34] Even while pointing to Cartagena's 15 percent unemployment rate to support its claim that, in Cartagena, "the gulf between Colombia's rich and poor is at its widest," the article fails to discuss which parts of the population are most likely to be unemployed and poor. The story reflects the way that these issues are often discussed in the Caribbean region itself, even among some of those who would be identified as "black." Discussions of disproportionate effects based on race draw attention to a painful history of slavery, exclusion, and persistent power differentials from which many prefer to distance themselves.[35]

Moreover, as the tourism industry has expanded and been dominated by megaprojects in the Caribbean, Afro-Colombian communities have been literally pushed to the margins, where they face ongoing threats to their livelihood. As noted in chapter 8, Afro-descendants are disproportionately represented among those Colombians internally displaced due to armed conflict. Not all displacements of Afro-Colombians are due directly to armed conflict, however, and they are not a recent phenomenon. In the Caribbean region, for instance, Afro-descendant fishing villages that had been located since colonial times in Boca Grande and El Laguito, today's tourist centers of Cartagena, were expelled at the beginning of the twentieth century.[36]

In more recent years, particularly since the 1970s, continued development along the coastline between Cartagena and Baranquilla has led to numerous displacements of Afro-Colombian communities.[37] Villa Gloria, a community that is part of the fishing village of La Boquilla, demonstrates how small coastal communities just outside Cartagena have been affected by the aspirations of tourism developers. Most of the people who live there are of African descent, and have moved (or been pushed) there in the past fifteen years due to the development of megatourism projects. There are no paved roads to the village, only tracks cut into the sand by motorcycle and bicycle taxis. The ocean waters it borders are contaminated. The community has no running water.

With or without collective title and with or without a formal right to autonomy or self-determination, Villa Gloria acts as a semi-autonomous community. It has set up its own schools and instituted programs of ethno-education. The community receives some funding for its schools, and the municipality delivers potable water (which is held in open, communal containers in the village). It is the recipient of little else in the way of development resources. The community possesses no sewer lines, and its members build their own houses and other structures that serve as shelter.

The community has established a community council, which seems essentially to govern the village in its day-to-day operations, primarily due to a lack of interest from any other administrative body. In this sense, the community resembles the description given some years ago by Jaime Arocha of communities in the Pacific basin, where Afro-Colombians "were able to develop relatively autonomous territorial, economic, and political formations, but were forgotten by the state. For example, even when offered, education, health care, marketing of agricultural products, and transportation are poorly delivered. This noticeable disregard has been a perverse form of racial discrimination."[38]

Despite—or perhaps because of—these conditions, in April 2000, Villa Gloria, along with nearby Marlinda (also in La Boquilla), submitted an application for title under Law 70. In accordance with an implementing decree,[39] the application was publicized so that anyone who considered that she or he had title over the land could object. One document shows that a citizen of Cartagena opposed the title, claiming ownership of part of the land.[40] In 2007, community leaders informed me that they had never heard back from INCODER with regard to their application.

I went to INCODER in 2008 to find out about the status of applications for collective title from Villa Gloria and a number of other communities I had been told had applied for title. Given that INCODER has not responded to most of the applications for collective title from the Caribbean region, I wondered whether its position might be that Law 70 does not apply to any communities outside the Pacific region (except perhaps to Palenque de San Basilio, due to its unique status described in chapter 8).

While at INCODER, I learned of another procedural twist. Although titling applications under Law 70 had been made to INCODER, the state had recently transferred most rural titling to UNAT (National Unity of Rural Lands), another office set up under the Ministry of Agriculture.[41] As a part of this reorganization, UNAT and the Ministry of the Interior entered into a cooperative agreement to resolve collective titling applications filed under Law 70 that are "in process,"[42] a stage at which many applications throughout the country seem to dwell indefinitely.[43] INCODER was therefore clarifying the status of the titling applications for UNAT. The latter had also taken responsibility for state decisions with regard to many areas where Afro-Colombian communities reside, including the Islas del Rosario.

A question the reorganization raised for me is whether UNAT will consider claims for collective title filed by Afro-descendant communities in the Caribbean, or whether it will decide that the communities are largely excluded from Law 70. Although I had expected that INCODER had essentially concluded that Law 70 did not apply to these communities, my visit to its offices challenged that expectation. On one hand, the official I spoke with at INCODER readily acknowledged that the law might well apply to communities in the Atlantic region. She even explained the "similar conditions" language to me. In fact, she showed me a chart showing the status of all applications from the department of Bolívar that are considered in process. That chart indicated that INCODER had initiated the process for five applications from the department, including that of Palenque de San Basilio. It turns out that this understanding of the possible application of Law 70 to the Caribbean, at least in principle, seems generally accepted by the state. The state's most recently passed development plan, for example, discusses the need to "explore the possibilities of collectively titling, under Law 70 of 1993, tierras baldías in regions like the basin of the Caribbean."[44]

On the other hand, the chart from INCODER indicated that the process had not in fact been initiated for four other communities on the list, even though their applications were identified as in process. For two of them, the process could not be begun because the applications did not clearly designate which land was to be titled; for the third, the requested title appeared to be for property that was privately owned. With regard to the fourth, the municipality had argued that the petitioning community council did not actually exist. Because community councils must, in the first instance, be recognized by municipalities, the withholding of such recognition would prevent a successful application. Of course, the chart did not tell the whole story, and I was unable to see the files. Yet the extent to which these applications were in fact in process was questionable. With regard to one of the applications that had not delineated the land to be titled, the official indicated that, in any event, the community did not abut water and therefore would not qualify. If that were the case, I do not understand why that application was not simply denied, along with the others that seemed not to meet the basic qualifications of the law. Why keep the application listed as in process?

Moreover, even with some of the five applications in which the process had been initiated, the story seemed to be more complicated than was at first suggested. One application process had been suspended, for example, because of the opposition of some community members. The other four were awaiting information, ranging from topographical maps to cultural, social, and ethnic histories of the communities.

At least fifteen community councils have been formed and recognized in the Caribbean region, but my understanding from the community leaders with whom I spoke is that only four or five had applied for collective title. In this sense, INCODER's inventory was longer than I had anticipated. But it also had glaring absences. In particular, I had been told of two communities (in addition to Orika) that had applied, and were nowhere on the list. Perhaps they were categorized differently—as applications that INCODER had refused even to consider. I was not, however, shown any document containing such a category.

At INCODER, I asked specifically about Villa Gloria, and I was initially told that the community had not applied for title. I insisted, and mentioned that I had found on the Internet that someone had opposed the title by claiming that he owned the land that Villa Gloria was claiming. When I finally noted that the file could be under another name, like Marlinda or La Boquilla, the official I spoke with requested from a colleague a file she remembered seeing in the back. She was then delivered a large file that contained the application, responses to it, and a report of an investigation that INCORA had done demonstrating that the individual who claimed the community overlapped with his private property was incorrect. Yet there was no resolution to the application. The most recent documents in the file were from 2002, although a revealing newspaper article was placed at the front. That article said that, after the community council had filed for collective title, the Office of the Prosecutor of Cartagena had come to the community to declare that its inhabitants were illegal occupants of the land.

The official with whom I spoke was reading the file in front of me, as though for the first time. She seemed genuinely perplexed by what she saw. There was no evidence of any resolution or of any continued action by INCORA. She pointed out that INCORA, not INCODER, seemed to have dropped the ball. Of course, the application should have been transferred to INCODER years before, so the distinction was not clear to me. She said that she would see what she could find out and would let me know. I have not heard from her since.

———

When I returned to Isla Grande in August 2008, the Constitutional Court had not reached a decision with regard to the community's right to apply for collective title. It had been eighteen months since the first attempted dislocation of Cuco, and he seemed to feel secure on his land. While it would not be fair to describe Cuco's business as booming, it did seem to have picked up a bit, in part because of the publicity about his case. He also had competition from another native-owned ecotourism hotel nearby.

No one on the island seemed to fault Cuco for having signed the agreement with INCODER, but the leaders of the community council were concerned that, even with (or perhaps because of) the pending lawsuit, INCODER had continued in its attemps to convince some natives to sign agreements of usufruct. One eighty-three-year-old man who cannot read, they told me, had signed such an agreement. Others were apparently considering signing, which had caused some tension among native residents. On one hand, the leaders of the community feared that, were individuals to sign these agreements, any collective title the community might eventually receive would no longer include their lands. Ever de la Rosa, the leader of the community council, explained that the contracts gave legitimacy to the idea that the state, rather than the community, was the rightful owner of the land. Indeed, in the form drafted by INCODER by which occupants on Isla Grande were to indicate their intention to enter into a usufruct contract, they expressly renounced any future claim or legal action against the state or any other public entity regarding the land.[45] On the other hand, even de la Rosa understood the intense pressure that could lead community members to forgo the possibility of long-term, though quite uncertain, collective titling prospects in favor of more immediate security, however short-lived.

Several hours after arriving on the island for my August visit, I was invited to join a meeting the community was to have with a social worker from a Cartagena-based foundation, who had been working full time with the community on strategies and plans for economic development. Much of her work focused on finding a way to address the community's needs for potable water, a sewage system, and electricity—basic services that the city of Cartagena has failed to provide for many of its residents. The foundation had raised money to provide these services to Orika in a green, low-impact way. Some of the materials had already been purchased, and the foundation and the community were preparing to move forward. An editorial in the Cartagena daily *El Universal* would later describe the project as one that would be difficult to oppose: "The project would be the dream of any environmentalist" and would have the modest potential of "help[ing] the natives ascend from the category of misery to that of poverty."[46]

That day, however, the social worker arrived with bad news. The foundation had contacted UNAT to ask for permission to install a water tank, dry toilets, and solar panels. UNAT had denied the request on the ground that the project was directed by unlawful occupants of the land. Although the resolution denying the request came from UNAT, in an example of the widespread confusion and uncertainty about the jurisdiction of each of these entities, everyone at the meeting referred to the decision as having been made by INCODER. The council needed to consider alternative plans for achieving the same result. One person asked why the community should even have to ask INCODER for permission. Another pointed to the contradiction between the state's official recognition of the community council and its claim that its members are not entitled to basic services.

Thus, the question of how the community might provide for itself was inseparable from its claimed right to collective territory. It was in a bind. Even if it were to win its case before the Constitutional Court, the judicial victory might only open up the possibility for the consideration of its application for collective title. The road ahead might entail a long process of application and consideration, during which time the community would continue to go without proper sanitation and sources of energy. Even if its main development project—native ecotourism (now with two hotels and fifteen tour guides)—were to become profitable, the residents would be unable to provide basic needs for themselves or the community.

If the community were to lose its case, individual members would presumably have the option of signing temporary contracts for usufruct, but they would then only be able to provide services for their small plots of land. There would be no communal resources. Nor would there be any guarantee beyond the eight-year period. The community leaders discussed the possibility of applying for collective usufruct for the life of current community members. Most, however, believed they should not compromise in such a way, as doing so could appear to concede that the state possessed legitimate authority over the fate of the land. While they spent significant time considering this option, I later learned that the lawyers involved in the case were doubtful that INCODER would or even could agree to such unprecedented terms, both in terms of collective ownership and the length of the agreement. A government lawyer for UNAT told me that the eight-year limit was inflexible, but suggested that a collective usufruct contract could be arranged by community members granting power of attorney to one representative who could then sign the contract for the land they collectively use.

In any event, the strategic response necessary to resolve these complicated issues was far from clear. The social worker and most leaders continued to insist that collective title was the only way to ensure development for the community. Yet the multiple jurisdictional levels of the state had put them in a precarious position. Somewhat inconsistent with its provision of education for the community, the municipality of Cartagena claimed to be limited in its ability to provide basic services because of the island's status as baldíos reservados de la nación. The federal government —in this case, through INCODER and UNAT—was insisting that, because community members did not legally occupy the land, they were not entitled to basic services. Given the pending tutela, it was difficult to imagine that INCODER could respond otherwise; if its position was that the community members were not entitled to own the land, it might well be inconsistent to allow them to continue to develop it. It seems that, at least initially, INCODER and UNAT saw the foundation's offer of assistance as a bargaining chip; if community members agreed to sign usufruct agreements, the government would permit them to accept the privately funded basic services. At the time, it appeared as though the tutela might have harmed the community politically by forcing the legalization issue far beyond what had been raised by Cuco's situation.

The parties seemed locked in disagreement. Indeed, when I visited

UNAT to learn more about the government's position, the lawyer I met with explained the fiscal code that predated the 1912 law, and noted that, as early as 1905, it referred to the islands as baldíos and as national property. He told me that "due to the ignorance of the community," the natives on Isla Grande did not understand that they needed to formalize their relationship to the land. He discussed the matter as though it were purely administrative. When I finally asked him about the foundation's proposal for dry toilets and solar panels, and why UNAT (or INCODER) wanted to deny the community the right to basic services and development, he seemed surprised that I would know such details. He finally informed me that the decision was under reconsideration. He seemed to know little about Law 70, simply reconfirming the position of INCODER and UNAT that the law does not apply to the islands.

On September 12, only a few weeks after I had visited the island, UNAT announced that it had reversed its opposition to the water tank, solar panels, and dry toilets. According to a story on its own webpage, "as a showing of its interest in maintaining the community in dignified conditions," UNAT was planning a trip to Isla Grande with the aim of resolving doubts and explaining to community members the benefits of legalizing their status—through usufruct contracts.[47] In other words, UNAT was still attempting to use the same bargaining chip, but this time as seduction rather than threat. It was now offering development (or agreeing not to block it) if the natives would give up their claim to collective title.

If autonomy was at stake in UNAT's discussion, it was the autonomy of UNAT—not of the community—with which the agency was preoccupied. The Cartagena newspaper had published an editorial criticizing UNAT's initial position and noting that INCODER had granted similar support to other islands in the archipelago. It referred to UNAT as a dependent entity of INCODER, and wondered how the two bodies could make such incongruent decisions. UNAT criticized the Cartagena newspaper for claiming that UNAT is a dependent part of INCODER, noting that UNAT "is an autonomous unit with a juridical personality."[48] With sad irony, UNAT had claimed for itself a legal status that likely would never be available to natives on Isla Grande.

In the best-case scenario, the community might eventually achieve collective land title. But that would be a far cry from autonomy. As discussed in chapter 8, the community would still be restricted, under

Law 70, to sustainable forms of development. Today, ecotourism might seem like a good option for development, but it is unlikely to affect the community—as opposed to a few individuals or even a small group—in a significant or direct way. Indeed, the one ecotourism business that existed on my first visit to the island had split into two by the second. These two were in the midst of significant disagreement over how to divide the assets of the business, especially those that had been granted to them by a non-profit foundation. As with many businesses operating inside collective land arrangements, it seems that proceeds from the hotels and businesses would go to the individuals or cooperatives that operate them. The communal arrangement would extend only to the land.

Given environmental and other restrictions throughout the island affecting whites and natives alike, perhaps ecotourism is more viable on Isla Grande than in other areas of the Caribbean. In the majority of those Caribbean coastal locales where natives live, restrictions are minimal and megatourism is the competition. As in the Pacific region, I would argue that Law 70 is only a partial—if arguably a necessary—solution for the long-term sustainability of Afro-Colombian communities throughout the region. Granting pockets, even islands, of rights to keep a few communities together on the land they occupy ultimately does little to question the state's larger development and environmental priorities. When those claiming alterity are forced to be the primary stewards of sustainable development, well-meaning, multicultural law-reform projects are unlikely to affect significantly the redistribution of wealth and resources. Indeed, they might even exacerbate preexisting disparities.

Perhaps Afro-Colombians in the Caribbean are more aware of this potential downside than others. Even if communities were guaranteed the right to have their applications for collective title seriously considered, differences within communities might ultimately lead to the denial or lack of resolution of those applications. Put another way, internal divisions might let the state off the hook by paralyzing attempts to apply the law to the region. I would contend, though, that just as calls to apply Law 70 to the Caribbean are symptomatic of gross inequality, so is internal community resistance to its application. As with those communities and community members interested in entering into agreements with the oil palm industry in the Pacific, they see their development choices as limited.

Conclusion

If I have done nothing else in this book, I hope that I have demonstrated the unpredictability of strategy—the inability of social movements ever to know that they are on the right long-term path—and the dangers of insisting that there is only one proper path.

I have attempted to show this unpredictability by describing the strategic dilemmas faced by indigenous people and peoples in the Americas over the past four decades in their pursuit of a range of rights and recognitions, which I see as principally guided by the quest for indigenous development. I have then considered the extent to which those same dilemmas have been mirrored at a relatively local level, for the Afro-Colombian rights movement over the past fifteen to twenty years.

The roots of these dilemmas, however, go deeper than the past half-century. Thus, I have attempted to place indigenous—and, to a certain extent, Afro-descendant—social movements in a historical context to trace the sources of the strategies they have chosen. From their early resistance to and attempts at negotiating colonialism and slavery, to efforts to assert their citizenship in post-colonial states in the Americas, to the deployment of international legal models of self-determination and human rights in transnational organizing, and to consideration of their place in the multicultural state, indigenous peoples and Afro-descendants throughout the Americas have covered significant ground.

Numerous factors, foreseen and unforeseen, have determined which path advocates have taken. Much of this book has been about those factors, such as the legal and political models that had developed before pan-indigenous organizing began in different contexts, and the extent to which the models seemed to fit the situation of indigenous peoples. The book has also considered how indigenous peoples throughout the Americas and Afro-descendants in Colombia have sought to pursue their own cosmovisions, and to adopt and adapt strategies that seemed most in line with their sense of their unique ways of thought. And, of course, it has concentrated on the successes of many of the strategies, as well as the downsides to those successes.

Whether advocates have chosen strategies of self-determination or of culture, I have argued throughout the book that the promise of indigenous development has, consciously or not, provided them with a guiding star. Thus, while on one level the book is about strategies for international legal recognition, I have sought to demonstrate that such recognition is often meant as a means (though maybe only one means) to an end. That end is economic justice.

While individual indigenous people have long left rural areas for cities in search of survival or a better way of making a living, indigenous social movements have attempted to provide remaining community members with other opportunities to survive and thrive. As part I illuminated, some movements have pursued this aim through organizing around campesino identity, while others have preferred to claim Fourth World identity. Some have called for self-determination, and others for cultural rights. Some have pursued capitalism, others Marxism, and still others hybrid forms of economic existence. Along the way, they have all forged new alliances, taken unexpected turns, and experienced successes and failures. Some have kept economic justice consciously at the forefront of their struggles, and others have lost sight of it—or, as discussed in part II, displaced it or deferred it for another day. Chapter 7 evinced how even, or sometimes especially, those focused on development have sometimes failed to recognize that gross inequalities of wealth and resources continue to structure and limit the options available to indigenous and Afro-descendant peoples for economic development.

Of course, the book has not merely been about economic justice. Assertions and understandings of cultural identity, autonomy, and sometimes self-determination do not simply mask a plea for economic justice. That they constitute the concepts and language often used to seek such justice elucidates the particular visions of social movements that, at least at times, have seen heritage, land, and development as inextricably intertwined. Notwithstanding postmodernism and postdevelopmentalism, assertions of culture, including those made in the context of development, continue to have some force for both indigenous social movements and international law. But these meanings do not need to be static. In fact, they have changed over time, largely in relationship to international law and politics. Even if the term "development" denotes modern notions of progress, I have used it as the promise held out for indigenous peoples. The promise is elusive because it represents an ever-shifting desire that neither indigenous social movements nor the individuals within them have abandoned. Chapter 7 revealed, for instance, how disagreements have tended to be more over the type of development that should be sought rather than whether it is a proper aim. Chapters 8 and 9 showed how many of these concerns have been repeated in the Afro-Colombian context.

Although I have argued for the unpredictability of strategy, the fact that each success has dark sides—I would contend—suggests a certain predictability about the persistence of structural inequality and the failure to attend to it. International human rights institutions will continue to adjudicate indigenous claims, perhaps on the basis of a right to culture today and one of self-determination tomorrow, but they cannot effectuate unequivocally positive results. Yet they provide important sites for struggle, even if the struggle never ceases. The UN General Assembly approved the Declaration on the Rights of Indigenous Peoples, but the OAS continues to work out its own declaration. At the same time that diplomats and indigenous peoples debate the OAS text, indigenous and Afro-descendant communities bring their claims to the Inter-American Commission and Court, which in turn decide cases that help to shape and mold future claims. Disappointments are nearly always embedded in apparent victories, and vice versa. The possibilities for legal and political change are endless. How could we possibly think that we could get the strategy right?

I want to conclude with a return to the discussion of defense mechanisms with which I ended the introduction. There, I challenged the instrumentalization of scholarly knowledge found in particular forms of activist research, especially those that rely on strategic essentialism. I questioned, in particular, the call for a separation of social science from cultural critique. Here, I would like to expand my plea for anti-essentialism, or at least for the continued critical study of the anti-anti-essentialist creed that seems to dictate the strategies of many social movements and their academic allies. If anti-anti-essentialism is a defense mechanism, what is the fear to which it is responding? Is essentialism, strategic or not, really less subject to manipulation, disappointment, and unintended consequences than other strategies or approaches?

At the risk of invoking another contested term, I would like to imagine a promise of indigenous development that is imbued with a constructivist understanding of culture. Here is how it might look. It would pursue an *embodied* historical and ethnographic understanding of culture, one that is connected to the multiple and sometimes seemingly contradictory lives of those people who form the groups that claim rights on the basis of their colonized status. And it would understand the extent to which colonialism and its legacy made impossible the claims to territory and the cultural practices connected to territory for many whose families were long ago displaced. It would be skeptical of indigenous groups' nationalist assertions that are based on cultural essence and separation in the same way that it would be skeptical of all nationalist assertions, but it would not require such essence for a group's autonomy, or maybe even for its self-determination in the strongest sense. Finally, despite its insistence that culture is constructed, it would understand the resonance, perpetuation, and even value of shared cultural practices, knowledges, and relationships. That there might be significant differences between current and past practices and beliefs would not constitute grounds for undermining their cultural basis.

Such an approach would self-consciously and admittedly connect culture to economic and political issues, in part by locating the initial assertion of indigenous culture in settlers' hegemonic practices. Indigenous groups have not simply lost a culture that was once real; rather, the colonial understandings of indigenous practices were as, if not more, problematic and essentialist as contemporary descriptions. The point is that inauthenticity is not a critique in the constructivist understanding, either for or against indigenous rights. In this way, the approach might complicate indigenous assertions of cultural identity, but it would not invalidate them. It would instead call for a more nuanced (and more "real") understanding of culture than that which is generally relied upon in indigenous advocacy. And it would at the same time attend to the background conditions and threats that might have led to the (re)assertion of identity in the first place. It would therefore aim to eliminate the defense mechanism altogether.

I understand that this call for constructivism is in many ways modest. My basic plea is to approach advocacy in a way that highlights rather than suppresses the underlying pathos. Only then will we begin to understand why legal and political victories do not necessarily lead to the major transformations that their advocates desire.

Notes

INTRODUCTION

1. Kennedy, *The Dark Sides of Virtue*.
2. Hale, "Between Che Guevara and the Pachamama," 14.
3. I take this term from Kingsbury, "Reconstructing Self-Determination," 25.
4. UN General Assembly, 61st Session, Declaration on the Rights of Indigenous Peoples.
5. This language was largely copied from the two major covenants on human rights—the International Covenant on Civil and Political Rights (ICCPR) and the International Covenant on Economic, Social and Cultural Rights (ICESCR)—which provide in their common Article 1 that "all peoples have the right of self-determination." By replacing the word "all" with "indigenous," the Declaration placed indigenous peoples among those entitled to self-determination.
6. UN General Assembly, 61st Session, Namibia. See also African Union, Assembly, 8th Session, Decision on the United Nations Declaration on the Rights of Indigenous Peoples, which expresses "concern at the political, economic, social and constitutional implications of the Declaration on the African Continent" and affirms "that the vast majority of the peoples of Africa are indigenous to the African Continent."
7. Cherrington, "United Nations General Assembly Declines Vote on Declaration on Indigenous Rights"; and Lutz, "Adoption of U.N. Declaration a Matter of Course."
8. Global Indigenous Peoples' Caucus, Steering Committee, "Report of the Global Indigenous Peoples' Caucus," 5.
9. U.S. Mission to the United Nations, "Explanation of Vote by Robert Hagen."
10. Povinelli, *The Cunning of Recognition*, 12.
11. Spivak, "Can the Subaltern Speak?"

12. This interview, originally published in *Thesis Eleven*, can be found at Spivak and Grosz, "Criticism, Feminism, and the Institution."

13. For one of the first discussions in which Spivak publicly abandons the term, see Danius, Jonsson, and Spivak, "An Interview with Gayatri Chakravorty Spivak."

14. In a provocative essay entitled "The Hyperreal Indian," Ramos writes: "The treatment of the Tukanoans in Brasilia exposes a tendency that has been around for a while in the indigenist circuit, viz., the fabrication of the perfect Indian whose virtues, sufferings, and untiring stoicism have won for him the right to be defended by the professionals of indigenous rights. That Indian is more real than the real Indian. He is the hyperreal Indian" (161).

15. Hale, "Activist Research v. Cultural Critique," 96.

16. Ibid., 100.

17. Ibid., 115.

18. Ibid., 113.

19. Hale contends that strategic essentialism fails to capture the extent to which indigenous peoples are essentialist in ways that are not properly described as strategic (ibid., 114). That said, I believe most strategic essentialists see their own use of essentialism as strategic, for some of the same reasons that Hale calls for the use of objective social science.

20. Ibid., 113.

21. Peter Brosius, for example, cautions against "accounts and critiques" of indigenous groups that "may be appropriated by the opponents of these movements and deployed against them. In a world of online library databases and internet search engines . . . there is no longer any such thing as a distanced academic critique safely ensconced in an obscure academic journal" ("On the Practice of Transnational Cultural Critique," 180–81). This concern is quoted sympathetically by Hodgson, "Introduction," 1044.

22. Stavenhagen, "Challenging the Nation-State in Latin America," 433.

CHAPTER 1: SETTING THE STAGE

1. See Thornberry, *Indigenous Peoples and Human Rights*, 21.

2. For a mention of this organization, which was begun in 1915, and discussion of thirty years of subsequent organizing by Andrew Paull, including the formation of the Native Brotherhood and the North American Indian Brotherhood, see Manuel and Posluns, *The Fourth World*, 84–121.

3. Rappaport, *Cumbe Reborn*, 14, 162–64, discusses the history and influence of Lame's treatise, Manuel Quintín Lame, *En defensa de mi raza* (Bogotá: Rosca de Investigación y Acción Social, 1971 [1939]).

4. Sanders, "The Re-Emergence of Indigenous Questions in International Law," 15.

5. These examples are not intended to be exhaustive, but merely representative of such movements. Of course, much earlier, there was significant indigenous resistance to colonialism throughout the Americas.

6. Colombres, *Hacia la Autogestión Indígena*, 39–41; Sanders, "Background Information on the World Council of Indigenous Peoples."

7. For a discussion of this meeting and the text of its conclusions, see Bonfil Batalla, *Utopía y revolución*, 189.

8. Brysk, "Turning Weakness into Strength," 41.

9. Ibid., 46.

10. Seed, *American Pentimento*, 1, quoting the *Oxford English Dictionary*, 2nd ed.

11. Ibid., 114.

12. See Anghie, *Imperialism, Sovereignty, and the Making of International Law*.

13. Ibid., 20.

14. Ibid.

15. Ibid., 21–22, quoting Francisco de Vitoria, *De Indis et De Ivre Belli Reflectiones* (Francisci de Victoria), trans. John Pawley (Buffalo: W. S. Hein, 1995 [1917]), 151.

16. Ibid., 22.

17. Povinelli, *The Cunning of Recognition*, 12.

18. Pagden, *Lords of All the World*, 65.

19. Ibid.

20. Seed, *American Pentimento*, 3.

21. Ibid., 115.

22. Pagden, *Lords of All the World*, 77.

23. Ibid., 91.

24. Pagden continues by explaining two further causes for lack of the terra nullius justification: "The first was the fact that, because of their origin in a papal charter, the Castilian crown's claims to rights of sovereignty and property in America had been made prior to actual occupation. Unlike the a posteriori contracts and treaties entered into by the French and the British in America, the Spanish 'titles' did not require any act of concession, or even of more than minimal recognition, on the part of the Native Americans themselves . . . The second reason . . . was the fact that the Castilian crown was as much concerned with its potential rights over the Indians themselves as with its rights over their property. The grants made by the crown to settlers in Spanish America—known as encomiendas—were precisely not feudatories as they were in Canada and the French Caribbean, nor were they entitlements to semi-independent occupation, as they were in British America. They were titles to labour." Ibid.

25. Miller, *Native America, Discovered and Conquered*, 13–14.

26. Pagden, *Lords of All the World*, 83.

27. Sanders, "The Re-Emergence of Indigenous Questions," 7.

28. Pagden, *Lords of All the World*, 83.

29. Seed, *American Pentimento*, 23–24.

30. Miller, *Native America, Discovered and Conquered*, 11.

31. Seed, *American Pentimento*, 25.

32. Ibid., 25–26, discussing the Oneida leaders' experiences of an agreement entered into with the governor of New York in 1790.

33. Banton, "International Norms and Latin American States' Policies on Indigenous Peoples," 90, quoting IWGIA, *International Working Group on Indigenous Affairs Yearbook 1988*, 159.

34. World Council of Indigenous Peoples, "Land Rights of the Indigenous Peoples."

35. Thornberry, *Indigenous Peoples and Human Rights*, 61–88, chapter entitled "Ambiguous Discourses: Indigenous Peoples and the Development of International Law."

36. Williams, "Encounters on the Frontiers of International Human Rights Law," 675.

37. Oquendo, "Indigenous Self-Determination in Latin America," 625.

38. Ibid.

39. Seed, *American Pentimento*, 132.

40. Rappaport, *Cumbe Reborn*, 27, citing Myriam Jimeno and Adolfo Triana, *Estado y minorías etnicas en Colombia* (Bogotá: Cuadernos del Jaguar, 1985).

41. Ibid. As Rappaport notes, that same law, also created a separate legal system for indigenous communities, which is perhaps the reason it is remembered. It did so, however, by placing Indians under the tutelage of the state, treating them as minors. The law remained in effect until the new Colombian constitution of 1991.

42. World Council of Indigenous Peoples, "Land Rights of the Indigenous Peoples."

43. Ibid.

44. Seed, *American Pentimento*, 156. She notes that Australia was exceptional in that it did not sign such agreements.

45. For an analysis of the debates about the status of Indian tribes under the U.S. Articles of Confederation through the constitutional convention, see Deloria and Wilkins, *Tribes, Treaties, and Constitutional Tribulations*, 13–25.

46. For a discussion of these cases, see Torres and Ruble, "Perfect Good Faith," 93.

47. U.S., Supreme Court, *Johnson v. M'Intosh*.

48. U.S., Supreme Court, *Worcester v. Georgia*.

49. U.S., Supreme Court, *Cherokee Nation v. Georgia*.

50. Midwest Alliance of Sovereign Tribes, "Trust Responsibility."

51. U.S. Department of Justice, "Department of Justice Policy on Indian Sovereignty."

52. U.S. Department of Justice, "Tribal Justice and Safety in Indian Country."

53. Ibid.

54. Macklem, *Indigenous Difference and the Constitution of Canada*, 116, citing UK Constitution Act (1867), 30 & 31 Victoria, c. 3, paragraph 91 (24).

55. Ibid., 117.

56. Ibid., 87.

57. Ibid., 57, citing S.C. 1867, c. 26 and S.C. 1876, c. 18.

58. Ibid.

59. Canada, Supreme Court, *Guerin v. The Queen*, 375–89. Leonard Rotman points out, however, that there is still much left to be said about the nature of this relationship:

"Clearly . . . describing Crown-Native relations as fiduciary is only the beginning of a process, not the final determination" ("Crown-Native Relations as Fiduciary," 368).

60. The rationale for the fiduciary duty is that indigenous peoples are made vulnerable by the legal regime that prohibits them from alienating their land. Canada, Supreme Court, *Guerin v. The Queen*. See also Macklem, *Indigenous Difference and the Constitution of Canada*, 255–56. I address issues surrounding the inalienability of indigenous lands in chapter 6.

61. A Canadian Supreme Court decision subsequent to *Guerin* and a report of the Royal Commission on Aboriginal Peoples call the relationship "trust-like" and based on the duty to protect indigenous Canadians. See Rotman, "Crown-Native Relations as Fiduciary," 364–65.

62. Rotman notes, for example, that, since *Guerin*, "the number of claims by First Nations alleging breaches of the Crown's fiduciary obligations has steadily increased" ("Provincial Fiduciary Obligations to First Nations," 736–37, citing six of the "more prominent" cases that took place between 1985 and 1993).

63. Oquendo, "Indigenous Self-Determination in Latin America," 625.

64. Ibid.

65. Ibid., 627, discussing Hans Gundermann, "Etnicidad y Ciudadanía en la Historia Andina Reciente (1930–1990)," in *Mapuches y Aymarás: El Debate en Torno al Reconocimiento y los Derechos Ciudadanos*, edited by Rolf Foerster et al. (Santiago: Universidad de Chile, 2003). The argument that liberalism and colonialism are not necessarily in conflict does not arise only in relationship to Latin America. Indeed, Uday Mehta (*Liberalism and Empire*) has argued that, at least in the context of the British empire, the two were inextricably intertwined: the British empire stemmed from liberal assumptions about reason and historical process, even as it continued to justify empire long after the independence of the Americas. Jennifer Pitts (*A Turn to Empire*) has also shown that liberal thinkers in France and Britain, particularly in the late nineteenth century, embraced colonialism. She argues that such an embrace was not necessary to liberal thought, even if it played a significant role in, for example, Tocqueville's justification of French colonialism.

66. Bolívar, *El Libertador*, 185. See also ibid., 187.

67. Ibid., 184–88.

68. Ibid., 189.

69. Ibid., 184, 189–90, 194–95.

70. Lynch, *Simón Bolívar*, 155.

71. Lynch is not alone in this analysis. According to another historian, Simon Collier, "Bolivar's vision of Indians, past or present, tended to be rather stereotyped; no serious analysis of Indian problems, no serious understanding of Indian culture, is to be found in his writings" ("Nationality, Nationalism, and Supranationalism in the Writings of Simón Bolívar," 45).

72. Lynch, *Simón Bolívar*, 155.

73. Ibid., 289.

74. Ibid.

75. Seed, *American Pentimento*, 152.

76. Banton, "International Norms and Latin American States' Policies on Indigenous Peoples," 91.

77. Rappaport, *Cumbe Reborn*, 27.

78. Ibid.

79. Ibid.

80. Knight, "Racism, Revolution, and *Indigenismo*," 80–81.

81. Ibid., 80, quoting Manuel Gamio, *Forjando patria* (Mexico, D.F.: Editorial Porrúa, 1960 [1916]).

82. See generally ibid.

83. Girón Cerna, "El Indigenismo y el Indio," 18. Original: "Es erróneo entonces para el verdadero indigenista creer que el problema es racial, cuando en realidad es económico, es social, es cultural, es gubernamental." Girón Cerna continues: "There are not superior or inferior races, only more or less advanced stages of culture, of economy, of sociology." Original: "No hay razas superiores o inferiores, sólo hay etapas más o menos avanzadas en cultura, en economía, en sociología."

84. Wade, *Race and Ethnicity in Latin America*, 32.

85. Ibid., 33.

86. Ibid.

87. Convention Providing for Creation of the Inter-American Indian Institute, Preamble.

88. Ryser, "Establishing a National Indian Institute."

89. Bonfil Batalla, *Utopía y revolución*, 14, citing "Acta final del Primer Congreso Indigenista Interamericano" of April 1940, *Actas finales de los tres primeros Congresos Indigenistas Interamericanos* (1959): 52 and 58. Original: "Estas políticas deben ser protectoras, porque se entiende al indio 'como un individuo, económica y socialmente débil,' deben tender hacia la incorporación integral de los indígenas en la vida nacional de cada país, y deben, simultáneamente, garantizar la permanencia y estimular el desarrollo de los aspectos de la culturas indias que sean 'positivos.' "

90. For further discussion of the pre-1957 history of the ILO's treatment of indigenous issues, see Swepston, "A New Step in the International Law on Indigenous and Tribal Peoples," 679–82. See also Thornberry, *Indigenous Peoples and Human Rights*, 320–23.

91. Rodríguez-Piñero, *Indigenous Peoples, Postcolonialism, and International Law*, 22.

92. Ibid., 18.

93. Sanders, "The Re-Emergence of Indigenous Questions in International Law," 19. For an analysis of ILO 107 that argues that the convention saw indigenous peoples as "ignoble primitives," as opposed to the more modern understanding of Indians as "noble primitives," see Tennant, "Indigenous Peoples," 48.

94. International Labor Organization, Convention 107, Article 4.

95. Ibid., Article 4(b).

96. Ibid., Article 11.

97. See ibid, Article 3, allowing for "special measures" to ensure the benefit of the general laws of a country, but only "so long as there is need for special protection and only to the extent that such protection is necessary."

98. Ibid., Article 4(c).

99. Ibid., Article 12. If, however, indigenous peoples were removed from their land for such reasons, they were entitled to compensation.

100. Ibid., Article 1(2).

101. Barsh, "Revision of ILO Convention No. 107," 757. See also Thornberry, *Indigenous Peoples and Human Rights*, 42–44 (discussing same language).

102. Rodríguez-Piñero, *Indigenous Peoples, Postcolonialism, and International Law*, 18.

103. See Knop, *Diversity and Self-Determination in International Law*, 18–19, 30–32 and the works cited there.

104. The Permanent Court of International Justice stated in 1935: "The idea underlying the treaties for the protection of minorities is to secure for certain elements incorporated in a State, the population of which differs from them in race, language or religion, the possibility of living peaceably alongside that population and cooperating amicably with it, while at the same time preserving the characteristics which distinguish them from the majority, and satisfying the ensuing special needs" (Permanent Court of International Justice, *Minority Schools in Albania*).

105. Berman, " 'But the Alternative Is Despair,' " 1823. *Minority Schools in Albania* was one case in which such special rights were held to be necessary to the achievement of equality. In its decision, the Permanent Court of International Justice found that the abolition of all private schools discriminated against minorities because state schools provided only members of the majority "nationality" with education in their own language and in accordance with their own traditions and customs. According to the court, "there could be no true equality between a majority and a minority if the latter were deprived of its own institutions, and were consequently compelled to renounce that which constitutes the very essence of its being as a minority" (Permanent Court of International Justice, *Minority Schools in Albania*).

106. For discussion of the plebiscite, the minority rights regime, and other interwar international legal approaches to the issue of the self-determination of nations, see Berman, " 'But the Alternative Is Despair.' "

107. For example, "certain communities formerly belonging to the Turkish Empire have reached a stage of development where their existence as independent nations can be provisionally recognized," while "other peoples, especially those of Central Africa, are at such a stage that the Mandatory must be responsible for the administration of the territory under conditions which will guarantee freedom of conscience and religion" (League of Nations, Covenant, Article 22). For a detailed discussion of this process and its resonances with modern-day international

economic policy, see Anghie, *Imperialism, Sovereignty, and the Making of International Law*, 115–95, 263–68.

108. Montevideo Convention on the Rights and Duties of States, Article 1.

109. Kirgis, "The Degrees of Self-Determination in the United Nations Era," 306–7.

110. Ibid., citing A. Rigo Sureda, *The Evolution of the Right of Self-Determination: A Study of United Nations Practice*, 1973, 99–101, which discusses U.N.C.I.O., vol. 18, 657–658). Sureda seems to have been referring to Palestinians.

111. UN Charter, Articles 73–74.

112. Ibid., Article 73(b).

113. For a concise history of this process, see Frankovits, "Towards a Mechanism for the Realization of the Right to Self-Determination."

114. Barsh, "Indigenous North America and Contemporary International Law," 85.

115. UN General Assembly, 15th Session, Declaration on the Granting of Independence to Colonial Countries and Peoples.

116. International Covenant on Civil and Political Rights, Article 1; International Covenant on Economic, Social and Cultural Rights, Article 1; and UN General Assembly, 61st Session, Declaration on the Rights of Indigenous Peoples, Article 3.

117. Frankovits, "Towards a Mechanism for the Realization of the Right to Self-Determination," 21.

118. UN General Assembly, 15th Session, Declaration on the Granting of Independence to Colonial Countries and Peoples, paragraph 6.

119. UN General Assembly, 25th Session, Declaration on Principles of International Law Concerning Friendly Relations and Cooperation among States in Accordance with the Charter of the United Nations.

120. Xanthaki, "The Right to Self-Determination," 17.

121. Ibid., 18–19.

122. Ibid., 32.

123. UN General Assembly, 3rd Session, Universal Declaration of Human Rights.

124. UN High Commissioner for Human Rights, "The Rights of Indigenous Peoples": "In the 1920s, American Indians approached the League of Nations. Their visit to Geneva attracted considerable attention, but there were no tangible results. In the early years of the United Nations, indigenous peoples' representatives made sporadic appeals to the world Organization. There was no specific reaction. A Bolivian Government initiative in the United Nations in 1948 to create a subcommission to study the social problems of aboriginal populations also came to nothing."

125. UN Commission on Human Rights, Subcommission on Prevention of Discrimination and Protection of Minorities, 36th Session, "Study of the Problem of Discrimination against Indigenous Populations," Final Report (Chapters XXI, XXII—Conclusions, proposals and recommendations), paragraph 6.

126. See UN Commission on Human Rights, Drafting Committee, 2nd Session, "Re-

port of the Drafting Committee to the Commission on Human Rights," quoting proposed texts for what would have been Article 31 by various states and UN committees.

127. See UN General Assembly, 3rd Session, Universal Declaration of Human Rights, Article 27(1): "Everyone has the right freely to participate in the cultural life of the community, to enjoy the arts and to share in scientific advancement and its benefits."

128. Several states that opposed the inclusion of "cultural genocide" in the Genocide Convention—drafted at the same time—argued that cultural minorities should be attended to in the UDHR (though many then voted against minority rights there). Morsink, *The Universal Declaration of Human Rights*, 274.

129. Banton, "International Norms and Latin American States' Policies on Indigenous Peoples," 91.

130. International Covenant on Civil and Political Rights.

131. Banton, "International Norms and Latin American States' Policies on Indigenous Peoples," 92.

132. Zion, "North American Indian Perspectives on Human Rights," 211. But see Carozza, "From Conquest to Constitutions," discussing Latin America's role in the drafting of the Universal Declaration of Human Rights and suggesting that the declaration can be read as more agreeable to collective rights and concerns for economic and social justice at the group level than is generally acknowledged.

133. American Anthropological Association, "Statement on Human Rights."

134. For the text of the questionnaire formulated by the UNESCO Committee on the Theoretical Bases of Human Rights, see UNESCO, ed., *Human Rights*, 251–57. For other responses to the questionnaire, see ibid.

135. For a more recent account of the origin of the document arguing that the invitation was originally extended to Herskovits in another capacity, see Goodale, *Surrendering to Utopia*, 19–23. Herskovits has long been considered to have drafted the text, in part because it is seen to reflect his style. See Renteln, *International Human Rights*, 83.

136. American Anthropological Association, "Statement on Human Rights," 539.

137. Ibid., 540.

138. Ibid.

139. Ibid., 542.

140. Ibid.

141. Ibid., 543.

142. Ibid., 540: "The consequences of [the point of view according to which 'an evangelical religious tradition' has 'translated the recognition of cultural differences into a summons to action'] have been disastrous to mankind. Doctrines of the 'white man's burden' have been employed to implement economic exploita-

tion and to deny the right to control their own affairs to millions of peoples over the world, where the expansion of Europe and America has not meant the literal extermination of whole populations."

143. Gandhi, "Letter to Julian Huxley."

CHAPTER 2: THE FOURTH WORLD MOVEMENT
AND *PANINDIANISMO*

1. See UN General Assembly, 61st Session, "Third Committee Approves Draft Resolution on Right to Development."

2. Colombia abstained, rather than voting yes, on final passage. Ibid.

3. An early *dependista*, Theotonio Dos Santos, described dependency as "a situation in which the economy of certain countries is conditioned by the development and expansion of another economy to which the former is subjected" ("The Structure of Dependence," 231). See also Frank, "Dependence Is Dead."

4. Frank, *Capitalism and Underdevelopment in Latin America*, 3.

5. Cardoso and Faletto, *Dependency and Development in Latin America*, xvii. Cardoso is perhaps the best known of a less radical, or reformist, group of dependistas. See also Cardoso, "Impedimentos estructurales e institucionales para el desarrollo."

6. Manuel and Posluns, *The Fourth World*, 40.

7. Griggs, "The Meaning of 'Nation' and 'State' in the Fourth World."

8. Manuel and Posluns, *The Fourth World*, 5.

9. Griggs, "The Meaning of 'Nation' and 'State' in the Fourth World."

10. Tinker, "The Full Circle of Liberation," 219.

11. Ibid.

12. Ibid.

13. Manuel and Posluns, *The Fourth World*, 6.

14. Dyck, "Representation and the 'Fourth World,' " 237.

15. Ryser, "The Legacy of Grand Chief George Manuel"; Colombres, *Hacia la Auto-gestión Indígena*, 39–41. Although this conference was considered "worldwide" at that time, it does not look like what would be a worldwide meeting today, given that it did not include representatives from Southeast Asia, South Asia, or Africa.

16. To the extent that the term "Fourth World" has been owned and deployed by indigenous peoples outside the global North, it has largely been used by groups in the Third World in their claims against the decolonized states in which they live. Tamilese nationalists, for example, have been using the term recently (Satyendra, "Fourth World—Nations without States").

17. Sanders, "Background Information on the World Council of Indigenous Peoples." This is not to say, however, that delegates from the global North were indifferent to the grave situations faced by Latin American indigenous peoples. One resolution from the October 1975 conference, for example, was dedicated to the unique circumstance of Brazilian Indians, whose government refused them permission to leave the country in order to participate in the conference. See

Resolución sobre la situación brasileña (British Columbia, Canada, 1975), reprinted in Colombres, *Hacia la Autogestión Indígena*, 54–55.

18. Sanders, "Background Information on the World Council of Indigenous Peoples."

19. Although the declaration states that it represents ninety-seven "Indian tribes and Nations from across North and South America," its contents make clear that its authors and intended subjects were almost exclusively indigenous peoples of the United States. Its references to indigenous peoples outside of that country are limited to general endorsements of solidarity between all "Native Nations" of the Western Hemisphere (International Indian Treaty Council, Declaration of Continuing Independence). For additional background, see "International Indian Treaty Council."

20. International Indian Treaty Council, Declaration of Continuing Independence.

21. Ibid.

22. Riggs, "American Indians, Economic Development, and Self-Determination in the 1960s," 433.

23. Deloria, *Behind the Trail of Broken Treaties*, 29.

24. Riggs, "American Indians, Economic Development, and Self-Determination in the 1960s," 432–33.

25. Ibid., 438–39.

26. Deloria, *Behind the Trail of Broken Treaties*, 20.

27. Ibid., 113.

28. Union of British Columbia Indian Chiefs, "Our History."

29. Union of British Columbia Indian Chiefs, *Stolen Lands, Broken Promises*, 30.

30. Union of British Columbia Indian Chiefs, UBCIC Declaration.

31. Ibid.

32. Bonfil Batalla, *Utopía y revolución*, 37. Original: "se postula que en América existe una sola civilización india."

33. Brysk, *From Tribal Village to Global Village*, 18.

34. "The Declaration of Barbados," 268. For a list of participants at Barbados I who signed the declaration, see ibid, 269.

35. Varese, "Memories of Solidarity," 24.

36. Ibid.

37. Ramos, "The Hyperreal Indian," 158. As this quotation indicates, "indigenism" is a word that is used in a variety of ways. Here Ramos is not talking of indigenism as the government ideology or strategy described in chapter 1, but is using the word to refer to indigenous activism or rights advocacy. Reflecting back on this time period from the vantage point of 1994, when she chronicles a divide between white and mestizo indigenous rights advocates and indigenous peoples themselves, she continues: "And so we reach 1990 with an indigenist panorama that has little to remind us of the solidarity, agitation and civic rapture of the seemingly remote days of the late 70s and early 80s."

38. Bonfil Batalla, *Utopía y revolución*, 20. Original: "La categoría de indio es supraét-

nica, es decir, no hace referencia ni da cuenta de la diversidad de pueblos que quedan englobados bajo el rubro de indios, porque la definición misma (el concepto de indio) parte de contraste con el no indio y esa distinción es lo único que importa, lo que da sentido al ser indio."

39. Ibid., 35–49. Original: "la negación del Occidente," "panindianismo: la afirmación de una civilización," "la recuperación de la historia," "revaloración de las culturas indias," "naturaleza y sociedad," "el hombre *es* naturaleza; no domina ni pretende dominar."

40. Ibid., 47, 49. Original: "folclorización," "banalización," "en interpretaciones deformadas," "defensa y recuperación de la tierra."

41. Ramos, "The Hyperreal Indian," 156.

42. "Conclusiones del Segundo Congreso Nacional de Pueblos Indígenas," 378. Original: "una política indigenista que sea paternal y protectora . . . Deseamos que se nos dé un trato de igual a igual y una participación más directa en todos los programas de la nación."

43. This conference was the continuation of what came to be called Barbados I, which—as noted above—had been held in 1971 with no indigenous representation. In the 1977 conference, many of the scholars who had participated in Barbados I met with a diverse group of Latin American indigenous activists, most of whom had traveled to the small Caribbean island in secret. See Varese, "Memories of Solidarity." Both Varese and Bonfil Batalla participated in Barbados I and Barbados II.

44. Bonfil Batalla, Mosonyi, Aguirre Beltran, and Arizpe, "La Declaración de Barbados II," 111–12.

45. Ibid., 112. Original: "nuestro pueblo."

46. Stavenhagen, "Challenging the Nation-State in Latin America," 430.

47. Ibid., 431.

48. Colombres, *Hacia la Autogestión Indígena*, 22. Original: "una identidad de clase que debe realizarse a expensas—y no a través—de su identidad étnica, o sea, la alienación para la liberación." Colombres, an Argentine lawyer and anthropologist clearly sympathetic to indigenous movements' resistance to what he calls "deculturation," further argues that "the Left's occidentalism does not conceive of the liberation of the indigenous without a prior proletarianization, even knowing that such proletarianization means the de-tribalization and death of the group as such." Original: "el occidentalismo de izquierda no concibe la liberación del indígena sin una previa proletarización, aun sabiendo que tal proletarización significa la destribalización y la muerte del grupo en cuanto tal" (21–22).

49. Reinaga, *La revolución india*, 54. Original: "una clase social sujeta a salario; clase explotada por una burguesía territorial . . . En Bolivia no existe la tal burguesía territorial o rural; el indio no es un asalariado . . . El indio no es una clase social . . . El indio es una raza, un pueblo, una Nación oprimida."

50. Ibid., 55. Original: "El indio no puede, no tiene que ser 'campesino' de la sociedad 'blanca'; el indio tiene que ser un *hombre libre*, en 'su' sociedad libre."

51. MINK'A, "Pueblo indio: Ultrajado, pero no vencido," 239. Original: "Cuando nos esclavizaban los patrones en las haciendas nos trataban de indios después de perder los latifundios nos tratan de campesinos. Ante todos estos hechos, nosotros declaramos con insistencia ¿por qué nos han de llamar campesinos?: que nos sigan llamando indios."

52. MITKA, "Manifiesto del Movimiento Indio Tupaj Katari," 264: "The simple revindication of class, as the dogmatic Marxists continue to repeat, weakens our fight and encloses it in foreign structures that—while perhaps applicable to other realities—are not to that of the Kollasuyo [the future state they advocated], demonstrating a lack of understanding of the real contradictions that exist in our subjugated and oppressed land." Original: "Que la simple reivindicación de clase, como los sostienen los dogmáticos repetidores del marxismo, debilita nuestra lucha y la encierra en esquemas foráneos, que pueden ser aplicables a otras realidades, pero no en el Kollasuyo, demostrando un desconocimiento de las verdaderas contradicciones existentes en nuestra tierra sojuzgada y oprimida."

53. Carnero Hoke, "Teoría y práctica de la indianidad," 123. Original: "Equivale, asimismo, a retomar el verdadero camino de la evolución social a partir del comunismo primitivo y desestimar, para siempre, la pesadilla del esclavismo, la feudalidad y el capitalismo."

54. Manifiesto de Tiawanacu. The manifesto explains that "the greatest good that governments and political parties can do for the campesinos is to let us . . . design our own socioeconomic policies taken from our cultural roots" (222). Original: "el mayor bien que los gobiernos y los partidos políticos pueden hacer a los campesinos es dejarnos elegir libre y democráticamente nuestros propios dirigentes y el que podamos elaborar nuestra propia política socioeconómica partiendo de nuestras raíces culturales."

55. "Tesis Política del Gran Pueblo Indio," 263. Original: "el sistema socialista más elevado que está latente en cada corazón indio, y que ha sido fuente de inspiración para todos los pueblos que hoy predican el socialismo como algo novedoso."

56. CRIC, "Nuestras luchas de ayer y de hoy," 291. Original: "una organización manejada por campesinos indígenas."

57. Rappaport, *Cumbe Reborn*, 15.

58. Colombres, *Hacia la Autogestión Indígena*, 161. Original: "la afirmación de un movimiento indígena multiétnico."

59. CRIC, "Nuestras luchas de ayer y de hoy," 295–96. Original: "Pero esta lucha no es sólo de medio millón de campesinos indígenas, sino de todos los campesinos explotados de Colombia."

60. Colombres, *Hacia la Autogestión Indígena*, 24, quoting an unnamed CRIC document. Original: "Dejamos constancia de que los indígenas hacemos parte del movi-

miento campesino, pero que por características propias tales como la organización interna, la lengua, costumbres, etc., tenemos derecho a nuestra organización particular, que debe ser respetada."

61. Rappaport, *Cumbe Reborn*, 15, citing Trino Morales, "El Movimiento Indígena en Colombia," in *Indianidad y Descolonización en América Latina: Documentos de la Segunda Reunión de Barbados* (Mexico: Nueva Imagen, 1979), 45.

62. Ibid., 16.

63. Ramos, "Cutting through State and Class," 261, quoting IWGIA, "Colombia: CRIC disassociates itself from guerrillas," *Newsletter* No. 33 (1983): 35.

64. Comisión Ideología y Filosofía Indianista del I Congreso Indio Sudamericana, "Conclusiones," in *Primer Congreso de Movimientos Indios de Sudamerica*, 136. Original: "Cuando el pueblo indio es mayoría, su finalidad inmediata será la toma del poder . . . Cuando el pueblo indio es minoría, debera lograr una autonomía, conservándose el derecho de decidir su acción inmediata junto a sectores populares, pero sin comprometer su independencia o identidad cultural."

65. Ibid. Original: "propugna la autodeterminación politica y autogestión económica de neustros pueblos."

66. For a discussion of the politics leading up to and following the manifesto, including the fracture of the Katarista movement that authored it, see Sanjinés C., *Mestizaje Upside-Down*, 154–58.

67. MITKA, "Conclusiones del Primer Congreso Histórico Político del Movimiento Indio Tupaj Katari," 251. Original: "El Movimiento Indio 'Tupaj Katari' no es un simple partido ni mucho menos una fracción: es la vanguardia política del pueblo indio del Kollasuyo, es un organismo autóctono, autónomo y autogestionario de esencia y presencia india; es antiimperialista, es antioccidental y es antirracista." Note that I have translated "autogestionario" as "self-managing." While there is no direct translation in English for "autogestión," a word sometimes used in Spanish during this period, the term appears to be used more to suggest autonomy or even economic self-sufficiency than anything akin to a strong form of self-determination. In this sense, the statements that use it differ markedly from those emerging in North America during the same period.

68. MITKA, "En el 196 aniversario del asesinato de Julián Apasa," 247. Original: "donde el hombre sea valorado por su condición humana y no por el color de su piel, por su actitud frente a la sociedad colectiva y no por sus intereses individuales."

69. CRIC, "Nuestras luchas de ayer y de hoy," 293.

70. Varese, "Memories of Solidarity," 23.

71. A contemporary overview of governmental and nongovernmental statistics of indigenous peoples throughout the world indicates that indigenous people comprise 13.3 million, or 13 percent, of the population of Mexico and between 1.2 and 1.4 million, or approximately 3 percent, of the population of Colombia. Sixty-two percent of the population of Bolivia aged fifteen or older self-identify as indigenous (Wessendorf, *The Indigenous World 2009*, 82, 124, 174). In 1978, Mayer and Masferrer

cited 8.042 million indigenous people as the official number in Mexico (12.4 percent of the population). In Bolivia, they estimated a population of 3.5 million indigenous people (59.2 percent), and in Colombia only 547,000 (2.2 percent), although they provided additional numbers of people identified as self-sufficient or tribal (*población autosuficiente y tribal*), which consisted of 187,000 people in Bolivia and 421,000 in Colombia ("La Población Indígena de América en 1978," 220–21).

72. Carta de Pátzcuaro, 374. Original: "todo lo que configura nuestra personalidad como pueblo."

73. Ibid. Original: "aceptamos lo positivo que la sociedad nacional nos ofrece."

74. Ibid., 373: "To facilitate our incorporation into the Mexican Revolution's objectives . . . [we demand] respect for the self-determination of indigenous communities, since the Republic's Constitution clearly posits its guarantees for all citizens . . . although in labor law and in agricultural and social security matters, we find ourselves far from implementing them fully." Original: "Para facilitar nuestra incorporación a los objetivos de la Revolución Mexicana . . . [exigimos] el respeto a la autodeterminación de las comunidades indígenas, pues si bien la Constitución de la Republica postula las garantías para todos los ciudadanos . . . aun en el derecho laboral, en materia agraria y de seguridad social, nos encontramos a una larga distancia de ejercerlo plenamente."

75. Brøsted et al., *Native Power*, 71–72.

76. Ibid.

77. Ibid., 72.

CHAPTER 3: SELF-DETERMINATION

1. Swepston, "Indigenous and Tribal Peoples and International Organizations," 15.

2. UN Commission on Human Rights, Subcommission on Prevention of Discrimination and Protection of Minorities, 36th Session, "Study of the Problem of Discrimination against Indigenous Populations," Final Report (Chapters XXI, XXII—Conclusions, proposals and recommendations). Other parts of the study may be found at http://www.un.org/esa/socdev/unpfii/en/spdaip.html.

   The decision to write the report stemmed from the suggestion by an expert on the subcommission that discrimination against indigenous people should not be included in his general 1976 study, but should be "singled out for special attention" (see Eide, "Indigenous Populations and Human Rights," 201–2).

3. For a somewhat pessimistic assessment, see Sanders, "The U.N. Working Group on Indigenous Populations," 408. For accounts that tie the Cobo Report directly to the establishment of the Working Group, see Daes, "United Nations Activities in the Field of Indigenous Rights," 12; and Eide, "Indigenous Populations and Human Rights," 202.

4. UN High Commissioner for Human Rights, "The Rights of Indigenous Peoples."

5. Swepston, "Indigenous and Tribal Peoples and International Organizations," 16.

6. UN Commission on Human Rights, Subcommission on Prevention of Discrimina-

tion and Protection of Minorities, 36th Session, "Study of the Problem of Discrimination against Indigenous Populations," Final Report (Chapters XXI, XXII—Conclusions, proposals and recommendations), paragraph 379.

7. A 1995 note by Erica-Irene Daes outlined definitions from various documents: "submit[ting] that an important first question to be addressed by the Working Group is the desirability of developing a definition of indigenous peoples" (UN Commission on Human Rights, Subcommission on Prevention of Discrimination and Protection of Minorities, WGIP, 13th Session, Note by the chairperson-rapporteur of the Working Group on Indigenous Populations, paragraph 4). For further discussion of various definitions and the question of whether a definition of indigenous peoples should be asserted at an international level, see Sanders, "Indigenous Peoples."

8. International Labor Organization, Convention 169, Article 1(2).

9. Ibid., Article 1(1). In chapter 4 I discuss how a number of advocates have nevertheless focused on self-identification as the principal criterion for determining indigeneity.

10. Corntassel and Primeau, "Indigenous 'Sovereignty' and International Law," 361.

11. Ibid., 344.

12. Ibid., 351.

13. For a discussion of many of these constitutions, with a detailed focus on Bolivia and Colombia, see Van Cott, *The Friendly Liquidation of the Past.*

14. Brysk, *From Tribal Village to Global Village,* 18.

15. Roy and Alfredsson, "Indigenous Rights," 21.

16. Ibid.

17. Sanders, "The Re-Emergence of Indigenous Questions in International Law," 25.

18. Montevideo Convention on the Rights and Duties of States. As noted in chapter 1, Article 1 of the convention says: "The state as a person of international law should possess the following qualifications: (a) a permanent population; (b) a defined territory; (c) government; and (d) capacity to enter into relations with the other states." For discussion of the use of the Montevideo Convention and other texts to support claims to statehood, see Roy and Alfredsson, "Indigenous Rights," 20 and 23, note 31.

19. Tennant, "Indigenous Peoples," 45.

20. Ibid., citing Glenn T. Morris, "In Support of the Right of Self-Determination for Indigenous Peoples under International Law," *German Year Book of International Law* (1986): 314. See also Roy and Alfredsson, "Indigenous Rights," 20.

21. Draft Declaration of Principles for the Defense of the Indigenous Nations and Peoples of the Western Hemisphere. Among the thirteen provisions are those that consider treaties (paragraphs 5 and 6), jurisdiction (7), claims to territory (8), cultural integrity (10), protection of the environment (11), and tribal membership (12).

22. Dunbar-Ortiz, "The First Decade of Indigenous Peoples at the United Nations," 68.

23. Ibid., 67. The atmosphere also may have been more welcoming of national liberation organizations, as "fewer governments participated than in 1977, due at least in part to the call by the Reagan administration for a government boycott of the conference." Reagan apparently argued that the conference organizers were either "Soviet fronts" or "Soviet dupes," according to Dunbar-Ortiz, who notes that "among Western countries, only the government of Norway registered, although other governments were present unofficially, and dozens of African, Asian, and Latin American governments registered and attended" (68).

24. Ibid.

25. Barsh, "Indigenous Peoples," 375–76, quoting the Mi'kmaq delegation.

26. Ibid., 376. See also ibid., 385, referring to the Ecuadorian representative's comment.

27. Ibid., 376.

28. Ibid. Also discussed in Sanders, "The Re-Emergence of Indigenous Questions in International Law," 29.

29. Barsh, "Indigenous Peoples," 376.

30. Sanders, "The Re-Emergence of Indigenous Questions in International Law," 29.

31. Lâm, *At the Edge of the State*, 52 and note 144, citing Julian Burger, *Report from the Frontier*, 56.

32. UN Commission on Human Rights, Subcommission on Prevention of Discrimination and Protection of Minorities, WGIP, 3rd Session, "Paper Submitted to the U.N. Working Group on Indigenous Populations by the Coalition of First Nations in conjunction with the International Indian Treaty Council."

33. For further discussion and contextualization of this argument under international and U.S. law, see Kauanui, "Hawaiian Nationhood, Self-Determination, and International Law"; Kauanui, "Colonialism in Equality," 643.

34. UN Commission on Human Rights, Subcommission on Prevention of Discrimination and Protection of Minorities, WGIP, 3rd Session, "Statement on Behalf of the Free Papua Movement (West Papuan People's Movement for Freedom and Independence)," paragraph 18.

35. Sanders, "The U.N. Working Group on Indigenous Populations," 428.

36. UN Commission on Human Rights, Subcommission on Prevention of Discrimination and Protection of Minorities, WGIP, 4th Session, Material Received from Non-Governmental Organizations in Consultative Status with the Economic and Social Council, paragraph 2.

37. UN Commission on Human Rights, Subcommission on Prevention of Discrimination and Protection of Minorities, WGIP, 3rd Session, "Paper Submitted to the U.N. Working Group on Indigenous Populations by the Coalition of First Nations in conjunction with the International Indian Treaty Council."

38. Torres, "The Rights of Indigenous Populations," 142–43.

39. UN Commission on Human Rights, Subcommission on Prevention of Discrimination and Protection of Minorities, 39th Session, "Declaration of Principles Adopted by the Indigenous Peoples' Preparatory Meeting," paragraph 16.

40. For a history of Treaty Six and a transcript of a meeting the Treaty Six Chiefs held in 1989 with the UN's special rapporteur on indigenous people, see Venne, Shulte-Tenckhoff, and Gray, *Honour Bound.*

41. UN Commission on Human Rights, Subcommission on Prevention of Discrimination and Protection of Minorities, WGIP, 6th Session, "Treaties and the Study of Treaties: Statement submitted by the Treaty Six Chiefs."

42. Ibid.

43. UN Commission on Human Rights, Subcommission on Prevention of Discrimination and Protection of Minorities, 46th Session, Agenda Item 15, "Discrimination against Indigenous Peoples," paragraph 35.

44. UN Commission on Human Rights, Subcommission on Prevention of Discrimination and Protection of Minorities, WGIP, 12th Session, Agenda Item 5, "Statement of the International Confederation of Autonomous Chapters of the American Indian Movement."

45. Others equated the term "peoples" with the right to statehood as well. Indeed, Warren and Jackson note that "the Draft U.N. Declaration on the Rights of Indigenous Peoples was unacceptable to many potential signatories because 'peoples' suggested self-determination with no specified limits, hypothetically permitting secession" ("Introduction," 34, note 31).

46. African Group of States, "Draft Aide Memoire: United Nations Declaration on the Rights of Indigenous People," paragraph 8.0. Note the title refers to "People" not "peoples."

47. Sanders, "The U.N. Working Group on Indigenous Populations," 428–29, citing a presentation that Diaz gave to a professional training program for indigenous representatives in Geneva in July 1985.

48. See, e.g., UN Commission on Human Rights, Subcommission on Prevention of Discrimination and Protection of Minorities, WGIP, 1st Session, "Study of the Problem of Discrimination against Indigenous Populations."

49. OAS, Inter-American Commission on Human Rights, "Report on the Situation of Human Rights of a Segment of the Nicaraguan Population of Miskito Origin," Part Two, B(8), describing the position articulated by Wiggins.

50. Ibid., paragraph 9

51. Ibid., paragraph 10.

52. Eide, "Indigenous Populations and Human Rights," 205.

53. UN Commission on Human Rights, Subcommission on Prevention of Discrimination and Protection of Minorities, WGIP, 6th Session, "Statement in Reference to the Study on the Significance of Indigenous Treaties presented by Rudolph C. Ryser."

54. Ibid.

55. Ryser, "Indian Nations and United States Debate Self-Determination and Self-Government in the United Nations."

56. Ibid.

57. UN Commission on Human Rights, Subcommission on Prevention of Discrimination and Protection of Minorities, WGIP, 11th Session, "Statement of Maivan C. Lam."

58. UN Commission on Human Rights, Subcommission on Prevention of Discrimination and Protection of Minorities, WGIP, 11th Session, "Statement by Dr. Rolf H. Lindeholm."

59. UN Commission on Human Rights, Subcommission on Prevention of Discrimination and Protection of Minorities, WGIP, 11th Session, "Statement of Kathryn Skipper."

60. Lâm, *At the Edge of the State*, 56.

61. Daes, "Striving for Self-Determination of Indigenous Peoples," 55.

62. UN Commission on Human Rights, Subcommission on Prevention of Discrimination and Protection of Minorities, 45th Session, "Explanatory Note Concerning the Draft Declaration on the Rights of Indigenous Peoples," paragraph 23.

63. Ibid., paragraph 21.

64. Daes, "Striving for Self-Determination of Indigenous Peoples," 57.

65. Ibid., 55.

66. Lâm, *At the Edge of the State*, 57.

67. Russell, *Recognizing Aboriginal Title*, 353, quoting Bill Barker speaking on behalf of the Australian delegation.

68. See Australian Human Rights Commission, "United We Stand," discussing an April 2009 statement made by the federal government in support of the UN Declaration.

69. UN Commission on Human Rights, Subcommission on Prevention of Discrimination and Protection of Minorities, 36th Session, "Study of the Problem of Discrimination against Indigenous Populations," Final Report (Chapters XXI, XXII—Conclusions, proposals and recommendations), paragraph 580.

70. Ibid., paragraph 581.

71. UN Commission on Human Rights, Subcommission on Prevention of Discrimination and Protection of Minorities, 35th Session, Agenda Item 15, "Study of the Problem of Discrimination against Indigenous Populations," paragraph 72.

72. Ibid., paragraph 82.

73. As Benedict Kingsbury explains decolonization, "the future relations between colonizer and colonized were then to be determined by free agreement, but the right to self-determination was concerned with the preconditions for such choice, not with the relationship itself" ("Reconstructing Self-Determination," 24). For discussion of the role that plebiscites played in self-determination in the interwar period, see Berman, "But the Alternative Is Despair," 1792.

74. Lâm, *At the Edge of the State*, 156, quoting Eide, "In Search of Constructive Alternatives to Secession," 140.

75. Barsh, "Evolving Conceptions of Group Rights in International Law," 9.

76. Torres, "The Rights of Indigenous Populations," 162.

77. Ibid., 163.

78. Niezen, "The Indigenous Claim for Recognition in the International Public Sphere," 598.

79. Ibid., 598–99.

80. Díaz Polanco, *Indigenous Peoples in Latin America*, 95.

81. Ibid.

82. Ibid., 98.

83. Ibid., 103.

84. Brøsted et al., *Native Power*, 72.

85. Torres, "The Rights of Indigenous Populations," 144.

86. UN Commission on Human Rights, Subcommission on Prevention of Discrimination and Protection of Minorities, WGIP, 12th Session, Declaration of Tlahuitoltepec on the Fundamental Rights of the Indigenous Nations, Nationalities and Peoples of Indo-Latin America, paragraphs 1 and 3.

87. Asamblea de Autoridades Mixes (ASAM), Servicios del Pueblo Mixe (SER) y la Escuela Nacional de Antropología e Historia, "Derechos indígenas en Naciones Unidas," 177. Original: "Autonomía no es lo mismo que separación . . . La lucha de los pueblos indígenas no es separatista, sino que da lugar a la unión de distintos y su concertación."

88. Ibid., 178. Original: "un efecto disgregador y prejudicial para todos los pueblos indios de América Latina."

89. Ibid., 178–79. Original: "Porque la autonomía siempre es integral, es decir, implica el ejercicio de derechos fundamentales en lo económico, en lo político, en lo cultural, etcétera."

90. Ibid., 181.

91. UN Commission on Human Rights, Subcommission on Prevention of Discrimination and Protection of Minorities, WGIP, 6th Session, "Submission by the Nordic Sami Council."

92. Ibid.

93. UN Commission on Human Rights, Subcommission on Prevention of Discrimination and Protection of Minorities, WGIP, 6th Session, "Statement by Dr. Atle Grahl-Madsen."

94. Lâm, *At the Edge of the State*, 60.

95. Karlsson, "Anthropology and the 'Indigenous Slot,'" 409.

96. Ibid.

97. Lâm, *At the Edge of the State*, 61, quoting Dodson, "The Human Rights Situation of Indigenous Peoples in Australia."

98. Anaya, *Indigenous Peoples in International Law,* 109.

99. Ibid., 100.

100. Ibid., 114–15.

101. Lâm, *At the Edge of the State*, 60–61, citing Anaya, *Indigenous Peoples in International Law*.

102. UN Commission on Human Rights, Subcommission on Prevention of Discrimination and Protection of Minorities, WGIP, 12th Session, Grand Council of the Crees (of Quebec), paragraphs 11 and 12.

103. UN Commission on Human Rights, Subcommission on Prevention of Discrimination and Protection of Minorities, WGIP, 12th Session, Declaration of Tlahuitoltepec on the Fundamental Rights of the Indigenous Nations, Nationalities and Peoples of Indo-Latin America.

104. UN Commission on Human Rights, Subcommission on Prevention of Discrimination and Protection of Minorities, WGIP, 11th Session, "Statement of Maivan C. Lam."

105. UN Commission on Human Rights, Subcommission on Prevention of Discrimination and Protection of Minorities, WGIP, 11th Session, "Review of Developments Pertaining to the Promotion and Protection of Human Rights and Fundamental Freedoms of Indigenous Populations, including Economic and Social Relations between Indigenous Peoples and States. Information received from Governments: Netherlands," paragraph 10.

106. Ibid., paragraph 8.

107. See Anaya, *Indigenous Peoples in International Law,* 129–56.

108. Lâm, *At the Edge of the State,* 179.

CHAPTER 4: HUMAN RIGHT TO CULTURE

1. OAS, Inter-American Commission on Human Rights, "Report on the Situation of Human Rights of a Segment of the Nicaraguan Population of Miskito Origin," paragraph 3.

2. Corntassel and Primeau, "Indigenous 'Sovereignty' and International Law," 365.

3. Anaya, "The Capacity of International Law to Advance Ethnic or Nationality Rights Claims," 408.

4. Svensson, "Right to Self-Determination," 363.

5. Ibid.

6. Zion, "North American Indian Perspectives on Human Rights," 209.

7. Muehlebach, "What Self in Self-Determination?" 255, citing Scheinin, "The Right to Self-Determination under the Covenant on Civil and Political Rights."

8. Corntassel and Primeau, "Indigenous 'Sovereignty' and International Law," 361.

9. Ibid.

10. UN Commission on Human Rights, Subcommission on Prevention of Discrimination and Protection of Minorities, 45th Session, "Report of the Working Group on Indigenous Populations on its Eleventh Session," paragraphs 68 and 69.

11. American Anthropological Association, Executive Board, "Committee for Human Rights Guidelines."

12. "The Declaration of Barbados," 268.

13. Ibid.

14. Ibid.

15. Nagengast and Turner, "Introduction," 270.

16. Messer, "Anthropology and Human Rights," 224.

17. Sponsel, "1995 Annual Report."

18. Ibid.

19. Messer, "Anthropology and Human Rights," 236.

20. American Anthropological Association, Executive Board, "Committee for Human Rights Guidelines."

21. American Anthropological Association, Committee for Human Rights, "Declaration on Anthropology and Human Rights."

22. Ibid.

23. Turner, "Human Rights, Human Difference," 273.

24. Barsh, "Revision of ILO Convention No. 107," 759.

25. ILO 169 has been ratified by the Latin American and Caribbean states of Argentina, Bolivia, Brazil, Chile, Colombia, Costa Rica, Dominica, Ecuador, Guatemala, Honduras, Mexico, Nepal, Paraguay, Peru, and Venezuela. It has also been ratified by Denmark, Fiji, the Netherlands, Norway, and Spain.

26. In *Indigenous Rights and United Nations Standards*, Xanthaki notes that over the years, ILO 107's assimilationist force has declined as a result of such interpretations by the ILO Committee of Experts on the Application of Conventions and Recommendations, 49–67.

27. International Labor Organization, Convention 169, Article 5(a).

28. Ibid., Article 14(1).

29. Ibid., Article 13(1).

30. Ibid., Article 1(1a).

31. Ibid., Article 1(1b).

32. Ibid., Article 1(2).

33. International Labor Organization, *Indigenous and Tribal Peoples Rights in Practice*, 9.

34. Ibid., 9–10.

35. See, e.g., Xanthaki, *Indigenous Rights and United Nations Standards*, discussing a draft of the UN Declaration: "As in the I.L.O. Convention No. 169, the criterion that defines indigenous peoples is that of self-identification" (105).

36. Thornberry, *Indigenous Peoples and Human Rights*, 339.

37. International Labor Conference, 76th Session, 1989, *Record of Proceedings*, 31 / 6. See also the statement made by Sharon Venne in ibid., 31 / 7.

38. Thornberry, *Indigenous Peoples and Human Rights*, 339.

39. For mention of this debate, as well as a general discussion of the international legal treatment of "peoples" and self-determination, see Myntti, "The Right of Indigenous Peoples to Self-Determination and Effective Participation."

40. International Labor Organization, Convention 169, Article 1(3). For further discussion of this provision, see Daes, "The Spirit and Letter of the Right to Self-Determination of Indigenous Peoples," 67. See also Myntti, "The Right of Indigenous Peoples to Self-Determination and Effective Participation," which argues

that the convention recognizes some indigenous political, if not territorial, autonomy, which Myntti calls "ethno-political self-government" (118).

41. Swepston, "Indigenous and Tribal Peoples and International Organizations," 17.

42. Colchester, "Indigenous Peoples and the International Labor Organization," 43.

43. International Labor Conference, 76th Session, 1989, *Record of Proceedings*, 31 / 6.

44. Ibid., 31 / 7.

45. Ibid., 31 / 6.

46. Ibid., 31 / 8.

47. I discuss the Zapatistas' use of ILO 169 below and in chapter 6. Chapters 8 and 9 examine its invocations by Colombian Afro-descendants. For the Mapuche challenge based on ILO 169, see International Labor Organization, Governing Body, "Report of the Committee Set Up to Examine the Representation Alleging Non-observance by Argentina of the Indigenous and Tribal Peoples Convention, 1989 (No. 169), made under article 24 of the ILO Constitution by the Education Workers Union of Río Negro (UNTER)."

48. Representations are the mechanisms through which reports of serious cases in which "any of the [state] Members has failed to secure in any respect the effective observance within its jurisdiction of any Convention to which it is a party" (International Labor Organization, Constitution, Article 24). Representations constitute only one of four submission options under the ILO. The others include "complaints," "special procedures for freedom of association," and "special surveys on discrimination." The Governing Body only accepts cases from government institutions, trade unions, and ILO delegates.

49. International Labor Organization, Governing Body, "Report of the Committee Set Up to Examine the Representation Alleging Non-observance by Peru of the Indigenous and Tribal Peoples Convention, 1989 (No. 169), Made under Article 24 of the ILO Constitution by the General Confederation of Workers of Peru (CGTP)," paragraph 30. This paragraph goes on to note that the committee's "experience acquired in the application of the Convention and its predecessor [suggests] that the loss of communal land often damages the cohesion and viability of the people concerned. For this reason, in the preparatory work for the Convention, many delegates took the position that lands owned by indigenous persons, and especially communal lands, should be inalienable." I will return to this issue in chapter 6. See also paragraphs 31 and 32(c) on the appropriate process for making decisions that affect indigenous land ownership.

50. International Labor Organization, Governing Body, "Report of the Committee Set Up to Examine the Representation Alleging Non-observance by Guatemala of the Indigenous and Tribal Peoples Convention, 1989 (No. 169), Made under Article 24 of the ILO Constitution by the Federation of Country and City Workers (FTCC)," paragraph 45. See also paragraphs 26 and 48.

51. Ibid., paragraph 48. The decision quotes from Article 15(2) of the convention.

52. Speed and Reyes, "Rights, Resistance, and Radical Alternatives," 66 and note 24.

When the project began in 2001, its focus was on three types of complaints. According to a statement at the time from the organization with which Proyecto 169 was associated, "the first will treat the theme of paramilitaries and the complicity of the state in their criminal acts; the second will focus on the right of self-definition and territory; and the final will present the injustices of presidential expropriations and the militarization they permit" (Red de Defensores Comunitarios por los Derechos Humanos, "Defensores Comunitarios Denuncian ante la OIT"). Original: "El primero tratará el tema de paramilitares y complicidad del Estado en sus actos delictivos; el segundo será enfocado a los derechos de auto-definición y territorios, y el último, presentará las injusticias de las expropiaciones presidenciales y la militarización que estas permiten."

53. Speed, "Global Discourses on the Local Terrain," 205.

54. Ibid., 223.

55. Slater, *Geopolitics and the Post-colonial*, 205, noting: "In fact, one of the first communiqués of the *Ejército Zapatista de Liberación Nacional* (EZLN) stated that NAFTA 'is a death certificate for the Indian peoples of Mexico, who are dispensable for the government of Carlos Salinas de Gortari' " (quoting Harvey, *The Chiapas Rebellion*, 39).

56. Colombia, Corte Constitucional, Sentencia T-379. Original: "se refiere a la autonomía de las comunidades indígenas al reconocer la aspiración de esos pueblos a asumir el control de sus propias instituciones y formas de vida, así como su desarrollo económico y social, manteniendo y fortaleciendo sus identidades, lenguas y religiones."

57. In contrast, when the Convention on the Rights of the Child went into effect over a decade later (in 1990), its guarantee of cultural rights for indigenous peoples was explicit: "In those States in which ethnic, religious or linguistic minorities or persons of indigenous origin exist, a child belonging to such a minority or who is indigenous shall not be denied the right, in community with other members of his or her group, to enjoy his or her own culture, to profess and practise his or her own religion, or to use his or her own language" (Article 30). Note that this language is identical to that used in Article 27 of the ICCPR, except that it adds the words "or who is indigenous."

58. Anaya, *Indigenous Peoples in International Law*, 100.

59. UN Human Rights Committee, Final Report, *Lovelace v. Canada*.

60. UN Human Rights Committee, Final Report, *Kitok v. Sweden*.

61. UN Human Rights Committee, Final Report, *Lovelace v. Canada*, paragraph 15.

62. Ibid., paragraph 16. This case has been the subject of much scholarly commentary, both because it was the first case to use Article 27 in the context of indigenous rights and because of its treatment of the gender discrimination claim. For an excellent critical discussion of the decision, see Knop, *Diversity and Self-Determination in International Law*, 358–72.

63. UN Human Rights Committee, Final Report, *Kitok v. Sweden*, paragraph 9.

64. Scheinin, "Indigenous Peoples' Land Rights under the International Covenant on Civil and Political Rights."

65. UN Human Rights Committee, 50th Session, CCPR General Comment No. 23, paragraph 7.

66. Ibid.

67. Charters, "Developments in Indigenous Peoples' Land Rights under International Law and Their Domestic Implications," 511, discussing the committee's 1999 Concluding Observations to Mexico, Chile, and Canada.

68. UN Human Rights Committee, Final Report, *Länsman et al. v. Finland*, paragraph 10.2. See also UN Human Rights Committee, Final Report, *Apirana Mahuika et al. v. New Zealand*, paragraph 9.3.

69. UN Human Rights Committee, Final Report, *Apirana Mahuika et al. v. New Zealand*, paragraph 9.4.

70. UN Human Rights Committee, Final Report, *Lubicon Lake Band v. Canada*.

71. Scheinin, "Indigenous Peoples' Land Rights Under the International Covenant on Civil and Political Rights."

72. Thornberry, *Indigenous Peoples and Human Rights*, 126.

73. UN Human Rights Committee, 50th Session, CCPR General Comment No. 23, paragraph 3.2, citing *Kitok v. Sweden*.

74. Scheinin, "The Right to Self-Determination under the Covenant on Civil and Political Rights," 179–80, discussing decision in *Kitok,* among others. The Article 1 claims were considered inadmissible because the committee found that the Optional Protocol recognizes only individual rights and, further, that individuals cannot be victims of a collective right to self-determination. In *Kitok,* the state had argued that the Sami did not constitute a people under Article 1 (UN Human Rights Committee, Final Report, *Kitok v. Sweden*, paragraph 4.1). The committee never needed to address that claim because of its finding that Article 1 did not apply to Kitok's individual application (paragraph 6.3).

75. UN Human Rights Committee, 50th Session, Final Report, *Lubicon Lake Band v. Canada*, paragraph 13.3.

76. UN Human Rights Committee, 50th Session, CCPR General Comment No. 23, paragraph 3.1.

77. See UN Human Rights Committee, Final Report, *Fongum Gorji-Dinka v. Cameroon*; UN Human Rights Committee, Final Report, *Diergaardt et al. v. Namibia*.

78. In UN Human Rights Committee, Final Report, *Apirana Mahuika et al. v. New Zealand*, the committee responded to a claim under the Optional Protocol brought by a group of individual Maori members under Articles 1 and 27, and noted not only that Article 1 might be relevant to understanding Article 27, but that only collective claims, not those brought by a "group of individuals, who claim to be commonly affected," are precluded. Because the committee did not ultimately find a violation of any of the claimed rights, it did not pursue the possible ways in which Article 1 might affect the interpretation of Article 27. For the committee's

connection of Article 1 to other articles, see UN Human Rights Committee, Final Report, *Diergaardt et al. v. Namibia*, paragraph 10.3, which notes that "the provisions of article 1 may be relevant in the interpretation of other rights protected by the Covenant, in particular Articles 25, 26 and 27"; and U.N. Human Rights Committee, Final Report, *Gillot et al. v. France*, paragraph 13.26, which indicates the relevance of Article 1 to the interpretation of Article 25.

79. Scheinin, "The Right to Self-Determination under the Covenant on Civil and Political Rights," 192.

80. Ibid., 193.

81. International Convention on the Elimination of All Forms of Racial Discrimination, Article 14(1) reads: "A State Party may at any time declare that it recognizes the competence of the Committee to receive and consider communications from individuals or groups of individuals within its jurisdiction claiming to be victims of a violation by that State Party of any of the rights set forth in this Convention." At the end of 2009, fifty-three states had recognized this competence.

82. UN CERD, 48th Session, "Report of the Committee," 1.

83. UN CERD, 68th Session, Early Warning and Urgent Action Procedure: Decision 1(68): United States of America, paragraph 10. The United States insisted in its later 2007 report to the CERD that Western Shoshone claims lay outside the CERD's purview. In particular, the United States contended that it had already successfully adjudicated the case in 1951 through the Indian Claims Commission, and that it had duly compensated the Western Shoshone for ancestral lands "that had been taken by private individuals or the government" (U.S. Department of State, "Periodic Report to the U.N. Committee on the Elimination of Racial Discrimination Concerning the International Convention on the Elimination of All Forms of Racial Discrimination" paragraph 1[a]). Therefore, the report notes, "in its Early Warning and Urgent Action Procedure, the CERD may be viewed as analyzing events that occurred well before the CERD existed and before the U.S. became a party to the CERD" (paragraph 18[a]). The United States argued that the petition resulted not from discrimination, but from a half-century-old "internal dispute among the Western Shoshone" over acceptable compensation for the group's lands (paragraph 1[c]).

84. Sanders, "The Re-Emergence of Indigenous Questions in International Law," 22–23.

85. Anaya, "Keynote Address," 257.

86. Ibid.

87. Banton, "International Norms and Latin American States' Policies on Indigenous Peoples," 93.

88. Ibid., 95–98.

89. Ibid., 97–98.

90. Ibid., 99.

91. Ibid., 100.

92. Specifically, Banton considers that "indigenous peoples in Costa Rica, Ecuador and

Peru could use article 14 of the Convention to maintain that the state has not protected their individual or shared rights." Ibid. Recall that Article 14(1) permits communications from groups as well as individuals.

93. UN CERD, 51st Session, General Recommendation No. 23, paragraph 1.

94. Anaya, "Keynote Address," 259.

95. Ibid., 260.

96. UN CERD, 51st Session, General Recommendation No. 23, paragraph 1.

97. Ibid., paragraph 5.

98. Ibid., paragraphs 5 and 4(c).

99. Ibid., paragraph 4(d).

100. International Convention on the Elimination of All Forms of Racial Discrimination, Article 5(d)(v).

101. UN CERD, 57th Session, Concluding Observations of the Committee: Finland, paragraph 11.

102. See, e.g., UN CERD, 70th Session, Concluding Observations of the Committee: India, paragraph 28.

103. The committee included in its 2006 recommendations to El Salvador: "The Committee urges the State party to take the necessary legislative steps to enable it to ratify ILO Convention No. 169" (UN CERD, 68th Session, Concluding Observations of the Committee: El Salvador, paragraph 10). For an excellent discussion of El Salvador's relationship with the CERD on the issue of indigenous rights, see Clark, "Confusion, Conformity, and Contradiction," 101–39.

104. UN CERD, 70th Session, Concluding Observations of the Committee: Canada, paragraph 27.

105. UN CERD, 72nd Session, Concluding Observations of the Committee: United States of America, paragraph 29.

106. Ibid., referencing Articles (d)(v), 5(e)(iv) and 5(e)(vi) of the convention.

107. Ibid.

108. UN CERD, 48th Session, General Recommendation No. 21, paragraph 4. To support its opposition to external self-determination, the General Recommendation relies on the Friendly Relations Declaration and UN secretary general, *An Agenda for Peace* (paragraph 6).

109. UN CERD, 48th Session, General Recommendation No. 21, paragraph 1.

110. Anaya, *Indigenous Peoples in International Law*, 232.

111. OAS, Inter-American Commission on Human Rights, "The Human Rights Situation of the Indigenous People in the Americas," Introduction.

112. In the discussion of commission and court decisions that follow, some refer to the declaration while others refer to the convention. The commission applies the declaration to those states that have not signed the convention. Because non-signatories to the convention have not accepted the jurisdiction of the court, the court has little reason to refer to the declaration and almost exclusively relies on the convention.

113. The court has the authority to hear cases that are referred to it by either the commission or a state party (American Convention on Human Rights, Article 61[1]). Because individuals cannot bring a case directly to the court, they must file a complaint with the commission alleging a rights violation. If the commission finds that the complaint is admissible, it will usually attempt a friendly settlement with the state party in question. In some special circumstances, or when the state and commission fail to reach a friendly settlement, the commission will bring a case against the state to the court. When it does so, the commission argues on behalf of the complainants, though since 2003, victims have been permitted to play an increasingly larger role in the proceedings.

114. OAS, Inter-American Commission on Human Rights, "The Human Rights Situation of the Indigenous People in the Americas," Introduction.

115. Ibid., chapter III, 6(B).

116. When the report was written, the commission had reached a decision or settlement regarding only five complaints that involved or implicated the cultural rights of indigenous or "tribal" groups. The commission passed resolutions in four cases between 1973 and 1985: *Coulter et al. v. Brazil, Paraguay: Tribu Aché-Guayaki*, "Report on the Situation of Human Rights of a Segment of the Nicaraguan Population of Miskito Origin," and *Guahibo Indians v. Colombia*. In 1999, it brokered a settlement in a land dispute in *Comunidades Indígenas Enxet-Lamenxay y Kayleyphapopyet-Riachito v. Paraguay*. It had decided to refer to the Inter-American Court three additional complaints, one of which had been decided at the time and two of which were pending: *Aloeboetoe v. Suriname, Plan de Sanchez Massacre v. Guatamala* and *The Mayagna (Sumo) Awas Tingni Community v. Nicaragua*.

117. For a summary of indigenous rights cases decided by the commission and the court through 2006, some of which implicate culture, see Pasqualucci, "The Evolution of International Indigenous Rights in the Inter-American Human Rights System."

118. OAS, Inter-American Court of Human Rights, *Aloeboetoe v. Suriname*, paragraph 97(a).

119. See, e.g., Pasqualucci, "The Evolution of International Indigenous Rights in the Inter-American Human Rights System," 299.

120. OAS, Inter-American Court of Human Rights, *Aloeboetoe v. Suriname*, paragraph 62: "As already stated . . . , here local law is not Surinamese law, for the latter is not effective in the region insofar as family law is concerned. It is necessary, then, to take Saramaka custom into account. That custom will be the basis for the interpretation of [the terms 'spouse' and 'ascendant'] to the degree that it does not contradict the American Convention. Hence, in referring to 'ascendants,' the Court shall make no distinction as to sex, even if that might be contrary to

Saramaka custom." At the end of this chapter, I discuss the exception in the last two sentences here as an example of the invisible asterisk.

121. OAS, Inter-American Court of Human Rights, *Bámaca Valásquez v. Guatemala*, Reparations and Costs, paragraph 52.

122. OAS, Inter-American Court of Human Rights, *Bámaca Valásquez v. Guatemala*, Merits, paragraph 165.

123. Ibid., paragraph 145(f).

124. OAS, Inter-American Court of Human Rights, *Plan de Sanchez Massacre v. Guatemala*, Reparations and Costs, paragraph 87(b).

125. Protocol One to the European Convention on Human Rights, which went into effect in 1953, and the African Charter on Human and Peoples' Rights, which entered into force in 1986, also include language protecting possession or property.

126. Article 23 of the American Declaration of the Rights and Duties of Man reads: "Every person has a right to own such private property as meets the essential needs of decent living and helps to maintain the dignity of the individual and of the home." It has been by the commission primarily in complaints against OAS member states that have not signed the convention.

127. UN General Assembly, 3rd Session, Universal Declaration of Human Rights, Article 17.

128. For a discussion of the debates over the right to property, which surprisingly did not align with cold war divisions, see Krause and Alfredsson, "Article 17," 363–74. Recall that discrimination in the granting of the right to property is prohibited by ICERD (Article 5). A similar provision can be found in Articles 15 and 16 of the UN Convention on the Elimination of All Forms of Discrimination against Women.

129. Van Banning, *The Human Right to Property*, 7.

130. Davis, *Land Rights and Indigenous Peoples*, 23, 34.

131. Many of the victims had been the targets of what the Colombian army saw as a counterinsurgency effort, which included the presence of the army's Seventh Brigade and the Rural Intelligence Service in San Rafael de Planas, in the eastern plains of Colombia. The Colombian government, under pressure from local elites, engaged in aggressive attempts to capture indigenous peoples who had fled to the forest because of the threat of forcible removal from their lands by large landowners. Ibid., 20–21.

132. Ibid., 21.

133. Ibid., 21, 22 and note 27.

134. Ibid., 23.

135. OAS, Inter-American Commission on Human Rights, "Informe Anual de la Comisión Interamericana de Derechos Humanos."

136. OAS, Inter-American Commission on Human Rights, "The Human Rights Situation of the Indigenous People in the Americas," chapters 3(I)(2) and 3(I)(6A).

137. OAS, Inter-American Commission on Human Rights, *Paraguay: Tribu Aché-Guayaki*.

138. Ibid. Even though the government did not respond directly to the commission, Davis discusses a speech given by Paraguay's ambassador to the OAS in a Permanent Council meeting following the commission's 1974 denunciation, in which he "praised the rich 'Indo-Hispanic' heritage of his country" (*Land Rights and Indigenous Peoples*, 33).

139. Specifically, the commission found violations of the following rights guaranteed under the American Declaration of the Rights and Duties of Man: life; liberty; personal security and integrity of the person; the constitution and protection of the family; the preservation of health and well-being; work and just remuneration; and leisure time (OAS, Inter-American Commission on Human Rights, *Paraguay: Tribu Aché-Guayaki*, paragraph 2).

140. Davis, *Land Rights and Indigenous Peoples*, 63.

141. OAS, Inter-American Commission on Human Rights, "Report on the Situation of Human Rights of a Segment of the Nicaraguan Population of Miskito Origin," Part Two, B(4).

142. Ibid., Part Two, B(15).

143. Ibid., Part Two, F(1).

144. Ibid., Part Two, F(7).

145. OAS, Inter-American Commission on Human Rights, *Coulter et al. v. Brazil*, Considerations paragraph 7.

146. Ibid., Considerations, paragraph 9.

147. Ibid., Considerations, paragraph 2.

148. Ibid., Resolution, paragraph 1.

149. Anaya combines the reliance on Article 27 of the ICCPR with the recommendations that the Brazilian government "proceed with plans to demarcate Yanomami lands and secure them from encroachment by outsiders" (*Indigenous Peoples in International Law*, 261). The commission's report discusses it under both the right to property and collective rights (OAS, Inter-American Commission on Human Rights, "The Human Rights Situation of the Indigenous People in the Americas").

150. OAS, Inter-American Court of Human Rights, *The Mayagna (Sumo) Awas Tingni Community v. Nicaragua*, paragraph 148.

151. Ibid., paragraph 149.

152. OAS, Inter-American Court of Human Rights, *Saramaka People v. Suriname*, paragraph 88. The court cites (note 79) two cases in which it had used identical language: *The Indigenous Community Sawhoyamaxa v. Paraguay*, paragraph 118; and *Yakye Axa Indigenous Community of the Enxet-Lengua People v. Paraguay*, paragraph 137.

153. In OAS, Inter-American Court of Human Rights, *Saramaka People v. Suriname* (paragraphs 92, 93, and 130), the court references for this point its own decisions in *Yakye Axa Indigenous Community of the Enxet-Lengua People v. Paraguay*, para-

graphs 127–30; and *The Indigenous Community Sawhoyamaxa v. Paraguay*, paragraph 117.

154. OAS, Inter-American Court of Human Rights, *Saramaka People v. Suriname*, paragraph 95.

155. Ibid., paragraph 99; see also paragraph 102.

156. Ibid., paragraph 103.

157. Ibid., paragraph 85. In ibid., note 75, the court cites *The Mayagna (Sumo) Awas Tingni Community v. Nicaragua*, paragraphs 148–49 and 151; *The Indigenous Community Sawhoyamaxa v. Paraguay*, paragraphs 118–21 and 131; and *Yakye Axa Indigenous Community of the Enxet-Lengua People v. Paraguay*, paragraphs 124, 131, 135–37 and 154.

158. OAS, Inter-American Court of Human Rights, *Saramaka People v. Suriname*, note 76.

159. Povinelli, *The Cunning of Recognition*, 12, 176. This repugnancy language comes from Australia, High Court, *Mabo v. the State of Queensland (No. 2)*, paragraph 68.

160. Sheleff, *The Future of Tradition*, 122.

161. Ibid., 123.

162. American Anthropological Association, Committee for Human Rights, "Declaration on Anthropology and Human Rights."

163. Ibid.

164. International Labor Organization, Convention 169, Article 8(2).

165. Okin, "Is Multiculturalism Bad for Women?" 22–23. For some of the critiques of this position, see Honig, " 'My Culture Made Me Do It' "; al-Hibri, "Is Western Patriarchal Feminism Good for Third World / Minority Women?"; and Post, "Between Norms and Choices." For a surprising level of agreement, see Kymlicka, "Liberal Complacencies." In response to some of the critiques, Okin later clarified her claim: "Neither do I conclude that 'feminism demands that we get rid of the offending cultures,' or that we engage in 'extinguishing cultures' [quoting Honig, " 'My Culture Made Me Do It' "]. I suggest, rather, that certain preconditions should obtain and discussions take place before groups are granted special rights designed to ensure the continuation of their cultures. There is a difference between urging caution about the extension of group rights and recommending the active extinction or wholesale condemnation of cultures" ("Reply," 117).

166. See, e.g., Humphry, "An Opportunity Lost for Aboriginal Self-Determination."

167. UN Human Rights Committee, 50th Session, CCPR General Comment No. 23, paragraph 8. Curiously, the committee has avoided stating this position in its Article 27, discussions under the Optional Protocol, even when asked to do so by individual complainants arguing that the state is either enabling or directly responsible for the group's violation of individual rights. The most obvious example is *Lovelace v. Canada*, where the committee avoided the sex discrimination claim by finding a violation of Article 27.

168. UN Human Rights Committee, 50th Session, CCPR General Comment No. 23, paragraph 6.2.

169. Ibid.

170. OAS, Inter-American Court of Human Rights, *Aloeboetoe v. Suriname*, paragraph 62.

171. OAS, Permanent Council, Committee on Juridical and Political Affairs, Working Group to Prepare the Draft American Declaration on the Rights of Indigenous Peoples, "Record of the Current Status of the Draft American Declaration on the Rights of Indigenous Peoples," 6. This language was chosen, however, over more specific language from the Indigenous Peoples Caucus, which would have made clear the range of spheres to be included: "Indigenous women have the right to the full enjoyment and protection of all human rights and fundamental freedoms in the civil, political, economic, social and cultural spheres, free of all forms of discrimination" (OAS, Permanent Council, Committee on Juridical and Political Affairs, Working Group to Prepare the Draft American Declaration on the Rights of Indigenous Peoples, "Note from the Chair").

172. OAS, Permanent Council, Committee on Juridical and Political Affairs, Working Group to Prepare the Draft American Declaration on the Rights of Indigenous Peoples, "Record of the Current Status of the Draft American Declaration on the Rights of Indigenous Peoples," 20. This language had been agreed upon in 2003.

173. The proposed American Declaration contains similar language, although some states are pushing for a provision to have state law limit the rights, suggesting that the limitation could be much broader than might be suggested by the UN Declaration. Article XXXVII in the 2009 draft reads (with brackets indicating contested language): "Any interpretation and application of the present Declaration [shall take into account the constitutional principles of each State and] shall be consistent with the international principles of justice, democracy, respect for human rights, nondiscrimination, [good governance,] and good faith" (OAS, Permanent Council, "Record of the Current Status of the Draft American Declaration on the Rights of Indigenous Peoples," 22).

174. Hernández Castillo, "Indigenous Law and Identity Politics in Mexico," 102.

175. Spivak, "Can the Subaltern Speak?" 296–97.

176. Hernández Castillo, "Indigenous Law and Identity Politics in Mexico," 103. The discourse of "women's rights," then, can be implicated in attempts "to disqualify indigenous cultures and traditions and to oppose indigenous peoples' demands for autonomy" (90).

177. Ibid., 103.

CHAPTER 5: CULTURE AS HERITAGE

1. MITKA, "Conclusiones del Primer Congreso Histórico Político del Movimiento Indio Tupaj Katari," 249–50. Original: "Restituir el uso para ocasiones trascendentales, de los símbolos y valores totémicos que representan a la personalidad del pueblo indio del Kollasuyo: la whiphala, la vara de mando, el cóndor, el pututu, el

poncho, el lluch'u, etcétera." A *pututu* is an Andean shell often used as a musical instrument. The *lluch'u* is a traditional wool cap worn in the Andes.

2. Niezen, "The Indigenous Claim for Recognition in the International Public Sphere," 593.

3. For a discussion of indigenous groups in other parts of the world, specifically Asia, see Kingsbury, "'Indigenous Peoples' in International Law."

4. See, e.g., Robin Wright's "Anthropological Presuppositions of Indigenous Advocacy," 369, where he discusses early-twentieth-century British structural functionalist anthropology, "which emphasized the uniqueness of cultures and the notion of diversity of cultures." This view has long had its critics as well (370). In fact, the criticism is now somewhat mainstream. A recent report by the United Nations Development Programme, for example, disparages the political use of outdated anthropological notions that the culture of any group is bounded, homogenous, and stable. "Preserving values and practices as an end in itself with blind allegiance to tradition," according to the report, constitutes not a service to "cultural liberty," but a threat against it (UNDP, *Human Development Report 2004*, 4).

5. Niezen, "The Indigenous Claim for Recognition in the International Public Sphere," 593.

6. Ibid.

7. See, e.g., Brown, *Who Owns Native Culture?*; Coombe, "Intellectual Property, Human Rights, and Sovereignty." For a review of some of these debates, and interventions in them, see Greene, "Indigenous People Incorporated?"

8. UNESCO, Convention for the Safeguarding of the Intangible Cultural Heritage, Article 2(2), (a)–(e).

9. Ibid., Article 1(b).

10. Ibid., Article 12.

11. Ibid., Article 11. In addition, Article 15 states: "Within the framework of its safeguarding activities of the intangible cultural heritage, each State Party shall endeavour to ensure the widest possible participation of communities, groups and, where appropriate, individuals that create, maintain and transmit such heritage, and to involve them actively in its management."

12. Daes, "Protection of the Heritage of Indigenous Peoples," iii.

13. Ibid.

14. Ibid.

15. See, e.g., UN Commission on Human Rights, Subcommission on Prevention of Discrimination and Protection of Minorities, 53rd Session, "Indigenous Peoples and Their Relationship to Land," paragraph 12: "In order to understand the profound relationship that indigenous peoples have with their lands, territories, and resources, there is a need for recognition of the cultural differences that exist between them and non-indigenous peoples, particularly in the countries in which they live. Indigenous peoples have urged the world community to attach positive value to this distinct relationship."

16. UN Human Rights Committee, Final Report, *Apirana Mahuika et al. v. New Zealand*, paragraph 8.2. The Maori applicants described the concept of the taonga in this context: "In the Maori idiom 'taonga' in relation to fisheries equates to a resource, to a source of food, an occupation, a source of goods for gift-exchange, and is a part of the complex relationship between Maori and their ancestral lands and water" (ibid.). I discuss this case further in chapter 7.

17. Tinker, "The Full Circle of Liberation," 219.

18. McGregor, "Coming Full Circle," 391.

19. Choquehuanca Céspedes, "Con energía milenaria salvemos al planeta," 3. Original: "Hermanas y hermanos, para salvar al mundo y al planeta ante esta amenaza contra la Vida, nos toca a los pueblos originarios indígenas, a las primeras naciones, representantes de pueblos y culturas ancestrales, ofrecer al mundo los valores de nuestra cultura, de La Cultura de la Vida que, fundamentada en el dar y recibir, en el complementarnos, en el bien común, el apoyo mutuo organizado, desenrolla sus capacidades sin destruir al hombre y la naturaleza, y levanta el consenso, el siempre ponernos de acuerdo, para que nadie oprima a nadie." Choquehuanca Céspedes, at the time of this statement, was the minister of foreign relations and religions.

20. Barsh, "Indigenous Peoples," 380, quoting UN Working Group on Indigenous Populations, Proposals of Several Organizations of Indigenous Populations and Participants, U.N. doc. E/CN.4/Sub.2/AC.4/1984/WP.1 (August 2, 1984). The Working Group statement continues by saying that the land should not be taken from indigenous groups, a perspective I discuss more fully below.

21. UN Commission on Human Rights, Subcommission on Prevention of Discrimination and Protection of Minorities, 53rd Session, "Indigenous Peoples and Their Relationship to Land," paragraph 13.

22. Ibid., paragraph 121.

23. UN Conference on Environment and Development, Rio Declaration on Environment and Development, Principle 22.

24. UNESCO, Convention for the Safeguarding of the Intangible Cultural Heritage, Article 1(1).

25. While the language of the exception could be interpreted fairly broadly, Janet Blake's commentary on the convention suggests a relatively narrow reading. She contends that the exception is "aimed at ensuring that certain traditional practices (such as infibulations or ritual scarring) that run contrary to universal human rights standards are not covered by the Convention" (*Commentary on the 2003 UNESCO Convention on the Safeguarding of Intangible Cultural Heritage*, 36).

26. Hale, "Rethinking Indigenous Politics in the Era of the 'Indio Permitido,'" 18–20.

27. Ulloa, "Las representaciones sobre los indígenas en los discursos ambientales y de desarrollo sostenible," 92. Original: "La primera asociada a nociones medievales imperantes sobre el determinismo ambiental que alimentaron las descripciones de

la Colonia en las que el trópico no permitía el florecimiento de la cultura y, por consiguiente, sus habitantes tenían un grado de cercanía a lo natural casi hasta su animalización. La segunda idea propendía al mejoramiento moral a través de disciplinas y actividades que promulgan la necesidad de una reconstrucción moral y social de los nativos de América."

28. Daes, "Protection of the Heritage of Indigenous Peoples," 21.

29. UNESCO, Declaration on the Principles of International Cultural Co-operation, Article 1 (emphasis added).

30. Daes, "Protection of the Heritage of Indigenous Peoples," iii.

31. Albro, "Diversity's Fate in Cultural Policymaking," 26.

32. World Commission on Environment and Development, *Our Common Future*, paragraph 105.

33. Burger, "Indigenous Peoples," 110.

34. Graham and Conklin, "The Shifting Middle Ground," 696.

35. Conklin, "Body Paint, Feathers, and VCRS," 711.

36. Ibid., 723. Manuel apparently rejected this tactic in the 1970s: "Remaining Indian does not mean wearing a breech-cloth or a buckskin jacket, any more than remaining English means wearing pantaloons, a sword, and a funny hat . . . 'I don't need to wear an Indian costume. I am an Indian,' was Buffy Ste. Marie's reply when someone at a concert asked her why she did not wear traditional clothing" (*The Fourth World*, 221).

37. Conklin, "Body Paint, Feathers, and VCRS," 722.

38. Ramos, "Pulp Fictions of Indigenism," 379.

39. Ibid.

40. Hogan, "Staging the Nation," 116.

41. Ibid.

42. Ramos, "Pulp Fictions of Indigenism," 374.

43. Wade, *Race and Ethnicity in Latin America*, 92.

44. Ibid.

45. Hendrickson, "Images of the Indian in Guatemala," 292.

46. Ibid., 293.

47. Ibid., 298.

48. Smith, *Decolonizing Methodologies*, 1.

49. Briggs, "The Politics of Discursive Authority in Research on the 'Invention of Tradition,'" 440.

50. McGregor, "Coming Full Circle," 390. She continues by contending that indigenous knowledge "does not lend itself to being fragmented into various discrete categories: 'No separation of science, art, religion, philosophy or aesthetics exists in Indigenous thought; such categories do not exist,'" quoting Marie Battiste and James (Sa'ke'j) Youngblood Henderson, *Protecting Indigenous Knowledge and Heritage: A Global Challenge* (Saskatoon: Purich Publishers, 2000), 43.

51. Povinelli, *The Cunning of Recognition*, 65, quoting M. M. Bakhtin, "The Problem of Speech Genre," in Michael Holquist, ed., *Speech Genres and Other Late Essays* (Austin: University of Texas Press, 1981), 68.

52. Ibid., 68–69.

53. Jackson, "Culture, Genuine and Spurious," 16, citing Richard Handler, *Nationalism and the Politics of Culture in Quebec* (Madison: University of Wisconsin Press, 1988).

54. Spivak, "In a Word," 124.

55. Dean and Levi, "Introduction," 15, citing Conklin, "Body Paint, Feathers, and VCRS." Conklin borrows the term "symbolic capital" from Pierre Bourdieu's *Outline of a Theory of Practice* (Richard Nice, trans. Cambridge: Cambridge University Press, 1977), which was originally published in 1972 as *Esquisse d'une théorie de la pratique précédé de Trois études d'ethnologie kabyle* (Geneva: Librairie Droz S.A.).

56. Dean and Levi, "Introduction," 16, quoting Laura Graham, "Eye on the Amazon: Brazilian Indians, the State, and Global Culture," *American Anthropologist* 100, no. 1 (1998): 165.

57. OAS, Permanent Council, Committee on Juridical and Political Affairs, Working Group to Prepare the Draft American Declaration on the Rights of Indigenous Peoples, "Record of the Current Status of the Draft American Declaration on the Rights of Indigenous Peoples," 8, reproducing the language in Article XII (3), and noting that it was adopted by consensus in 2007.

58. Ibid., 7.

59. Ibid., 7–8, note 2.

60. Ibid., 8, note 3.

61. Ibid., 8.

62. Robinson, "MFA Won't Relinquish Guatemalan Artifacts," quoting a June 26, 1998, letter by the museum's director, Malcolm Rogers, to Carlos Enrique Zea Flores, Guatemala's vice minister of culture.

63. Lubow, "The Possessed."

64. Yale University, Office of Public Affairs, "Yale Seeks Collaborative Relationship with Peru."

65. U.S., District Court, District of Columbia, *Republic of Peru v. Yale University*.

66. How the Peruvian state intends to apply these international treaties to a nonstate actor is unclear.

67. Yale University, Office of Public Affairs, "Yale Seeks Collaborative Relationship with Peru."

CHAPTER 6: CULTURE AS GROUNDED IN LAND

1. Ramos, "The Hyperreal Indian," 162. Rondon founded the Brazilian Indian Service in 1910. Ramos describes him as "the quasi-mythical father figure of indigenism in Brazil who ardently adhered to the principle that the helpless Indians need the protection of whites against other whites" (ibid., note 9).

2. Brown, "Who Owns Native Culture?" 220. He continues: "In the United States,

the 1990 census revealed that 56 percent of American Indians lived in urban areas. In Canada, Australia, and New Zealand, the corresponding figures for aboriginal peoples in the 1990s were 70, 73, and 83 percent. In these four settler democracies, then, residence and everyday social relations are difficult to reconcile with the Daes Report's assumption that a people harbors a culture in a given patch of real estate" (220–21).

3. Daes, "Protection of the Heritage of Indigenous Peoples," paragraph 164.

4. International Alliance of the Indigenous and Tribal Peoples of the Tropical Forests, "Charter of the Indigenous and Tribal Peoples of the Tropical Forests," Article 3.

5. UN Human Rights Committee, 50th Session, CCPR General Comment No. 23, paragraph 7.

6. Burger, "Indigenous Peoples," 101.

7. Ibid.

8. Anaya, *Indigenous Peoples in International Law*, 141. See ibid., note 91 for citations to indigenous statements about land.

9. International Labor Organization, Convention 169, Article 13(1).

10. UN General Assembly, 61st Session, Declaration on the Rights of Indigenous Peoples, Article 25.

11. UN Commission on Human Rights, Subcommission on Prevention of Discrimination and Protection of Minorities, 45th Session, "Draft Declaration on the Rights of Indigenous Peoples," Article 25 (emphasis added).

12. Muehlebach, "What Self in Self-Determination?" 251.

13. Eide, "Indigenous Populations and Human Rights," 204.

14. OAS, Inter-American Court of Human Rights, *The Mayagna (Sumo) Awas Tingni Community v. Nicaragua*.

15. Ibid., paragraph 149.

16. OAS, Inter-American Commission on Human Rights, *Maya Indigenous Community of the Toledo District v. Belize*, paragraph 113.

17. Ibid., note 112 and paragraph 114, note 113. Article 13(1) of ILO 169 states: "In applying the provisions of this Part of the Convention governments shall respect the special importance for the cultures and spiritual values of the peoples concerned of their relationship with the lands or territories, or both as applicable, which they occupy or otherwise use, and in particular the collective aspects of this relationship."

18. Ramos, "The Hyperreal Indian," 164.

19. Canada, Supreme Court, *Delgamuukw v. British Columbia*, 128.

20. Ibid.

21. UN Commission on Human Rights, Subcommission on Prevention of Discrimination and Protection of Minorities, 53rd Session, "Indigenous Peoples and Their Relationship to Land," paragraph 39.

22. Scheinin, "The Right to Enjoy a Distinct Culture," 198. Scheinin explains: "By the notion of *pathological situations* I refer to circumstances created by a series of

historical injustices, where a land resource conflict no longer appears as one between indigenous use determined by tradition and a competing use typical for 'modernization' but where even the substance of the actual present-day indigenous claims can be questioned as to their suitability for preserving or furthering a distinctive indigenous culture or way of life" (ibid., note 156).

23. UN Commission on Human Rights, Subcommission on Prevention of Discrimination and Protection of Minorities, 36th Session, "Study of the Problem of Discrimination against Indigenous Populations," Final Report (Chapters XXI, XXII— Conclusions, proposals and recommendations), paragraph 379.

24. Nelson, *A Finger in the Wound*, 302–3.

25. ILO 169, for example, states its applicability to "peoples in independent countries who are regarded as indigenous on account of their descent from the populations which inhabited the country, or a geographical region to which the country belongs, at the time of conquest or colonisation or the establishment of present state boundaries and who, irrespective of their legal status, retain some or all of their own social, economic, cultural and political institutions" (Article 1[b]). The convention also applies to "tribal peoples in independent countries whose social, cultural and economic conditions distinguish them from other sections of the national community, and whose status is regulated wholly or partially by their own customs or traditions or by special laws or regulations" (Article 1[a]). For more on the opposition of indigenous advocates to define the term "indigenous," see chapter 3 of the present work, as well as Sanders, "Indigenous Peoples."

26. Muehlebach, "What Self in Self-Determination?" 250.

27. Global Exchange, "Stop the Forced Displacement of Indigenous Communities in Chiapas, Mexico."

28. Ibid.

29. Ibid. The legal advocacy on behalf of these groups avoids this question altogether, arguing instead that government relocations threaten the cultural integrity of the groups in violation of Article 27 of the ICCPR, and calling for government consultation with the groups under ILO 169. See Red de Defensores Comunitarios por los Derechos Humanos, Solicitud de Medidas Cautelares en favor de las comunidades ubicadas en los Montes Azules, seeking precautionary measures from the Inter-American Commission of Human Rights; Centro de Derechos Humanos Fray Bartolomé de las Casas, "Amenazas de desalojo y hostigamiento a Pueblos Indígenas en la Selva Lacandona," an urgent call for action to Mexican officials regarding the continued threat of dislocation of several communities.

30. Maderas del Pueblo del Sureste, "Breve historia de la llamada 'Comunidad Lacadona.'" Original: "Breve historia de la llamada 'Comunidad Lacandona' . . . O cómo los caribes se sacaron la lotería sin comprar billete."

31. México, Secretaria de la Reforma Agraria, "El Gobierno de la República cumple su palabra con los Lacandones."

32. ARIC-ID, "Boletín de Prensa: sobre el desalojo que SEMARNAT implementará en

Montes Azules, Chiapas." Original: " . . . es patrimonio de la humanidad y de todos los mexicanos no solo de un grupo de empresarios y un grupo de indígenas que son manejados al antojo de sector ambiental." ARIC-ID released this statement to the press in Ocosingo, Chiapas, on April 18, 2007, directing it in particular toward the secretary of environment and natural resources, the secretary of agricultural reform, and the Government of the State of Mexico. See also Bellinghausen Enviado, "Indígenas en Montes Azules."

33. Henriquez and Mariscal, "Desalojo en Montes Azules." Original: "indígenas lacandones y personal de la Semarnat arribaron a la zona para destruir las viviendas y potreros que construyeron los pobladores durante tres décadas."

34. Jackson, "Culture, Genuine and Spurious," 8.

35. Ibid.

36. Conklin, "Body Paint, Feathers, and VCRS," 728.

37. Macklem, *Indigenous Difference and the Constitution of Canada*, 255.

38. Canada, Supreme Court of Canada, *Guerin v. The Queen* (1984), 382.

39. Ankersen and Ruppert, "Defending the Polygon," 745. Four countries that no longer have these provisions are Mexico, Peru, Nicaragua, and El Salvador (ibid., note 398).

40. See, for example, the Fifth Amendment to the United States Constitution.

41. The American Convention on Human Rights, Article 21(2), for example, provides: "No one shall be deprived of his property except upon payment of just compensation, for reasons of public utility or social interest, and in the cases and according to the forms established by law."

42. In the United States, property is often referred to as a "bundle of rights." For a history and analysis of different theories of property in the United States and elsewhere, see Alexander, *The Global Debate over Constitutional Property*.

43. UN Commission on Human Rights, Subcommission on Prevention of Discrimination and Protection of Minorities, 53rd Session, "Indigenous Peoples and Their Relationship to Land," paragraph 38.

44. International Labor Organization, Convention 169, Article 17(2).

45. UN Commission on Human Rights, Subcommission on Prevention of Discrimination and Protection of Minorities, 53rd Session, "Indigenous Peoples and Their Relationship to Land," paragraph 39.

46. Ibid., paragraph 147.

47. International Labor Organization, Convention 169, Article 16.

48. UN General Assembly, 61st Session, Declaration on the Rights of Indigenous Peoples, Article 28(1).

49. In 2005, the World Peace Council proposed the inclusion of the following language in the UN Declaration: "All indigenous peoples have the ancestral right to collective ownership" (UN Commission on Human Rights, Drafting Committee, 61st Session, "Report of the Working Group Established in Accordance with Commission on Human Rights Resolution 1995 / 32 of 3 March 1995"). Such language had not

been included in the 1993 draft, nor did it make it into the final document. Article 26 of the final version of the UN Declaration does, however, require that states "give legal recognition and protection to these lands, territories and resources. Such recognition shall be conducted with due respect to the customs, traditions and land tenure systems of the indigenous peoples concerned." To the extent that indigenous peoples have traditionally held land in common, it might be argued that collective title would seem to be the required legal recognition.

50. International Labor Organization, Governing Body, "Report of the Committee Set Up to Examine the Representation Alleging Non-observance by Peru of the Indigenous and Tribal Peoples Convention, 1989 (No. 169), Made under Article 24 of the ILO Constitution by the General Confederation of Workers of Peru (CGTP)," paragraph 26.

51. Gilbert, *Indigenous Peoples' Land Rights under International Law*, 93, citing Jennifer Roback, "Exchange, Sovereignty, and Indian-Anglo Relations," in *Property Rights and Indian Economies*, edited by Terry L. Anderson, 5–26 (Lanham, Md.: Rowman and Littlefield, 1992) and Nell Jessup Newton, "Compensation, Reparations, and Restitution: Indian Property Claims in the United States," *Georgia Law Review* 28 (1994): 453–480.

52. Ibid., 92–96.

53. For two classic works that treat the formation of ejidos and the Mexican Revolution, see Tutino, *From Insurrection to Revolution in Mexico*, and Knight, *The Mexican Revolution*. For a recent work that examines ejidos throughout the twentieth century, see Harvey, *The Chiapas Rebellion*.

54. Thornberry, "Self-Determination and Indigenous Peoples," 56.

55. Ibid.

CHAPTER 7: CULTURE AS DEVELOPMENT

1. Stavenhagen, "Ethnodevelopment," 93.

2. Manuel and Posluns, *The Fourth World*, 221–22.

3. Trubek and Santos, "Introduction."

4. Kennedy, "The 'Rule of Law,' Political Choices, and Development Common Sense," 150.

5. Stavenhagen, "Challenging the Nation-State in Latin America," 429.

6. Robin Wright discusses how military conquest and forced acculturation provided two responses to the view of many, including the nineteenth-century anthropological "cultural theorists," that the "backwardness" of indigenous peoples "impeded their development as well as the progress of Western society" ("Anthropological Presuppositions of Indigenous Advocacy," 368–69).

7. Stavenhagen, "Challenging the Nation-State in Latin America," 430. When this article was published in 1992, Stavenhagen was serving as the External Research Coordinator at the UN Research Institute for Social Development. Later, from 2001

to 2008, he served as the UN special rapporteur on the situation of human rights and fundamental freedoms of indigenous peoples.

8. Ibid., discussing the work of José Carlos Mariátegui in Peru.

9. Ibid., 431, citing Fernando Cardoso and Enzo Faletto, *Dependence and Development in Latin America*.

10. Ibid., 430.

11. Ibid.

12. International Labor Organization, Convention 107, Preamble.

13. Thornberry, *Indigenous Peoples and Human Rights*, 27, citing Gray, *Indigenous Rights and Development*.

14. Wright, "Anthropological Presuppositions of Indigenous Advocacy," 373.

15. Burger, "Indigenous Peoples," 105.

16. UN Commission on Human Rights, Subcommission on Prevention of Discrimination and Protection of Minorities, 53rd Session, "Indigenous Peoples and Their Relationship to Land," paragraph 67.

17. Ibid., paragraphs 66–69.

18. Stavenhagen, "Ethnodevelopment," 80.

19. In "La diversidad cultural en el desarrollo de las Américas," for example, Stavenhagen explains: "The profound economic inequalities between indigenous and nonindigenous people, the social marginalization of the indigenous, and their political exclusion and cultural subordination, constitute an historical picture of persistent discrimination that cannot be labeled anything other than structural racism, which is to say, it is rooted in the structures of the power and domination that have been characterizing Latin American societies for centuries" (9). Original: "Las profundas desigualdades económicas entre indígenas y no-indígenas, la marginación social de aquellos, su exclusión política y su subordinación cultural, conforman un cuadro histórico de discriminación persistente que no puede calificarse más que de racismo estructural, es decir, enraizado en las estructuras del poder y del dominio que han venido caracterizando a las sociedades latinoamericanas durante siglos."

20. Stavenhagen, "Ethnodevelopment," 77.

21. Ibid., 85.

22. Blaser, Feit, and McRae, *In the Way of Development*, 6.

23. Ibid.

24. Ryser, "The Legacy of Grand Chief George Manuel."

25. Wright, "Anthropological Presuppositions of Indigenous Advocacy," 377.

26. Blaser, Feit, and McRae, *In the Way of Development*, 6–7, discussing Peru, Bolivia, Ecuador, Guatemala, and Mexico.

27. Stavenhagen, "Ethnodevelopment," 90.

28. Ibid.

29. Ibid., 91.

30. Ibid., 92. I have discussed elsewhere a similar assertion of culture, in the form of "Asian values," by some Asian states in the 1990s. See Engle, "Culture and Human Rights."

31. Gray, *Indigenous Rights and Development*, 244.

32. For example, Gray, *Indigenous Rights and Development*, uses "self-development"; Hettne, *Development Theory and the Three Worlds*, discusses "another development" (see below); Laurie, Andolina, and Radcliffe, "Ethnodevelopment," as well as van Nieuwkoop and Uquillas, "Defining Ethnodevelopment in Operational Terms," use "development with identity" and "ethnodevelopment"; and Blaser, Feit, and McRae, *In the Way of Development*, write about "life projects." Partridge and Uquillas point out that "this process is referred to by many different names such as, self-development, self-managed development, transformation, autonomous development, free-determination, and self-determination" ("Including the Excluded," paragraph 13).

33. Blaser, Feit, and McRae, *In the Way of Development*, 9.

34. Ibid.

35. Gray, *Indigenous Rights and Development*, 244. Gray self-consciously refers to "indigenous self-development," which he argues "operates on the basis of an 'alternative programme' or, 'another development,'" citing Hettne, *Development Theory and the Three Worlds*, for the term "another development."

36. World Commission on Environment and Development, *Our Common Future*, paragraph 63.

37. Escobar, *Encountering Development*, 192. See also Blaser, Feit, and McRae, *In the Way of Development*, 9.

38. Escobar, *Encountering Development*, 193. Although *Our Common Future* represents a convergence of the environmental and indigenous rights movements, environmentalists have since been criticized by many for exploiting indigenous peoples and their knowledge to further the environmental cause. At the same time, the mid-1980s convergence of the movements was not supported by all environmentalists. Mac Chapin—noting that indigenous and environmental groups had little to do with each other before the mid-1980s, when the World Wildlife Fund embarked upon a USAID-financed program called Wildlands and Human Needs—contends that many within the World Wildlife Fund "viewed the new program as an unwanted diversion from strict conservation, which they saw as their mission" ("A Challenge to Conservationists," 19). As demonstrated by the environmentalist criticisms of some indigenous groups in Chiapas detailed in chapter 6, conflicts continue between these social movements.

39. The CDF, which the World Bank considers a "vision" or "process" rather than a "blueprint," was outlined in a document by then Senior Vice President Joseph Stiglitz in 1998, and was both proposed by then President James Wolfensohn and endorsed by the Bank's Development Committee in 1999. See Stiglitz, "Towards a

New Paradigm for Development," and Wolfensohn, "A Proposal for a Comprehensive Development Framework."

40. World Bank, *Making Sustainable Commitments*, 39.

41. Ibid.

42. For an excellent discussion and critique of the inclusion of the social in what she calls "second generation reforms" in law and development, see Rittich, "The Future of Law and Development."

43. UN, *The Millennium Development Goals Report 2008*, 3.

44. See Davis, "Indigenous Peoples, Poverty, and Participatory Development," 233–34.

45. World Bank, *The World Bank Operational Manual*, Operational Directive 4.20, paragraph 6. This directive was in effect until 2005, when it was replaced by Operational Policy 4.10 and Bank Policy 4.10. Together, these policies appear to elaborate on and strengthen the requirements of OD 4.20, particularly with regard to prior consultation (World Bank, *The World Bank Operational Manual*, Operational Policy 4.10). As I discuss below, however, the new provisions have been subject to criticism by many indigenous rights advocates, who would like even stronger provisions on consent.

46. World Bank, *The World Bank Operational Manual*, Operational Directive 4.20, paragraph 8.

47. See Santos, "The World Bank's Uses of the 'Rule of Law' Promise in Economic Development." For a discussion of the ways that the World Bank has managed different positions on balancing indigenous rights and development, see Sarfaty, "The World Bank and the Internationalization of Indigenous Rights Norms."

48. Hale, "Does Multiculturalism Menace?" 488.

49. Ibid., 487.

50. Hale characterizes Davis as an "activist anthropologist turned World Bank sociologist, [who] led with remarkable success a two-decade-long campaign from within the organization to reform World Bank policies toward indigenous peoples." Hale goes on to note that Davis was "playing strategically off rising cries of protest over World Bank 'mega-projects' and their deleterious effects on indigenous peoples," a protest that Davis himself helped to ignite ("Neoliberal Multiculturalism," 18).

51. Hale makes this argument explicitly in "Does Multiculturalism Menace?" 508–9.

52. Laurie, Andolina, and Radcliffe, "Ethnodevelopment," 473.

53. Hale, "Does Multiculturalism Menace?" 490. Laurie, Andolina, and Radcliffe suggest they come to the project by looking at possibilities rather than limitations (the latter of which they equate with Hale's work), but I think their difference from Hale is primarily one of focus. Specifically, Laurie, Andolina, and Radcliffe state that "our approach differs from Charles Hale's discussion of neoliberal multiculturalism, in that it recognizes indigenous people's and other social actors' (including anthropologists employed by bilateral and multilateral agencies) active

role in shaping contemporary development, and wider racial projects" ("Ethno-development," 491, note 3).

54. UN Conference on Environment and Development, Rio Declaration on Environment and Development, Article 22. Again, I do not mean either to suggest that this focus is not important for indigenous peoples or that it is not taken advantage of by them. As Blaser, Feit, and McRae put it: "The focus on the environment is important to Indigenous peoples in part because it provides a narrative anchor by which their concerns with survival can be articulated with non-Indigenous peoples' concerns for survival," even if it "often involve[s] important distortions of Indigenous perspectives that eventually resurface and often create feelings of betrayal between former allies" (*In the Way of Development*, 10–11).

55. International Labor Organization, Convention 169, Part IV: Vocational Training, Handicrafts and Rural Industries, and Part VI: Education and Means of Communication.

56. Ibid., Article 29.

57. UN Human Rights Committee, Final Report, *Länsman et al. v. Finland*, paragraph 10.2; UN Human Rights Commitee, Final Report, *Apirana Mahuika et al. v. New Zealand*, paragraph 9.3.

58. UN Human Rights Committee, Final Report, *Apirana Mahuika et al. v. New Zealand*, paragraph 9.4; see also UN Human Rights Committee, Final Report, *Länsman et al. v. Finland*, paragraph 9.3.

59. UN CERD, 51st Session, General Recommendation No. 23, paragraph 4(c). Similarly, paragraph 5 states: "The Committee especially calls upon States parties to recognize and protect the rights of indigenous peoples to own, develop, control and use their communal lands, territories and resources and, where they have been deprived of their lands and territories traditionally owned or otherwise inhabited or used without their free and informed consent, to take steps to return those lands and territories. Only when this is for factual reasons not possible, the right to restitution should be substituted by the right to just, fair and prompt compensation. Such compensation should as far as possible take the form of lands and territories."

60. OAS, Inter-American Court of Human Rights, *Saramaka People v. Suriname*, paragraph 95.

61. UN General Assembly, Human Rights Council, 9th Session, "Report on the Situation of Human Rights and Fundamental Freedoms of Indigenous People," paragraph 36.

62. UN General Assembly, 61st Session, Declaration on the Rights of Indigenous Peoples, Article 20(1).

63. Partridge and Uquillas, "Including the Excluded," paragraph 16.

64. Ibid.

65. Gow, *Countering Development*, 1.

66. Ibid., 97–98. I discuss the 1991 Colombian constitution at great length in chapters 8 and 9, although I focus primarily on its provision granting collective land rights to

Afro-Colombians. For more on the constitution as it pertains to indigenous peoples and development, see Dover and Rappaport, "Introduction," and Rappaport and Dover, "The Construction of Difference by Native Legislators."

67. Gow, *Countering Development*, 12, citing Trinh T. Minh-ha, *When the Moon Waxes Red: Representation, Gender and Cultural Politics* (London: Routledge, 1991) and Akhil Gupta, *Postcolonial Developments: Agriculture in the Making of Modern India* (Durham: Duke University Press, 1998). I believe that most indigenous peoples would count as "inappropriate Others" under Gow's usage of the term.

68. Ibid., 114–15.

69. Ibid., 197.

70. Ibid., 199.

71. Escobar, *Encountering Development*, 195.

72. Gow, *Countering Development*, 199 (emphasis added).

73. Brysk, "Turning Weakness into Strength," 41.

74. Ibid.

75. Laurie, Andolina, and Radcliffe, "Ethnodevelopment," 474.

76. Ulloa, "Las representaciones sobre los indígenas," 104. Original: "El conocimiento indígena ha sido reconocido como válido y esperanzador con relación al medio ambiente y esto ha repercutido en una aparente autonomía para manejar sus territorios, pero está sujeta a la inclusión de proyectos de explotación sostenible que hacen parte de ideologías occidentales."

77. Ibid. Original: "un doble discurso que implica la permanencia de lógicas paternalistas y coloniales." Only now, she continues, the discourse takes place within "the new environmentalist context." Original: "el nuevo contexto ambientalista."

78. Gow, *Countering Development*, 108.

79. International Labor Organization, Convention 169, Article 15(2).

80. Ibid.

81. Ibid., Article 7(1).

82. Ibid., Article 7(3).

83. Ibid., Article 6(2).

84. UN Human Rights Committee, *Apirana Mahuika et al. v. New Zealand*, paragraph 9.5.

85. Ibid., paragraph 9.6.

86. UN Human Rights Committee, Final Report, *Anni Äärelä and Jouni Näkkäläjärvi v. Finland*, paragraph 7.6.

87. Anaya, "Indigenous Peoples' Participatory Rights in Relation to Decisions about Natural Resource Extraction," 12, discussing *Länsman et al. v. Finland*. Dinah Shelton has also criticized these and other decisions, complaining that the committee failed to "articulate any standards for determining whether the government had acted in good faith" ("The U.N. Human Rights Committee's Decisions," 33).

88. OAS, Inter-American Court of Human Rights, *Saramaka People v. Suriname*, paragraph 121, citing OAS, Inter-American Commission on Human Rights, *Yakye Axa*

Indigenous Community of the Enxet-Lengua People v. Paraguay, paragraph 137, and OAS, Inter-American Court of Human Rights. *The Indigenous Community Sawhoyamaxa v. Paraguay*, Merits, Reparations and Costs, paragraph 118.

89. Ibid., paragraph 126.

90. Ibid., paragraph 143.

91. Ibid., paragraph 133. It further calls for any consultation to "take account of the Saramaka people's traditional methods of decision-making."

92. Colombia, Corte Constitucional, Sentencia SU-039. In this case concerning the U'wa, the court ruled that prior consultation is a fundamental right for indigenous peoples under the Colombian constitution, as well as under the international law that forms a part of Colombian law. Despite the fact that there had been a number of meetings between representatives of the U'wa, the state, and private companies seeking concessions on U'wa land, the court found that the state's granting of a license had not been done in a way that respected "the fundamental right of the U'wa community with regard to the formal and substantive consultation they should have." Original: "El procedimiento para la expedición de la licencia ambiental se cumplió en forma irregular y con desconocimiento del derecho fundamental de la comunidad U'wa, en relación con la consulta que formal y sustancialmente ha debido hacérsele."

93. UN General Assembly, Human Rights Council, 15th Session, "La situación de los pueblos indígenas en Colombia, paragraphs 41 and 44. For a discussion of the consequences of the Peruvian state's failure to apply a consent requirement included in its own investment law, see Laplante and Spears, who argue that indigenous communities affected by the extractive industries are "increasingly aware that they do in fact have that right under both international and domestic law, but lack a domestic forum in which to exercise it [and] . . . often 'end up seeing protest, even violent protest, as their only means of expression'" ("Out of the Conflict Zone," 102, quoting an interview by Laplante with Miguel Levano, Staff Member of Social Conflict Unit, Peruvian Ombudsman, Lima, Peru [Aug. 25, 2007]).

94. OAS, Inter-American Court of Human Rights, *Saramaka People v. Suriname*, paragraph 134.

95. Ibid., paragraph 136 and note 136, citing UN CERD, 62nd Session, Concluding Observations of the Committee: Ecuador, paragraph 16. In fact, the CERD's 1997 General Recommendation 23, which I discussed in chapter 4, may provide the strongest wording for the recognition of the right to free and informed consent, calling on states to "ensure that members of indigenous peoples have equal rights in respect of effective participation in public life and that no decisions directly relating to their rights and interests are taken without their informed consent" (UN CERD, 51st Session, General Recommendation No. 23, paragraph 4[d]).

96. UN General Assembly, 61st Session, Declaration on the Rights of Indigenous Peoples, Article 32.

97. Fromherz reports: "Noting 'significant concerns with respect to the wording of

the [adopted] text,' Canada's ambassador to the UN, John McNee, focused on three specific areas when speaking to the GA on September 13, 2007: 'the provisions on lands, territories and resources'; the provisions on 'free, prior and informed consent when used as a veto'; and 'dissatisfaction with the process'" ("Indigenous Peoples' Courts," 1346).

98. UN Commission on Human Rights, Subcommission on Prevention of Discrimination and Protection of Minorities, 45th Session, "Draft Declaration on the Rights of Indigenous Peoples," Article 30.

99. In this sense, the language is similar to that in ILO 169 regarding good faith (discussed above). That the ultimate objective (though not the required outcome) of consultation is consent or consensus for the ILO is reflected in reviews of complaints ("representations") alleging state violations of Convention 169. See, e.g., International Labor Organization, Governing Body, "Report of the Committee Set Up to Examine the Representation Alleging Non-observance by Guatemala of the Indigenous and Tribal Peoples Convention, 1989 (No. 169), Made under Article 24 of the ILO Constitution by the Federation of Country and City Workers (FTCC)," paragraphs 56 and 60(g).

100. Laplante and Spears, "Out of the Conflict Zone," 88. Indeed, that the provision was kept intact (and not watered down further) from the immediately preceding version was one of the reasons that indigenous peoples agreed to the limiting language on self-determination in the declaration's final passage (Global Indigenous Peoples' Caucus, Steering Committee, "Report of the Global Indigenous Peoples' Caucus," 2).

101. World Bank, *The World Bank Operational Manual*, Operational Directive 4.20, paragraph 1 (emphasis added) and note 4.

102. For a critical assessment of the Bank's will to carry out new (then draft) requirements, and a call for a complaint mechanism, see MacKay, "The Draft World Bank Operational Policy 4.10 on Indigenous Peoples," 97–98. Again, the Bank has not been of one mind in its policies in the area. Laplante and Spears noted in 2008 that "more than ten years have passed since the organizer of a World Bank-sponsored conference on mining and the community predicted 'that the move from consultation to participation in decision-making is the next logical (albeit difficult) step in the evolution of [extractive industry]-community relations'" ("Out of the Conflict Zone," 88).

103. Dulitzky, "When Afrodescendants Became Tribal Peoples," 13.

104. International Labor Organization, Convention 169, Article 7(4).

105. UN General Assembly, 61st Session, Declaration on the Rights of Indigenous Peoples, Article 29.

106. OAS, Inter-American Court of Human Rights, *Saramaka People v. Suriname*, paragraph 140. Dulitzky suggests, however, that in the consideration of reparations, the Saramaka were not granted as much autonomy as might have been anticipated. He notes that, although the Court awarded the community reparations in

the form of a community development fund for damage done to its traditional lands and resources over the years, it dictated that a three-member committee be established to determine how the fund should be spent. The committee includes one representative of the community, one of the state, and one jointly chosen ("When Afrodescendants Became Tribal Peoples," 15–16, citing *Saramaka People v. Suriname*, paragraphs 201 and 202, as well as other cases.

107. Keller, "Goshute Nuclear Waste Repository." For the case study, see Keller, "Case Study."

108. Keller, "Case Study," 82–83.

109. Keller, "Goshute Nuclear Waste Repository."

110. Quoted in Keller, "Case Study," 83.

111. National Environmental Coalition of Native Americans, "Nuclear Free Zones."

112. U.S., Court of Appeals, District of Columbia, *Devia v. Nuclear Regulatory Commission*, 4–5.

113. For a summary of the grounds, see ibid., 5.

114. Stolz and Wald, "Interior Department Rejects Interim Plan for Nuclear Waste."

115. U.S. Court of Appeals, District of Columbia, *Devia v. Nuclear Regulatory Commission*, 2–3.

116. UN General Assembly, 61st Session, Declaration on the Rights of Indigenous Peoples, Article 29(2).

117. Partridge and Uquillas, "Including the Excluded," paragraph 21.

118. World Bank, *The World Bank Operational Manual*, Operational Directive 4.20, paragraph 15(c).

119. Ibid.

120. World Bank, *The World Bank Operational Manual*, Operational Policy 4.10, paragraph 17.

121. Van den Berg, "Mainstreaming Ethnodevelopment." For the World Bank's 1994 survey, see Psacharopoulos and Patrinos, *Indigenous People and Poverty in Latin America*, especially the executive summary, the introduction, and chapters 1 and 2, all of which van den Berg cites.

122. Van den Berg, "Mainstreaming Ethnodevelopment."

123. Ibid., citing Plant and Hvalkof, *Land Titling and Indigenous Peoples*, 14.

124. Ibid., citing Inter-American Development Bank, *The Path out of Poverty: The Inter-American Bank's Approach to Reducing Poverty* (Washington: Inter-American Development Bank, 1998). Of course, even those who agree that economic growth is the most powerful tool for combating equality disagree over the ways to achieve growth. See, e.g., Rodrik, *One Economics, Many Recipes*.

125. Santos, "The World Bank's Uses of the 'Rule of Law' Promise," 256.

126. Partridge and Uquillas, "Including the Excluded," paragraph 13.

127. Ibid., paragraph 14.

128. For a discussion on the origins of large-scale gaming, see Cattelino, *High Stakes*, chapter 1.

129. IGRA defines gaming in three classes. Cattelino explains: "Traditional games (class I) are wholly regulated by tribes; many card games, bingo, and games similar to it (class II) can be operated and regulated by tribes, but only if they are legal in the surrounding state (even in dissimilar contexts such as charity bingo); and slot machines, blackjack, and other 'Las Vegas style' games (class III) are restricted by the rules for class II plus the requirement that tribes and states negotiate a gaming compact in good faith" (*High Stakes*, 15). For details on the classes of gaming, see U.S. Congress, Indian Gaming Regulatory Act, 25 U.S.C. §2703(6)–(8). For limits on uses of casino revenues, see ibid., 25 U.S.C. §2701.

130. Class I gaming, not subject to regulation by IGRA, includes "traditional forms of Indian gaming."

131. Mezey, "The Distribution of Wealth, Sovereignty and Culture through Indian Gaming."

132. See Butterfield, "Indians' Wish List," for a discussion of the offer by Cheyenne and Arapaho Indians to pay $1 billion and give up ancestral claims to half of the area of Colorado, from which they were driven out of in 1864, in exchange for 500 acres near Denver to build a casino and resort.

133. Cattelino, *High Stakes*, 9.

134. Ibid., 58, quoting Cornell and Kalt, "Reloading the Dice: Improving the Chances for Economic Development on American Indian Reservations," in *What Can Tribes Do? Strategies and Institutions in American Indian Economic Development*, edited by S. Cornell and J. P. Kalt, 2–50 (Los Angeles: American Indian Studies Center, University of California, 1992), 5.

135. Ibid., 209, note 10, provides both quantitative and qualitative details. For instance, Cattelino points out that Jonathan Taylor and Joseph Kalt's 2005 study shows that "American Indian incomes increased at a higher rate than the general U.S. population between 1990 and 2000, with gaming tribes exhibiting greater gains. Nonetheless, the same study emphasized that 2000 Census figures showed the real per capita income of Indians living in Indian Country was less than half the U.S. level. Indian unemployment was more than double the U.S. rate, and family poverty was triple the U.S. rate," quoting Taylor and Kalt, *American Indians on Reservations: A Databook of Socioeconomic Change between the 1990 and 2000 Censuses* (Cambridge: The Harvard Project on American Indian Economic Development, Harvard University, 2005).

136. Cattelino, *High Stakes*, 101. See 7–8 and 101–2 for Cattelino's discussion of the effects on popular culture and politics of the "rich Indian" stereotype.

137. Ibid., 100. See 100–103 for Cattelino's elaboration of this double bind. In particular, she references the Dawes Act of 1887, which "aimed to shape Indians' character and, importantly, to prepare them for U.S. citizenship by promoting agricultural and individual property ownership"; the U.S. Supreme Court decision in *Northwestern Bands of Shoshone Indians v. United States*, 324 U.S. 335 (1945), in which

the "Shoshones' nomadic subsistence practices undermined their land claims in the eyes of the court"; and House Concurrent Resolution 108 in 1953, which would "terminate" federal relations with several American Indian tribes, including those that were economically self-sufficient.

138. Ibid., 14.

139. Kennedy, "The 'Rule of Law,' Political Choices and Development Common Sense," 165.

140. Ibid., 158, Table 7. This table outlines a variety of left, center, and right positions that Kennedy identifies within a "chastened neoliberalism" from 1995–2005.

141. Escobar, *Encountering Development*, 215. Escobar has since traced the emergence of the postdevelopment project, which he dates to the early 1990s. See, e.g., Escobar, "Imaginando un Futuro," and Escobar, "Post-development as Concept and Social Practice."

142. Escobar, *Encountering Development*, 222.

143. Ibid., 225.

144. Ibid., 210.

145. Gow, *Countering Development*, 115.

146. Ibid.

147. Gray, *Indigenous Rights and Development*, 251.

148. Ibid., 261.

149. Ibid., 273.

150. Escobar, *Encountering Development*, 226.

151. Ibid., 247 note 17. Eduardo Restrepo reminds me that most of the book was actually written in 1988, before the movement had begun to consolidate, thus explaining its treatment in a footnote.

152. Escobar, *Territories of Difference*, 171.

153. Ibid., 162–63.

154. Ibid., 198.

155. Ibid., 100.

156. Ibid.

157. Ibid., 102. For Escobar, in this view, "the economy constitutes a realm of heterogeneity and difference rather than a monolithic embodiment of an abstract capitalist essence, makes visible noncapitalist practices and leads to a rethinking of production from cultural and ecological perspectives."

158. Ibid., 332–33, note 27.

159. Ibid., 95.

160. Ibid., 83.

161. Escobar, "Whose Knowledge, Whose Nature?" 66.

162. Escobar, *Territories of Difference*, 7.

163. Ibid., 146.

164. Escobar, "Whose Knowledge, Whose Nature?" 75–76.

165. Escobar, *Territories of Difference*, 310.

1. Wade, *Race and Ethnicity in Latin America*, 37.

2. Colombia, Congreso de la República, Ley 70, Article 1. Original: "La presente ley tiene por objeto reconocer a las comunidades negras que han venido ocupando tierras baldías en las zonas rurales ribereñas de los ríos de la Cuenca del Pacífico, de acuerdo con sus prácticas tradicionales de producción, el derecho a la propiedad colectiva, de conformidad con lo dispuesto en los artículos siguientes. Así mismo tiene como propósito establecer mecanismos para la protección de la identidad cultural y de los derechos de las comunidades negras de Colombia como grupo étnico, y el fomento de su desarrollo económico y social, con el fin de garantizar que estas comunidades obtengan condiciones reales de igualdad de oportunidades frente al resto de la sociedad colombiana."

3. Juliet Hooker points out that, in general, indigenous peoples in Latin America had more success than their Afro-descendant counterparts in gaining collective rights during this period of reform. Afro-Latin Americans whose advocacy revolved principally around their cultural difference (as opposed to, for example, racial discrimination) were most likely to be included in multicultural reforms. Colombia is one such case, even though, as Hooker points out, it did not constitute one of those few examples in which Afro-descendant group rights were equal to indigenous rights ("Indigenous Inclusion / Black Exclusion").

4. Offen, "The Territorial Turn," 43–44.

5. Restrepo, "Afrocolombianos, antropología y proyecto de modernidad en Colombia," 298. Original: "la definición constitucional de la 'nacionalidad colombiana' como pluriétnica y multicultural representa un quiebre con respecto al modelo de Estado-nación configurado en la ideología política del mestizaje, en lo hispánico-mestizo como paradigma cultural necesario para el logro de la civilización, del progreso." For a discussion of the ongoing tension between the constitution's desire for political unity and for self-government of indigenous peoples, see Bonilla Maldonado, *La Constitución multicultural*.

6. Colombia, Political Constitution of Colombia of 1991, Transitory Article 55. Original: "Dentro de los dos años siguientes . . . una ley que les reconozca a las comunidades negras que han venido ocupando tierras baldías en las zonas rurales ribereñas de los ríos de la Cuenca del Pacífico, de acuerdo con sus prácticas tradicionales de producción."

7. Ibid. Original: "establecerá mecanismos para la protección de la identidad cultural y los derechos de estas comunidades, y para el fomento de su desarrollo económico y social."

8. Colombia, Vicepresidencia, "La Población Afrocolombiana." For a more detailed list of titles given to communities from 1996 to 2005, see Grueso Castelblanco, "Documento propuesta para la formulación del plan integral de largo plazo," Anexo 3.

9. Colombia, Political Constitution of Colombia of 1991, Transitory Article 55, paragraph 1. Original: "podrá aplicarse a otras zonas del país que presenten similares condiciones."

10. Colombia, Presidente de la República, Decreto 1332, Articles 2(c)–(d). This decree establishes the Comisión Especial para las Comunidades Negras. Original: "(c) Identificar y proponer mecanismos para la protección de la identidad cultural y los derechos de las Comunidades Negras; (d) Proponer a las autoridades competentes programas de fomento del desarrollo económico y social de las Comunidades Negras."

11. Ibid., Article 1(a)–(f). These institutions are INCORA (Instituto Colombiano de la Reforma Agraria), DNP (Departamento Nacional de Planeación), INDERNA (Instituto Nacional de los Recursos Naturales Renovables y del Medio Ambiente), Instituto Geográfico Agustín Codazzi, and ICAN (Instituto de Investigaciones Culturales y Antropológicas).

12. Ibid., Article 1(g). Those named under this category were: Gustavo de Roux, Jaime Arocha, Otilia Dueñas, Edgar Eulises Torres Murillo, Omar Torres Angulo, Jesús Rosero Ruano, Piedad Córdoba de Castro, Guillermo Panchano, Silvio Garcés, and Luis Jaime Perea Ramos.

13. Ibid., Article 1(h). See also Article 3, which lists all the organizations to be included in the consultative commissions.

14. For a discussion of some of the early organizing, including on the part of the church, see Restrepo, "Eventualizing Blackness in Colombia," Restrepo, "Políticas de la alteridad," Pardo, "Movimientos sociales y actores no gubernamentales," and Wade, "Identidad y Ethnizidad."

15. Restrepo, "Afrocolombianos, antropología y proyecto de modernidad en Colombia," 299. Original: "Si bien es cierto la emergencia de la cuestión étnica afrocolombiana se sitúa en el cruce de factores de orden nacional e internacional, en ningún momento se le puede reducir a dichos factores. Por lo menos desde los años sesenta, en algunos círculos de intelectuales urbanos se encuentran los antecedentes de la emergencia de la cuestión étnica afrocolombiana, aunque en aquellos años el discurso se construía a partir de una reivindicación racial fundada en la común experiencia histórica de esclavitud y marginamiento económico y social."

16. Ibid., 312, citing Carlos Rosero, Conferencia "Comunidades negras y Ley 70," en Taller Laboratorio de Culturas Negras, Universidad del Valle-Ican-Colciencias, Cali, Colombia, 1995. Original: "Según Rosero este paradigma de la alteridad de la comunidad negra, de la afrocolombianidad, lejos se encuentra aún de lograr claridad sobre muchos aspectos; todavía está sometido a un proceso de destilación del cuál no se sabe a ciencia cierta cuáles serán los resultados. Por ello, desde la perspectiva de las organizaciones que le apuestan a este paradigma de representación, la etnicidad afrocolombiana es una construcción que aunque ha permitido

unas fronteras en la negociación con el Estado y en la constitución de un particular movimiento de base, aún se encuentra en plena elaboración."

17. Black urban identity and the effects of internal displacements on its construction are the subject of much contemporary scholarship in Colombia. See, for example, Agier and Hoffmann, "Pérdida de lugar, despojo y urbanización"; Agudelo, "No todos vienen del río"; Barbary et al., "Ser negro-a"; Aponte, "El cuerpo étnico en la constitución del espacio urbano y el proyecto nacional de José María Samper"; Hoffmann and Quintín, "Organización social, dinámicas culturales e identidades de las poblaciones afrocolombianas del Pacífico y suroccidente en un contexto de movilidad y urbanización"; Urrea and Quintín, "Urbanización y construcción de identidades de las poblaciones Afrocolombianas de la Región Pacífica Colombiana"; Urrea, Ramírez, and Viáfara, "Perfiles sociodemográficos de la población afrocolombiana en contextos urbano-regionales del país a comienzos del siglo XXI"; and Mosquera, Pardo, and Hoffmann, "Las trayectorias sociales e identitarias de los afrodescendientes."

18. Colombia, Departamento Administrativo Nacional de Estadísticas (DANE), *Censo General 2005*, 130. The exact figures in this census are the following: a national population of 41,468,384, with 4,273,722 counted as "Negro, mulato, afrocolombiano."

19. Colombia, Departamento Administrativo Nacional de Estadística (DANE), *Los grupos etnicos de colombia en el censo de 1993*, 9. According to a later World Bank report, the data are "inferior and distant from the estimates done by research carried out from specialized surveys" (Sánchez and García, *Más Allá de los Promedios*, 14). Original: "inferior y distante de los estimativos hechos por investigaciones realizadas a partir de encuestas especializadas."

20. Sánchez and García, *Más allá de los Promedios*, 15, citing Olivier Barbary et al., "Perfiles contemporáneos de la población afrocolombiana," in *Gente negra en Colombia*, 69–112 (CIDSE, Universidad del Valle-IRD, Colciencias, 2003).

21. World Bank, Environmentally and Socially Sustainable Development Unit, "The Gap Matters," x. The precise figures are 8,300,000 Afro-Colombians out of a total national population of 43 million. These estimates, near 19 percent, accord with other studies. For example, Offen notes that "a 1997 U.N. report estimated that blacks make up 6 million or 16 percent of the Colombian population" ("The Territorial Turn," 67, note 12, citing Comisión Interamericana de Derechos Humanos, *Tercer Informe Sobre la Situación de los Derechos Humanos en Colombia, Capítulo XI: Los Derechos de las Comunidades Negras*, OEA / SET.L / V / II.102 (Washington, 1999). Offen also notes other estimates, such as 10–12 percent, citing Odile Hoffmann, "Titling Collective Lands of the Black Communities in Colombia: Between Innovation and Tradition," in *The Challenge of Diversity: Indigenous Peoples and Reform of the State in Latin America*, edited by G. W. Assies, V. D. Haar, and A. Hoekema, 123–136 (Amsterdam: Thela Thesis, 2000), 123; and 14–21 percent, citing Rodolfo Monge Oviedo, "Are We or Aren't We?" *NACLA* 24, no. 4: 19.

22. Colombia, Congreso de la República, Address (*ponencia*) by José Renán Trujillo García.

23. See Colombia, Departamento Nacional de Planeación, "Mapa 1," which includes a table listing municipalities with a high percentage of Afro-Colombians in both the Pacific and Atlantic regions. According to Offen, "about 90 percent of the Pacific's inhabitants are black, or Afro-Colombian, with various indigenous groups making up about 4–5 percent" ("The Territorial Turn," 54).

24. Colombia, Congreso de la República, Address (*ponencia*) by José Renán Trujillo García, 14.

25. Martínez, "The Black Blood of New Spain," 7. The terms to describe having nonwhite blood or illegitimacy—such as a "stain" on one's lineage and a "defect in birth"—were used by colonial subjects themselves and in legal documents.

26. Twinam, *Public Lives, Private Secrets*, 43. For an excellent discussion of the Old World origins of *limpieza de sangre* (originally designed to protect whiteness from Moor or Jewish blood) and how these shifted dramatically with the new mixtures of blood that arose in the New World contexts, see ibid., 41–50. For an analysis of both the official and informal means whereby some with black blood could "pass" as white, see Twinam, "Racial Passing."

27. Larson, "Andean Highland Peasants and the Trials of Nation Making during the Nineteenth Century," 581.

28. Ibid.

29. Ibid., 582.

30. For more on the position of Afro-Colombians in the Pacific region, see Wade, *Blackness and Race Mixture*; for the Caribbean region, see Helg, *Liberty and Equality in Caribbean Colombia, 1770–1835*.

31. Cunin, *Identidades a flor de piel*, 39, citing Nina S. de Friedemann, "Estudios de negros en la antropología colombiana," in *Un siglo de investigación social. Antropología en Colombia*, edited by Jaime Arocha and Nina S. de Friedemann, 507–572 (Bogotá: Colciencias-FES, 1984), 510. Original: "Friedemann, en 1984 define la invisibilidad como una negación de la actualidad y de la historia de los africanos y sus descendientes en América."

32. Offen, "The Territorial Turn," 57, citing Jorge I. del Valle, "Practicas tradicionales de producción y ordenamiento territorial," in *Renacientes del Guandal: "grupos negros" de los ríos Satinga y Sanquianga*, edited by Eduardo Restrepo and Jorge I. del Valle, 455–473 (Bogotá: Universidad Nacional de Colombia, Medellín, 1996).

33. Ibid., citing Arturo Escobar, "Viejas y Nuevas Formas de Capital y los Dilemas de la Biodiversidad," in *Pacífico: ¿Desarrollo o diversidad? Estado, capital y movimientos sociales en el Pacífico colombiano*, edited by Arturo Escobar and Alvaro Pedrosa, 109–131 (Bogotá: CEREC, 1996).

34. Offen states that because the "Agrarian Law of 1961 not only ignored the customary land claims of resident Afro-Colombians in the Pacific, but [also] used accusations of 'irrational land use' by black communities to justify the need to title lands

to individuals," it achieved its "intended" goal and "sparked large-scale colonization and land privatization." He notes that "18% of the Pacific region became privatized at this time, although some of these titles were granted to black families" (ibid., 57–58, citing Enrique Sánchez Gutierrez and Roque Roldán Ortega, *Titulación de los territorios comunales afrocolombianos e indígenas en la Costa Pacífica de Colombia*, Dirección Sectorial para el Desarrollo Social y Ecológicamente Sostenible. [Washington: World Bank, 2002], 5).

35. Wade, "The Colombian Pacific in Perspective," 5; Offen, "The Territorial Turn," 57–58, citing Escobar, "Viejas y Nuevas Formas de Capital."

36. Escobar, *Territories of Difference*, 57.

37. I am grateful to Eduardo Restrepo for encouraging me to analyze the proceedings of the Special Commission, and for providing me with copies of the minutes (*actas*) and recordings of those meetings. The minutes are also available through Restrepo's web-based directory, http://www.unc.edu/restrepo/actascomiespecial/actas/.

38. For further discussion of this earlier coalescence of the black social movement, see Restrepo, "Eventalizing Blackness in Colombia," chapter 2, especially 55–107. Specifically, Restrepo locates this efflorescence of the movement in the debates leading up to and during the National Constituent Assembly. For him, this dynamic atmosphere, combined with the production of the new constitutional language providing for the Special Commission for the Black Communities, ultimately "articulated an unusual political culture around a black ethnicity anchored in the cultural, the territorial, the community, the traditional, and the identity among others" (55). For an examination of the critical role of many Catholic priests who had been trained as anthropologists in the development of the black social movement during this earlier period, see 96–107.

39. Brazil, Constitution of the Federative Republic of Brazil of 1988, Temporary Constitutional Provisional Act, Article 68. Original: "Aos remanescentes das comunidades dos quilombos que estejam ocupando suas terras."

40. For a discussion of the contemporary challenges facing *quilombo* communities and an analysis of the extent to which the provision has been implemented over the past twenty years, see Bernard and Audre Rapoport Center for Human Rights and Justice, "Between the Law and Their Land."

41. For a discussion of transnational organizations in which the PCN has participated since 1995, see Escobar, *Territories of Difference*, 264–69.

42. Offen, "The Territorial Turn," 59.

43. Ibid., quoting Peter Wade, "The Cultural Politics of Blackness in Colombia," *American Ethnologist* 22, no. 2 (1995): 346.

44. Colombia, Comisión Especial para las Comunidades Negras, Acta 006, 6–7, paraphrasing Commissioner Jaime Arocha. Original: "Los pueblos negros han sufrido un proceso histórico, prosiguió, comparable y simétrico con las comunidades indígenas, como la desterritorialización, el etnocidio y el marginamiento cultural,

y fueron destruidos, al igual que los pueblos indígenas, del género humano, mediante posiciones filosóficas, éticas y morales."

45. Colombia, Comisión Especial para las Comunidades Negras, Acta de la Sesión de las Subcomisiones de Territorio y Desarrollo, 4. Original: "La comisionada Zulia Mena presentó . . . que el terrritorio que han habitado tradicionalmente las comunidades negras es una unidad . . . [S]e ha hablado también que la situación territorial para las comunidades negras no se puede homologar a la situación de las comunidades indígenas, porque básicamente estas últimas están asentadas en las zonas rurales . . . Frente a como debe darse el proceso de titulación colectiva de estos territorios, han surgido una serie de planteamientos en el interior de estas comunidades. Uno de ellos es que este reconocimiento debe comprender la integralidad del territorio de las comunidades negras dentro de la relación campo-poblado, que se caracteriza por el semi-nomadismo, la multiplicidad de residencias, y que se basa en una economía de actividades complementarias (prácticas tradicionales de producción) y multiopcionales."

46. Colombia, Comisión Especial para las Comunidades Negras, Acta 001, 4. Original: "El comisionado Saturnino Moreno afirmó que el problema territorial entre indios y negros es el mismo, en el sentido de que se trata de minorías étnicas, tradicionalmente marginadas, que necesitan un territorio para poder desarrollar su cultura y su tradición que difieren del resto del pueblo colombiano."

47. Ibid. ("El señor Viceministro intervino argumentando que la Constitución dió un reconocimiento diferente a la problemática indígena en relación con el tratamiento dado a las comunidades negras, puesto que a los primeros les reconoció, a sus territorios, el carácter de entidades territoriales indígenas").

48. Colombia, Political Constitution of Colombia of 1991, Article 286. Original: "Son entidades territoriales los departamentos, los distritos, los municipios y los territorios indígenas." The vice minister specifically referred to this provision, as well as to Article 285, using the direct inclusion of indigenous territories (and lack of reference to black territories) to reinforce his argument that that the constitution does not recognize ethnic territorial entities for black Colombians in the same way it does for indigenous groups. Colombia, Comisión Especial para las Comunidades Negras, Acta 001, 7.

49. Colombia, Comisión Especial para las Comunidades Negras, Acta 001, 3–4. Original: "[Jaime Arocha expresó] que los síntomas de conflicto [entre etnias] surgen ahora a raíz de la Nueva Constitución donde se estableció una asimetría en la territorialidad de los negros y de los indios al negarle a los primeros algunos derechos territoriales." For Arocha, the job of the Special Commission was "to reverse this asymmetry," noting that, beyond seeking simple land tenancy, Afro-descendants were aiming for territorial rights. Original: "reversar esta asimetría."

50. Offen, "The Territorial Turn," 62, citing Jean Jackson, "The Impact of Recent National Legislation in the Vaupés Region of Colombia," *Journal of Latin American*

Anthropology 1, no. 2 (1996): 120–151; and Bettina Ng'weno, *On Titling Collective Property, Participation, and Natural Resource Management: Implementing Indigenous and Afro-Colombian Demands* (Washington: World Bank, 2001).

51. Ibid., 63, citing Silvio Garcés Mosquera, Director del Programa de Comunidades Negras, INCORA, Bogotá, Colombia, interview with author, May 16, 2003 (emphasis added).

52. Colombia, Corte Constitucional, Sentencia C-169.

53. Escobar explains that "for at least a millennium, indigenous communities occupied the territory with particular forms of appropriation of the environment . . . practicing until recent decades a type of subsistence livelihood appropriate to the humid forest." He notes that the early (precolonial) disappearance of much of the indigenous culture in the area "is thought to have been caused by natural disaster, perhaps tsunamis and earthquakes that pushed the survivors to migrate out of the area." Escobar emphasizes that the remaining groups are "demographically, culturally and politically important groups such as the Embera and Wounaan in the northern Chocó province" (*Territories of Difference*, 45).

54. Bernard and Audre Rapoport Center for Human Rights and Justice, "Unfulfilled Promises and Persistent Obstacles to the Realization of the Rights of Afro-Colombians," 15–16, 24. See also Colombia, Presidente de la República, Decreto 1745, Article 22.

55. For a detailed ethnographic account of both conflicts and alliances in the late 1990s between indigenous and Afro-descendant communities in the Pacific Department of Cauca, see Ng'Weno, *Turf Wars*.

56. Escobar, *Territories of Difference*, 61.

57. Colombia, Congreso de la República, Ley 70, Article 2(5). Original: "Comunidad negra. Es el conjunto de familias de ascendencia afrocolombiana que poseen una cultura propia, comparten una historia y tienen sus propias tradiciones y costumbre dentro de la relación campo-poblado, que revelan y conservan conciencia de identidad que las distinguen de otros grupos étnicos."

58. Colombia, Comisión Especial para las Comunidades Negras, Acta 004, 24. Original: "expresó que efectivamente se trata de una sola comisión, pero en su interior hay dos visiones de la vida, dos culturas: la cultura afro-colombiana y la cultura tradicional, dominante de este país. Se debe dar este reconocimiento para lograr verdaderos resultados."

59. Colombia, Comisión Especial para las Comunidades Negras, Subcomisión de Identidad Cultural, Acta 02, 2. Original: "La noción de afro tiene para nosotros mucha relevancia, a pesar del desconocimiento de algunos antropólogos de la convención histórica que existe entre Africa y nuestra presencia . . . [E]s claro que somos americanos, pero también es claro que tenemos una ascendencia africana, reflejada no sólo en la pigmentación, en el color, sino en nuestra particular cosmovisión y manifestaciones culturales."

60. Ibid., 6. Original: "[Mario Martínez notó que] es una realidad, concluyó, que las comunidades negras tienen una identidad propia, resultante de una imposición, adaptación y transformación, que no se ha logrado globalizar porque el Estado no las reconoce."

61. Ibid., 7. Original: "no puede afirmarse que el pueblo negro no ama la tierra, pues hace parte de él, y es evidente su convivencia en armonía con la naturaleza."

62. Ibid., 12. Original: "Señaló cómo las comunidades han recreado el lenguaje y lo han adecuado a su propia cosmovisión, han expresado, a través de éste, su relación con la naturaleza, su relación de afecto, su sexualidad, que tiene particularidades muy propias" (paraphrasing Garcés).

63. Ibid., 13. Original: "la *calentura* que siente un negro cuando se enamora de una mujer."

64. Colombia, Congreso de la República, Ley 70, Article 34. Original: "La educación para las comunidades negras debe tener en cuenta el medio ambiente, el proceso productivo y toda la vida social y cultural de estas comunidades. En consecuencia, los programas curriculares asegurarán y reflejarán el respeto y el fomento de su patrimonio económico, natural, cultural y social, sus valores artísticos, sus medios de expresión y sus creencias religiosas."

65. Ibid., Articles 32 and 35. Article 32 states: "The Colombian state recognizes and guarantees black communities the right to an education process that accords with their ethno-cultural needs and aspirations." Original: "El Estado colombiano reconoce y garantiza a las comunidades negras el derecho a un proceso educativo acorde con sus necesidades y aspiraciones etnoculturales." Article 35 provides: "State educational programs and services for black communities must . . . respond to their particular needs and must embrace their history, their knowledges and methods, their value systems, their linguistic and dialectical forms, and all of their other social, economic, and cultural aspirations." Original: "Los programas y los servicios de educación destinados por el Estado a las comunidades negras deben desarrollarse y aplicarse en cooperación con ellas, a fin de responder a sus necesidades particulares y deben abarcar su historia, sus conocimientos y técnicas, sus sistemas de valores, sus formas lingüísticas y dialectales y todas sus demás aspiraciones sociales, económicas y culturales."

66. For a description and discussion of these works, see Museo Nacional de Colombia, *Velorios y santos vivos*, 18–20.

67. Colombia, Congreso de la República, Ley 70, Article 39. Original: "el conocimiento de las prácticas culturales propias de las comunidades negras y sus aportes a la historia y a la cultura colombiana, a fin de que ofrezcan una información equitativa y formativa de las sociedades y culturas de estas comunidades."

68. Ibid., Article 42. Original: "El Ministerio de Educación formulará y ejecutará una política de etnoeducación para las comunidades negras y creará una comisión pedagógica, que asesorará dicha política con representantes de las comunidades."

69. A presidential decree elucidated the particulars of this "Comisión Pedagógica de

Comunidades Negras" established by Law 70. For details on the commission's operation, see Colombia, Presidente de la República, Decreto 2249. Nevertheless, a December 2008 meeting of Afro-Colombian communities and organizations produced a "Document of Consent," which recommends that the government "prioritize within [its development] Plan public policies that attend to sectors and groups that encounter special situations of exclusion." It therefore advocates for "Policies of Ethno-education (to speed up processes of formulation under way)" and asks "the government to authorize an inspection of the United Nations independent expert on minority issues and the United Nations special rapporteur on the right to education." Reunión de Consejos Comunitarios y Organizaciones Afrocolombianas, Negras, Palenqueras y Raizales, "Documento de Consenso," 9. Original: "Priorizar dentro del Plan las políticas públicas que atienden sectores y grupos que enfrentan situaciones de exclusión especiales . . . [incluyendo] Políticas de Etnoeducación (agilizar procesos de formulación en curso) [y] Solicitamos al gobierno autorizar la visita de las relatoras de Naciones Unidas sobre Minorías Étnicas, y contra la Discriminación en la Educación."

70. There has, however, been criticism of government efforts here. For example, some communities have asserted that: "Despite that [Presidential] Decree 1627 of 1996 created a fund of loan forgiveness [*créditos condonables*] for Afro-Colombian students, administered by ICETEX, which facilitated the entry and sustainability of many Afro-Colombian students in the country's public and private universities, the current government has reduced and almost eliminated the fund by not allocating resources for it for the past two years" (Consejos Comunitarios, "¡No a la Palma, Sí a los Derechos Territoriales y a la Vida!"). Original: "A pesar de que el decreto 1627 de 1996 creó el fondo de créditos condonables para estudiantes afro-colombianas administrado por el ICETEX, posibilitó el ingreso y sostenibilidad de muchos estudiantes afrocolombianos en las universidades públicas y privadas del país, en este gobierno se ha reducido y casi eliminado el fondo de créditos condonables para afrocolombianos, pues el gobierno que debe adjudicarle los recursos para su funcionamiento cada seis meses, no lo ha hecho desde hace 2 anos."

The Minority Rights Group International has also pointed out the trend of higher-education disparities for Afro-Colombians: "According to recent World Bank reports, Afro-Colombians attend primary schools at a level higher than the national average, with 42 percent of blacks in school compared to 32 percent of all Colombians, but black students are less likely to attend high school, because secondary education is available to only 62 percent of Afro-Colombians compared to 75 percent of all Colombians. The quality of secondary schools available to blacks is extremely low, according to the ICFES, a national college entrance exam board, 65 percent of schools in Afro-Colombian communities are identified as poor quality or very poor quality. Only 14 percent of blacks pursue higher education compared to 26 percent of all adults in the nation, although blacks and whites have roughly the same high literacy rates (89 percent for blacks and 94 percent for the country as a whole)" (*World Directory of Minorities and Indigenous Peoples*).

71. Wade, *Race and Ethnicity in Latin America*, 32.

72. Ibid., 33.

73. Colombia, Congreso de la República, Address (*ponencia*) by José Renán Trujillo García, 1. Original: "Se presumía, y todavía hay quienes incurren en este error, que tales seres privados de libertad, desnudos, hambrientos, carentes de una lengua inteligible, pudieran tener algo distinto que aportar a la aculturación americana, que sus manos y sus músculos."

74. Ibid. Original: "Se ignoraba que un ser humano aún colocado en la más extrema situación de incomunicación, extraño en su tierra, expoliado de su cultura, mientras tenga uso de razón, constituye una célula cultural capaz de crear ideas, hacerse a medios expresivos, formas y herramientas adecuadas para generar por sí solo o en asocio de otros, los valores tradicionales de la cultura de donde proceda."

75. UNESCO, "The Cultural Space of Palenque de San Basilio."

76. Ibid.

77. Wade, *Race and Ethnicity in Latin America*, 33.

78. See, e.g., Perry, "The Roots of Black Resistance."

79. Colombia, Congreso de la República, Ley 70, Article 2(6). Original: "Ocupación colectiva. Es el asentamiento histórico y ancestral de comunidades negras en tierras para su uso colectivo, que constituyen su hábitat, y sobre los cuales desarrollan en la actualidad sus prácticas tradicionales de producción."

80. Colombia, Comisión Especial para las Comunidades Negras, Acta de la Subcomisión de Desarrollo, 9. Original: "Para entrar en materia de esta Subcomisión, la doctora Myriam Jimeno propuso fusionar las subcomisiones de Identidad Cultural con la de Territorio, pues concidera que las dos están relacionadas y el objetivo es ampliar el tema y no reducirlo."

81. Colombia, Comisión Especial para las Comunidades Negras, Acta 003, 15. Original: "El proceso de recuperación de tierras por vías de hecho dio inicio en 1987 por medio de organizaciones campesinas que si bien defienden el derecho a la tierra no tiene en cuenta el carácter cultural que nos hace hablar de territorio como un cuerpo que incluye lengua propia, tradición y producción."

82. Colombia, Comisión Especial para las Comunidades Negras, Acta de la Sesión de las Subcomisiones de Territorio y Desarrollo, 5. Original: "Lo que se ha venido hablando es que para proteger las tres zonas debe otorgarse una titulación colectiva del bloque, comprendiendo los tres niveles descritos por el asesor Pastor Murillo."

83. Ibid. Original: "recoge legitimamente los usos y costumbres en cuanto a derechos territoriales de la comunidad negra."

84. Colombia, Congreso de la República, Ley 70, Article 6(b). Original: "Las areas urbanas de los municipios."

85. Colombia, Comisión Especial para las Comunidades Negras, Acta de la Sesión de

las Subcomisiones de Territorio y Desarrollo, 13. Original: "para los indígenas ya existen los cabildos, para las comunidades negras de lo que se trata es de ir reconstruyendo esas autoridades propias de las comunidades que han existido y existen y que están amenazadas por toda la influencia externa."

86. Colombia, Comisión Especial para las Comunidades Negras, Acta 003, 5. Original: "Es por eso que tenemos que demostrar en la lucha y en la práctica que las comunidades negras necesitan un territorio para poder desarrollar su propia cultura . . . Serán ellos los responsables de que el futuro de la nueva generación desaparezca, porque ningún pueblo sin territorio puede desarrollarse."

87. Colombia, Comisión Especial para las Comunidades Negras, Acta de la Sesión de Subcomisiones de Territorio y Desarrollo, 11. Original: "no es por capricho, sino porque obedece a una racionalidad del uso de esos recursos, que es lo que finalmente permite que esa cultura y ese pueblo se reproduzca."

88. Colombia, Comisión Nacional Especial para las Comunidades Negras, Acta 005, 13–14. Original: "[Jaime Arocha propuso que] el análisis de una subregionalización del litoral Pacífico, que muestre las diferencias en el funcionamiento de las organizaciones representantes, permitiría definir quiénes serían los beneficiarios de los títulos colectivos: las organizaciones, las familias extendidas o los municipios. Esto, agregó, debe abordarse a partir de los resultados de los censos de la ACIA [Asociación Campesina Integral del Atrato], de la concepción territorial de las propiedades comunales y cómo esa concepción territorial va a enfrentarse con la concepción que tenga el Instituto Geográfico, por lo que se requiere de un cronograma que contemple reflexionar sobre esto." See also Colombia, Comisión Nacional para las Comunidades Negras, Acta de la Sesión de las Subcomisiones de Territorio y Desarrollo, 11.

89. Colombia, Congreso de la República, Ley 70, Article 9 (b) and (d). Original: "Antecedentes etnohistóricos" and "Prácticas tradicionales de producción."

90. Colombia, Presidente de la República, Decreto 1745, Article 20(7). Original: "Prácticas tradicionales de producción, especificando: a) Formas de uso y aprovechamiento individual y colectivo de los recursos naturales; b) Formas de trabajo de los miembros de la comunidad; c) Otras formas de uso y apropiación cultural del territorio."

91. Colombia, Congreso de la República, Ley 70, Article 6. Original: "Con respecto a los suelos y los bosques incluidos en la titulación colectiva, la propiedad se ejercerá en función social y le es inherente una función ecológica."

92. Colombia, Comisión Especial para las Comunidades Negras, Acta 002, 18. Original: "Desde el punto de vista histórico, señalamos la presencia de nuestros antepasados, quienes desde el año 1709, han venido dominando la zona, trabajando incansablemente para la adquisición de sus sustento y mediante la explotación equilibrada de sus recursos, han contribuido al país, para levantar el nivel socioeconómico del mismo."

93. Colombia, Comisión Especial para las Comunidades Negras, Subcomisión de

Identidad Cultural, Acta 02, 7. Original: "El hombre negro y el indígena son quienes tienen la autoridad para sostener y equilibrar el ecosistema."

94. Colombia, Congreso de la República, Exposición de Motivos, 8. Original: "Los artículos pertinentes al manejo de los recursos naturales en las tierras que sean entregadas en forma colectiva a las comunidades negras apuntan hacia la necesidad de proteger la biodiversidad, como base fundamental para el desarrollo económico y social de esas comunidades y como un valioso recurso para el país. Por eso se señala la necesidad de hacer un desarrollo sostenible de los recursos naturales renovables de la zona, siguiendo el mandato constitucional según el cual la propiedad privada cumple una función ecológica."

95. Colombia, Congreso de la República, Ley 70, Article 6(b). Original: "En consecuencia los adjudicatarios desarrollarán prácticas de conservación y manejo compatibles con las condiciones ecológicas."

96. Ibid. Original: "Para tal efecto se desarrollarán modelos apropiados de producción como la agrosilvicultura, la agroforestería u otros similares, diseñando los mecanismos idóneos para estimularlos y para desestimular las prácticas ambientalmente insostenibles."

97. Ibid. Article 7. Original: "inalienable, imprescriptible e inembargable." In principle, this provision works in tandem with Article 52, discussed below.

98. Colombia, Comisión Especial para las Comunidades Negras, Acta 008, 14. Original: "Un aspecto que no está claro es la definición de las condiciones en que se podrán enajenar estas tierras [comunales]."

99. Ibid. Original: "el carácter inalienable a las tierras que aquí se adjudiquen significaría que se inmovilizaría, desde el punto de vista comercial, el movimiento de tierras en el Pacífico."

100. Colombia, Congreso de la República, Ley 70, Article 49. Original: "El diseño, ejecución y coordinación de los planes, programas y proyectos de desarrollo económico y social que adelante el gobierno y la Cooperación Técnica Internacional para beneficio de las comunidades negras de que trata esta ley, deberá hacerse con la participación de los representantes de tales comunidades, a fin de que respondan a sus necesidades particulares, a la preservación del medio ambiente, a la conservación y cualificación de sus prácticas tradicionales de producción, a la erradicación de la pobreza y al respeto y reconocimiento de su vida social y cultural. Estos planes, programas y proyectos deberán reflejar las aspiraciones de las comunidades negras en materia de desarrollo."

101. Ibid., Article 50. Original: "fomentará y financiará actividades de investigación orientadas . . . al estudio de las realidades y potencialidades de las comunidades negras, de manera que se facilite su desarrollo económico y social."

102. Comisión Especial para las Comunidades Negras, Acta de la Sesión de las Subcomisiones de Territorio y Desarrollo, 22. Original: "Sobre el tema de desarrollo concretamente, el dr. Pastor Murillo planteó que hay consenso entre las organizaciones, en el sentido de partir del mismo artículo 55 Transitorio, que habla

de prácticas tradicionales de producción. Esto se contraopone al modelo de desarrollo que ha venido planteando el Estado colombiano en el territorio del Pacífico, y no responde a las necesidades de la población."

103. Colombia, Comisión Especial para las Comunidades Negras, Acta 003, 25. Original: "El próximo siglo será del Pacífico, y ya las empresas transnacionales y los grupos con poder económico del país y del exterior, tienen los ojos puestos en esa región, no sólo para apropiarse de sus recursos, sino para liderar su desarrollo. Desarrollo, que sino se hace de manera concertada con las comunidades, va a terminar generando una economía de colonias, como las que se vivieron en la región con la explotación aurífera por parte de empresas extranjeras."

104. For more on the history of gold mining in the Pacific region, see Offen, "The Territorial Turn," 55–56.

105. Colombia, Comisión Especial para las Comunidades Negras, Acta 003, 13. Original: "han venido explotando los recursos naturales en perfecta armonía con la naturaleza, conservando el medio ambiente."

106. Ibid., 14, referencing Articles 79 and 80 of the constitution.

107. Colombia, Comisión Especial para las Comunidades Negras, Acta 003, 6. Specifically, the statement said: "For example, we do not understand how it is that the Special Commission is defining the communal titling of our territory (by drafting legislation) while, at the same time, the same government is granting concessions to the timber companies." Original: "Por ejemplo, no entendemos como, mientras se define mediante la Comisión Especial, la titulación comunitaria de nuestro territorio (Proyecto de Ley), por otro lado el mismo gobierno concede permisos a las empresas madereras."

108. Ibid., 7. Original: "Rechazar todos los permisos vigentes y en trámite a las grandes empresas madereras (Maderas de Urabá, Maderas del Darién): Balsa II, Larga Boba, Guamal, Sábalos, Cacarica, Domingodó, Truandó y otros."

109. Colombia, Comisión Especial para las Comunidades Negras, Acta 005, 24. Original: "Con respecto a los permisos, la posición de la Gerencia es que no es posible suspender totalmente la concesión de permisos de aprovechamiento maderero en el Pacífico, entre otras porque hay unas comunidades negras que viven de ese aprovechamiento."

110. Colombia, Comisión Especial para las Comunidades Negras, Acta 003, 7. Original: "Exigimos un desarrollo economico y social acorde a nuestra cultura, necesidades e intereses."

111. Colombia, Comisión Especial para las Comunidades Negras, Acta de la Sesión de las Subcomisiones de Territorio y Desarrollo, 22. Original: "Dentro de ese contexto, el dr. Murillo identificó dos factores fundamentales, sobre los cuales hay acuerdo entre las organizaciones. En primer lugar, que las comunidades afrocolombianas tienen una visión distinta a la que el Estado colombiano les ha impuesto. Segundo, estas comunidades tienen unas especificidades que ameritan concebir un módelo de desarrollo acorde con esas particularidades."

112. Ibid. Original: "módelo de etnodesarrollo, entendido como el ejercicio de la capacidad social que tiene un pueblo para construir su futuro, aprovechando los recursos reales y potenciales de su cultura, de acuerdo a un proyecto definido conforme a sus propios valores y aspiraciones."

113. Escobar, *Territories of Difference*, 156–57.

114. Offen, "The Territorial Turn," 52.

115. Escobar, *Territories of Difference*, 188, quoting and translating the plan.

116. Ibid.

117. Ibid., 158.

118. Ibid., 157.

119. Ibid.

120. For discussion of the meeting in October 1992 in which Franco described Balsa II, see Pantoja, *Colombia, País de regiones*, chapter 3a.

121. Colombia, Comisión Especial para las Comunidades Negras, Acta de la Sesión de las Subcomisiones de Territorio y Desarrollo, 22. Original: "Grandes obras de desarrollo, para lo cual hay que considerar el impacto ambiental, cultural y social que causarían sobre las comunidades."

122. Ibid.

123. Colombia, Congreso de la República, Ley 70, Article 58. Original: "En los fondos estatales de inversión social habrá una unidad de gestión de proyectos para apoyar a las comunidades negras en los procesos de capacitación, identificación, formulación, ejecución y evaluación de proyectos."

124. Ibid., Article 55. Original: "El Gobierno adecuará los programas de crédito y asistencia técnica a las particulares condiciones socioeconómicas y ambientales de las comunidades negras."

125. Ibid., Article 52. The provision states in part: "In order to guarantee credit, the value of the goods authorized for exploitation can be taken into account." Original: "para garantizar los créditos, se podrá tener en cuenta el valor de los bienes que se autoriza aprovechar."

126. Ibid., Article 57. Original: "El Gobierno Nacional creará una comisión de estudios para la formulación de un plan de desarrollo de las comunidades negras."

127. Ibid. Original: "propondrá las políticas de largo plazo y será el marco de referencia para que las políticas del Plan Nacional de Desarrollo respeten la diversidad étnica de la Nación y promuevan el desarrollo sostenible de esas comunidades de acuerdo a la visión que ellas tengan del mismo."

128. Ibid., Article 49. Original: "El diseño, ejecución y coordinación de los planes, programas y proyectos de desarrollo económico y social . . . deberá hacerse con la participación de los representantes de tales comunidades."

129. See, for example, Escobar, *Territories of Difference*; Bernard and Audre Rapoport Center for Human Rights and Justice, "Unfulfilled Promises and Persistent Obstacles to the Realization of the Rights of Afro-Colombians"; Grueso Castel-

blanco, "Documento propuesta para la formulación del plan integral de largo plazo"; Global Rights and AFRODES, *Los Derechos Humanos de las Comunidades Afrocolombianas*; Proceso de Comunidades Negras en Colombia (PCN), *Informe*; Sánchez and García, *Más allá de los Promedios*; Reunión de Consejos Comunitarios y Organizaciones Afrocolombianas, Negras, Palenqueras y Raizales, "Documento de Consenso."

130. Colombia, Corte Constitucional, Sentencia C-030.

131. As happened with restrictions on the inalienability of land discussed in chapter 6 and issues regarding nuclear waste storage facilities considered in chapter 7, some people argued that black communities should simply not be given the option of ceding rights to their land (or forest) in this way. The PCN took such a position, as did some environmentalists. One news story described the position of the latter: "If a clear ban is not defined, the necessities and, in some cases, the organisational weakness of the communities will lead to deals with individual lumber companies and exploitation of forests on an industrial scale, says activist Mariela Osorno, of Ecofondo, an umbrella organisation linking more than 100 environmental groups in Colombia" (Parra, "Environment—Colombia").

132. Colombia, Corte Constitucional, Sentencia C-030, 72.

133. Colombia, Departamento Nacional de Planeación, Consejo Nacional de Política Económica y Social, *Política Para la Población Afrocolombiana*. The Ministry of the Interior and the Departments of Housing and Public Credit, Agriculture and Rural Development, Environment, Mining and Energy, and Economic Development were to work with the DNP, the Colombian Institute of Agrarian Reform (INCORA, now INCODER), and Afro-Colombian representatives. The focus was to be on Articles 21, 24, 50, 54, 58, 61, and 64 of Law 70.

134. Colombia, Ministerio de Ambiente y Desarrollo Territorial, *Proyecto de Ley Reglamentario de los Capítulos IV, V y VII de Ley 70 de 1993*, 6.

135. Ibid., 7. Original: "se hizo referencias a medidas de realización de derechos económicas y sociales; nuevas líneas en fondos existentes, y adopción de programas diferenciales a favor del desarrollo de las comunidades negras."

136. Consejos Comunitarios, "¡No a la Palma, Sí a los Derechos Territoriales y a la Vida!"

137. In fact, as Escobar points out, a significant number of Afro-Colombians in the Pacific region are themselves producers of oil palm, either as small farmers or as laborers for agro-business. Specifically, he notes that "the production of palm by small farmers is by no means negligible. In 1999, there were 1,427 farms with fewer than 5 hectares planted in palm, and 350 with between 5 and 20, amounting to about 3,500 hectares, representing 18 percent of the total area under cultivation and between 10 and 15 percent of the total production" (*Territories of Difference*, 82, citing FEDEPALMA, *Censo Nacional de Palma de Aceite, Colombia 1997–1998* [Bogotá: FEDEPALMA, 1999]).

138. Bernard and Audre Rapoport Center for Human Rights and Justice, "Unfulfilled Promises and Persistent Obstacles to the Realization of the Rights of Afro-Colombians," 33. Escobar subsequently has made similar observations, noting that, despite small farmers' formidable presence, they face rising pressures, for "since the late 1990s . . . capitalists, local politicians, and development agencies have pushed to transform small farm practices to resemble those of the large plantations. They have done so chiefly through a strategy spearheaded by a regional mixed corporation, Cordeagropaz, set up with the collaboration of the large growers. If successful, this program will result in a significant rupture in customary cultivation practices" (*Territories of Difference*, 82–83). Escobar, nevertheless, chooses to "bracket the assumption that these enterprises can be described in purely capitalist terms" (83).

139. Consejos Comunitarios, "¡No a la Palma, Sí a los Derechos Territoriales y a la Vida!" Original: "el racismo, la exlcusión y la discriminación institucionalizada, no ha permitido intervención positiva del estado desde las aspiraciones de las propias comunidades."

140. Ibid. Original: "las pretensiones de este gobierno de profundizar el desequilibrio ambiental de nuestra región insertando grandes extensiones de monocultivos como el de la palma aceitera lo cual en conjunto que la coca son parte de las grandes amenazas que tienen nuestras comunidades."

141. Ibid. Original: "nuestras prácticas ancestrales de producción, como son, la minería, la pesca, la agricultura, aprovechamiento maderero, la medicina ancestral entre otras."

142. Colombia, Ministerio del Interior y de Justica, Proyecto de Decreto de los Capítulos IV, V y VII de Ley 70 de 1993 (Propuesta Integral), Article 56; and Colombia, Ministerio del Agricultura y Desarrollo Rural, Proyecto de Decreto de Capítulo VII de Ley 70 de 1993, Article 22. Original: "las comunidades negras titulares del derecho de propiedad colectiva . . . podrán celebrar contratos de asociación y / o de colaboración, con empresarios del sector privado nacional o internacional, o con entidades públicas o privadas de cualquier naturaleza, para el desarrollo de proyectos. Igualmente podrán asociarse para el procesamiento y comercialización de la producción." The integrated proposal was put together as part of an inter-institutional process, led by the Office of Black, Afro-Colombian, *Raizal* and *Palenquero* Communities in the Ministry of the Interior, in consultation with black community representatives and the High Level Consultative Commission created by Law 70. The draft regulations for only Chapter VII were proposed by the Colombian Institute for Rural Development (INCODER) within the Ministry of Agriculture. I am grateful to Pastor Murillo for providing background on these various drafts.

143. Colombia, Ministerio del Interior y de Justica, Proyecto de Decreto de los Capítulos IV, V y VII de Ley 70 de 1993 (Propuesta Integral), Article 1. Original: "Es el derecho exclusivo de las comunidades negras al aprovechamiento de los recursos forestales en sus territorios colectivos, en observancia de las normas tutelares de conservación y el aprovechamiento forestal sostenible."

144. Ibid., Article 11. Original: "se harán conforme a la función social y ecológica que les es inherente . . . está referida a mantener sus condiciones de conservación y sostenibilidad."

CHAPTER 9: THE PERIPHERY OF LAW 70

1. Because of the technical nature of the term and the difficulty of translating it precisely, I will refer to it in Spanish throughout the chapter.

2. Colombia, Congreso de la República, Ley 110, Article 45. Original: "Se reputan baldíos, y por consiguiente, de propiedad nacional . . . Las islas de uno y otro mar pertenecientes al Estado, que no están ocupadas por poblaciones organizadas, o apropiadas por particulares, en virtud de título traslaticio de dominio."

3. The community council's full name is Consejo Comunitario de Comunidades Negras de la Unidad Comunera de Gobierno Rural de Isla del Rosario Caserío de Orika. The founders of the Orika settlement are said to have named it in honor of the daughter of Domingo "Benkos" Bioho, the revered leader of seventeenth-century slave rebellions in northern Colombia, whose followers included the former slaves who established Palenque de San Basilio. Interestingly, Orika herself is remembered for having been sentenced to death by her fellow maroons after attempting to help her Spanish lover—whom they had taken prisoner—escape. Durán Bernal, ¿Es nuestra isla para dos?, 95, 183–84; Escalante, "Palenques in Colombia," 78.

4. Consejo Comunitario de Comunidades Negras de la Unidad Comunera de Gobierno de Isla del Rosario Caserío de Orika (Application for Collective Title), 6.

5. See Colombia, Ministerio de Agricultura y Desarrollo Rural, Unidad Nacional de Tierras Rurales (UNAT), "Orika podrá adelantar proyecto de saneamiento básico."

6. I asked one of the self-identified natives on Isla Grande—a community activist in his thirties who had moved there with his family from Barú when he was a child—if he had always identified himself as native. He answered "yes," but he went on to explain that those on the islands use the term largely to distinguish themselves from *Cartageneros*, or those from Cartagena, including the majority black population there. According to him, Cartagena thus serves as a reference point for those on the island. Since then, others have offered different perspectives, suggesting that "native" is a relatively recent description, even self-description, for those who live full-time in the Islas del Rosario. In any event, it would appear that Cartageneros do not derive their identity from a contrast with natives. When I asked a Cartagenera of African descent of about the same age, who is working with natives on Isla Grande, when she first heard the term "native" in reference to the black community living on the island, she answered that it was when she went to college and started working with the community. If her experience is representative, it would seem that those from Cartagena define themselves by location—they are Cartageneros, not *Barranquilleros* or *Palenqueros*—rather than by the

amount of time their ancestors have been in the place where they currently live, or by whether their ancestors were there before the mestizos.

7. Consejo Comunitario de Comunidades Negras de la Unidad Comunera de Gobierno de Isla del Rosario Caserío de Orika (Application for Collective Title), 7–8.

8. See Bolaños, "No titularán predios en las Islas."

9. Consejo Comunitario de Comunidades Negras de la Unidad Comunera de Gobierno de Isla del Rosario Caserío de Orika (Application for Collective Title), 2; María Paula Saffon, interview with the author, March 30, 2007.

10. As with the term "baldíos reservados de la nación," there exists no precise English equivalent for the term "tierras baldías," so I have generally retained the Spanish version.

11. Colombia, Political Constitution of Colombia of 1991, Transitory Article 55, paragraph 1. Original: "Lo dispuesto en el presente artículo podrá aplicarse a otras zonas del país que presenten similares condiciones, por el mismo procedimiento y previos estudio y concepto favorable de la comisión especial aquí prevista."

12. Colombia, Congreso de la República, Ley 70, Article 1. Original: "Esta ley se aplicará también en las zonas baldías, rurales y ribereñas que han venido siendo ocupadas por comunidades negras que tengan prácticas tradicionales de producción en otras zonas del país y cumplan con los requisitos establecidos en esta ley."

13. Colombia, Presidente de la República, Decreto 1745, Article 19(9). Original: "Los baldíos que constituyan reserva territorial del Estado."

14. In the 1950s, a number of Afro-Colombians living in Barú apparently sold some of their land on Isla Grande to whites due to economic hardship, caused by a disease that had harmed their coconut crops. For a discussion of this history, see Consejo Comunitario de Comunidades Negras de Isla del Rosario Caserío Orika, *Acción de tutela contra la nación*, Anexo 1 principal, quoting Ever de la Rosa and Roberto Lemaitre, "Transcripción de la reunión de los representantes de la comunidad negra de las Islas del Rosario con los propietarios blancos de casas y hoteles para informarles su decisión de solicitar la titulación colectiva de la tierra."

15. The entity I am referring to here is called the Sala de Consulta y Servicio Civil del Estado (Consultation and Civil Service Room of the Council of State).

16. Colombia, Consejo de Estado, Sala de Consulta y Servicio Civil, Decision of March 21, 2007, paragraphs 1 and 2.

17. Ibid., paragraph 3.

18. Ibid., paragraph 6.

19. Consejo Comunitario de Comunidades Negras de Isla del Rosario Caserío Orika, *Acción de tutela contra la nación*, 2.

20. Ibid., 1 and 20 (fundamental right to petition), 30 (fundamental right to due process).

21. Ibid., 2 and 58 (fundamental rights to existence, cultural and social existence, cultural identity, and autonomy of ethnic community).

22. Colombia, Political Constitution of Colombia of 1991, Article 93. For an extensive

discussion of the development of and implications for the "block of constitutionality," see Arango Olaya, "El bloque de constitucionalidad en la jurisprudencia de la corte constitucional colombiana," which explains that the "block of constitutionality" is outlined by the Colombian constitution and statutory and "organic" law as well as international treaties and international human rights law.

23. Consejo Comunitario de Comunidades Negras de Isla del Rosario Caserío Orika, *Acción de tutela contra la nación*, 49 and note 81, citing Colombia, Corte Constitucional, Sentencia SU-383.

24. Consejo Comunitario de Comunidades Negras de Isla del Rosario Caserío Orika, *Acción de tutela contra la nación*, 67, citing Colombia, Corte Constitucional, Sentencia T-379. Original: "[ILO 169] se refiere a la autonomía de las comunidades indígenas al reconocer la aspiración de esos pueblos a asumir el control de sus propias instituciones y formas de vida, así como su desarrollo económico y social, manteniendo y fortaleciendo sus identidades, lenguas y religiones."

25. See Roldán Ortega, "Models for Recognizing Indigenous Land Rights in Latin America," 5, 20, 21, 25; Uprimny Yepes, "The Enforcement of Social Rights by the Colombian Constitutional Court," discussing the Colombian Constitutional Court's willingness to enforce social rights.

26. Consejo Comunitario de Comunidades Negras de Isla del Rosario Caserío Orika, *Acción de tutela contra la nación*, 68. Original: "Para determinar su propio destino, definiendo las prioridades de su desarrollo y sus formas de vida, así como decidiendo la manera de ejecutarlas dentro de su territorio." This part of the tutela also connects the court's jurisprudence on ILO 169 to a number of constitutional provisions, including TA 55. Indeed, it is through that connection, that the right becomes "fundamental."

27. Operation Genesis has been well documented, and its occurrence has led to claims before the Inter-American Commission on Human Rights (OAS, Inter-American Commission on Human Rights, *Marino López et al. v. Colombia*). See also Norwegian Refugee Council, "Resisting Displacement by Combatants and Developers." For one account of the story of Cariaca, see Fundación CEPS, *Colombia*, 86–89.

28. Fundación CEPS, *Colombia*, 88–89.

29. Primer Encuentro Nacional Agrominero Interétnico, "Declaración Pública."

30. Foro Andino Nacional, Eje de Derechos Culturales, "La Mirada de los Derechos Culturales desde la Perspectiva de las Etnias en el D.C." (Relatoría). Original: "El primer derecho cultural es la autodeterminación de los pueblos, sin esa autodeterminación no hay derechos culturales."

31. World Bank, "Colombia." As discussed in chapter 8, reliable statistics on race in Colombia are difficult to come by, due to difficulties with the census. The numbers used by the World Bank, however, appear to be widely accepted.

32. Universidad de San Buenaventura, Grupo de Investigación en Desarrollo Social—Gides, "Perspectivas del desarrollo comunitario y la calidad de vida en Cartagena," 8.

33. UNDP, "En el Caribe Colombiano."

34. Associated Press, "Poverty, Crime Cloud Cartagena's Tourism Hopes." The quotation from the priest is short but telling, though only if one already knows the context: "We're a historic and cultural heritage site and yet have the uncivilization of the most bitter and trying problems of injustice, of decadence, of inequity."

35. See Cunin, "De la esclavitud al multiculturalismo," 145.

36. Asociación de Afrocolombianos Desplazados (AFRODES) et al., "Misión de Observación a la Situación de las Comunidades Afrodescendientes en Colombia: Desplazamiento Forzado Interno, Violaciones al Derecho Internacional Humanitario y Situación de Personas Afrocolombianas en las Carceles," Annex 1.

37. Ibid., discussing other, more recent, displacements dating from the 1970s, as well as ongoing threats of displacement due to current and proposed megaprojects in the region. For a description of Afro-Colombian identity in the Caribbean, including the effects of Law 70, globalization, racism, and megaprojects on that identity, see Hernández Cassiani, "El caribe colombiano."

38. Arocha, "Inclusion of Afro-Colombians," 76.

39. Colombia, Presidente de la República, Decreto 1745, Article 21.

40. Carlos Jaime Barjuch of Cartagena was reported to have opposed the collective title. See Asociación de Afrocolombianos Desplazados (AFRODES) et al., "Misión de Observación a la Situación de las Comunidades Afrodescendientes en Colombia," paragraph 67, which cites 2001 data from the Instituto Colombiano de la Reforma Agraria.

41. Colombia, Congreso de la República, Ley 1152 ("por la cual se dicta el Estatuto de Desarrollo Rural, se reforma el Instituto Colombiano de Desarrollo Rural, Incoder, y se dictan otras disposiciones"). Among other things, the law liquidated much of INCODER and transferred many of its responsibilities to UNAT.

42. Colombia, Ministerio de Agricultura y Desarrollo, Unidad Nacional de Tierras Rurales (UNAT), "Se firma convenio UNAT-Min Interior," 3.

43. Bernard and Audre Rapoport Center for Human Rights and Justice, "Unfulfilled Promises and Persistent Obstacles to the Realization of the Rights of Afro-Colombians," 23–24.

44. Porras Vallejo, *Plan Nacional de Desarrollo 2006–2010*, 60. Original: "Explorar posibilidades de titular tierras baldías en la Cuenca del Caribe y en el Putamayo, zonas de colonización, valles interandinos, a comunidades afrocolombianas."

45. Colombia, Ministerio de Agricultura y Desarrollo Rural, INCODER-UNAT, Grupo de Empalme, "Procesos de Legalización de Tierra a Comunidades Negras de Bolívar."

46. "La 'suerte' de Orika." Original: "El proyecto . . . sería el sueño de cualquier ambientalista [y] . . . ayudaría a los nativos a ascender de la categoría de miseria a la de pobreza."

47. Colombia, Ministerio de Agricultura y Desarrollo, Unidad Nacional de Tierras Rurales (UNAT), "Orika podrá adelantar proyecto de saneamiento básico."

48. Ibid.

Bibliography

A print copy of all documents listed as "on file with the author" may be found in an archive for the book deposited at the Nettie Lee Benson Latin American Collection at the University of Texas. Digital copies are also available for most of those documents.

African Group of States. "Draft Aide Memoire: United Nations. Declaration on the Rights of Indigenous People." November 9, 2006. http://www.ipacc .org.za / uploads / docs / Africanaidememoire.pdf (accessed January 12, 2010). Copy on file with the author.

African Union. Assembly. 8th Session. Decision on the United Nations Declaration on the Rights of Indigenous Peoples. Dec. 141, Doc. Assembly / AU / 9 (VIII). January 30, 2007.

Agier, Michel, and Odile Hoffmann. "Pérdida de lugar, despojo y urbanización: un estudio sobre los desplazados en Colombia." In *Desplazados, migraciones internas y reestructuraciones territoriales*, edited by Fernando Cubides and Carlos Domínguez, 104–26. Bogotá: CES-Universidad Nacional y Ministerio del Interior, 1999.

Agudelo, Carlos Efrén. "No todos vienen del río: Construcción de identidades negras urbanas y movilización política en Colombia." In *Conflicto e (in)visibilidad: retos de los estudios de la gente negra en Colombia*, edited by Eduardo Restrepo and Axel Rojas, 171–192. Popayán: Editorial Universidad del Cauca, 2004.

Aikio, Pekka, and Martin Scheinin, eds. *Operationalizing the Right of Indigenous Peoples to Self-Determination*. Turku, Finland: Institute for Human Rights, Åbo Akademi University, 2000.

Albro, Robert. "Diversity's Fate in Cultural Policymaking." *Anthropology News* 46, no. 9 (December 2005): 26.

Alexander, Gregory S. *The Global Debate over Constitutional Property: Lessons for American Takings Jurisprudence*. Chicago: University of Chicago Press, 2006.

Alfredsson. Gudmunder, and Asbjørn Eide, eds. *The Universal Declaration of Human Rights: A Common Standard of Achievement.* Boston: Martinus Nijhoff, 1999.

al-Hibri, Azizah Y. "Is Western Patriarchal Feminism Good for Third World / Minority Women?" In *Is Multiculturalism Bad for Women?* edited by Joshua Cohen, Matthew Howard, and Martha C. Nussbaum, 7–24. Princeton, N.J.: Princeton University Press, 1999.

American Anthropological Association. Committee for Human Rights. "Declaration on Anthropology and Human Rights." Adopted by American Anthropological Association membership June 1999. http://www.aaanet.org/stmts/humanrts.htm (accessed February 8, 2009). Copy on file with the author.

——. Executive Board. "Committee for Human Rights Guidelines." Adopted October 7, 1995. http://www.aaanet.org/committees/cfhr/guide.htm (accessed February 8, 2009). Copy on file with the author.

——. "Statement on Human Rights." *American Anthropologist* 49 (1947): 539–43.

American Convention on Human Rights. Adopted November 21, 1969. O.A.S. T.S. No. 36, 1144 U.N.T.S. 143.

American Declaration of the Rights and Duties of Man. Res. XXX. Final Act of the Ninth International Conference of American States (Pan American Union). Bogotá, Colombia. March 30–May 2, 1948. Reprinted in *Basic Documents Pertaining to Human Rights in the Inter-American System.* OAS / Ser.L / v / 1.4 Rev. 9 (2003).

Anaya, S. James. "The Capacity of International Law to Advance Ethnic or Nationality Rights Claims." *Human Rights Quarterly* 13 (1991): 403–11.

——. *Indigenous Peoples in International Law.* 2nd ed. New York: Oxford University Press, 2004.

——. "Indigenous Peoples' Participatory Rights in Relation to Decisions about Natural Resource Extraction: The More Fundamental Issue of What Rights Indigenous Peoples Have in Lands and Resources." *Arizona Journal of International and Comparative Law* 22, no. 1 (2005): 7–17.

——. "Keynote Address: Indigenous Peoples and Their Mark on the International Legal System." *American Indian Law Review* 31, no. 2 (2006–7): 257–72.

Anghie, Antony. *Imperialism, Sovereignty, and the Making of International Law.* New York: Cambridge University Press, 2005.

Ankersen, Thomas T., and Thomas K. Ruppert. "Defending the Polygon: The Emerging Human Right to Communal Property." *Oklahoma Law Review* (winter 2006): 681–757.

An-Na'im, Abdullahi, ed. *Human Rights in Cross-Cultural Perspectives.* Philadelphia: University of Pennsylvania Press, 1992.

Aponte, Lola. "El cuerpo étnico en la constitución del espacio urbano y el proyecto nacional de José María Samper." In *Chambacú, la historia la escribes tú: ensayos sobre cultura afrocolombiana,* edited by Lucía Ortiz, 349–60. Madrid: Iberoamericana. 2007.

Apthorpe, Raymond, and András Kráhl, eds. *Development Studies: Critique and Renewal.* Leiden: E. J. Brill, 1986.

Arango Olaya, Mónica. "El bloque de constitucionalidad en la jurisprudencia de la corte constitucional colombiana." In *Precedente: Anuario Jurídico*, 79–102. Cali: Universidad ICESI, 2004. http://www.icesi.edu.co (accessed February 9, 2009). Copy on file with the author.

ARIC-ID. "Boletín de Prensa: sobre el desalojo que SEMARNAT implementará en Montes Azules, Chiapas." Press release. April 23, 2007. http://www.cencos.org/es/node/10297 (accessed January 8, 2010). Copy on file with the author.

Arocha, Jaime. "Inclusion of Afro-Colombians: Unreachable National Goal?" *Latin American Perspectives* 25, no. 3 (May 1998): 70–89.

Asamblea de Autoridades Mixes (ASAM). Servicios del Pueblo Mixe (SER) y la Escuela Nacional de Antropología e Historia. "Derechos indígenas en Naciones Unidas: reflexiones y propuestas." *Boletín de Antropología Americana*, no. 19 (1989): 173–186.

Asociación de Afrocolombianos Desplazados (AFRODES) et al. "Misión de Observación a la Situación de las Comunidades Afrodescendientes en Colombia: Desplazamiento Forzado Interno, Violaciones al Derecho Internacional Humanitario y Situación de Personas Afrocolombianas en las Carceles." June 2002. http://www.nadir.org/nadir/initiativ/agp/free/colombia/txt/2002/afrocolombians.htm (accessed December 15, 2009). Copy on file with the author.

Associated Press. "Poverty, Crime Cloud Cartagena's Tourism Hopes." April 22, 2007.

Australia. High Court. *Mabo v. the State of Queensland (No. 2)*. [1992] HCA 23; 175 CLR I.

Australian Human Rights Commission. "United We Stand—Support for United Nations Indigenous Rights Declaration, a Watershed Moment for Australia." Press release. April 3, 2009. http://www.hreoc.gov.au/about/media/media_releases/2009/21_09.html (accessed January 18, 2010). Copy on file with the author.

Banton, Michael. "International Norms and Latin American States' Policies on Indigenous Peoples." *Nations and Nationalism* 2 (1996): 89–103.

Barbary, Olivier, et al. "Ser negro-a: Entre una identidad étnica-territorial y una urbano-racial; Análisis estadístico, resultados etnográficos de percepciones colectivas e interpretaciones sociológicas." Marseille: Institut de Recherche pour le Développement, 2001.

Barsh, Russel L. "Evolving Conceptions of Group Rights in International Law." *Transnational Perspectives* 13, no. 1 (1987): 6–10.

———. "Indigenous North America and Contemporary International Law." *Oregon Law Review* 62 (1983): 73–125.

———. "Indigenous Peoples: An Emerging Object of International Law." *American Journal of International Law* 80, no. 2 (1986): 369–85.

———. "Revision of ILO Convention No. 107." *American Journal of International Law* 81, no. 3 (1987): 756–62.

Bellinghausen Enviado, Hermann. "Indígenas de Montes Azules, en alerta ante un anuncio de posible desalojo." *La Jornada* (Mexico City), April 22, 2007. www.jornada.unam.mx/2007/04/22/index.php?article=017n1pol&section=politica (accessed August 15, 2009). Copy on file with the author.

Berman, Nathaniel. "'But the Alternative Is Despair': European Nationalism and the Modernist Renewal of International Law." *Harvard Law Review* 106, no. 8 (1993): 1792–1903.

Bernard and Audre Rapoport Center for Human Rights and Justice. "Between the Law and Their Land: Afro-Brazilian Quilombo Communities' Struggle for Land Rights: A Report by the Rapoport Delegation on Afro-Brazilian Land Rights." September 22, 2008. http://www.utexas.edu/law/academics/centers/humanrights/projects_and_publications/brazil-report.pdf (accessed August 15, 2009). Copy on file with the author.

——. "Unfulfilled Promises and Persistent Obstacles to the Realization of the Rights of Afro-Colombians: A Report on the Development of Ley 70 of 1993." July 18, 2007. http://www.utexas.edu/law/academics/centers/humanrights/ projects_and_ publications/colombia-report.pdf (accessed August 15, 2009). Copy on file with the author.

Blake, Janet. *Commentary on the 2003 UNESCO Convention on the Safeguarding of the Intangible Cultural Heritage.* Leicester, England: Institute of Art and Law, 2006.

Blaser, Mario, Harvey A. Feit, and Glenn McRae. *In the Way of Development: Indigenous Peoples, Life Projects and Globalization.* London: Zed, 2004.

Bolaños, Santiago Burgos. "No titularán predios en las Islas." *El Universal* (Cartagena, Colombia), April 13, 2007. Copy on file with the author.

Bolívar, Simón. *El Libertador: Writings of Simón Bolívar.* Translated by F. H. Fornoff and edited by David Bushnell. New York: Oxford University Press, 2003.

Bonfil Batalla, Guillermo, ed. *Utopía y revolución: El pensamiento político contemporáneo de los indios en América Latina.* Mexico City: Editorial Nueva Imagen, 1981.

Bonfil Batalla, Guillermo, Esteban Emilio Mosonyi, Gonzalo Aguirre Beltran, and Lourdes Arizpe. "La Declaración de Barbados II y Comentarios." *Nueva Antropologia* No. 7 (1977): 109–25.

Bonilla Maldonaldo, Daniel. *La Constitución multicultural.* Bogotá: Siglo del Hombres Editores, 2006.

Brazil. Constitution of the Federative Republic of Brazil of 1988. https://www.planalto .gov.br/ccivil_03/Constituicao/Constituiçao.htm (accessed December 9, 2009).

Briggs, Charles L. "The Politics of Discursive Authority in Research on the 'Invention of Tradition.'" *Cultural Anthropology* 11 (November 1996): 435–69.

Brosius, Peter. "On the Practice of Transnational Cultural Critique." *Identities* 6, no. 2–3 (1999): 179–200.

Brøsted, Jens, et al., eds. *Native Power: The Quest for Autonomy and Nationhood of Indigenous Peoples.* Bergen, Norway: Universitetsforlaget, 1985.

Brown, Michael F. *Who Owns Native Culture?* Cambridge: Harvard University Press, 2003.

Brysk, Alison. *From Tribal Village to Global Village: Indian Rights and International Relations in Latin America.* Stanford: Stanford University Press, 2000.

——. "Turning Weakness into Strength: The Internationalization of Indian Rights." *Latin American Perspectives* 23, no. 2 (spring 1996): 38–57.

Burger, Julian. "Indigenous Peoples: New Rights for Old Wrongs." In *Human Rights*, edited by Peter Davies, 99–110. New York: Routledge, 1988.

———. *Report from the Frontier: The State of the World's Indigenous Peoples*. Atlantic Highlands, N.J.: Zed Books, 1987.

Butterfield, Fox. "Indians' Wish List: Big-City Sites for Casinos." *The New York Times*, April 8, 2005.

Canada. Supreme Court. *Delgamuukw v. British Columbia*. [1997] 3 S.C.R. 1010.

———. *Guerin v. The Queen*. [1984] 2 S.C.R. 335.

Cardoso, Fernando H. "Impedimentos estructurales e institucionales para el desarrollo." *Revista Mexicana de Sociología* 32, no. 6 (1970): 1461–82.

Cardoso, Fernando Henrique, and Enzo Faletto. *Dependency and Development in Latin America*. Berkeley: University of California Press, 1979.

Carnero Hoke, Guillermo. "Teoría y práctica de la indianidad." 1979. Reprinted in *Utopía y revolución: el pensamiento político contemporáneo de los indios en América Latina*, edited by Guillermo Bonfil Batalla, 111–25. Mexico City: Editorial Nueva Imagen, 1981.

Carozza, Paolo. "From Conquest to Constitutions: Retrieving a Latin American Tradition of the Idea of Human Rights." *Human Rights Quarterly* 25 (2003): 281–313.

"Carta de Pátzcuaro." 1975. Reprinted in *Utopía y revolución: el pensamiento político contemporáneo de los indios en América Latina*, edited by Guillermo Bonfil Batalla, 372–77. Mexico City: Editorial Nueva Imagen, 1981.

Cattelino, Jessica R. *High Stakes: Florida Seminole Gaming and Sovereignty*. Durham: Duke University Press, 2008.

"Carta de Pátzcuaro." 1975. Reprinted in *Utopía y revolución: el pensamiento político contemporáneo de los indios en América Latina*, edited by Guillermo Bonfil Batalla, 372–77. Mexico City: Editorial Nueva Imagen, 1981.

Centro de Derechos Humanos Fray Bartolomé de las Casas. "Amenazas de desalojo y hostigamiento a Pueblos Indígenas en la Selva Lacandona." July 19, 2006. http://www.frayba.org.mx/archivo/acciones_urgentes/060719_amenazas_montes_azules.pdf (accessed August 16, 2009). Copy on file with the author.

Chapin, Mac. "A Challenge to Conservationists." *World Watch Magazine* 17, no. 6 (November–December 2004): 17–31.

Charters, Claire. "Developments in Indigenous Peoples' Land Rights under International Law and Their Domestic Implications." *New Zealand Universities Law Review* 21 (2005): 511–53.

Cherrington, Mark. "United Nations General Assembly Declines Vote on Declaration on Indigenous Rights." *World Indigenous News*. December 8, 2006.

Choquehuanca Céspedes, David. "Con energía milenaria salvemos al planeta: Mensaje a las naciones indígenas del mundo." Statement, Misión Permanente de Bolivia ante las Naciones Unidas, New York, May 15, 2006. Copy on file with the author.

Clark, Joshua P. "Confusion, Conformity, and Contradiction: The Salvadoran State's Reluctant Engagements with Indigenous Recognition." Master's thesis, University of Texas, Austin, 2007.

Cohen, Joshua, Matthew Howard, and Martha C. Nussbaum, eds., *Is Multiculturalism Bad for Women?* Princeton, N.J.: Princeton University Press, 1999.

Colchester, Marcus. "Indigenous Peoples and the International Labour Organisation." *Interights Bulletin* 4 (1989): 43–45.

Collier, Simon. "Nationality, Nationalism, and Supranationalism in the Writings of Simón Bolívar." *Hispanic American Historical Review* 63, no. 1 (February 1983): 37–64.

Colombia. Comisión Especial para las Comunidades Negras. Actas. These minutes (*actas*) from the Special Commission are available at Eduardo Restrepo's website: http://www.unc.edu/restrepo/actascomiespecial/actas/. Copies are also on file with the author.

——. Acta 001. August 11, 1992.

——. Acta 002. September 3–4, 1992.

——. Acta 003. October 2–3, 1992.

——. Acta 004. November 5, 1992.

——. Acta 005. January 28–29, 1993.

——. Acta 006. April 23, 1993.

——. Acta 008. May 6, 1993.

——. Acta de la Sesión de las Subcomisiones de Territorio y Desarrollo. February 25, 1993.

——. Acta de la Subcomisión de Desarrollo. October 15, 1992.

——. Acta 02 de la Subcomisión de Identidad Cultural. February 26, 1993.

Colombia. Congreso de la República. Address (*ponencia*) by José Renán Trujillo García. *Gaceta del Congreso*. June 19, 1993.

——. Exposición de Motivos. *Gaceta del Congreso*. June 2, 1993.

——. Ley 70 (1993). *Diario Oficial* No. 41.013. August 31, 1993.

——. Ley 110 (1912). *Diario Oficial* No. 14.845 a 14.847. Bogotá, Colombia, November 23, 1912.

——. Ley 1152 (2007). *Diario Oficial* No. 46.700. July 25, 2007.

Colombia. Consejo de Estado, Sala de Consulta y Servicio Civil. Decision of March 21, 2007. Copy on file with the author.

Colombia. Corte Constitucional. Sentencia SU-039. February 3, 1997. Copy on file with the author.

——. Sentencia C-169. February 14, 2001. Copy on file with the author.

——. Sentencia T-379. May 9, 2003. Copy on file with the author.

——. Sentencia C-030. January 23, 2008. Copy on file with the author.

Colombia. Departamento Administrativo Nacional de Estadística (DANE). *Censo General 2005*. Bogotá: Departamento Administrativo Nacional de Estadística, 2005.

——. *Los grupos etnicos de colombia en el censo de 1993: Análisis de resultados*. Bogotá: Departamento Administrativo Nacional de Estadística, 2000.

Colombia. Departamento Nacional de Planeación (DNP). "Mapa 1: Distribución de la población afro-colombiana en el territorio nacional." In "Eje Temático de Medio Ambiente y Territorio—Genero en el Marco del Proceso de Formulación del Plan

Integral de Largo Plazo para la Población Negra o Afrocolombiana: Anexo 8, Mapas de Población." Contrato No. CON0202360004. August 2006. http://www.dnp.gov.co/archivos/documentos/DDTS_Ordenamiento_Desarrollo_Territorial/3hMAAnexo%208.pdf (accessed August 14, 2009). Copy on file with the author.

——. Consejo Nacional de Política Económica y Social. *Política Para la Población Afrocolombiana.* Bogotá: May 23, 2002.

Colombia. Ministerio de Agricultura y Desarrollo Rural. INCODER-UNAT. Grupo de Empalme. "Procesos de Legalización de Tierra a Comunidades Negras de Bolívar." May 28, 2008. Copy on file with the author.

——. Proyecto de Decreto de Capítulo VII de Ley 70 de 1993. Copy on file with the author (received September 2008).

——. Unidad Nacional de Tierras Rurales (UNAT). "Orika podrá adelantar proyecto de saneamiento básico." Copy on file with the author.

——. Unidad Nacional de Tierras Rurales (UNAT). "Se firma convenio UNAT-Min Interior: Para adelantar los procesos agrarios de negritudes e indígenas." *Noticias de la UNAT* (July 2008).

Colombia. Ministerio de Ambiente y Desarrollo Territorial. *Proyecto de Ley Reglamentario de los Capítulos IV, V y VII de Ley 70 de 1993.* Bogotá, Version of June 2007 (Published Draft). Copy on file with author.

Colombia. Ministerio del Interior y de Justica. Proyecto de Decreto de los Capítulos IV, V y VII de Ley 70 de 1993 (Propuesta Integral). Copy on file with the author (received September 2008).

Colombia. Political Constitution of Colombia of 1991. http://web.presidencia.gov.co/constitucion/index.pdf (accessed August 15, 2009).

Colombia. Presidente de la República. Decreto 1332 (1992). *Diario Oficial* No. 40.538. August 12, 1992.

——. Decreto 1745 (1995). *Diario Oficial* No. 42.049. October 13, 1995.

——. Decreto 2249 (1995). *Diario Oficial* No. 42.163. December 26, 1995.

Colombia. Vicepresidencia. "La Población Afrocolombiana: Títulos Colectivos Adjudicados a las Comunidades Negras Cuenca del Pacífico (Años 1996–2007)." http://www.vicepresidencia.gov.co/iniciativas/c_afrocolombiana/titulos.asp (accessed January 29, 2009). Copy on file with the author.

Colombres, Adolfo, ed. *Hacia la Autogestión Indígena: Documentos.* Quito: Ediciones del Sol, 1977.

Comisión Ideología y Filosofía Indianista del I Congreso Indio Sudamericana. "Conclusiones." In *Primer Congreso de Movimientos Indios de Sudamerica.* Ollantaytambo (Cuzco, Peru), 27 Febrero–3 Marzo de 1980, 136–39. Paris: Ediciones Mitra, 1980.

"Conclusiones del Segundo Congreso Nacional de Pueblos Indígenas." March 4, 1977. Reprinted in *Utopía y revolución: el pensamiento político contemporáneo de los indios en América Latina,* edited by Guillermo Bonfil Batalla, 377–383. Mexico City: Editorial Nueva Imagen, 1981.

Conklin, Beth A. "Body Paint, Feathers, and VCRS: Aesthetics and Authenticity in Amazonian Activism." *American Ethnologist* 24, no. 4 (1997): 711–37.

Consejo Comunitario de Comunidades Negras de Isla del Rosario Caserío Orika. *Acción de tutela contra la nación (Ministerio de Agricultura, Instituto Colombiano de Desarrollo Rural [INCODER]).* November 2007. Copy on file with the author.

Consejo Comunitario de Comunidades Negras de la Unidad Comunera de Gobierno de Isla del Rosario Caserío de Orika. (Application for Collective Title). February 2006. Copy on file with the author.

Consejos Comunitarios. "¡No a la Palma, Sí a los Derechos Territoriales y a la Vida!" November 14, 2008. http://colombia.indymedia.org/news/2008/11/95406.php (accessed January 18, 2010). Copy on file with the author.

Convention on the Rights of the Child. Adopted November 20, 1989. 1577 U.N.T.S. 3.

Convention Providing for Creation of the Inter-American Indian Institute. Adopted November 29, 1940. 1272 U.N.T.S. 330.

Coombe, Rosemary J. "Intellectual Property, Human Rights, and Sovereignty: New Dilemmas in International Law Posed by the Recognition of Indigenous Knowledge and the Conservation of Biodiversity." *Indiana Journal of Global Legal Studies* 6 (1998): 59–115.

Corntassel, Jeff J., and Thomas Hopkins Primeau. "Indigenous 'Sovereignty' and International Law: Revised Strategies for Pursuing 'Self-Determination.'" *Human Rights Quarterly* 17, no. 2 (1995): 343–65.

CRIC. "Nuestras luchas de ayer y de hoy." 1973. Reprinted in *Utopía y revolución: el pensamiento político contemporáneo de los indios en América Latina,* edited by Guillermo Bonfil Batalla, 279–96. Mexico City: Editorial Nueva Imagen, 1981.

Cubides, Fernando, and Carlos Domínguez, eds. *Desplazados, migraciones internas y reestructuraciones territoriales.* Bogotá: CES-Universidad Nacional y Ministerio del Interior, 1999.

Cunin, Elisabeth. "De la esclavitud al multiculturalismo: El antropólogo entre identidad rechazada e identidad instrumentalizada." In *Conflicto e (in)visibilidad: Retos en los estudios de la gente negra en Colombia,* edited by Eduardo Restrepo and Axel Rojas, 141–56. Popayán, Colombia: Editorial Universidad del Cauca, 2004.

———. *Identidades a flor de piel: Lo "negro" entre apariencias y pertenencias: categorías raciales y mestizaje en Cartagena (Colombia).* Bogotá: Instituto Colombiano de Antropología e Historia, 2003.

Daes, Erica-Irene. "Protection of the Heritage of Indigenous Peoples." UN Study Series no. 10/1997.

———. "The Spirit and Letter of the Right to Self-Determination of Indigenous Peoples: Reflections on the Making of the United Nations Draft Declaration." In *Operationalizing the Right of Indigenous Peoples to Self-Determination,* edited by Pekka Aikio and Martin Scheinin, 67–83. Turko/Åbo: Åbo Akademi University, 2000.

———. "Striving for Self-Determination for Indigenous Peoples." In *Pursuit of the Right to Self-Determination: Collected Papers & Proceedings of the First International Conference on the Right to Self-Determination & the United Nations,* edited by Yussuf Naim Kly and Diana Kly, 50–62. Atlanta: Clarity, 2001.

——. "United Nations Activities in the Field of Indigenous Rights." *Transnational Perspectives* 13 (1987): 11–14.

Danius, Sara, Stefan Jonsson, and Gayatri Chakravorty Spivak. "An Interview with Gayatri Chakravorty Spivak." *Boundary 2* 20, no. 2 (1993): 24–50.

Davies, Peter, ed. *Human Rights*. New York: Routledge, 1988.

Davis, Shelton H. "Indigenous Peoples, Poverty, and Participatory Development: the Experience of the World Bank in Latin America." In *Multiculturalism in Latin America*, edited by Rachel Sieder, 227–51. Basingstoke: Palgrave, 2002.

——. *Land Rights and Indigenous Peoples: The Role of the Inter-American Commission on Human Rights*. Cambridge, Mass.: Cultural Survival, 1998.

Dean, Bartholomew, and Jerome M. Levi. "Introduction." In *At the Risk of Being Heard: Identity, Indigenous Rights, and Postcolonial States*, edited by Bartholomew Dean and Jerome M. Levi, 1–43. Ann Arbor: University of Michigan Press, 2003.

"The Declaration of Barbados: For the Liberation of the Indians." *Current Anthropology* 14, no. 3 (June 1973): 267–70.

Deloria, Vine, Jr. *Behind the Trail of Broken Treaties: An Indian Declaration of Independence*. New York: Delacorte, 1974.

Deloria, Vine, Jr., and David E. Wilkins. *Tribes, Treaties, and Constitutional Tribulations*. 1st edition. Austin: University of Texas Press, 1999.

Díaz Polanco, Héctor. *Indigenous Peoples in Latin America: The Quest for Self-Determination*. Translated by Lucía Rayas. Boulder, Colo.: Westview, 1997.

Dodson, Michael. "The Human Rights Situation of Indigenous Peoples in Australia." *Indigenous Affairs* 1 (Jan.–Feb.–March 1999): 32–45.

Dos Santos, Theotonio. "The Structure of Dependence." *American Economic Review* 60, no. 2 (1970): 231–36.

Dover, Robert V. H., and Joanne Rappaport. "Introduction." In Ethnicity Reconfigured: Indigenous Legislators and the Colombian Constitution of 1991. Joanne Rappaport, ed. Special Issue. *Journal of Latin American Anthropology* 1, no. 2 (1996): 2–17.

Draft Declaration of Principles for the Defense of the Indigenous Nations and Peoples of the Western Hemisphere. (Drafted and circulated by indigenous participants at the Non-Governmental Organization Conference on Discrimination Against Indigenous Populations, Geneva, 1977.) Reprinted in *Indigenous Peoples in International Law*, by James S. Anaya, 293–296. 2nd ed. New York: Oxford University Press, 2004.

Dulitzky, Ariel. "When Afrodescendants Became Tribal Peoples: The Inter-American Human Rights System and Rural Black Communities." Paper presented at the Congress of the Latin American Studies Association, Rio de Janeiro, June 11–14, 2009. Copy on file with the author.

Dunbar-Ortiz, Roxanne. "The First Decade of Indigenous Peoples at the United Nations." *Peace & Change* 31, no. 1 (January 2006): 58–74.

Durán Bernal, Carlos Andrés. *¿Es nuestra isla para dos? Conflicto por el desarrollo y la conservación en Islas del Rosario, Cartagena*. Bogotá, Colombia: Universidad de Los Andes, Facultad de Ciencias Sociales-Ceso, Departamento de Antropología, 2007.

Dyck, Noel. "Representation and the 'Fourth World': A Concluding Statement." In *Indigenous Peoples and the Nation-State: Fourth World Politics in Canada, Australia, and Norway*, edited by Noel Dyck, 236–41. St. John's, Newfoundland: Institute of Social and Economic Research, 1985.

Eide, Asbjørn. "Indigenous Populations and Human Rights: The United Nations Efforts at Mid-Way." In *Native Power: The Quest for Autonomy and Nationhood of Indigenous Peoples*, edited by Jens Brøsted et al., 196–212. Bergen, Norway: Universitetsforlaget, 1985.

———. "In Search of Constructive Alternatives to Secession." In *Modern Law of Self-Determination*, edited by Christian Tomuschat, 139–76. Dordrecht, Netherlands: Martinus Nijhoff, 1993.

Engle, Karen. "Culture and Human Rights: The Asian Values Debate in Context." *New York University Journal of International Law and Politics* 32, no. 2 (2000): 291–333.

Escalante, Aquiles. "*Palenques* in Colombia." In *Maroon Societies: Rebel Slave Communities in the Americas*. 3rd ed., edited by Richard Price, 74–81. Baltimore: Johns Hopkins University Press, 1996.

Escobar, Arturo. *Encountering Development: The Making and Unmaking of the Third World*. Princeton, N.J.: Princeton University Press, 1995.

———. "Imaginando un Futuro: Pensamiento Crítico, Desarrollo y Movimientos Sociales." In *Desarrollo y Democracia*, edited by Margarita López Maya, 135–70. Caracas: Nueva Sociedad, 1991.

———. " 'Post-development' as Concept and Social Practice." In *Exploring Post-Development: Theory and Practice, Problems and Perspectives*, edited by Aram Ziai, 18–31. Hoboken: Taylor and Francis, 2007.

———. *Territories of Difference: Place, Movements, Life, Redes*. Durham: Duke University Press, 2008.

———. "Whose Knowledge, Whose Nature? Biodiversity, Conservation, and the Political Ecology of Social Movements." *Journal of Political Ecology* 5 (1998): 53–82.

Foro Andino Nacional. Eje de Derechos Culturales. "La mirada de los derechos culturales desde la perspectiva de las etnias en el D.C." (Relatoría). Remarks of Ayden Salgado. Bogotá, September 24–26, 2007. Copy on file with the author.

Frank, André Gunder. *Capitalism and Underdevelopment in Latin America: Historical Studies of Chile and Brazil*. New York: Monthly Review, 1967.

———. "Dependence Is Dead, Long Live Dependence and the Class Struggle: An Answer to Critics." *Latin American Perspectives* 1, no. 1 (1974): 87–106.

Frankovits, André. "Towards a Mechanism for the Realization of the Right to Self-Determination." In *In Pursuit of the Right to Self-Determination, Collected Papers & Proceedings of the First International Conference on the Right to Self-Determination & the United Nations*, edited by Yussaf Naim Kly and Diana Kly, 19–35. Atlanta: Clarity, 2001.

Fromherz, Christopher J. "Indigenous Peoples' Courts: Egalitarian Juridical Pluralism, Self-Determination, and the United Nations Declaration on the Rights of Indigenous Peoples." *University of Pennsylvania Law Review* 156, no. 5 (2008): 1341–82.

Fundación CEPS. *Colombia: Un país formal y otro real.* Valencia, Spain: Centro de Estudios Políticos y Sociales, October 2006. http://www.omal.info/www/IMG/pdf/Colombia_unpaisformal_y_otroreal_ceps.pdf (accessed December 9, 2009). Copy on file with the author.

Gandhi, Mahatma. "Letter to Julian Huxley, Director General of UNESCO." Reprinted in *Human Rights: Comments and Interpretations*, edited by UNESCO, 18. New York: Columbia University Press, 1949.

Gargarella, Roberto, Pilar Domingo, and Theunis Rous, eds. *Courts and Social Transformation in New Democracies: An Institutional Voice for the Poor?* Burlington, Vt.: Ashgate, 2006.

Ghanea, Nazila, and Alexandra Xanthaki, eds. *Minorities, Peoples and Self-Determination.* Boston: Martinus Nijhoff, 2005.

Gilbert, Jérémie. *Indigenous People's Land Rights under International Law: From Victims to Actors.* Ardsley, N.Y.: Transnational, 2006.

Girón Cerna, Carlos. "El Indigenismo y el Indio." *América Indígena* 1, no. 1 (1941): 17–20.

Global Exchange. "Stop the Forced Displacement of Indigenous Communities in Chiapas, Mexico." Press release. March 14, 2003. Copy on file with the author.

Global Indigenous Peoples' Caucus. Steering Committee. "Report of the Global Indigenous Peoples' Caucus." August 31, 2007. Reprinted at http://www.hreoc.gov.au/social_Justice/declaration/screport_070831.pdf (accessed February 9, 2009). Copy on file with the author.

Global Rights and AFRODES. *Los Derechos Humanos de las Comunidades Afrocolombianas.* Washington: Global Rights, 2006. Copy on file with the author.

Goodale, Mark. *Surrendering to Human Rights: An Anthropology of Human Rights.* Palo Alto, Calif.: Stanford University Press, 1999.

Gow, David D. *Countering Development: Indigenous Modernity and the Moral Imagination.* Durham: Duke University Press, 2008.

Graham, Laura R., and Beth Conklin. "The Shifting Middle Ground: Amazonian Indians and Eco-Politics." *American Anthropologist* 97, no. 4 (1995): 695–710.

Graham, Richard, ed. *The Idea of Race in Latin America, 1870–1940.* Austin: University of Texas Press, 1990.

Gray, Andrew. *Indigenous Rights and Development: Self-Determination in an Amazonian Community.* Oxford: Berghahn, 1997.

Greene, Shana. "Indigenous People Incorporated?" *Current Anthropology* 45 (2004): 211–37.

Griggs, Richard. "The Meaning of 'Nation' and 'State' in the Fourth World." Paper 18. Olympia, Wash.: Center for World Indigenous Studies, 1992. http://cwis.org/fourthw.htm (accessed December 9, 2009).

Grueso Castelblanco, Libia Rosario. "Documento propuesta para la formulación del plan integral de largo plazo: población negra/afrocolombiana, palenquera y raizal, 2007–2019." Bogotá: May 31, 2007. http://www.dnp.gov.co/archivos/documentos/DDTS_Portadas/DOC_EJEC_FINAL_PLAN_INTEGRAL.pdf (accessed December 15, 2009). Copy on file with the author.

Hale, Charles R. "Activist Research v. Cultural Critique: Indigenous Land Rights and the Contradictions of Politically Engaged Anthropology." *Cultural Anthropology* 21, no. 1 (2006): 96–120.

———. "Between Che Guevara and the Pachamama: Mestizos, Indians and Identity Politics in the Anti-quincentenary Campaign." *Critique of Anthropology* 14, no. 1 (1994): 9–39.

———. "Does Multiculturalism Menace? Governance, Cultural Rights and the Politics of Identity in Guatemala." *Journal of Latin American Studies* 34 (2002): 485–524.

———. "Neoliberal Multiculturalism: The Remaking of Cultural Rights and Racial Dominance in Central America." *POLAR: Political and Legal Anthropology Review* 28, no. 1 (2005): 9–19.

———. "Rethinking Indigenous Politics in the Era of the 'Indio Permitido.'" *NACLA Report on the Americas* 38, no. 2 (2004): 16–21.

Hallman, David G., ed. *Ecotheology: Voices from South and North.* Maryknoll, N.Y.: Orbis, 1994.

Harasym, Sarah, ed. *The Post-Colonial Critic: Interviews, Strategies, Dialogues.* New York: Routledge, 1990.

Harvey, Neil. *The Chiapas Rebellion: The Struggle for Land and Democracy.* Durham: Duke University Press, 1998.

Helg, Aline. *Liberty and Equality in Caribbean Colombia, 1770–1835.* Chapel Hill: University of North Carolina Press, 2004.

Hendrickson, Carol. "Images of the Indian in Guatemala: The Role of Indigenous Dress in Indian and Ladino Constructions." In *Nation States and Indians in Latin America*, edited by Greg Urban and Joel Sherzer, 286–306. Austin: University of Texas Press, 1991.

Henriquez, Elio, and Angeles Mariscal. "Desalojo en Montes Azules; arrestan a 6 jefes de familia." *La Jornada* (Mexico City). April 19, 2007.

Hernández Cassiani, Ruben D. "El caribe colombiano: Entre la identidad y la diferencia." In *Procesos históricos-culturales: Diplomado en etnoeducación e interculturalidad*, compiled by Ruben D. Hernandez Cassiani, 7–34. [s.l.]: Editorial Changó, 2006. Copy on file with the author.

Hernández Castillo, Aída R. "Indigenous Law and Identity Politics in Mexico: Indigenous Men's and Women's Struggle for a Multicultural Nation." *Political and Legal Anthropology Review* 24, no. 2 (2002): 90–109.

Hettne, Björn. *Development Theory and the Three Worlds: Towards an International Political Economy of Development.* 2nd ed. New York: John Wiley and Sons, 1995.

Hodgson, Dorothy L. "Introduction: Comparative Perspectives on the Indigenous Rights Movement in Africa and the Americas." *American Anthropologist* 104, no. 4 (2002): 1037–49.

Hoffmann, Odile, and Pedro Quintín. "Organización social, dinámicas culturales e identidades de las poblaciones afrocolombianas del Pacífico y suroccidente en un contexto de movilidad y urbanización." *Boletín socioeconómico*, no. 31 (1999): 134–40.

Hogan, Jackie. "Staging the Nation: Gendered and Ethnicized Discourses of National Identity in Olympic Ceremonies." *Journal of Sport and Social Issues* 27 (2003): 100–123.

Honig, Bonnie. " 'My Culture Made Me Do It.' " In *Is Multiculturalism Bad for Women?* edited by Joshua Cohen, Matthew Howard, and Martha C. Nussbaum, 7–24. Princeton, N.J.: Princeton University Press, 1999.

Hooker, Juliet. "Indigenous Inclusion/Black Excusion: Race, Ethnicity and Multicultural Citizenship in Latin America." *Journal of Latin American Studies* 37, no. 2 (2005): 285–310.

Humphry, Alison. "An Opportunity Lost for Aboriginal Self-Determination: Australia's Compliance with ILO 169." *Murdoch University Electronic Journal of Law* 2, no. 1 (April 1995). http://www.murdoch.edu.au/elaw/issues/v2n1/humphry21.html (accessed February 8, 2009).

"International Indian Treaty Council." *The Encyclopedia of Native American Legal Tradition*, edited by Bruce Elliott Johansen, 154–55. Westport, Conn.: Greenwood, 1998.

International Alliance of the Indigenous and Tribal Peoples of the Tropical Forests. "Charter of the Indigenous and Tribal Peoples of the Tropical Forests." February 15, 1992; revised November 22, 2002. http://www.international-alliance.org (accessed October 25, 2009). Copy on file with the author.

International Convention on the Elimination of All Forms of Racial Discrimination (ICERD). Adopted December 21, 1965. 660 U.N.T.S. 195.

International Covenant on Civil and Political Rights (ICCPR). Adopted December 16, 1966. 999 U.N.T.S. 171.

International Covenant on Economic, Social and Cultural Rights (ICESCR). Adopted December 16, 1966. 993 U.N.T.S. 3.

International Indian Treaty Council. Declaration of Continuing Independence by the First International Indian Treaty Council at Standing Rock Indian Country June 1974. http://www.treatycouncil.org/pdfs/declaration_of_continuing_independence .pdf (accessed August 16, 2009). Copy on file with the author.

International Labor Conference. 76th Session, 1989. *Record of Proceedings*. Geneva: International Labor Organization, 1990.

International Labor Organization. Constitution (as amended). Adopted October 9, 1946. 15 U.N.T.S. 40.

———. Convention 107. Concerning the Protection and Integration of Indigenous and Other Tribal and Semi-Tribal Populations in Independent Countries (ILO 107). Adopted June 26, 1957. 328 U.N.T.S. 247.

———. Convention 169. Concerning Indigenous and Tribal Peoples in Independent Countries (ILO 169). Adopted June 27, 1989. 1650 U.N.T.S. 383.

———. *Indigenous and Tribal Peoples' Rights in Practice: A Guide to ILO Convention No. 169*. Geneva: International Labor Organization, 2009.

International Labor Organization. Governing Body. "Report of the Committee Set Up to Examine the Representation Alleging Non-observance by Peru of the Indigenous and Tribal Peoples Convention, 1989 (No. 169), Made under Article 24 of the ILO

Constitution by the General Confederation of Workers of Peru (CGTP)." Submitted 1997. Copy on file with the author.

——. "Report of the Committee Set Up to Examine the Representation Alleging Non-observance by Argentina of the Indigenous and Tribal Peoples Convention, 1989 (No. 169), Made under Article 24 of the ILO Constitution by the Education Workers Union of Río Negro (UNTER)." I.L.O. Doc. GB.303/19/7. November 12, 2008. Copy on file with the author.

——. "Report of the Committee Set Up to Examine the Representation Alleging Non-observance by Guatemala of the Indigenous and Tribal Peoples Convention, 1989 (No. 169), Made under Article 24 of the ILO Constitution by the Federation of Country and City Workers (FTCC)." I.L.O. Doc. GB.299/6/1. June 4, 2007. Copy on file with the author.

IWGIA. *International Working Group on Indigenous Affairs Yearbook 1988.* Copenhagen: IWGIA, 1989.

Jackson, Jean E. "Culture, Genuine and Spurious: The Politics of Indianness in the Vaupés, Colombia." *American Ethnologist* 22 (1995): 3–27.

Johansen, Bruce Elliott, ed. *The Encyclopedia of Native American Legal Tradition.* Westport, Conn.: Greenwood, 1998.

Karlsson, Bengt G. "Anthropology and the 'Indigenous Slot': Claims to and Debates about Indigenous Peoples' Status in India." *Critique of Anthropology* 23, no. 4 (2003): 403–23.

Kastrup, José Paulo. "The Internationalization of Indigenous Rights from the Environmental and Human Rights Perspective." *Texas International Law Journal* 32, no. 1 (1997): 97–122.

Kauanui, J. Kehaulani. "Colonialism in Equality: Hawaiian Sovereignty and the Question of U.S. Civil Rights." *South Atlantic Quarterly* 107, no. 4 (2008): 635–650.

——. "Hawaiian Nationhood, Self-Determination, and International Law," In *Transforming the Tools of the Colonizer: Collaboration, Knowledge, and Language in Native Narratives,* edited by Florencia E. Mallon. Durham: Duke University Press, forthcoming 2010.

Keller, David R. "Case Study: Un-American or Very-American? The Goshute Nuclear Waste Repository." http://davidkeller.us/publications/TeachingEthics1_2001_79–87.pdf (accessed October 26, 2009). Copy on file with the author.

——. "Goshute Nuclear Waste Repository: Un-American or Very American?" *Salt Lake Tribune,* December 29, 2002. http://davidkeller.us/publications/SaltLakeTribune12–29–02.pdf (accessed October 26, 2009). Copy on file with the author.

Kennedy, David. *The Dark Sides of Virtue: Reassessing International Humanitarianism.* Princeton, N.J.: Princeton University Press, 2004.

——. "The 'Rule of Law,' Political Choices, and Development Common Sense." In *The New Law and Economic Development: A Critical Appraisal,* edited by David M. Trubek and Alvaro Santos, 95–173. New York: Cambridge University Press, 2006.

Kingsbury, Benedict. "Reconstructing Self-Determination: A Relational Approach." In

Operationalizing the Right of Indigenous Peoples to Self-Determination, edited by Pekka Aikio and Martin Scheinin, 19–37. Turko / Åbo: Åbo Akademi University, 2000.

——. " 'Indigenous Peoples' in International Law: A Constructivist Approach to the Asian Controversy." *American Journal of International Law* 92, no. 3 (1998): 414–457.

Kirgis, Frederic L., Jr. "The Degrees of Self-Determination in the United Nations Era." *American Journal of International Law* 88, no. 2 (1994): 304–10.

Kly, Yussaf Naim, and Diana Kly, eds. *In Pursuit of the Right to Self-Determination: Collected Papers and Proceedings of the First International Conference on the Right to Self-determination and the United Nations*. Atlanta: Clarity, 2001.

Knight, Alan. *The Mexican Revolution*. Vol. 1: *Porfirians, Liberals, and Peasants*. Cambridge: Cambridge University Press, 1986.

——. "Racism, Revolution, and *Indigenismo*: Mexico, 1910–1940." In *The Idea of Race in Latin America, 1870–1940*, edited by Richard Graham, 71–113. Austin: University of Texas Press, 1990.

Knop, Karen. *Diversity and Self-Determination in International Law*. New York: Cambridge University Press, 2002.

Krause, Catarina, and Gudmunder Alfredsson. "Article 17: The Right to Property in Other Human Rights Instruments." In *The Universal Declaration of Human Rights: A Common Standard of Achievement*, edited by Gudmunder Alfredsson and Asbjørn Eide, 359–78. Boston: Martinus Nijhoff, 1999.

Kymlicka, Will. "Liberal Complacencies." In *Is Multiculturalism Bad for Women?*, edited by Joshua Cohen, Matthew Howard, and Martha C. Nussbaum, 7–24. Princeton, N.J.: Princeton University Press, 1999.

Lâm, Maivân. *At the Edge of the State: Indigenous Peoples and Self-determination*. Ardsley, N.Y.: Transnational, 2000.

Laplante, Lisa J., and Suzanne A. Spears. "Out of the Conflict Zone: The Case for Community Consent Processes in the Extractive Sector." *Yale Human Rights and Development Law Journal*, vol. 11 (2008): 69–117.

Larson, Brooke. "Andean Highland Peasants and the Trials of Nation Making during the Nineteenth Century." In *The Cambridge History of the Native Peoples of the Americas*, Vol. 3, *South America: Part 2*, edited by Frank Salomon and Stuart B. Schwartz, 558–703. Cambridge: Cambridge University Press, 1999.

Laurie, Nina, Robert Andolina, and Sarah Radcliffe. "Ethnodevelopment: Social Movements, Creating Experts and Professionalising Indigenous Knowledge in Ecuador." *Antipode* 37, no. 3 (2005): 470–96.

League of Nations Covenant. Adopted April 11, 1919. 225 Consol. T.S. 195.

López Maya, Margarita, ed. *Desarrollo y Democracia*. Caracas: Nueva Sociedad, 1991.

Lubow, Arthur. "The Possessed." *The New York Times Magazine*. June 24, 2007.

Lutz, Ellen. "Adoption of U.N. Declaration a Matter of Course." *Indian Country Today*, June 1, 2007. http://www.indiancountrytoday.com/archive/28147794.html (accessed December 18, 2009). Copy on file with the author.

Lynch, John. *Simón Bolívar: A Life*. New Haven, Conn.: Yale University Press, 2006.

MacKay, Fergus. "The Draft World Bank Operational Policy 4.10 on Indigenous Peoples: Progress or More of the Same?" *Arizona Journal of International and Comparative Law* 22, no. 1 (2005): 65–98.

Macklem, Patrick. *Indigenous Difference and the Constitution of Canada.* Toronto: University of Toronto Press, 2001.

Maderas del Pueblo del Sureste. "Breve historia de la llamada 'Comunidad Lacandona.'" Pamphlet. December 2002. Copy on file with the author.

"Manifiesto de Tiawanacu." July 30, 1973. Reprinted in *Utopía y revolución: el pensamiento político contemporáneo de los indios en América Latina,* edited by Guillermo Bonfil Batalla, 216–23. Mexico City: Nueva Imagen, 1981.

Manuel, George, and Michael Posluns. *The Fourth World: An Indian Reality.* New York: Free Press, 1974.

Martínez, María Elena. "The Black Blood of New Spain: *Limpieza de Sangre*, Racial Violence, and Gendered Power in Early Colonial Mexico." *William and Mary Quarterly* 61, no. 3 (2004): 479–520.

Mato, Daniel, ed. *Políticas de economía, ambiente y sociedad en tiempos de globalización.* Caracas: Universidad Central de Venezuela, 2005.

Mayer, Enrique, and Elio Masferrer. "La Población Indígena de América en 1978." *América Indígena* 39, no. 2 (1979): 217–337.

McGregor, Deborah. "Coming Full Circle: Indigenous Knowledge, Environment, and Our Future." *American Indian Quarterly* 28, nos. 3–4 (2004): 385–410.

Mehta, Uday Singh. *Liberalism and Empire: A Study in Nineteenth-Century British Liberal Thought.* Chicago: University of Chicago Press, 1999.

Messer, Ellen. "Anthropology and Human Rights." *Annual Review of Anthropology* 22 (1993): 221–49.

México. Secretaria de la Reforma Agraria. "El Gobierno de la República cumple su palabra con los Lacandones: Salazar Adame." Press release SRA / 021. March 27, 2006.

Mezey, Naomi. "The Distribution of Wealth, Sovereignty and Culture through Indian Gaming." *Stanford Law Review* 48, no. 3 (February 1996): 711–37.

Midwest Alliance of Sovereign Tribes. "Trust Responsibility." http://m-a-s-t.org/TrustResponsibility.htm (accessed October 21, 2008). Copy on file with the author.

Miller, Robert J. *Native America, Discovered and Conquered.* Westport, Conn.: Praeger, 2006.

MINK'A. "Pueblo indio: Ultrajado, pero no vencido." 1975. Reprinted in *Utopía y revolución: el pensamiento político contemporáneo de los indios en América Latina,* edited by Guillermo Bonfil Batalla, 234–40. Mexico City: Editorial Nueva Imagen, 1981.

Minority Rights Group International. *World Directory of Minorities and Indigenous Peoples– Colombia: Afro-Colombians.* Minority Rights Group International, 2008. http://www.unhcr.org/refworld/docid/49749d3cc.html (accessed February 1, 2009). Copy on file with the author.

MITKA. "Conclusiones del Primer Congreso Histórico Político del Movimiento Indio

Tupaj Katari." Press release. April 26, 1978. Reprinted in *Utopía y revolución: el pensamiento político contemporáneo de los indios en América Latina*, edited by Guillermo Bonfil Batalla, 248–52. Mexico City: Editorial Nueva Imagen, 1981.

———. "En el 196 aniversario del asesinato de Julián Apasa." 1977. Reprinted in *Utopía y revolución: el pensamiento político contemporáneo de los indios en América Latina*, edited by Guillermo Bonfil Batalla, 245–48. Mexico City: Editorial Nueva Imagen, 1981.

———. "Manifiesto del Movimiento Indio Tupaj Katari." 1978. Reprinted in *Utopía y revolución: el pensamiento político contemporáneo de los indios en América Latina*, edited by Guillermo Bonfil Batalla, 252–65. Mexico City: Editorial Nueva Imagen, 1981.

Montevideo Convention on the Rights and Duties of States. Adopted December 26, 1933. 165 L.N.T.S. 19.

Moore, Donald S., Jake Kosek, and Anand Pandian, eds. *Race, Nature, and the Politics of Difference*. Durham: Duke University Press, 2003.

Morsink, Johannes. *The Universal Declaration of Human Rights: Origins, Drafting, and Intent*. Philadelphia: University of Pennsylvania Press, 1999.

Mosquera, Claudia, Mauricio Pardo, and Odile Hoffmann. "Las trayectorias sociales e identitarias de los afrodescendientes." In *Afrodescendientes en las Américas: Trayectorias sociales e identitarias*, edited by Claudia Mosquera, Mauricio Pardo, and Odile Hoffmann, 13–42. Bogotá: Universidad Nacional de Colombia-ICANH-IRD-ILAS, 2002.

Muehlebach, Andrea. "What Self in Self-Determination? Notes from the Frontiers of Transnational Indigenous Activism." *Identities: Global Studies in Culture and Power* 10, no. 2 (April–June 2003): 241–68.

Museo Nacional de Colombia. *Velorios y santos vivos: Comunidades negras, afrocolombianas, raizales y palenqueras*. Bogotá: Ministerio de Cultura, 2008.

Myntti, Kristian. "The Right of Indigenous Peoples to Self-Determination and Effective Participation." In *Operationalizing the Right of Indigenous Peoples to Self-Determination*, edited by Pekka Aikio and Martin Scheinin, 85–130. Turko / Åbo: Åbo Akademi University, 2000.

Nagengast, Carole, and Terence Turner. "Introduction: Universal Human Rights versus Cultural Relativism." *Journal of Anthropological Research* 53, no. 3 (1997): 269–72.

National Environmental Coalition of Native Americans. "Nuclear Free Zones." http:// necona.indigenousnative.org / nfz.html (accessed August 16, 2009). Copy on file with the author.

Nelson, Cary, and Lawrence Grossberg, eds. *Marxism and the Interpretation of Culture*. Urbana: University of Illinois Press, 1988.

Nelson, Diane M. *A Finger in the Wound: Body Politics in Quincentennial Guatemala*. Berkeley: University of California Press, 1999.

Ng'weno, Bettina. *On Titling Collective Property, Participation, and Natural Resource Management: Implementing Indigenous and Afro-Colombian Demands. A Review of Bank Experience in Colombia*. Washington: World Bank, 2001.

——. *Turf Wars: Territory and Citizenship in the Contemporary State*. Stanford: Stanford University Press, 2007.

Niezen, Ronald. "The Indigenous Claim for Recognition in the International Public Sphere." *Florida Journal of International Law* 17, no. 3 (2005): 583–601.

Norwegian Refugee Council. "Resisting Displacement by Combatants and Developers: Humanitarian Zones in North-west Colombia." Internal Displacement Monitoring Centre: Geneva, November 2007. http://www.internal-displacement.org (accessed December 9, 2009). Copy on file with the author.

OAS (Organization of American States). Inter-American Commission on Human Rights. *Coulter et al. v. Brazil (Yanomami Case)*, Res. No. 12/85, Case No. 7615, OAS/Ser.L/v/II.66, doc. 10, rev. 1. March 5, 1985.

——. *Guahibo Indians v. Colombia*. Case 1690. *Annual Report 1973* 21–23. O.A.S. Doc OEA/Ser.L/v/II.30, doc. 45, rev. 1. February 26, 1973.

——. "The Human Rights Situation of the Indigenous People in the Americas." OEA/Ser.L/v/II.108, doc. 62. October 20, 2000.

——. "Informe Anual de la Comisión Interamericana de Derechos Humanos." OEA/Ser.L/v/II.32, doc. 3. February 1974.

——. *Marino López et al. v. Colombia (Operation Genesis)*, Report No. 86/06, Petition 499–04. October 21, 2006. (Declared admissible.)

——. *Maya Indigenous Community of the Toledo District v. Belize*. Case 12.053, Report No. 40/04, OEA/Ser.L/v/II.122, doc. 5, rev. 1. October 12, 2004.

——. *Paraguay: Tribu Aché-Guayaki*. Case 1802. May 27, 1977. Reprinted *Ten Years of Activities, 1971–1981* by Inter-American Commission on Human Rights, 151–52. Washington: OAS, 1982.

——. "Report on the Situation of Human Rights of a Segment of the Nicaraguan Population of Miskito Origin." OEA/Ser.L/v.II.62, doc. 10, rev. 3. November 29, 1983.

——. *Yakye Axa Indigenous Community of the Enxet-Lengua People v. Paraguay*. Case 11.713, Report No. 90/99, OEA/Ser.L/v/II.106 Doc. 3. September 29, 1999.

OAS. Inter-American Court of Human Rights, *Aloeboetoe v. Suriname*. Reparations and Costs. (Series C) No. 15. September 10, 1993.

——. *Bámaca Velásquez v. Guatemala*. Merits. (Series C) No. 70. November 25, 2000.

——. *Bámaca Velásquez v. Guatemala*. Reparations and Costs. (Series C) No. 91. February 22, 2002.

——. *The Indigenous Community Sawhoyamaxa v. Paraguay*. Merits, Reparations and Costs. (Series C) No. 146. March 29, 2006.

——. *The Mayagna (Sumo) Awas Tingni Community v. Nicaragua*. Merits, Reparations, and Costs. (Series C) No. 79. August 31, 2001.

——. *Plan de Sánchez Massacre v. Guatemala*. Case 11.763, Report No. 31/99. OEA/Ser.L/v/II.95, doc. 7. March 11, 1999. (Declared admissible).

——. *Plan de Sánchez Massacre v. Guatemala*. Reparations and Costs. (Series C) No. 116. November 19, 2004.

——. *Saramaka People v. Suriname*. Preliminary Objections, Merits, Reparations, and Costs. (Series C) No. 172. November 28, 2007.

OAS. Permanent Council. Committee on Juridical and Political Affairs. Working Group to Prepare the Draft American Declaration on the Rights of Indigenous Peoples. "Note from the Chair of the Working Group on the Proposals to Amend Section VI of the Chair's Consolidated Text." OEA / Ser.K / XVI GT / DADIN / doc.244 / 06. January 26, 2006.

——. "Record of the Current Status of the Draft American Declaration on the Rights of Indigenous Peoples." OEA / Ser.K / XVI GT / DADIN / doc.334 / 08 rev. 5. December 3, 2009.

Offen, Karl H. "The Territorial Turn: Making Black Territories in Pacific Colombia." *Journal of Latin American Geography* 2, no. 1 (2003): 43–73.

Okin, Susan Moller. "Is Multiculturalism Bad for Women?" In *Is Multiculturalism Bad for Women?*, edited by Joshua Cohen, Matthew Howard, and Martha C. Nussbaum, 7–24. Princeton, N.J.: Princeton University Press, 1999.

——. "Reply." In *Is Multiculturalism Bad for Women?*, edited by Joshua Cohen, Matthew Howard, and Martha C. Nussbaum, 115–131. Princeton, N.J.: Princeton University Press, 1999.

Oquendo, Angel R. "Indigenous Self-Determination in Latin America." *Florida Journal of International Law* 17, no. 3 (December 2005): 625–31.

Orlin, Theodore S., et al., eds. *The Jurisprudence of Human Rights Law: A Comparative Interpretive Approach*. Turku, Finland: Institute for Human Rights, Åbo Akademi University, 2000.

Ortiz, Lucía, ed. *Chambacú, la historia la escribes tú: Ensayos sobre cultura afrocolombiana*. Madrid: Iberoamericana, 2007.

Pagden, Anthony. *Lords of All the World: Ideologies of Empire in Spain, Britain and France c.1500–c.1800*. New Haven, Conn.: Yale University Press, 1995.

Pantoja, Fabio Zambrano. *Colombia, País de regiones*. Bogotá: CINEP, 1998.

Pardo, Mauricio. "Movimientos sociales y actores no gubernamentales." In *Antropología en la modernidad: Identidades, Etnicidades y Movimientos Sociales en Colombia*, edited by María Victoria Uribe and Eduardo Restrepo, 207–52. Bogotá: Instituto Colombiano de Antropología, 1997.

Pardo, Mauricio, Claudia Mosquera, and María Clemencia Ramírez. *Panorámica afrocolombiana: Estudios sociales en el Pacífico*. Bogotá: ICANH-Universidad Nacional de Colombia, 2004.

Parra, Sonia. "Environment—Colombia: Controversy over Forestry Law Simmers On." Inter Press Service, October 5, 2008. http://ipsnews.net/news.asp?idnews= 35002 (accessed August 15, 2009). Copy on file with the author.

Partridge, William L., and Jorge E. Uquillas, with Kathryn Johns. "Including the Excluded: Ethnodevelopment in Latin America." Paper presented at the annual World Bank Conference on Development in Latin America and the Caribbean, Bogotá, June 30–July 2, 1996. http://info.worldbank.org/etools/docs/library/136 160/tslg/pdf/including.pdf (accessed December 9, 2009). Copy on file with the author.

Pasqualucci, Jo Marie. "The Evolution of International Indigenous Rights in the Inter-American Human Rights System." *Human Rights Law Review* 6 (2006): 281–322.

Permanent Court of International Justice. *Minority Schools in Albania.* P.C.I.J. (Ser. A / B) No. 64. April 6, 1935.

Perry, Keisha-Khan. "The Roots of Black Resistance: Race, Gender and the Struggle for Urban Land Rights in Salvador, Bahia, Brazil." *Social Identities* 10, no. 6 (2004): 811–31.

Pitts, Jennifer. *A Turn to Empire: The Rise of Imperial Liberalism in Britain and France.* Princeton, N.J.: Princeton University Press, 2006.

Plant, Roger, and Soren Hvalkof. *Land Titling and Indigenous Peoples.* Technical Study No. IND-109, Indigenous Peoples and Community Development Unit, Sustainable Development Department. Washington: Inter-American Development Bank, 2000. http://www.iadb.org / sds / doc / IND-109E.pdf (accessed February 9, 2009). Copy on file with the author.

Porras Vallejo, Oswaldo Aharón. "Plan Nacional de Desarrollo 2006–2010: 'Estado Comunitario: Desarrollo para Todos.'" Departamento Nacional de Planeación. http://www.dnp.gov.co / PortalWeb / PND / PND20062010 / tabid / 65 / Default.aspx (accessed February 9, 2009). Copy on file with the author.

Post, Robert. "Between Norms and Choices." In *Is Multiculturalism Bad for Women?*, edited by Joshua Cohen, Matthew Howard, and Martha C. Nussbaum, 65–68. Princeton, N.J.: Princeton University Press, 1999.

Povinelli, Elizabeth A. *The Cunning of Recognition: Indigenous Alterities and the Making of Australian Multiculturalism.* Durham: Duke University Press, 2002.

Price, Richard, ed. *Maroon Societies: Rebel Slave Communities in the Americas.* 3rd ed. Baltimore: Johns Hopkins University Press, 1996.

Primer Encuentro Nacional Agrominero Interétnico. "Por el territorio, la dignidad y la autodeterminación. No a las transnacionales en nuestros territorios." July 24, 2007. http://www.dhcolombia.info / spip.php?article407 (accessed December 9, 2009). Copy on file with the author.

Proceso de Comunidades Negras en Colombia (PCN). *Informe: Avance Ley 70 de 1993.* Bogotá: 2003. Copy on file with the author.

Psacharopoulos, George, and Harry Anthony Patrinos, eds. *Indigenous People and Poverty in Latin America: An Empirical Analysis.* Washington: World Bank, 1994.

Ramos, Alcida Rita. "Cutting through State and Class." In *Indigenous Movements, Self-Representation, and the State in Latin America,* edited by Kay B. Warren and Jean E. Jackson, 251–79. Austin: University of Texas Press, 2003.

——. "The Hyperreal Indian." *Critique of Anthropology* 14, no. 2 (1994): 153–71.

——. "Pulp Fictions of Indigenism." In *Race, Nature, and the Politics of Difference,* edited by Donald S. Moore, Jake Kosek, and Anand Pandian, 356–79. Durham: Duke University Press, 2003.

Rappaport, Joanne. *Cumbe Reborn: An Andean Ethnography of History.* Chicago: University of Chicago Press, 1994.

Rappaport, Joanne, and Robert V. H. Dover. "The Construction of Difference by Native Legislators: Assessing the Impact of the Colombian Constitution of 1991." *Journal of Latin American Anthropology* 1, no. 2 (1996): 22–45.

Red de Defensores Comunitarios por los Derechos Humanos. "Defensores Comunitarios Denuncian ante la OIT: Con su 'Ley' el Gobierno Viola la Legislación Internacional." Ojarasca. *La Jornada* (Mexico City), July 2001 supplement. http://www.jornada.unam.mx/2001/07/16/oja51-defensores.html (accessed November 9, 2009). Copy on file with the author.

———. Solicitud de Medidas Cautelares en favor de las comunidades ubicadas en los Montes Azules (to Inter-American Commission on Human Rights). April 23, 2002. Copy on file with the author.

Reinaga, Fausto. *La revolución india.* La Paz: Ediciones Partido Indio de Bolivia, 1969.

Renteln, Alison Dundes. *International Human Rights: Universalism versus Relativism.* Newbury Park, Calif.: Sage, 1990.

Restrepo, Eduardo. "Afrocolombianos, antropología y proyecto de modernidad en Colombia." In *Antropología en la Modernidad: Identidades, Etnicidades y Movimientos Sociales en Colombia,* edited by María Victoria Uribe and Eduardo Restrepo, 279–320. Bogotá: Instituto Colombiano de Antropología, 1997.

———. "Eventalizing Blackness in Colombia." Ph.D. diss., University of North Carolina, 2009.

———. "Políticas de la alteridad: Etnización de 'comunidad negra' en el Pacífico sur colombiano." *Journal of Latin American Anthropology* 7, no. 2 (2002): 34–59.

Restrepo, Eduardo, and Axel Rojas, eds. *Conflicto e (in)visibilidad: Retos en los estudios de la gente negra en Colombia.* Popayán, Colombia: Editorial Universidad del Cauca, 2004.

Reunión de Consejos Comunitarios y Organizaciones Afrocolombianas, Negras, Palenqueras y Raizales. "Documento de Consenso." San Andrés de Tumaco. December 17–18, 2008. http://odr.uniandes.edu.co/pdfs/DerHechos/reuniondeconsejos comunitariosyorganizaciones.pdf (accessed February 9, 2009). Copy on file with the author.

Riggs, Christopher K. "American Indians, Economic Development, and Self-Determination in the 1960s." *Pacific Historical Review* 69, no. 3 (August 200): 431–63.

Rittich, Kerry. "The Future of Law and Development: Second Generation Reforms and the Incorporation of the Social." In *The New Law and Economic Development: A Critical Appraisal,* edited by David M. Trubek and Alvaro Santos, 203–52. New York: Cambridge University Press, 2006.

Robinson, Walter V. "MFA Won't Relinquish Guatemalan Artifacts." *Boston Globe,* July 9, 1998.

Rodriguez Garavito, Cesar, and Tatiana Alfonso. *Derecho a la consulta y grupos etnicos en Colombia: La disputa por el territorio, los recursos naturales y los planes de desarrollo.* Bogota: Uniandes, 2009.

Rodríguez-Piñero, Luis. *Indigenous Peoples, Postcolonialism, and International Law: The ILO Regime, 1919–1989.* New York: Oxford University Press, 2005.

Rodrik, Dani. *One Economics, Many Recipes*. Princeton, N.J.: Princeton University Press, 2007.

Roldán Ortega, Roque. "Models for Recognizing Indigenous Land Rights in Latin America." Biodiversity Series, Paper 99. Washington: World Bank Environment Department, 2004. http://siteresources.worldbank.org/ BOLIVIA / Resources / Roque _Roldan.pdf (accessed December 10, 2009). Copy on file with the author.

Rotman, Leonard I. "Crown-Native Relations as Fiduciary: Reflections Almost 20 Years after *Guerin*." *Windsor Yearbook of Access to Justice* 22 (2003): 363–98.

———. "Provincial Fiduciary Obligations to First Nations: The Nexus between Governmental Power and Responsibility." *Osgoode Hall Law Journal* 32, no. 4 (1994): 735–83.

Roy, Bernadette Kelly, and Gudmundur Alfredsson. "Indigenous Rights: The Literature Explosion." *Transnational Perspectives* 13, no. 1 (1987): 19–24.

Russell, Peter H. *Recognizing Aboriginal Title: The Mabo Case and Indigenous Resistance to English-Settler Colonialism*. Toronto: University of Toronto Press, 2005.

Ryser, Rudolph C. "Establishing a National Indian Institute: A U.S. Treaty Commitment Unfulfilled." National Indian Institute. Olympia, Wash.: Center for World Indigenous Studies, 1993. Copy on file with the author.

———. "Indian Nations and United States Debate Self-Determination and Self-Government in the United Nations." *Center for World Indigenous Studies Publication Catalogue*. Olympia, Wash.: Center for World Indigenous Studies, August 20, 1993.

———. "The Legacy of Grand Chief George Manuel." Center for World Indigenous Studies. http://www.cwis.org/ manuel.htm (accessed February 4, 2009). Copy on file with the author.

Salomon, Frank, and Stuart B. Schwartz, eds. *The Cambridge History of the Native Peoples of the Americas*. Vol. 3: *South America: Part 2*. Cambridge: Cambridge University Press, 1999.

Sánchez, Enrique, and Paola García. *Más allá de los Promedios: Afrodescendientes en América Latina: Los Afrocolombianos*. Washington: World Bank, 2006. http://www-wds.worldbank.org (accessed February 9, 2009). Copy on file with the author.

Sanders, Douglas. "Background Information on the World Council of Indigenous Peoples: The Formation of the World Council of Indigenous Peoples." World Council of Indigenous Peoples. 1980. http://www.cwis.org/ fwdp / International / wcipinfo.txt (accessed October 21, 2008). Copy on file with the author.

———. "Indigenous Peoples: Issues of Definition." *International Journal of Cultural Property* 8, no. 1 (1999): 4–13.

———. "The Re-Emergence of Indigenous Questions in International Law." *Canadian Human Rights Yearbook* 3 (1983): 3–30.

———. "The U.N. Working Group on Indigenous Populations." *Human Rights Quarterly* 11 (August 1989): 406–33.

Sanjinés C., Javier. *Mestizaje Upside-down: Aesthetic Politics in Modern Bolivia*. Pittsburgh: University of Pittsburgh Press, 2004.

Santos, Alvaro. "The World Bank's Uses of the 'Rule of Law' Promise." In *The New*

Law and Economic Development: A Critical Appraisal, edited by David M. Trubek and Alvaro Santos, 253–300. New York: Cambridge University Press, 2006.

Sarfaty, Galit A. "The World Bank and the Internationalization of Indigenous Rights Norms." *Yale Law Journal* 114, no. 7 (2005): 1791–1818.

Satyendra, Nadesan. "Fourth World—Nations without States." Tamil Nation. http://www.tamilnation.org/selfdetermination/fourthworld/index.htm (accessed February 4, 2009). Copy on file with the author.

Scheinin, Martin. "Indigenous Peoples' Land Rights under the International Covenant on Civil and Political Rights." Oslo: Norwegian Centre for Human Rights, University of Oslo, 2004. http://www.galdu.org/govat/doc/ind_peoples_land_rights.pdf (accessed February 8, 2009). Copy on file with the author.

———. "The Right to Enjoy a Distinct Culture: Indigenous and Competing Uses of Land." In *The Jurisprudence of Human Rights Law: A Comparative Interpretive Approach*, edited by Theodore S. Orlin, et al., 159–222. Turku, Finland: Institute for Human Rights, Åbo Akademi University, 2000.

———. "The Right to Self-determination under the Covenant on Civil and Political Rights," In *Operationalizing the Right of Indigenous Peoples to Self-Determination*, edited by Pekka Aikio and Martin Scheinin, 179–99. Turko/Åbo: Åbo Akademi University, 2000.

Seed, Patricia. *American Pentimento: The Invention of Indians and the Pursuit of Riches*. Minneapolis: University of Minnesota Press, 2001.

Sheleff, Leon Shaskolsky. *The Future of Tradition: Customary Law, Common Law, and Legal Pluralism*. Portland, Ore.: F. Cass, 2000.

Shelton, Dinah. "The U.N. Human Rights Committee's Decisions." *Human Rights Dialogue* 2, no. 12 (spring 2005), 31–33.

Sieder, Rachel, ed. *Multiculturalism in Latin America*. Basingstoke: Palgrave, 2002.

Slater, David. *Geopolitics and the Post-colonial: Rethinking North-South Relations*. Malden, Mass.: Blackwell, 2004.

Smith, Linda Tuhiwai. *Decolonizing Methodologies: Research and Indigenous Peoples*. New York: Zed, 1999.

Smolenski, John, and Thomas J. Humphrey, eds. *New World Orders: Violence, Sanction, and Authority in the Colonial Americas*. Philadelphia: University of Pennsylvania Press, 2005.

Speed, Shannon. "Global Discourses on the Local Terrain: Human Rights and Indigenous Identity in Chiapas." *Cultural Dynamics* 14, no. 2 (2002): 205–28.

Speed, Shannon, and Alvaro Reyes. "Rights, Resistance, and Radical Alternatives: The Red de Defensores Comunitarios and Zapatismo in Chiapas." *Humboldt Journal of Social Relations* 29, no. 1 (2005): 47–83.

Spivak, Gayatri Chakravorty. "Can the Subaltern Speak?" In *Marxism and the Interpretation of Culture*, edited by Cary Nelson and Lawrence Grossberg, 271–313. Urbana: University of Illinois Press, 1988.

———. "In a Word: Interview with Ellen Rooney." *Differences: A Journal of Feminist Cultural Studies* 1 (1989): 124–56.

Spivak, Gayatri, and Elizabeth Grosz. "Criticism, Feminism, and the Institution: An Interview with Gayatri Spivak." *Thesis Eleven* nos. 10/11 (1985): 175–187. Reprinted in *The Post-Colonial Critic: Interviews, Strategies, Dialogues*, edited by Sarah Harasym, 1–16. New York: Routledge, 1990.

Sponsel, Leslie E. "1995 Annual Report: Commission for Human Rights." American Anthropological Association. http://www.aaanet.org/committees/cfhr/ar95.htm (accessed February 8, 2009). Copy on file with the author.

Stavenhagen, Rodolfo. "Challenging the Nation-State in Latin America." *Journal of International Affairs* 45, no. 2 (winter 1992): 421–40.

——. "La diversidad cultural en el desarrollo de las Américas: Los pueblos indígenas y los estados nacionales en Hispanoamérica." Organization of American States. http://www.oas.org/udse/wesiteold/estudios-cult.html (accessed August 16, 2009). Copy on file with the author.

——. "Ethnodevelopment: A Neglected Dimension in Development Thinking." In *Development Studies: Critique and Renewal*, edited by Raymond Apthorpe and András Kráhl, 71–94. Leiden: E. J. Brill, 1986.

Stiglitz, Joseph E. "Towards a New Paradigm for Development: Strategies, Policies and Process." Prebisch Lecture. UN Conference on Trade and Development (UNCTAD). Geneva. October 19, 1998.

Stolz, Martin, and Matthew L. Wald. "Interior Rejects Interim Plan for Nuclear Waste." *New York Times*, September 9, 2006.

"La 'suerte' de Orika." *El Universal* (Cartagena). September 9, 2008.

Svensson, Tom G. "Right to Self-Determination: A Basic Human Right Concerning Cultural Survival: The Case of the Sami and the Scandinavian State." In *Human Rights in Cross-Cultural Perspectives*, edited by Abdullahi An-Na'im, 363–84. Philadelphia: University of Pennsylvania Press, 1992.

Swepston, Lee. "Indigenous and Tribal Peoples and International Organizations: New Perspectives." *Transnational Perspectives* 13, no. 1 (1987): 15–18.

——. "A New Step in the International Law on Indigenous and Tribal Peoples: ILO Convention No. 169 of 1989." *Oklahoma City University Law Review* 15, no. 3 (1990): 677–714.

Tennant, Chris. "Indigenous Peoples, International Institutions, and the International Legal Literature from 1945–1993." *Human Rights Quarterly* 16, no. 1 (1994): 1–57.

Tesis Política del Gran Pueblo Indio. La Paz, 1971. Reprinted in *Hacia la Autogestión Indígena: Documentos*, edited by Adolfo Colombres. Quito: Ediciones del Sol, 1977.

Thornberry, Patrick. *Indigenous Peoples and Human Rights*. Manchester, England: Manchester University Press, 2002.

——. "Self-Determination and Indigenous Peoples: Objections and Responses." In *Operationalizing the Right of Indigenous Peoples to Self-Determination*, edited by Pekka Aikio and Martin Scheinin, 39–64. Turko/Åbo: Åbo Akademi University, 2000.

Tinker, George. "The Full Circle of Liberation: An American Indian Theology of

Place." In *Ecotheology: Voices from South and North*, edited by David G. Hallman, 218–24. Maryknoll, N.Y.: Orbis, 1994.

Torres, Gerald, and Erin Ruble. "Perfect Good Faith." *Nevada Law Journal* 5, no. 1 (2004): 93–125.

Torres, Raidza. "The Rights of Indigenous Populations: The Emerging International Norm." *Yale Journal of International Law* 16, no. 1 (1991): 127–75.

Trubek, David M., and Alvaro Santos. "Introduction: The Third Moment in Law and Development Theory and the Emergence of a New Critical Practice." In *The New Law and Economic Development: A Critical Appraisal*, edited by David M. Trubek and Alvaro Santos, 1–18. New York: Cambridge University Press, 2006.

Turner, Terence. "Human Rights, Human Difference: Anthropology's Contribution to an Emancipatory Cultural Politics." *Journal of Anthropological Research* 53, no. 3 (autumn 1997): 273–91.

Tutino, John. *From Insurrection to Revolution in Mexico: Social Bases of Agrarian Violence, 1750–1940*. Princeton, N.J.: Princeton University Press, 1986.

Twinam, Ann. *Public Lives, Private Secrets: Gender, Honor, Sexuality, and Illegitimacy in Colonial Spanish America*. Stanford: Stanford University Press, 1999.

———. "Racial Passing: Informal and Official 'Whiteness' in Colonial Spanish America." In *New World Orders: Violence, Sanction, and Authority in the Colonial Americas*, edited by John Smolenski and Thomas J. Humphrey, 249–72. Philadelphia: University of Pennsylvania Press, 2005.

Ulloa, Astrid. "Las representaciones sobre los indígenas en los discursos ambientales y de desarrollo sostenible." In *Políticas de economía, ambiente y sociedad en tiempos de globalización*, edited by Daniel Mato, 89–109. Caracas: Universidad Central de Venezuela, 2005.

UN. CERD (Committee on the Elimination of Racial Discrimination). 48th Session. "Report of the Committee: Annex III—Prevention of Racial Discrimination, Including Early Warning and Urgent Procedures." UN doc. A / 48 / 18, Supp. 18. 1994.

———. 48th Session. General Recommendation No. 21: Right to Self-determination. UN doc. A / 51 / 18, UNGAOR, 51st Session., Supp. 18, annex VIII. August 23, 1996.

———. 51st Session. General Recommendation No. 23: Indigenous Peoples. UN doc. A / 52 / 18, UNGAOR, 52nd Session, Supp. 18, annex V. August 18, 1997.

———. 57th Session. Concluding Observations of the Committee: Finland. UN doc. CERD / C / 304 / Add.107. 2001.

———. 62nd Session. Concluding Observations of the Committee: Ecuador. UN doc. CERD / C / 62 / CO / 2. June 2, 2003.

———. 68th Session. Concluding Observations of the Committee: El Salvador. UN doc. CERD / C / SLV / CO / 13. April 4, 2006.

———. 68th Session. Early Warning and Urgent Action Procedure: Decision 1(68): United States of America. UN doc. CERD / C / USA / DEC / 1. April 11, 2006.

———. 70th Session. Concluding Observations of the Committee: Canada. UN doc. CERD / C / CAN / CO / 18. May 25, 2007.

———. 70th Session. Concluding Observations of the Committee: India. UN doc.CERD /
C / IND / CO / 19. May 5, 2007.

———. 72nd Session. Concluding Observations of the Committee: United States of
America. UN doc. CERD / C / USA / CO / 6. May 8, 2008.

UN. Charter. Adopted June 26, 1945. 59 Stat. 1031; T.S. No. 993; 3 Bevans 1153.

UN. Commission on Human Rights. Drafting Committee. 2nd Session. "Report of the
Drafting Committee to the Commission on Human Rights." UN doc. E / CN.4 / 95.
May 21, 1948. Copy on file with the author.

———. 61st Session. "Report of the Working Group Established in Accordance with
Commission on Human Rights Resolution 1995 / 32 of 3 March 1995." (Submitted by
Chairperson-Rapporteur Luis-Enrique Chavez.) UN doc. E / CN.4 / 2005 / 89 / Add.1.
February 24, 2005. Copy on file with the author.

UN. Commission on Human Rights. Subcommission on Prevention of Discrimination
and Protection of Minorities. 35th Session. Agenda Item 15. "Study of the Problem
of Discrimination against Indigenous Populations. Report of the Working Group
on Indigenous Populations on its First Session. Chairman-Rapporteur: Mr. Asbjörn
Eide." UN doc. E / CN.4 / Sub.2 / 1982 / 33. August 25, 1982. Copy on file with the
author.

———. 36th Session. "Study of the Problem of Discrimination against Indigenous Populations." Final Report (Chapters XXI, XXII—Conclusions, proposals and recommendations). (Submitted by the special rapporteur, José Martínez Cobo.) UN doc.
E / CN.4 / Sub.2 / 1983 / 21 / Add.8. September 30, 1983. All parts of the report available
at http://www.un.org / esa / socdev / unpfii / en / spdaip.html (accessed January 10,
2010).

———. 39th Session. "Declaration of Principles Adopted by the Indigenous Peoples'
Preparatory Meeting Held at Geneva 27–31 July 1987." UN doc. E / CN.4 / Sub.2 /
1987 / 22, Annex V. August 24, 1987. Copy on file with the author.

——— .45th Session. "Draft Declaration on the Rights of Indigenous Peoples." (Sub-
mitted by the chairperson-rapporteur, Erica-Irene A. Daes.) In "Report of the
Working Group on Indigenous Populations on its Eleventh Session." UN doc. E /
CN.4 / Sub.2 / 1993 / 29 / Annex I, August 23, 1993. Copy on file with the author.

———. 45th Session. "Explanatory Note Concerning the Draft Declaration on the Rights
of Indigenous Peoples." (By Erica-Irene A. Daes, Chairperson of the Working Group
on the Rights of Indigenous Peoples.) UN doc. E / CN.4 / Sub.2 / 1993 / 26 / Add.1.
July 19, 1993. Copy on file with the author.

———. 45th Session. "Report of the Working Group on Indigenous Populations on its
Eleventh Session." UN doc. E / CN.4 / Sub.2 / 1993 / 29. August 23, 1993. Copy on file
with the author.

———. 46th Session. Agenda Item 15. "Discrimination against Indigenous Peoples: Report of the Working Group on Indigenous Populations on its Twelfth Session.
chairperson-rapporteur: Ms. Erica-Irene A. Daes." UN doc. E / CN.4 / Sub.2 / 1994 / 30.
August 17, 1994. Copy on file with the author.

——. 53rd Session. "Indigenous Peoples and Their Relationship to Land." UN doc. E / CN.4 / Sub.2 / 2001 / 21. June 11, 2001. Copy on file with the author.

UN. Commission on Human Rights. Subcommission on Prevention of Discrimination and Protection of Minorities. WGIP (Working Group on Indigenous Populations). Many of these documents were found as a result of the work of the Fourth World Documentation Project. Its complete collection of United Nations Documents and Submissions are available at http://cwis.org/fwdp/un.html (accessed January 12, 2010). A copy is also on file with the author.

——. 1st Session. "Study of the Problem of Discrimination against Indigenous Populations." UN doc. E / CN.4 / Sub.2 / AC.4 / 1982 / R.1. August 26, 1982. http://cwis.org/fwdp/International/82–11964.txt (accessed January 18, 2010). Copy on file with the author.

——. 3rd Session. "Paper Submitted to the U.N. Working Group on Indigenous Populations by the Coalition of First Nations in conjunction with the International Indian Treaty Council." July 31, 1984. http://cwis.org/fwdp/Americas/1st_nat.txt (accessed January 18, 2010). Copy on file with the author.

——. 3rd Session. "Statement on Behalf of the Free Papua Movement (West Papuan People's Movement for Freedom and Independence)." July 30–August 3, 1984. http://cwis.org/fwdp/Oceania/w_papua.txt (accessed January 18, 2010). Copy on file with the author.

——. 4th Session. Material Received from Non-Governmental Organizations in Consultative Status with the Economic and Social Council. In "Standard-Setting Activities: Evolution of Standards Concerning the Rights of Indigenous Populations. Drafting of a Body of Principles on Indigenous Rights, Based on Relevant National Legislation, International Instruments and Other Juridical Criteria." UN doc. E / CN.4 / Sub.2 / AC.4 / 1985 / WP.4 / Add.4. July 29, 1985. http://cwis.org/fwdp/International/dec_prin.txt (accessed January 18, 2010). Copy on file with the author.

——. 6th Session. "Statement by Dr. Atle Grahl-Madsen." UN doc. E / CN.4 / Sub.2 / AC.4. August 1–5, 1988. http://cwis.org/fwdp/Eurasia/sami88.txt (accessed January 18, 2010). Copy on file with the author.

——. 6th Session. "Statement in Reference to the Study on the Significance of Indigenous Treaties presented by Rudolph C. Ryser." August 1988. http://cwis.org/fwdp/International/uncwis88.txt (accessed January 18, 2010). Copy on file with the author.

——. 6th Session. "Submission by the Nordic Sami Council." UN doc. E / CN.4 / Sub.2 / AC.4. August 1–5, 1988. http://cwis.org/fwdp/Eurasia/nsc_un88.txt (accessed January 18, 2010). Copy on file with the author.

——. 6th Session. "Treaties and the Study of Treaties: Statement submitted by the Treaty Six Chiefs." August 1988. http://cwis.org/fwdp/Americas/tret6_88.txt (accessed January 18, 2010). Copy on file with the author.

——. 11th Session. "Review of Developments Pertaining to the Promotion and Protection of Human Rights and Fundamental Freedoms of Indigenous Populations, including Economic and Social Relations between Indigenous Peoples and States. Information received from Governments: Netherlands." UN doc. E/CN.4/Sub.2/AC.4/1993/CRP.3. July 1, 1993. http://cwis.org/fwdp/International/nethr-93.txt (accessed January 18, 2010). Copy on file with the author.

——. 11th Session. "Statement by Dr. Rolf H. Lindeholm." July 20, 1993. http://cwis.org/fwdp/International/sweden.txt (accessed January 18, 2010). Copy on file with the author.

——. 11th Session. "Statement of Kathryn Skipper." July 21, 1993. http://cwis.org/fwdp/International/skipper.txt (accessed January 18, 2010). Copy on file with the author.

——. 11th Session. "Statement of Maivan C. Lam." July 21, 1993. http://cwis.org/fwdp/International/maivan.txt (accessed January 18, 2010). Copy on file with the author.

——. 12th Session. Agenda Item 5. "Statement of the International Confederation of Autonomous Chapters of the American Indian Movement." July 27, 1994. http://cwis.org/fwdp/Americas/aim-un94.txt (accessed January 18, 2010). Copy on file with the author.

——. 12th Session. Declaration of Tlahuitoltepec on the Fundamental Rights of the Indigenous Nations, Nationalities and Peoples of Indo-Latin America. In "Review of Developments Pertaining to the Promotion and Protection of Human Rights and Fundamental Freedoms of Indigenous Populations." UN doc. E/CN.4/Sub.2/AC.4/1994/7/Add.1. June 20, 1994. Copy on file with the author.

——. 12th Session. Grand Council of the Crees (of Quebec). In "Standard-Setting Activities: Evolution of Standards Concerning the Rights of Indigenous Populations." UN doc. E/CN.4/Sub.2/AC.4/1994/4. June 3, 1994. Copy on file with the author.

——. 13th Session. Note by the chairperson-rapporteur of the Working Group on Indigenous Populations, Ms. Erica-Irene A. Daes, on criteria which might be applied when considering the concept of indigenous peoples. In "Standard-Setting Activities: Evolution of Standards Concerning the Rights of Indigenous People—New Developments and General Discussion of Future Action." UN doc. E/CN.4/Sub.2/AC.4/1995/3. June 21, 1995. Copy on file with the author.

UN Conference on Environment and Development. Rio Declaration on Environment and Development. June 14, 1992. UN doc. A/CONF.151/26/Rev.1 (vol. I) (1993).

UNDP (United Nations Development Programme). "En el Caribe Colombiano, el PNUD impulsa Acuerdo Regional por la Seguridad Alimentaria." http://www.pnud.org.co (accessed February 9, 2009). Copy on file with the author.

——. *Human Development Report 2004: Cultural Liberty in Today's Diverse World*. New York: United Nations Development Program, 2004.

UNESCO (United Nations Educational, Scientific and Cultural Organization). Convention for the Safeguarding of the Intangible Cultural Heritage. Adopted October 17, 2003. 2368 U.N.T.S. 3.

——. Convention on the Protection and Promotion of the Diversity of Cultural Expressions. Adopted October 20, 2005.

——. "The Cultural Space of Palenque de San Basilio." http://www.unesco.org/cultu re/ich/index.php?RL=00102 (accessed December 7, 2009).

——. Declaration on the Principles of International Cultural Co-operation. Records of the General Conference, 14th Session. 1966.

——, ed. *Human Rights: Comments and Interpretations*. New York: Columbia University Press, 1949.

UN. General Assembly. 3rd Session. Universal Declaration of Human Rights. G.A. Resolution 217 (III). UN doc. A/810. December 10, 1948.

——. 15th Session. Declaration on the Granting of Independence to Colonial Countries and Peoples. Resolution 1514 (XV), December 14, 1960.

——. 25th Session. Declaration on Principles of International Law Concerning Friendly Relations and Cooperation among States in Accordance with the Charter of the United Nations. Resolution 2625 (XXV). October 24, 1970.

——. 61st Session. Declaration on the Rights of Indigenous Peoples. Resolution 61/295. September 13, 2007.

——. 61st Session. Namibia: Amendments to Draft Resolution on Behalf of the Group of African States. UN doc. A/C.3/61/L.57/Rev.1. November 21, 2006.

——. 61st Session. "Third Committee Approves Draft Resolution on Right to Development." UN Press Release. GA/SHC/3878. November 28, 2006.

UN. High Commissioner for Human Rights. "The Rights of Indigenous Peoples." Fact Sheet No. 9 (Rev. 1). http://www.ohchr.org/Documents/Publications/Fact Sheet9 rev.1en.pdf (accessed February 4, 2009). Copy on file with the author.

UN. Human Rights Committee. Final Report, *Anni Äärelä and Jouni Näkkäläjärvi v. Finland*. Communication No. 779/1997, UN doc. CCPR/C/73/D/779/1997. 2001.

——. Final Report, *Apirana Mahuika et al. v. New Zealand*. Communication No. 547/1993, UN doc. CCPR/C/70/D/547/1993. 2000.

——. Final Report, *Diergaardt et al. v. Namibia*. Communication No. 760/1997, UN doc. CCPR/C/69/D/760/1997. 2000.

——. Final Report, *Fongum Gorji-Dinka v. Cameroon*. Communication No. 1134/2002, UN doc. CCPR/C/83/D/1134/2002. 2005.

——. Final Report, *Gillot et al. v. France*. Communication No. 932/2000, UN doc. CCPR/C/75/D/932/2000. 2002.

——. Final Report, *Kitok v. Sweden*. Communication No. 197/1985, UN doc. CCPR/C/33/D/197/1985. 1988.

——. Final Report, *Länsman et al. v. Finland*. (Submitted by Jouni E. Länsman.) Communication No. 671/1995, UN doc. CCPR/C/58/D/671/1995. 1996.

——. Final Report, *Lovelace v. Canada*. Communication No. 24/1977, UN doc. CCPR/C/13/D/24/1977. 1981.

——. Final Report, *Lubicon Lake Band v. Canada*. Communication No. 167/1984, UN doc. CCPR/C/38/D/167/1984. 1990.

———. 50th Session. CCPR General Comment No. 23: The rights of minorities (Art. 27). UN doc. CCPR / C / 21 / Rev.1 / Add.5. 1994.

UN. Human Rights Council. 9th Session. "Report on the Situation of Human Rights and Fundamental Freedoms of Indigenous People." (Submitted by the special rapporteur, S. James Anaya.) UN doc. A / HRC / 9 / 9. August 11, 2008.

———. 15th Session. "La situación de los pueblos indígenas en Colombia." (Submitted by the special rapporteur, S. James Anaya.) UN doc. A / HRC / 15 / 34. January 8, 2009.

UN. *The Millennium Development Goals Report 2008*. New York: United Nations, 2008.

UN. Secretary General. *An Agenda for Peace: Preventive Diplomacy, Peacemaking, and Peacekeeping: Report of the Secretary-General*. 47th Session. UN Doc. A / 47 / 277-S / 24111. June 17, 1992. http://www.un.org/Docs/sg/agpeace.html (accessed January 8, 2010).

Union of British Columbia Indian Chiefs. "Our History." http://www.ubcic.bc.ca/about/history.htm (accessed February 4, 2009). Copy on file with the author.

———. *Stolen Lands, Broken Promises: Researching the Indian Land Question in British Columbia*. 2nd ed. Vancouver: Union of British Columbia Indian Chiefs, 2005.

———. UBCIC Declaration. Adopted by the UBCIC General Assembly May 17, 1976. http://www.ubcic.bc.ca/Resources/declaration.htm (accessed February 4, 2009). Copy on file with the author.

Universidad de San Buenaventura. Grupo de Investigación en Desarrollo Social–Gides. "Perspectivas del desarrollo comunitario y la calidad de vida en Cartagena: Estudio de caso en Los Barrios, La Central, El Milagro y San José de Los Campanos —Zona Sur Occidental." Cartagena: Centro de Investigaciones, 2003. http://www.disaster-info.net/desplazados/documentos/perspectivasdesarrollo/index.html (accessed May 6, 2010). Copy on file with the author.

Uprimny Yepes, Rodrigo. "The Enforcement of Social Rights by the Colombian Constitutional Court: Cases and Debates." In *Courts and Social Transformation in New Democracies: An Institutional Voice for the Poor?*, edited by Roberto Gargarella, Pilar Domingo, and Theunis Rous. Burlington, Vt.: Ashgate Publishing, 2006.

Urban, Greg, and Joel Sherzer, eds. *Nation States and Indians in Latin America*. Austin: University of Texas Press, 1991.

Uribe, María Victoria, and Eduardo Restrepo, eds. *Antropología en la Modernidad: Identidades, Etnicidades y Movimientos Sociales en Colombia*. Bogotá: Instituto Colombiano de Antropología, 1997.

Urrea, Fernando, and Pedro Quintín. "Urbanización y construcción de identidades de las poblaciones Afrocolombianas de la Región Pacífica Colombiana." *Documento de trabajo*, No. 7. Cali: Proyecto Cidse-Orstom, 1997.

Urrea, Fernando, Héctor Fabio Ramírez, and Carlos Viáfara. "Perfiles sociodemográficos de la población afrocolombiana en contextos urbano-regionales del país a comienzos del siglo XXI." In *Panorámica afrocolombiana. Estudios sociales en el Pacífico*, edited by Mauricio Pardo, Claudia Mosquera, and María Clemencia Ramírez, 213–68. Bogotá: ICANH-Universidad Nacional de Colombia, 2004.

U.S. Congress. Indian Gaming Regulatory Act. Public Law 100–497 (1988), codified at 25 U.S.C. §2701 *et seq.*

U.S. Court of Appeals. District of Columbia Circuit. *Devia v. Nuclear Regulatory Commission*, 492 F.3d 421 (2007).

U.S. Department of Justice. "Department of Justice Policy on Indian Sovereignty and Government-to-Government Relations with Indian Tribes." June 1, 1995. http://www.usdoj.gov/ag/readingroom/sovereignty.htm (accessed August 16, 2009). Copy on file with the author.

———. "Tribal Justice and Safety in Indian Country: Government to Government Relationship." http://www.tribaljusticeandsafety.gov/govt2govt.htm (accessed February 4, 2009). Copy on file with the author.

U.S. Department of State. "Periodic Report to the U. N. Committee on the Elimination of Racial Discrimination Concerning the International Convention of the Elimination of All Forms of Racial Discrimination: Annex 2, April 2007." http://www.state.gov/documents/organization/83519.pdf (accessed August 16, 2009). Copy on file with the author.

U.S. District Court. District of Columbia. *Republic of Peru v. Yale University*, no. 1:08-cv-02109 (filed December 5, 2008).

U.S. Mission to the United Nations. "Explanation of vote by Robert Hagen, U.S. Advisor, on the Declaration on the Rights of Indigenous Peoples, to the UN General Assembly." Press release. September 13, 2007. http://www.archive.usun.state.gov/press_releases/20070913_204 (accessed February 9, 2009). Copy on file with the author.

U.S. Supreme Court. *Cherokee Nation v. Georgia*, 30 U.S. 1 (1831).

———. *Johnson v. M'Intosh*, 21 U.S. 543 (1823).

———. *Northwestern Bands of Shoshone Indians v. United States*, 324 U.S. 335 (1945).

———. *Worcester v. Georgia*, 31 U.S. 515 (1832).

Van Banning, Theo R. G. *The Human Right to Property.* Antwerp, Belgium: Intersentia, 2002.

Van Cott, Donna Lee. *The Friendly Liquidation of the Past: The Politics of Diversity in Latin America.* Pittsburgh: University of Pittsburgh Press, 2000.

Van den Berg, Maarten H. J. "Mainstreaming Ethnodevelopment: Poverty and Ethnicity in World Bank Policy." Paper presented at the Towards a New Political Economy of Development Conference, the University of Sheffield, England, July 4–6, 2002. http://www.risq.org/article17.html (accessed January 10, 2010). Copy on file with the author.

Van Nieuwkoop, Martien, and Jorge E. Uquillas. "Defining Ethnodevelopment in Operational Terms: Lessons from the Ecuador Indigenous and Afro-Ecuadoran Peoples Development Project." Sustainable Development Working Paper No. 6. World Bank, Latin America and Caribbean Regional Office, 2000. http://www-wds.worldbank.org/external/default/main?pagePK=64193027&piPK=64187937&theSitePK=523679&menuPK=64187510&searchMenuPK=64187283&siteName=

WDS&entityID=000094946_01112904005522 (accessed January 12, 2010). Copy on file with the author.

Varese, Stefano. "Memories of Solidarity: Anthropology and the Indigenous Movement in Latin America." *Cultural Survival Quarterly* 21, no. 3 (October 1997): 23–26.

Venne, Sharon, Isabelle Shulte-Tenckhoff, and Andrew Gray. *Honour Bound: Onion Lake and the Spirit of Treaty Six: The International Validity of Treaties with Indigenous Peoples.* Copenhagen: IWGIA, 1997.

Wade, Peter. *Blackness and Race Mixture: The Dynamics of Racial Identity in Colombia.* Baltimore: Johns Hopkins University Press, 1993.

——. "The Colombian Pacific in Perspective." *Journal of Latin American Anthropology* 7, no. 2 (2002): 2–33.

——. "Identidad y etnicidad." In *Pacífico: ¿Desarrollo o diversidad? Estado, capital y movimientos sociales en el Pacífico colombiano*, edited by Arturo Escobar and Alvaro Pedrosa, 283–98. Bogotá: CEREC, 1996.

——. *Race and Ethnicity in Latin America.* Chicago: Pluto, 1997.

Warren, Kay B., and Jean E. Jackson. "Introduction: Studying Indigenous Activism in Latin America." In *Indigenous Movements, Self-Representation, and the State in Latin America*, edited by Kay B. Warren and Jean E. Jackson, 1–33. Austin: University of Texas Press, 2003.

Wessendorf, Kathrin, ed. *The Indigenous World 2009.* Copenhagen: International Work Group for Indigenous Affairs, 2009.

Williams, Robert. "Encounters on the Frontiers of International Human Rights Law: Redefining the Terms of Indigenous Peoples' Survival in the World." *Duke Law Journal* 1990, no. 4 (September 1990): 660–704.

Wolfensohn, James D. "A Proposal for a Comprehensive Development Framework." Memo to the board, management, and staff of the World Bank Group. January 21, 1999. Washington: World Bank, 1999. Copy on file with the author.

World Bank. "Colombia: Social Safety Net project." Washington: World Bank, June 30, 2005. http://go.worldbank.org/0LO5INFON0 (accessed January 18, 2010). Copy on file with the author.

——. *Making Sustainable Commitments: An Environmental Strategy for the World Bank.* Washington: World Bank, 2001.

——. *The World Bank Operational Manual.* Operational Policy 4.10: Indigenous Peoples. July 2005. http://go.worldbank.org/TE769PDWN0 (accessed January 10, 2010). Copy on file with the author.

——. *The World Bank Operational Manual.* Operational Directive 4.20: Indigenous Peoples. September 1991. http://graduateinstitute.ch/faculty/clapham/hrdoc/docs/wBOD4.20.htm (accessed January 10, 2010). Copy on file with the author.

World Bank. Environmentally and Socially Sustainable Development Unit. "The Gap Matters: Poverty and Well-Being of Afro-Colombians and Indigenous Peoples." Report No. 33014-CO. July 20, 2005. http://go.worldbank.org/PM4WUV2UTI (accessed January 12, 2010). Copy on file with the author.

World Commission on Environment and Development. *Our Common Future*. (Report submitted to the UN General Assembly, 42nd Session). UN doc. A/42/427. June 1987. http://www.un-documents.net/ocf.htm (accessed February 9, 2009). Copy on file with the author.

World Council of Indigenous Peoples. "Land Rights of the Indigenous Peoples, International Agreements and Treaties, Land Reform and Systems of Tenure." Paper presented at the International NGO Conference on Indigenous Peoples and the Land, Geneva, September 1981. http://cwis.org/fwdp/International/lndright.txt (accessed January 10, 2010). Copy on file with the author.

Wright, Robin M. "Anthropological Presuppositions of Indigenous Advocacy." *Annual Review of Anthropology* 17 (1988): 365–90.

Xanthaki, Alexandra. *Indigenous Rights and United Nations Standards: Self-determination, Culture and Land*. New York: Cambridge University Press, 2007.

——. "The Right to Self-Determination: Meaning and Scope." In *Minorities, Peoples and Self-Determination,* edited by Nazila Ghanea and Alexandra Xanthaki, 15–34. Boston: Martinus Nijhoff, 2005.

Yale University. Office of Public Affairs. "Yale Seeks Collaborative Relationship with Peru." Press release. December 9, 2008. http://opa.yale.edu/news/article.aspx?id=1997 (accessed February 9, 2009). Copy on file with the author.

Ziai, Aram, ed. *Exploring Post-Development: Theory and Practice, Problems and Perspectives*. Hoboken, N.J.: Taylor and Francis, 2007.

Zion, James W. "North American Indian Perspectives on Human Rights." In *Human Rights in Cross-Cultural Perspectives*, edited by Abdullahi An-Na'im, 191–220. Philadelphia: University of Pennsylvania Press, 1992.

Index

Chiapas, Mexico (*cont.*)
vention 169 and, 112, 173; Zapatista
movement and, 57, 94, 112–13, 301–
2n52, 302n55
Choquehuanca Céspedes, David, 146–47
CISA (Congress of the Indian Council of
South America), 63–66, 75, 92
class identity, 60–62, 65, 186, 188–90, 275,
291n52. *See also campesino* (peasant)
identity
Coalition of First Nations, 77–78
Cobo, José Martinez, 68
Cobo Report, 68–69, 81, 89, 170, 293n2
cold war, 43, 48–49, 60, 126, 188
collective land rights: Afro-Colombians in
Caribbean region and, 8, 253–60, 264,
266–70, 272–73, 346n14; Afro-
Colombians in Pacific region and, 1, 8–
9, 224–26, 228–29, 232–33, 240–43, 332–
33n34; Brazil and, 229; culture as development, 208; culture as land and,
167–68, 177, 180–81, 239–43, 317n39; CERD
and, 120–21, 322n59; dark sides of, 102,
253–60, 264, 266–70, 272–73, 345n3,
346n14; *ejidos* and, 181; human right to
culture and, 85, 106–13, 124, 130–31, 163–
68, 276, 306n116, 315n17, 322n59; ICCPR,
Article 27 and, 241, 303–4n78; ILO Convention 169 and, 85, 97, 106–13, 168,
301n49, 315n17; indigenous movements
and, 25, 31; indigenous peoples in Latin
America and, 25, 31, 127–28, 177, 282n41,
306n116, 307n131; Inter-American Commission on Human Rights and, 124, 127,
130, 163, 167–68, 276, 306n116; Inter-
American Court of Human Rights and,
127–33, 240, 306n113, 306n116, 308n152,
308–9n153; Law 70 and, 8–9, 224–25,
228–29, 240–41, 253–55, 257–61, 267, 332–
33n34; Peru and, 31, 301n49; *resguardos*
and, 25, 232–33; UN Human Rights Committee and, 322n59
Collier, Simon, 283n71
Colombia: Constitution of 1991 and, 223–
24, 228, 233, 260–63, 271, 282n41, 329n3,

329n6, 346–47n22; FARC and, 62–63; PBP
and, 246–47; UN Declaration and,
288n2. *See also* Afro-Colombians in Caribbean region; Afro-Colombians in
Pacific region; indigenous peoples of
Colombia; Law 70
Colombian Institute of Agrarian Reform
(INCORA), 254, 256, 258, 268–69. *See also*
Colombian Institute of Rural Development (INCODER)
Colombian Institute of Rural Development (INCODER), 256–62, 266–72,
348n41. *See also* Colombian Institute of
Agrarian Reform (INCORA)
colonialism: British model of, 18–19, 20–
22, 24–25, 281n24, 283n65; Canada and,
18–19, 21–23, 25, 281n24; Fourth World
thought and effects of, 50–51; French
model of, 18–19, 21–22, 281n24, 283n65;
human right to culture and, 19, 25; ILO
and, 36; indigenous movements and, 1,
274; Latin American and, 21–22, 24, 30,
36, 60–62; liberalism and, 30, 53, 283n65;
Portuguese model of, 18–19, 21–22;
self-determination and, 4–5, 280n5;
Spanish model of, 18–22, 24–25,
281n24; treaties and 23, 25–27, 30, 47,
54–55, 79–80; U.S. and, 18–19, 21–23, 25,
281n24; "white man's burden" assumption under, 45, 287–88n142
Committee on the Elimination of Racial
Discrimination (CERD), 119–23, 195, 203,
205–6, 304n83, 305n103, 322n59, 324n95
communal land (*ejidos*), 181
communal land holdings (*resguardos*), 25,
232–33
Comprehensive Association of Small
Farmers of the Atrato (ACIA), 240
Comprehensive Development Frame-
work (CDF), 192, 320–21n39
Congress of the Indian Council of South
America (CISA), 63–66, 75, 92
Conklin, Beth, 151–52, 156, 176
Consejo Regional Indígena del Cauca
(CRIC), 62–65

Garcés, Silvio, 235, 242, 244, 330n12

García, Paola, 331n19

genocide, 71, 82, 101, 104, 187

Genocide Convention (UN Convention against Genocide), 43, 101, 287n128

Girón Cerna, Carlos, 284n83

Global Exchange, 172–73

Global Indigenous Peoples' Caucus, 325n100

Goshute band, 206–8

Gow, David, 197–99, 215, 323n67

Graham, Laura, 151, 157

Grahl-Madsen, Atle, 94

Gray, Andrew, 190–91, 215–16, 320n35

Griggs, Richard, 49–52

Guahibo Indians, 127–28, 306n116, 307n131

Guatemala: culture as heritage and, 149, 154, 159; ILO representations and, 111–12, 301n48; indigenous populations as majority in, 92–93; Plan de Sanchez Massacre and, 125, 159, 306n116, 307n124; statehood and, 81–82, 92–93

Hale, Charles, 2–3, 11–12, 149, 193–94, 280n19, 321n50, 321–22n53

Harvey, Neil, 302n55

Hendrickson, Carol, 154, 159

heritage. *See* culture as heritage

Hernández Castillo, Aída R., 136–37, 310n176

Herskovits, Melville, 44, 287n135

Hogan, Jackie, 153

Hooker, Juliet, 329n3

Human Rights Committee. *See* UN Human Rights Committee

human right to culture, 3, 7–8, 100–103; AAA and, 103–6; Afro-Colombians in Caribbean region and, 264–66, 348n34; Afro-Colombians in Pacific region and, 223–24, 237, 329n3; Brazil and, 128–30, 306n116, 308n145, 308n149; Canada and, 114–16, 121–22, 302n62; collective land rights and, 85, 106–13, 124, 130–31, 163–68, 276, 306n116, 315n17, 322n59; colonialism and, 19, 25; culture as develop-

ment and, 190–96, 322n54; culture as land and, 126–33, 306n116, 308n149, 308n152, 308–9n153; dark sides of, 1–4, 7, 14, 20–21, 133–37, 178–79, 309n165, 309n167, 310nn171–73, 310n176; education and, 1, 100, 110, 192; ethnodevelopment and, 190–96, 322n54; ethno-education and, 235, 237, 265–66; ICCPR, Article 27 and, 43, 101, 113–18, 129–32, 135, 146, 164–65, 303–4n78, 309n167, 316n29; ILO Convention 169 and, 108–9, 134, 178–79, 200–201; indigenous movements and, 43–45, 287n132, 287–88n142; indigenous peoples of Colombia and, 127–28, 203, 223–24, 262–64, 306n116, 307n131; inter-American system of human rights and, 123–24, 128–30, 132–33, 135–36, 163, 276, 306n116, 308n138; "invisible asterisk" proviso and, 7, 20–21, 102, 106, 133–37; Law 70 and, 223–24, 261–63, 329n3; legal instruments and, 85, 97–98, 102, 106–14, 119–23, 146, 168, 303–4n78, 304n83, 315n17; multiculturalism and, 223–24; Nicaragua and, 11, 130–31, 167–68, 306n116, 308n150, 309n157, 315n14; *panindianismo* and, 55–59; self-determination and, 8, 73, 96–99; special rights and, 100, 106–7, 118–24, 129–30, 132–33; Suriname and, 124–25, 131–32, 135–36, 306n116, 306n118, 306–7n120, 308–9n153, 309n154; sustainable development and, 14; tribal peoples and, 80; UN Declaration and, 102; UN Human Rights Committee and, 97–98, 102, 114; U.S. and, 54, 102, 118–23, 304n83; women's rights and, 135–37, 309n165, 310n171, 310n176. *See also* culture as development; culture as heritage; culture as land

human right to property, 3, 116, 121, 124, 126–33, 158–60, 163–68, 177–78, 195, 201–2, 307n125, 307n126; 307n128, 308n149. *See also* collective land rights; culture as land

"The Hyperreal Indian" (Ramos), 162, 280n14, 289n37

ICCPR (International Covenant on Civil and Political Rights). *See* ICCPR, Article 1; ICCPR, Article 27

ICCPR, Article 1, 97–98, 116–18, 195, 303n74, 303–4n78

ICCPR, Article 27: collective land rights and, 241, 303–4n78; culture as development and, 194–95, 201–2, 312n16; culture as land and, 102, 121, 302n62, 308n149; human right to culture and, 43, 101, 113–18, 129–32, 135, 146, 164–65, 303–4n78, 309n167, 316n29; prior consultation and, 118, 201–202; tribal peoples and, 114

ICERD (International Convention on the Elimination of All Forms of Racial Discrimination), 106, 118–23, 304n81, 304n83, 304–5n92, 307n128

ICESCR (International Covenant on Economic, Cultural and Social Rights), 97–98, 113–14, 126, 132, 195, 279n5

identity: Afro-Colombians in Pacific region and, 216, 218–19, 220, 328n151; *campesino*, 59–64, 94, 225, 240, 291n54; class and, 60–62, 65, 186, 188–90, 275, 291n52; ethnodevelopment and, 183–85, 190–96, 205–6, 208–9, 245–47, 320n32, 322n54; ethno-education and, 235, 237, 265–66; national, 33, 35. *See also* indigenous identity

IGRA (Indian Gaming Regulatory Act), 211–13, 215, 327nn129–30, 327n132, 327n135

IITC (International Indian Treaty Council), 52–53, 75–79, 165, 289n19

IITC Declaration of Continuing Independence, 52–53, 289n19

ILO (International Labor Organization), 33–38, 67, 111–12, 301n48. *See also* ILO Convention 107; ILO Convention 169

ILO Convention 107: informed consent and, 121; integrationism and, 19, 36–38, 46–47, 106–7, 182, 186, 284n93, 285n97, 285n99, 300n26; populations, use of term in, 109; tribal peoples and, 37–38

ILO Convention 169: Afro-Colombians in Caribbean region and, 124, 201, 262; Afro-Colombians in Pacific region and, 232; autonomy within the state and, 111, 113, 262; collective land rights and, 85, 97, 106–13, 168, 301n49, 315n17; culture as development and, 194, 200–201; culture as land and, 111–12, 173, 178–79, 301n48, 316n29; history of, 38; human right to culture's dark sides and, 108–9, 134, 178–79, 200–201; indigenous, use of term in, 70, 85, 97, 106–13, 168, 170, 180, 300n25, 315n17, 316n25; informed consent and, 109, 200–201, 325n99; integrationism rejection in, 107, 300–301n40; mineral rights and, 200; peoples, use of term in, 109, 300–301n40; prior consultation and, 109, 112, 121, 200–201, 316n29, 325n99; self-determination rejection in, 106–11, 262; sustainable development and, 116; tribal peoples and, 38, 107–8, 124, 262; Zapatista movement and, 112–13, 301–2n52, 302n55

INCODER (Colombian Institute of Rural Development), 256–62, 266–72, 348n41. *See also* INCORA (Colombian Institute of Agrarian Reform)

INCORA (Colombian Institute of Agrarian Reform), 254, 256, 258, 268–69. *See also* INCODER (Colombian Institute of Rural Development)

INDERNA (National Institute of Natural Resources), 245, 247

Indian Gaming Regulatory Act (IGRA), 211–13, 215, 327nn129–30, 327n132, 327n135

Indian Law Resource Center, 75–76, 82, 93

indigenismo, 32–35, 55–66, 58, 199, 284n83, 289n37. *See also* indigenous identity

indigenous advocacy, 4–6, 274–78. *See also* indigenous advocacy in the 1970s; indigenous advocacy since 1980; indigenous advocacy since 1990

indigenous advocacy in the 1970s: cold

indigenous advocacy in the 1970s (*cont.*)
war and, 48–49, 60; culture as development in opposition and, 185–90, 318n6, 319n19, 320n30; dependency theory and, 48, 186, 213, 288n3, 288n5; Marxism and, 58, 60–61, 65, 291n52; overview of, 46–49. *See also* Fourth World Movement; *panindianismo*

indigenous advocacy since 1980, 67–73, 188, 293n2. *See also* autonomy within the state; self-determination; statehood; UN Declaration on the Rights of Indigenous Peoples (UN Declaration); Working Group (Working Group on Indigenous Populations; WGIP)

indigenous advocacy since 1990, 7, 133–37, 309n165, 309n167, 310nn171–73, 310n176

indigenous identity, 69–71, 108–9, 170–71, 316n25; Afro-Colombians in Caribbean region and, 253–54, 265; Afro-Colombians in Pacific region and, 229, 238; *campesino* identity versus, 59–64, 94, 225, 240, 291n54; culture as development and, 184, 188–90, 199, 205, 220; as defense mechanism, 13–14, 276–77; development's dark sides and differences in, 216, 218–19, 328n141, 328n151, 328n157; Fourth World Movement and, 50–52, 188–89, 288nn15–16, 288–89n17; identity politics and, 2–3, 190; *indigenismo* and, 32–35, 55–66, 58, 199, 284n83, 289n37; Law 70 and, 229–33; *mestizo* identity and, 29, 33, 60–61, 66, 92, 224; neoliberalism and, 2, 112–13, 184; use of term, 70, 85, 97, 106–13, 168, 170, 180, 300n25, 315n17, 316n25

indigenous movements, 1–3, 6–7, 275–76; Canada and, 17, 49, 52, 54–55, 286n124; class identity and, 60–62, 65, 186, 188–90, 275, 291n52; colonialism and, 1, 17–19, 274, 280n5, 282n44; education and, 34, 38, 285n105; human right to culture and, 43–45, 287n132, 287–88n142; identity politics and, 2–3, 190; state-indigenous relations and, 63–66; Tupaj

Katari movement, 64, 141, 291n52, 292n67; U.S. and, 17; Zapatista movement, 57, 94, 113, 301–2n52, 302n5, 302n55. *See also* indigenous advocacy in the 1970s; indigenous advocacy since 1980; indigenous advocacy since 1990

"Indigenous Peoples and Their Relationship to Land" (UN Report), 169–70, 177–78, 187, 311n15

indigenous peoples of Colombia: autonomy within the state and, 64–65; *campesino* identity and, 62–63; collective land rights and, 25, 127–28, 282n41, 306n116, 307n131; CRIC and, 62–65; culture as development and, 197–98, 243–45, 249; culture as heritage and, 176, 233–39, 253; culture as land and, 239–42, 307n131; forest reserves and, 249; human right to culture and, 127–28, 203, 223–24, 262–64, 306n116, 307n131; integrationism and, 31–32, 228; Law 70 and, 229–33; as model for Afro-Colombians, 228–33; prior consultation and, 203, 249, 324n92; state-indigenous relations and, 63–65; statistics of, 65, 292–93n71. *See also* Colombia

"Indigenous 'Sovereignty' and International Law" (Corntassel and Primeau), 100

indio (Indian) concept, 58

informed consent: Canada and, 203; culture as development and, 198–208, 210; CERD and, 121, 205–6, 322n59, 324n95; Draft American Declaration on the Rights of Indigenous Peoples, 158, ILO Convention 107 and, 121; ILO Convention 169 and, 109, 200–201, 325n99; Inter-American Court of Human Rights and, 203, 205–6; Peru and, 324n93; UN Declaration and, 5, 179, 203–4, 208, 324–25n97, 325n100; World Bank and, 193, 204, 321n45, 325n102. *See also* prior consultation

Instituto Indigenista Interamericano (Inter-American Indian Institute), 34–35

method and sources for research, 9–14

Mexico: culture as land's dark sides and, 171–76, 181, 199, 316n29, 317n39; *ejidos* and land reform in, 181; integrationism and, 32–33, 284n83; Marxism and, 65; model of colonialism and, 22; national identity and, 33; paternalism and, 58, 199; self-determination, 93–94, 98; state-indigenous relations and, 63, 65; statistics of indigenous peoples in, 65, 292–93n71; UN Declaration and, 48, 93. *See also* Chiapas, Mexico

Mezey, Naomi, 211

Midwest Alliance of Sovereign Tribes, 27

Mi'kmaq tribe, 75

Millennium Development Goals (MDGS), 192

Miller, Robert J., 22–23

minority rights, 38, 40, 43, 72, 114, 285nn104–6

Miskito Indians, 71–72, 82–83, 93–96, 100, 129–30, 296n49, 299n1, 306n116, 308n141

MITKA (Movimiento Indio Tupaj Katari), 64, 141, 291n52, 292n67

Mixe people, 93–94, 98

Montes Azules Integral Biosphere Reserve, 171–76, 181, 199, 316n29

Montevideo Convention on the Rights and Duties of States, 39, 73, 294n18

Moreno, Saturnino, 231

Muehlebach, Andrea, 102, 166, 170–71

multiculturalism, 65–66, 71, 73, 92, 149, 152–53, 193; constitutions of Latin America and, 71, 92, 223–24, 233, 329n3; culture as development and, 193, 273, 321–22n53; culture as heritage and, 149, 152–53, 233–34; human right to culture and, 223–24; statehood and, 65–66, 71, 73, 92, 223–24, 233, 274, 329n3

Murillo, Pastor, 234, 239–40, 244–45, 344n142

NAFTA (North American Free Trade Agreement), 112–13, 302n55

Nasa communities, 197–98

National Congress of American Indians (NCAI), 53–54

National Institute of Natural Resources (INDERNA), 245, 247

National Planning Department (DNP), 248–49, 343n133

National Unity of Rural Lands (UNAT), 266–67, 271–72, 348n41

native Hawaiian people, 52, 77

NCAI (National Congress of American Indians), 53–54

Nelson, Diane, 170–71

neoliberalism, 2, 112–13, 184, 191–93, 199, 213, 215, 219–20, 321–22n53. *See also* chastened neoliberalism (post–Washington Consensus)

New Zealand: culture as development and, 195, 201–2; culture as heritage and, 146, 303–4n78, 312n16; culture as land and, 19, 314–15n2; Fourth World Movement and, 50, 51; prior consultation and, 201; UN Declaration and, 5, 82; WCIP delegates from, 52, 288n15

NGO Conference on Discrimination Against Indigenous Populations, 17–18, 68, 70, 74–75, 87–88, 97, 294n21, 295n23, 310n173

Nicaragua: culture as land and, 167–68, 315n14, 317n39; human right to culture and, 11, 130–31, 306n116, 308n150, 309n157; self-determination and, 71–72, 82–83, 93–96, 100, 129–30, 296n49, 299n1, 306n116, 308n141

Niezen, Ronald, 90–91, 141–42

North American Free Trade Agreement (NAFTA), 112–13, 302n55

North American Indians. *See* Canada; United States

Norway. *See* Sami people

OAS (Organization of American States): American Convention on Human Rights, 43, 106, 123, 126, 129, 167, 195, 305n112, 317n41; American Declaration

OAS (*cont.*)
of the Rights and Duties of Man, 43–44, 106, 123, 126–27, 130, 167, 307n126, 308n139; Draft American Declaration on the Rights of Indigenous Peoples, 123–24, 136, 157–59, 310nn171–73, 314n57. *See also* Inter-American Commission on Human Rights; Inter-American Court of Human Rights

Offen, Karl, 224, 228, 230, 232, 246, 331n21, 332n23, 332–33n34

oil palm production, 217, 219, 228, 244, 250–53, 263, 343n137, 344n138

Okin, Susan Muller, 135, 309n165

Olympic Games, 152–53

Ontiveros Yulquila, Asunción, 110

Oquendo, Angel, 24, 30

Organization of American States (OAS). *See* OAS (Organization of American States)

Orika community, 254–64, 269–72, 345n3, 346–47n22. *See also* Islas del Rosario archipelago

Our Common Future (World Commission on Environment and Development), 151, 191, 320n38

Pagden, Anthony, 21–22, 281n24

Palenque de San Basilio, 227, 236, 238–39, 259, 262–64, 267

panindianismo: *campesino* identity and, 60–63; human right to culture and, 55–59; *indigenismo* and, 32–35, 55–66, 199, 284n83, 289n37; *indio* concept and, 58; Marxism and, 58, 60–61, 65, 291n52; state-indigenous relations and, 63–66

Paraguay, 34, 127, 128, 306n116, 308nn137–39

Parra, 343n131

Partridge, William L., 197, 208–10, 320n32

paternalism, 58, 199

PBP (Plan Biopacífico), 246–47

PCN (Proceso de Comunidades Negras en Colombia), 225–26, 229, 232, 248–51, 253, 343n131

peasant (*campesino*) identity, 59–64, 94, 225, 240, 291n54

peoples, use of term, 73, 80, 109, 294n7, 296n45, 300–301n40

Permanent Court of International Justice, 285nn104–5

Peru: *campesino* identity and, 61; collective land rights and, 31, 301n49; culture as development and, 215–16; culture as land and, 31, 180, 317n39; informed consent and, 324n93; model of colonialism and, 22; national identity and, 33; tangible heritage and, 159–60, 314n65; UN Declaration and, 48

Pitts, Jenifer, 283n65

place-based practices, 217–18

Plan Biopacífico (PBP), 246–47

Plan de Sanchez Massacre, 125, 159, 306n116, 307n124

population / populations, use of term, 80, 109

Portuguese model of colonialism, 18–19, 21–22

Posluns, Michael, 49

post–Washington Consensus (chastened neoliberalism), 184, 199, 213, 219, 228n140. *See also* neoliberalism; Washington Consensus

Povinelli, Elizabeth, 7, 21, 133, 148, 155, 176

property as bundle of rights, 177–78, 181, 317n42

Primeau, Thomas Hopkins, 70, 100, 102

prior consultation: Afro-Colombians and, 249, 251, 261; culture as development and, 199–207, 210, 323n87, 324n92; ICCPR, Article 27 and, 118, 201–2; ILO Convention 169 and, 109, 112, 121, 200–201, 316n29, 325n99; indigenous peoples of Colombia and, 203, 249, 324n92; Inter-American Court of Human Rights and, 202–4; New Zealand and, 201; UN Declaration and, 203–4, 324–25n97; UN Human Rights Committee and, 201–2, 323n87; World Bank and, 193, 204, 321n45, 325n102. *See also* informed consent

Spanish model of colonialism, 18–22, 24–25, 281n24

Spears, Suzanne A., 324n93, 325n102

Special Commission for Black Communities (Special Commission), 224–27, 229–34, 239, 244–46, 333n38, 341n107

special rights, 100, 106–7, 118–24, 129–30, 132–33

Speed, Shannon, 112

Spivak, Gayatri, 10, 137

statehood, 73–74, 294n18; "blue water" thesis and, 40–41, 73, 83; Canada and, 19, 47–48, 52–56; decolonization model for, 19, 39–42, 69, 74–78, 285–86n107; Fourth World Movement and, 52–55, 77; indigenous populations as majority and, 63–64, 81–82, 92–93, 291n52, 292n67; land rights as basis for, 19, 52–55, 75, 77–81, 85; Latin America and, 61, 63–64, 81–82, 92–93; multiculturalism and, 65–66, 71, 73, 92, 223–24, 233, 274, 329n3; self-determination equation with, 2, 52–55, 68–69, 82–85; UN Declaration and, 68–69, 78–83; U.S. and, 47–48, 52–54, 85, 88. See also self-determination

state-indigenous relations, 63–66. See also "invisible asterisk" proviso

state sovereignty, 4–5, 19, 57, 80, 81, 279n6

Stavenhagen, Rodolfo, 13–14, 60, 183, 186–90, 318–19n7, 319n19

strategic essentialism, 10–13, 152–54, 156–57, 160, 276–77, 280n14, 280n19, 280n21, 313n36; anti-essentialism versus, 14, 217–19, 276–77

structural racism, 1–3, 179, 184, 187–88, 238–39, 276

Suriname: culture as development and, 195, 202–4, 325–26n106; human right to culture and, 124–25, 131–32, 135–36, 306n116, 306n118, 306–7n120, 308–9n153, 309n154

sustainable development, 8, 14, 116, 147–48, 151–52, 165, 172–73, 216–19, 241–53, 272–73, 313n36. See also environmentalism

Svensson, Tom, 101

Sweden, 85, 94, 102. See also Sami people

Swepston, Lee, 68, 109

TA 55 (Transitory Article 55 of Law 70), 224, 231, 244–45, 258, 261–62

Tennant, Chris, 73

Territories of Difference (Escobar), 214, 216–18, 228–29, 335n53, 343n137, 344n138

Third World, 48–51, 77–79, 188–90, 216, 288n16; Fourth World Movement and, 49–55, 77, 188–89, 288nn15–16, 288–89n17

Thornberry, Patrick, 24, 117, 181–82, 186

tierras baldías (empty or unused land), 223–24, 257–59, 267

Tinker, George, 50–51, 146

Torres, Raidza, 79, 90, 92–93

Transitory Article 55 of Law 70 (TA 55), 224, 231, 244–45, 258, 261–62

transnational indigenous movements. *See* indigenous advocacy in the 1970s; indigenous advocacy since 1980; indigenous advocacy since 1990; indigenous movements

treaties: Canada and, 23, 25–26, 30, 47, 54–55, 79–80; colonialism and, 23, 25–27, 30, 47, 54–55, 79–80; Latin America and, 23, 30; self-determination and, 53–54, 110; U.S. and, 23, 25–27, 30, 47, 52–54

Treaty Six Chiefs, 79–80

tribal peoples: culture as development and, 189, 195, 202; culture as heritage and, 146, 151–52; culture as land and, 164–67; human right to culture and, 80; ICCPR, Article 27 and, 114; ILO Convention 107 and, 37–38; ILO Convention 169 and, 38, 107–8, 124, 262; Inter-American Court of Human Rights, 124–26, 131–32

Tribu Aché-Guayaki, 127–28, 306n116, 308nn137–39

Trubek, David, 184

trust responsibility, 27–29, 32, 53–54, 179

Tupaj Katari movement, 64, 141, 291n52, 292n67

van Banning, Theo R. G., 126
van den Berg, Maarten H. J., 209–10, 326n124
Varese, Stefano, 57
Venne, Sharon, 110
Villa Gloria community (La Boquilla), 265–66, 268
Vitoria, Francisco de, 20
Viveros, Trífilo, 234–35, 241

Wade, Peter, 33–34, 154, 223, 230, 237–38
Warren, Kay B., 296n45
Washington Consensus, 192–93. *See also* neoliberalism; post–Washington Consensus (chastened neoliberalism)
WCIP (World Council of Indigenous Peoples), 17, 23, 25, 52, 75–76, 288n15, 288–89n17
Western Shoshone, 118–20, 304n83,
WGIP (Working Group on Indigenous Populations; Working Group), 4, 67–68, 70–71, 73–87, 89–90, 92–97, 102, 111, 147, 157–59, 166, 169, 203, 293n3, 294n7, 310n171, 312n20, 317–18n49. *See also* UN Declaration on the Rights of Indigenous Peoples
"white man's burden" assumption, 45, 287–88n142
Wiggins, Armstrong, 82
Williams, Robert, 24
women's rights, 135–37, 309n165, 310n171, 310n176
Working Group (Working Group on Indigenous Populations; WGIP), 4, 67–68,

70–71, 73–87, 89–90, 92–97, 102, 111, 147, 157–59, 166, 169, 203, 293n3, 294n7, 310n171, 312n20, 317–18n49. *See also* UN Declaration on the Rights of Indigenous Peoples
World Bank: Afro-Colombian statistics, 226–27, 331n19, 331n21; culture as development and, 192–93, 205, 246–47, 320–21n39, 321n45, 321n50; dependency displacement of land and, 208–10; development aid and, 192; ethnodevelopment and, 246–47; informed consent and, 193, 204, 321n45, 325n102; prior consultation and, 193, 204, 321n45, 325n102
World Commission on Environment and Development (*Our Common Future*; Brundtland Commission), 151, 191, 320n38
World Council of Indigenous Peoples (WCIP), 17, 23, 25, 52, 75–76, 288n15, 288–89n17
Wright, Robin, 189, 311n4, 318n6

Xanthaki, Alexandra, 42, 300n26, 300n35

Yale University, 159–60, 314n65
Yanomami people, 128–30, 306n116, 308n145, 308n149

Zapatista movement, 57, 94, 111–13, 171–72, 301–2n52, 302n55
Zion, James, 101–2

Portions of chapters 1 and 4 first appeared in the article "From Skepticism to Embrace: Human Rights and the American Anthropological Association from 1947–1999," in *Human Rights Quarterly* 23 (2001). A brief summary of some of the arguments from chapters 3–7 was published as "Indigenous Rights Claims in International Law: Self-Determination, Culture and Development," in the *Routledge Handbook of International Law*, edited by David Armstrong (London: Routledge, 2009). Parts of chapter 9 were taken from a short piece I published after my first trip to Colombia, titled "Rapoport Center Investigates Afro-Colombian Territorial Rights," in *Portal: LLILAS Annual Review* (Austin: Lozano Long Institute for Latin American Studies, 2007).

Karen Engle is the Cecil D. Redford Professor in
Law and the director of the Rapoport Center for
Human Rights and Justice at the University of
Texas School of Law.

Engle, Karen.
The elusive promise of indigenous development :
rights, culture, strategy / Karen Engle.
p. cm.
Includes bibliographical references and index.
ISBN 978-0-8223-4750-7 (cloth : alk. paper)
ISBN 978-0-8223-4769-9 (pbk. : alk. paper)
1. Indigenous peoples—Civil rights—America.
2. America—Civilization. I. Title. K3247.E54 2010
342.08′72—dc22   2010017007